CIVIL WAR SENATOR

CONFLICTING WORLDS

New Dimensions of the American Civil War

T. MICHAEL PARRISH, *Series Editor*

CIVIL WAR

SENATOR

WILLIAM PITT FESSENDEN AND THE FIGHT TO SAVE THE AMERICAN REPUBLIC

ROBERT J. COOK

LOUISIANA STATE UNIVERSITY PRESS)|(BATON ROUGE

For Andrea

Published with the assistance of the V. Ray Cardozier Fund

Published by Louisiana State University Press
Copyright © 2011 by Louisiana State University Press
All rights reserved
Manufactured in the United States of America
First printing

DESIGNER: *Mandy McDonald Scallan*
TYPEFACE: *Whitman*
TYPESETTER: *Thomson Digital*
PRINTER: *McNaughton & Gunn, Inc.*
BINDER: *John Dekker and Sons, Inc.*

Library of Congress Cataloging-in-Publication Data

Cook, Robert J., 1958–
  Civil War senator : William Pitt Fessenden and the fight to
save the American republic / Robert J. Cook.
    p. cm.
  Includes bibliographical references and index.
  ISBN 978-0-8071-3707-9 (cloth : alk. paper) 1. Fessenden,
William Pitt, 1806-1869. 2. Cabinet officers—United States—
Biography. 3. Legislators—United States—Biography.
4. United States—Politics and government—1861-1865.
5. Maine—Biography. I. Title.
  E415.9.F4C66 2010
  973.7092—dc22
  [B]

                                            2010019744

Apply your eye-glass and minutely scan
The form and features of a wondrous man—
Sharp in his physique—you could well expect
Sharpness and boldness in his intellect.
Ready in thought and irony—not wit—
Behold in FESSENDEN our modern Pitt.
He speaks; and steel-clad weapons from his brain
Sweep like a tempest o'er the hills of Maine.
Then like the storm-king, with unpitying eye,
He views the prostrate forms around him lie.
Cold in his temper and of icy glow,
He shines like his Katahdin crowned with snow.
No smiles or blushes leave their genial trace
Upon his Norman, frigid, thoughtful face;
For beams of sunshine and of cheer would mar
The scene and advent of his natal star,
Tho' seeming strange, the truth must be confessed,
That fervid elements control his breast,
Like fires which in volcanic mountains glow
Whose summits glisten with eternal snow.

—J. B. MANSFIELD AND D. M. KELSEY,
    *Personal Sketches of the Members of the Fortieth Congress
    of the United States of America: Maine Delegation*
    (Baltimore: The Authors, 1867).

William Pitt Fessenden
Library of Congress

Contents

Preface

I have incurred numerous debts while writing this biography. There are three principal repositories of Fessenden correspondence: Bowdoin College, the Library of
Congress, and the Western Reserve Historical Society. For hospitality and friendship
in Brunswick, Maine, Silver Spring, Maryland, and Cleveland, Ohio, my thanks go,
respectively, to Deborah Zorach, Barbara Holmlund and Julianne Borton, and Mary
and Drew Nicholls. Barb, Juli, and I shared with wonder-cook Bob Depue the rare
privilege of driving into the District of Columbia to locate Fessenden Street, the
only physical reminder of the senator's eventful presence in Washington. I am also
grateful to Karen Canter and Russ Erickson for hosting me so warmly in Portland, to
Mary and Joe Fenstermacher for making me welcome on a memorable summer visit
to Long Island before I caught the ferry across to New England, and to my old (I use
the word advisedly) friends John Zeller—who searched in vain for a bust of William
Pitt Fessenden that had once been owned by Fessenden's Senate colleague, James
W. Grimes of Iowa—and Trevor Griffiths who, over the years, has never ceased to
inquire politely about the state of this project before adeptly moving the conversation on to more esoteric topics such as cricket and Scottish cinema.

I undertook much of the archival work on this book when I was Mellon Research
Fellow at Cambridge University. There I was sustained by the warm friendship and
strong support of Peter Searby and the late Charlotte Erickson—both highly accomplished historians from whom I learned a great deal—and of three postgrad-
uate students of considerable promise (each one now a professor): Peter Coates,
Steve Hindle, and Brian Ward. Other academic friends and colleagues have helped
to shape this book, especially Bill Dusinberre, my inspirational tutor at the University of Warwick, who first alerted me to Fessenden's importance and urged the need
for a modern biography of the senator. I have benefited greatly over the years from
conversations with many fellow members of that peerless organization, the British
American Nineteenth Century Historians group (BrANCH), including the much-
missed Robert Harrison and Peter Parish. I recall, too, a particularly fruitful conversation with Owen Dudley Edwards at a conference of the British Association for

American Studies which met under leaden skies somewhere in the British Isles (it may have been Aberystwyth). The subject was father-son relations and the imprint of Owen's insightful remarks can be found in chapter one. More recent contacts with Michael Todd Landis, a keen Fessenden scholar, and Marilyn Green Day, a direct descendant of Fessenden's mother, have also helped to improve this study in significant ways.

Even in these technologically advanced times writing books remains a solitary endeavor. I've been fortunate over the years to have supportive colleagues in the History Department at Sheffield and the American Studies Department at Sussex. The names of David Brown, Richard Carwardine, Richard Follett, Simon Hall, Ian Kershaw, Linda Kirk, Simon Loseby, Simon Middleton, Patrick Renshaw, Jarod Roll, Stephen Salter, Dominic Sandbrook, Joe Street, Simon Walker, Clive Webb, and Hugh Wilford spring to mind immediately. David Brown (a touchingly proud Saddlers fan and notorious doubter of Fessenden's historical import, now happily converted to an advocate of the Great Man's Treasury policy) and Richard Carwardine merit especial thanks for their trenchant comments on a draft of this manuscript, as do Heather Cox Richardson, Adam Smith, the series editor T. Michael Parrish, and a remarkably conscientious anonymous reader for LSU Press. While this biography is all the stronger for their contributions, the errors that remain are, of course, entirely my own.

Writing books costs time and money. I'm grateful therefore to the Mellon Fund for a life-changing fellowship at Cambridge in 1987–90, to the universities of Sheffield and Sussex for a period of leave in 2007–8, to the United Kingdom Arts and Humanities Research Council for research funding in the first half of 2008, and to the Huntington Library in San Marino for a one-month Mellon Research Fellowship in 2006. Andrea Greengrass gave up her own valuable time to provide expert assistance with copyediting and indexing.

Those dearest to academic scholars pay the biggest price for projects like this one. My greatest debt is to those who have lived closest to William Pitt Fessenden for far too long: my beloved family: Andrea, Martha and Daniel, and my parents, John and Margaret. Quite simply, this book would never have seen the light of day without them.

CIVIL WAR SENATOR

Introduction

Late in the evening of Friday, March 4, 1854, the Washington correspondent of Horace Greeley's *New-York Tribune* entered the gallery of the United States Senate to observe debate on a most contentious item of legislation. Denounced by its Free Soil opponents "as part and parcel of an atrocious plot" to spread slavery across the trans-Missouri West, the Kansas-Nebraska Bill undermined existing safeguards against expansion of the South's "peculiar institution."[1] Controversial though it was, the bill had every chance of success in the upper chamber, where the antislavery forces were particularly weak. The *Tribune* correspondent was thus delighted to find beneath him in the flaring gaslight a trim, bewhiskered New Englander named William Pitt Fessenden in full flow during his maiden speech before the Senate. It was, commented the reporter, "a most gallant onslaught upon the Nebraska conspirators . . . manly, caustic and defiant." Here was no craven northerner prepared to do the bidding of his southern antagonists but a bold new presence determined to call the bluff of arrogant slave-drivers:

> All around him were the bullying, braggart majority, flushed with anticipated victory, and some of them, I am mortified to say beastly drunk. He nevertheless with undaunted courage held them all at bay. Twice Senator [Andrew] Butler of South Carolina advanced toward the Senator from Maine with clenched fists and flushed face, as if to commit a personal assault, but this only brought forth renewed and redoubled blows of eloquence and logic from the new Senator. He told the South what they should have been told in 1850, that if they desire to leave the Union they need not delay their departure an hour on account of the North.

While such defiance may have inspired *Tribune* readers, it did not change hearts and minds in the polarized antebellum Senate. Debate finally closed on the bill before dawn broke on Saturday morning. The measure passed by thirty-seven votes to fourteen. "And so ended," wrote Greeley's correspondent forebodingly, "the first step in this great iniquity."[2] The second step occurred on May 22 when, after President Franklin Pierce and his proslavery allies had made Kansas-Nebraska a party issue, significant numbers of northern Democrats joined southern delegates to pass the bill in the House of Representatives. At the end of the month Pierce put his seal on the villainy by signing into law an act rightly described by historian William E. Gienapp as "one of the most fateful measures ever approved by Congress."[3]

The "great iniquity" of Kansas-Nebraska precipitated a chain of events that would culminate seven years later in a calamitous civil war. For more than a decade the Yankee politician who so impressed observers with his opening salvos in the Senate was at the storm-center of an unfolding crisis that nearly destroyed the United States. When William Pitt Fessenden died at the age of 62 in September 1869, four years after the southern rebellion had been defeated, contemporaries paid fulsome tribute to his patriotism and ability. "[H]e was almost perfection as a legislator," commented *The Nation*, and "has left to his country the legacy of a character and a career as lofty as that of any American who ever led a public life."[4] To an obituarist in the *Chicago Tribune* he was "the most acute debater . . . the most commanding and judicious leader, the most accomplished and persuasive orator, and for years . . . the model senator of the United States."[5]

Historians of nineteenth-century America have not always looked so positively on Fessenden's career but generally they have concurred that he was one of the leading politicians of his divided generation. A brilliant young lawyer who was also godson of the famous Massachusetts politician, Daniel Webster, he largely fulfilled the promise noted by observers of his pugnacious contribution to debate over the Kansas-Nebraska Act. During the 1840s and 1850s he played a crucial role in the country's growing political crisis by using sectional issues to gain national office and by cooperating with likeminded politicians to make the new northern Republican Party an election-winning coalition capable of curbing the power of proslavery southerners. When secessionists rejected Abraham Lincoln's triumph at the ballot box in 1860 and tried to sunder the Union in 1860–61, he rejected compromise with the slave states and girded himself for war. Rapidly emerging as one of the most effective senators in Washington, he employed his matchless legislative skills in the service of the republic. In July 1864 President Abraham Lincoln appointed him secretary of the treasury at one of the lowest points of the northern war effort. By the time he left office early the following year to return to the Senate, northern military might had brought the Confederacy to the point of total collapse. Fessenden was no financial miracle worker but his indefatigable labors as chairman of the Senate

Finance Committee and treasury secretary helped keep the North's armed forces in the field at a critical juncture in American history. After Appomattox, he returned to the Senate to play a decisive role in formulating congressional policy for the post-emancipation South. Balancing the need for a lasting peace with a desire to protect the fruits of the North's hard-won victory, he strove consistently for practical solutions to the seemingly intractable problems facing a country shattered by war, burdened with debt, and desperate to move on toward a brighter future. His historical reputation as a brake on congressional Reconstruction was cemented in May 1868 when he dramatically voted against the conviction of Andrew Johnson at the end of the first presidential impeachment trial in the nation's history.

Fessenden's opposition to impeachment won him plaudits not only from contemporary conservatives but also late nineteenth- and early twentieth-century historians who lauded his integrity, ability, and "powerful, impressive Cato-like" opposition to supposedly irresponsible Radicals eager to impose corrupt black rule on courageous white southerners.[6] The civil rights movement of the early 1960s, however, discredited this racist interpretation of Reconstruction, rendering the majority of professional historians sympathetic to the humanitarian objectives of abolitionists and Radical Republicans. Subsequently tempered by a more cynical approach to the American past, this paradigmatic shift heightened awareness of those so-called moderate Republicans who had helped to prevent Reconstruction from revolutionizing southern society.

Eric McKitrick contended in 1960 that historians can learn "a great deal more about the government crisis that was precipitated in the winter and early spring of 1865–66 by following the course of things along *his* [Fessenden's] angle of vision—and that of his colleagues Trumbull, Grimes, and Sherman—than by following the phillipics of Charles Sumner and Thaddeus Stevens."[7] It was a judgment broadly confirmed by later scholars such as Michael Les Benedict and Eric Foner who endorsed the view that congressional Reconstruction was more conservative than its racist critics had once claimed, owing largely to the efforts of centrists like Fessenden. Significantly, however, modern historians' preoccupation with, and admiration for, the abolitionists has tended to restrict scholarly interest in the moderate Republicans to the ever-fascinating Abraham Lincoln. The recent trend in Reconstruction historiography away from high politics to socio-cultural topics, while a positive development in many respects, has done nothing to expand awareness of the moderates. This is unfortunate, to say the least, for the centrists' views were more representative of prevailing northern opinion than those of the Radicals. If we want to make sense of the deepest crisis ever faced by the United States, it is time we came to a better understanding of men like Fessenden—however difficult it may be to incorporate them into a usable past for the multicultural present.

Despite agreeing about Fessenden's significance as a bellwether politician during Reconstruction, Foner and Benedict failed to concur on how to categorize him. While the former described the powerful senator as a pre- and postwar "moderate," Benedict labeled him "a consistent conservative" after Appomattox.[8] To add to the apparent confusion, Allan Bogue's quantitative analysis of the Civil War Senate revealed Fessenden's ability to construct a radical voting record.[9] Indeed, Abraham Lincoln himself considered the senator from Maine a Radical.[10] Given that Fessenden's views on a range of subjects were marked by a good deal of intellectual consistency, this semantic diversity may seem surprising. However, it illustrates perfectly the difficulty of labeling precisely a politician whose ideology was a composite one and whose actions were essentially pragmatic (though not unprincipled) responses to the most cataclysmic sequence of events in American history.

Conscious of the dangers inherent in categorization, I have avoided describing Fessenden as a moderate on the grounds that this description furnishes a misleading impression of both his character and his tenacious opposition to slavery expansion and southern power before and during the Civil War. I have also avoided the term "conservative" because, notwithstanding values and prejudices typical of his elite class, he helped to facilitate the political and economic changes remaking America in the nineteenth century and was both supportive of hard-war policies against the Confederacy and opposed to the unthinking prejudices and fossilized constitutionalism of genuine conservatives. He was, essentially, a centrist-oriented antislavery republican who, radicalized by the fight against the slaveocracy, worked to save the United States through decisive governmental action in war, and who, after the fall of the Confederacy, attempted to lay the foundations for a permanent peace between North and South without betraying the Union dead of both races.

Unlike professional biographers, historians tend to be more interested in the times than individual lives—to be concerned primarily with what one person's brief spell on earth can tell readers about broader historical themes and events, rather than about how and why their subject acted in particular ways during the course of his or her worldly career. Sensible of this problem, I have chosen to press ahead with this study in the knowledge that biographers can no more resurrect dead souls than historians can fully uncover the remote past. Much of what William Pitt Fessenden did, thought, or felt is gone for good. But abundant traces of his privileged span remain. Printed congressional debates, Treasury records, newspaper reports and editorials, and hundreds of letters to his wife and sons, to fellow politicians, and to his beloved cousin Elizabeth Warriner (who thankfully disregarded injunctions to burn his correspondence) all attest to his significance as one of the republic's leading politicians in the fevered years of what was once called the "middle period." These traces allow the historian to reconstruct portions of Fessenden's life, to advance plausible explanations for his actions, and to connect those actions to some of the most momentous events of the nineteenth century. I would be dishonest if I claimed to be more interested in the life than in the events and the structures that underpinned them. However, I have endeavored to provide a sympathetic (though not uncritical) assessment of a fellow human being without losing sight of the fact that his political career can help us answer important questions about U.S. economic development, the role of party in nineteenth-century America, the coming of the Civil War, the reasons for Union military victory, and the failure of the ruling Republicans during Reconstruction to safeguard the rights of the emancipated slaves.

In a caustic review of Charles A. Jellison's 1962 biography of Fessenden, LaWanda Cox questioned whether conventional biography, especially when unaccompanied by "literary skill and mellowed historical perception," is sufficiently equipped to answer important questions about major historical developments.[11] More recently Patrick O'Brien has assailed poltical biography as a form of historical analysis unless scholars can demonstrate that their subjects exercised a direct and transformative impact on history.[12] While this last criticism privileges the lives of rich and famous men, both O'Brien and Cox make reasonable points. The biography of a single figure cannot possibly tell us everything we want to know about complex historical events but some remarkably powerful individuals have had a greater effect on past societies than others. William Pitt Fessenden had a disproportionate impact on Civil War America because he held high office in the U.S. government in the mid-nineteenth century. His influence on federal policymaking at a time of acute national crisis was immense from the moment southern delegates left Washington during the secession crisis. In this sense he passes O'Brien's stringent test for biography. Readers will judge for themselves the extent to which this "life" answers LaWanda Cox's skepticism. A comprehensive understanding of the terrible violence Americans meted out to one another in the 1860s and of the resulting triumph of the Union requires more than a critical biography of one human being, whether that individual be William Pitt Fessenden, Abraham Lincoln, Jefferson Davis, or anyone else—male or female, black or white, rich or poor—caught up in the maelstrom of the Civil War.

This said, Fessenden's political career contains much of value to those who seek that understanding, especially those with an inkling that Congress played as vital a role in saving the Union as Lincoln, his soldiers, or the millions of African Americans literally in transit between slavery and freedom.

William Pitt Fessenden was never quite the independent Whig or Republican he liked to think he was. While this self-image helps to explain his course on impeachment, it is clear that he was a party animal in a period when parties dominated the American political landscape. Party was the agency through which he rose to prominence and subsequently exercised power. Even when his enemies tried to eject him from the Republican fold after the failure of impeachment, Fessenden resisted tenaciously—well aware that his influence was gone if he jumped the Republican ship. He was an unusually influential partisan in an age that was often ambivalent about intense partisanship yet broadly tolerant of the role that party organizations played in the functioning of America's evolving democracy. His attachment to party was the result of a combination of ideological commitment and the desire for personal political advancement. A loyal Whig in the 1840s because of that organization's support for ordered progress and government-assisted economic development, he abandoned the party in the 1850s when it became clear that the Republicans presented the optimal vehicle for his ambitions and, no less important, for achieving the final triumph of northern free-soil nationalism over proslavery Unionism—a triumph that he and countless other northerners believed was necessary to guarantee the future welfare and greatness of the United States.

Fessenden was not a democrat: his republican worldview was striated with class, gender, and racial prejudices. But nor was he a reactionary. A Yankee patriot in an era when the interests of New England were more closely identified with those of the United States than they had been under the administrations of Thomas Jefferson and James Madison, he understood that his section and the republic to which it belonged were changing inexorably. On the whole, he embraced that change and identified with party as the agent of change. The younger Pitt was dynamic, forward-looking, and supremely confident in his own abilities and his country's future. It is to him that we turn first.

The Younger Pitt, 1806–1836

A Federalist Boyhood

William Pitt Fessenden was born on October 6, 1806. A moderate by reputation, he was not born into a world marked by moderation. The Napoleonic Wars, the most global conflict of any up to that point in history, had yet to reach their midpoint and, after a period of relative calm, the armies of the Old World were again laying waste to the earth. Just eight days after his birth French troops crushed two Prussian armies at the battles of Jena and Auerstädt before marching on Berlin. The United States, independent from Britain for less than a quarter of a century, had managed to avoid direct entanglement in the Great Power conflagration but its neutral status was threatened regularly by British and French depredations on its maritime trade. Although proud of their achievements during and since the Revolution, Americans were deeply divided by politics. In the month of Fessenden's birth, Aaron Burr, the disgraced vice president who had killed Alexander Hamilton in a duel two years earlier, was at liberty in Kentucky possibly intriguing to separate the western portion of the country under his leadership. Closer to home, New England was riven by partisan competition, much of it generated by European events, between Federalists and Jeffersonian Republicans. Pitt Fessenden was not by nature a violent man but his life was touched by warfare and party conflict from the beginning and would be until it ended.

The circumstances of his birth are shrouded in mystery. His father was the fifth son of a bookish Congregational minister from Maine (then a district of Massachusetts). Samuel Fessenden was 21 at the time of his son's conception, a student at Dartmouth College in Hanover, New Hampshire, where he studied with reasonable assiduity, fretted about the future like all young men, wrote a four-act anti-French tragedy entitled "The Conspiracy," and derided attempts by one of the professors to spread religious revivalism. To help pay his way through college he taught school in

Boscawen, a quaint village on the banks of the Merrimack River just north of the soon-to-be state capital, Concord. One of the major attractions here was Ruth Green, the 18-year-old daughter of a prominent local lawyer and farmer, Nathaniel Green. Patriarchal controls over young people, rigid in Puritan New England, had declined during the eighteenth century and premarital pregnancy was far from uncommon.[1] At some point in the winter of 1805–6 Ruth and Samuel—a powerfully built, handsome man who always wore his heart on his sleeve—yielded unpuritanically to their passions. Subsequently Ruth gave birth to an illegitimate boy at her father's home in Boscawen. Daniel Webster, a talented Dartmouth alumnus (class of 1801) who had tutored Samuel at nearby Fryeburg Academy, had recently opened a law office in Boscawen. "[Samuel] Fessenden has a fine son," reported the future statesman (who may have introduced his friend to Ruth) a month after the event. "I have not seen him, but he is said to be the image & superscription, & to carry proof of his parentage in his countenance." When the baby was "about a week old," he added, "he was put out at nurse."[2]

Ruth Green and Samuel Fessenden did not marry, as one might have expected. Instead the boy was dispatched to his father's family home in Fryeburg, where he was nurtured for nearly six years by Samuel's mother, Sarah, and her daughters. We can only speculate about what happened, for hard evidence is lacking. Clearly the amorous liaison ended at some point in 1806, possibly because Ruth ended the affair before she discovered she was pregnant. The absence of a parental union left the baby in an ambiguous, potentially dangerous legal position. Customary practice would have been for the bastard child to stay with the mother. American authorities were keen to limit the number of illegitimate children on the poor law roll and courts in the early republic proved increasingly willing to grant custody rights to unmarried mothers. But if the mother or the mother's family did not want the child because of the accompanying social stigma and monetary costs, then care of that child would have devolved upon the locality unless the father agreed to accept responsibility.[3] It would appear in this case that neither party, young as they both were, was financially equipped to look after the baby but that Samuel and his extended family were positively willing to assume full parental responsibilities. In this respect the baby was exceedingly lucky.

Only a few facts are known about this early period of the boy's life. First, at some point in late 1806, Samuel asked his friend Daniel Webster to be the child's godfather. Webster agreed—an act that would, after Webster attained fame, prove enormously useful to his godson's political career. Second, we know that his father gave the baby two forenames. Although "William" was chosen primarily because it was his paternal grandfather's name, the appellation "Pitt" branded the youngster as the offspring of a devoted Federalist. William Pitt the Younger, prime minister of Great Britain, died on January 23, 1806, at about the same time the child was conceived. A relatively successful war leader, he had spearheaded Britain's struggle to defeat Napoleonic France. This made him a hero for many Massachusetts Federalists who were waging their own political campaign against French influence as it manifested itself in the policies of the ruling Jeffersonian party. Samuel Fessenden's decision to name his lad after an English patriot so soon after the American War of Independence signaled an attachment to Francophobe New England Federalism which informed his entire political career and could hardly fail to influence young Pitt in his early years.

Massachusetts Federalism was a form of politics rooted in what had once been the relatively stable and ordered society of New England, a society dominated by patriarchal values and institutions (foremost among them the family and the Congregational Church) and a sense of cultural superiority over the rest of the country. The main threat to the region's conservative elites in the late eighteenth century came from the quickening pace of economic activity occasioned by steady population growth and inexorable market penetration into areas like the Connecticut River valley and the Atlantic coast. Federalists were not necessarily opposed to the development of a capitalist society characterized by entrepreneurial zeal and the search for profit through trade in agricultural products, but they fretted over signs that their God-fearing, hierarchical, and republican society was under attack. Casting around for the source of the problem they found the culprit in their reading of classical history, specifically their observation that republics were fragile entities vulnerable to would-be despots conspiring to undermine the tree of liberty. The first decade of the nineteenth century, as these Yankee Federalists saw it, boasted one Caesar par excellence: Napoleon Bonaparte, spawn of the bloody French Revolution (which had terrified American conservatives) and the alleged puppet-master of the Francophile president, Thomas Jefferson, whose radical, irreligious supporters seemed intent on demolishing every pillar of good order in the country.

At the close of 1806 Samuel Fessenden returned to his home town of Fryeburg in the District of Maine where his babe could be nurtured by female relatives while he trained for the bar. In the summer of 1809, having passed that hurdle, he scouted the countryside for somewhere to practice. The fastest growing area in the United States, Maine was an attractive destination for young New Englanders seeking cheaper land or success in professional vocations filled by older men in more settled portions of Massachusetts. His chosen venue was New Gloucester, home to a group of Shakers. The backcountry was an attractive location for radical Protestant sects like this; in the wake of the "New Light stir," a series of religious revivals in the region, Maine's remote interior was becoming a stronghold of Methodists and Baptists whose poor-to-middling adherents tended to be hostile to the established Congregational Church and supportive of the Jeffersonian Republicans (or Democrats).[4] Although New Gloucester might have seemed a surprising choice of location for a Federalist, it held certain attractions outlined by Samuel to his sister Mary in July. It was, he reckoned, "a very pleasant town finely situated, with a good society. Democracy has there long been triumphant, but its influence is on the wane. There are two lawyers in town, of talents not above mediocrity, the one a Demo, the other a Fed." Added Samuel, "Kiss my dear *Bill Pitt* for me, and love him for my sake."[5]

Uncertain of his talents and short of money (at one stage he begged a loan from his friend Webster), Samuel was forced to board in town while he established himself. Building a client base in New Gloucester proved hard and he was often depressed. How he regretted leaving Fryeburg, he told Mary in December 1811: "Happiness is not to be found in the sphere in which I am now fixed."[6] In fact, by this time the tide was already turning. He had joined the Freemasons and was one of the most active Federalists in the community—so active that his co-partisans had invited him to deliver the ritual Independence Day oration four months previously. This lurid speech was a ripe example of extreme Federalism dripping with classical republican imagery and political paranoia rooted in fears conjured up by the horrors of the French Revolution.

Composed at a moment when leading Massachusetts Federalists like Timothy Pickering were lambasting Jefferson's successor, James Madison, for conspiring with France to try and drag the United States into war with Britain, Samuel Fessenden's tirade was an eighteenth-century republican's clarion call for vigilance in the early nineteenth century. He began with a warning to all those complacent Americans "indulging in a thoughtless security, while craft and corruption, aided by cowardice and ambition" were undermining the Columbian edifice. "[T]he blessings of freedom and civil government . . .," he intoned, "may be taken from us. Republic after republic has been formed and destroyed." Moving effortlessly from generalities to specifics, he cited the European wars as the driver of instability, revolution, atheism, and mindless innovation and reform. And now President Madison, he moaned, "the dagon of democracy," had declared the United States to be on the verge of joining the conflict. "That it is the consequence of a systematic design," he continued, "to involve us in a state of warfare, thereby to effect a dissolution of our present form of government, and build on its ruins a military, or some other despotism, I am not disposed to deny." Federalists like him were assailed for speaking up but they would not be silenced. "[W]hile I remain in a land of freedom," he thundered, "while I can stand in an assembly of freemen, my voice shall be raised to deprecate the impending ruin of my country, till my heart-strings crack! My tongue shall move, till my head be severed from my body by the axe of the executioner, and, while it yet quivers from the stroke, it shall lisp our danger!"[7]

When war with Britain finally came in 1812, elite Massachusetts Federalists such as Harrison Gray Otis found it difficult to rein in men like Samuel who were publicly thirsting for conflict with the Madison administration.[8] Fessenden's radicalism, which resembled that of the fire-breathing Pickering (verging at times in support for outright secession), may have prevented him from being elected to the 1814 Hartford convention which, along with General Andrew Jackson's victory at New Orleans early the next year, kept New England separatism narrowly in check. But it did not hamper his career as one of the district's most combative Federalists. Profiting politically and financially from his role as counsel for the owners of extensive landholdings in Maine, he served five times in the Massachusetts legislature between 1814 and 1819. There he was a constant thorn in the side of the Jeffersonian Republicans, vigorously opposing their attempts to separate predominantly Jeffersonian Maine from Federalist-controlled Massachusetts—a fight that ended in defeat in March 1820, when Maine finally became a state of the Union as part of the Missouri Compromise—and to undercut the power of Bowdoin College, a bastion of Federalism in the district.[9]

This uncompromising politician was also an indulgent, if exacting, parent who adhered to the affectionate childrearing practices increasingly common among the middling classes of New England in the late eighteenth century. Initially Samuel shared the role of nurturing Pitt with his mother and sisters, who spoiled the boy with love and attention. Yet even when absent from Fryeburg, the aspiring lawyer took steps to exert a controlling influence on young Bill, particularly in the sphere of education which, as he knew from his own relatively privileged experience, held the key to character and worldly fame. "My little Boy, as I hear does finely, and you will kiss him for me," he instructed his sister Mary in September 1810: "Tell him that if he will be good & learn to read his bible, when I come again, he shall have a fine new book."[10] He held out further material incentives to the lad the following year when, from New Gloucester, he promised "a *watch* and a new coat & pantaloons & hat" if the youngster should begin writing and committing more texts to memory.[11]

When Pitt turned 7, his father sent for him. His matriarchal Fryeburg cocoon rudely shattered, he soon found his world altered beyond measure when Samuel married a New Gloucester woman, Deborah Chandler, in December 1813. Again the boy was fortunate. His stepmother treated him kindly even though she had borne Samuel four children of her own by the end of the decade.[12] Predictably, in view of his cosseted upbringing, Pitt was extremely precocious. One of Deborah's young cousins remembered him as "tall, thin, and very graceful," an indication that he had inherited his looks from his mother rather than the broad-framed Samuel. She also recalled "that he learned very rapidly, and read nearly all the books that came in his way." Other recollections of this time confirm Pitt's prodigious capacity for learning, instilled in him from an early age by his father: his ability to read Virgil in the vernacular at the age of 10 and his attendance at Master Woodman's school, where he became so advanced in his studies that he had to be instructed by his father's law students.[13]

For all his intellectual precocity, Pitt was neither a dull nor a sedentary boy. He played zestfully and interacted well with his new Chandler cousins. One of them described him as "bright, active, quick, energetic, overbearing, honest, truthful, and honorable, and never vicious."[14] His fondness for swimming nearly ended in tragedy. Diving into a mill pond outside town, he cracked his head on a stone, resulting in a long scar on his brow. As well as engaging in strenuous physical activity, he was also quick witted. One day while out with friends, the group yelled insults at a bizarrely dressed old man. On learning of the incident his father prepared to administer a beating whereupon Pitt, thinking on his feet, avowed that his playmates had told him that the stranger was Napoleon Bonaparte. Having heard his father call Boney "a wicked monster," he had thought it right to abuse him. Samuel let the child off with a stern warning.[15] Though Pitt was pushed hard by his earnest parent, his boyhood appears to have been a relatively happy one. He was unusually spoiled and studious and perhaps more solitary and less physically strong than some of his peers. But he learned "masculine" traits of courage, loyalty, and action through play and was by no means unprepared for life away from home.

At the tender age of 11 Pitt traveled to Brunswick near the coast to be presented for examination at Bowdoin College wearing "a jacket and trousers with a broad ruffle about his neck."[16] The new president, William Allen, who had assumed his post at a moment in the college's history when Federalist influence was beginning to wane, sent him home because he looked so young. The boy returned the next year and was admitted to the college in the fall of 1819. His student career began the following spring. It was an eventful one and—like that of novelist Nathaniel Hawthorne who entered Bowdoin two years later, chafed at the strictness of the rules, and was always short of money—it was not an entirely happy experience.[17] His initial problems were due partly to his young age and partly to the fact that he started at Bowdoin by boarding with homespun relatives in Gorham, thirty miles from campus. (Because of his son's youth, Samuel Fessenden had prevailed on the college authorities to allow him to live with family.) Unable to attend classes on a regular basis, Pitt found it difficult to settle. Especially galling was the poor quality of the food, principally the breakfasts of mashed brown bread and potatoes and dinners of boiled meat "which would be good if it was not so tuff, & baked blue beans, & once in a while a piece of stuffed veal."[18] Life improved when he moved into college as a sophomore in late 1820. Conquering homesickness, he began to make friends among his classmates, included among whom was William G. Crosby, a future governor of Maine.[19] He spent his days studying classical history, Greek, Latin, moral philosophy, trigonometry, algebra, and geometry—all core subjects in the university curriculum of the early republic.

During the holidays he taught school in nearby Lewiston. There he met an impoverished youth named James Brooks, later a New York Whig, with whom he shared his love of reading. The two lads became firm friends and spent much of their time in the modest village library devouring leather-bound tomes on modern and classical history. Among the books they read was Charles Rollin's *Ancient History* (1730–38), a popular and unashamedly didactic French work that confirmed the Revolutionary generation's cyclical view of history.[20] Empires, Rollin taught, rose and fell through time, their progress dependent on the attachment of leaders and citizens alike to moral virtues such as frugality, endeavor, and incorruptibility, and on the judgments of an immanent Creator.[21] Although we have no evidence of Pitt's response to Rollin, his reading can only have deepened his commitment to the elitist, religion-infused republicanism of the Federalists. What it did not do, could not do at this stage of his development, was teach him how to govern the passions that burned within.

While Pitt coped well with the intellectual demands of the Bowdoin curriculum, traces of ill-discipline began to spot his record, as it did that of many of his peers. The first sign of any problem occurred in December 1820. He and his classmates took strong drink to an impromptu party hosted by two of their friends to celebrate the end of algebra tuition. Alcohol consumption was common among students at this time but when the company began to get rowdy, the wiser members of the group began to slip away. Pitt and another boy clambered out of a window and caught up with the others between the old and new college buildings. At some point, either before or after his departure from the group, a window was broken. One youth was suspended by the Bowdoin authorities for his part in "the irregularities"; others, including Fessenden, were fined $2 for their role in the disorder.[22]

The next two and a half years were the most rebellious of Pitt's life. He received many additional fines from the college, thirteen in total for a range of minor offenses, including absence from prayers, neglect of public duties, and playing bowls during study hours. He spent freely on cigars, alcohol, and off-campus suppers. By September 1822 he had run up modest debts and was complaining to his father about his lack of spending money. He exhibited also a waning deference to what he called "this rascally government." The college authorities had given him a room that he, now a senior, adjudged unworthy of his status. "All I could get from the old scamp," he wrote after an unsuccessful interview with President Allen, "was that the [college] government had assigned me that room and I had no right to grumble."[23] Although Samuel chided his haughty son for his conduct toward Allen, Pitt's pride had been hurt. "I did not talk very saucily to the Pres.," he replied. "I only told him that in my opinion and that of my class that I had been used very unjustly by the Gov[ernment]."[24]

The youth's wayward conduct did not improve during his final months at the college. In fact, it nearly cost him his degree. On the night of June 30, 1823, he went drinking at Wardsworth's tavern on the road to Bath without permission. Two weeks later he joined a mob of students who had gathered with sticks to repel an anticipated assault from local townsmen who were rumored (falsely as it turned out) to have attacked one of their classmates. When Pitt was ordered to return to his room he was found guilty of what the authorities deemed "disrespectful conduct." He had not calmed down the following morning. When interviewed about his behavior he apparently swore profusely and hurled insults at college officers from his window. In view of these events "& considering his general character & the bad influence of his example," the Bowdoin authorities sent the insubordinate young blood home to his father with the recommendation that he should not be allowed to graduate with his peers.[25] President Allen then penned a forthright letter to Samuel Fessenden's new law partner, Thomas A. Deblois. There was, he said, a disturbing subtext to the story. "[T]he Government," he avowed, "consider young Fessenden, notwithstanding his youth, as one of the most unprincipled and corrupt young men in college, & they are able to explain the grounds of their persuasion if it be necessary to vindicate the justice of their measures." By "corrupt" the president meant immoral. Wardsworth's tavern, he added, was a disreputable lower-class establishment which, on the night of Fessenden's visit, had been frequented by "several harlots from Portland." As for the boy's profaneness, concluded Allen, "I understand that young Fessenden has been in the *habit* of it, even most indecently at his boarding-table."[26]

If William Allen and his fellow faculty members thought these revelations would prompt remorse and an apology, they were much mistaken. Pitt was deeply stung by his first major crisis. He promised his father that he hoped the "scrape" would teach him "prudence." Hitherto, he said, he had "learnt to manage and restrain my propensity to wildness" and would redouble his efforts "to learn discretion with regard to my temper and my feelings." Yet, he averred proudly, "I am not of a disposition to lie still & be trodden . . . They [the members of the college government] may [be] great men but they are no less mortals, and as such I am their equal although a boy and Wm Pitt Fessenden."[27] Determined that his father should appeal the suspension, the angry senior insisted not only that he could prove the absence of prostitutes at Wardsworth's and the steady improvement of his habits, but also that President Allen was "frightened."[28] Although one cannot know for certain if Pitt visited Wardsworth's to gratify his sexual appetites and may find it difficult to accept his claim to be a reformed character, he was right to contend that Allen's belated reference to moral corruption was meant to intimidate Samuel. The letter to Deblois bore the hallmarks of an attempt to forestall an appeal and it says much for Pitt's innate political sense and remarkable self-confidence that he was able to discern the president's tactics. Samuel Fessenden took his son's word for what had happened and appealed to the college trustees for redress—principally on the grounds of Pitt's "extreme youth" (he was still only 17) and his contention that the tyrannical punishment did not fit the crime.[29] The petition was rejected but, in the late summer of 1824, the board of trustees overruled the faculty and voted to confer a bachelor of arts degree on Fessenden, who thereafter was listed officially as a member of the Class of 1823.[30]

One should be wary of reading too much into this catalogue of misdeeds. Student unrest was rampant in the colleges of the early republic.[31] Pitt engaged in no act of insubordination comparable to riots that had occurred previously at Harvard, Princeton, and William and Mary. University authorities, particularly faculty members as distinct from trustees (who tended to be wary of losing income through excessive discipline), were often religious and political conservatives intent on keeping a tight rein on their charges. The result was an irksome panoply of petty regulations unlikely to garner unyielding assent from the male offspring of relatively wealthy parents. Authority came under challenge everywhere in the early republic: any behavior that smacked of monarchy and aristocracy was suspect. Fessenden learned from his father that it was acceptable to speak one's truth to unrestrained power. But his wayward conduct and readiness to confront the college authorities was probably as much the product of youthful striving for peer respect and personal independence as it was of Samuel's extreme brand of Federalism. He was by no means the only Bowdoin alumnus to fall foul of college authorities. Nathaniel Hawthorne (who graduated in 1825) was fined alongside Pitt for gambling at cards for a quart of wine.[32] Pitt's misdeeds at Bowdoin were not untypical of the time. What is more significant is the defiant manner in which he responded to the punishments. As he prepared to make his way in an increasingly competitive society, it was clear he possessed the self-worth, if not yet the application, to survive and prosper.

The Making of a Politician

While his unruly behavior was far from unrepresentative, the same cannot be said of his attendance at college. Only a small minority of boys in the early republic attended university. Most, like Abraham Lincoln, worked on the family farm. Pitt Fessenden may not have been the most diligent of scholars but he was an exceptionally bright youth whose privileged education, encouraged from boyhood by his father, enhanced the likelihood that he would enjoy a leading position in society. His ability to memorize long passages of text, to organize his thoughts in a logical fashion, and to expound publicly upon historical and contemporary issues were all assisted by his Bowdoin education. The central place of rhetoric in the curriculum was of particular value to him as an aspiring lawyer and, perhaps even at this early stage, politician. Students were expected to learn and recite long classical texts and, toward the end of the school year, to declaim confidently before a large audience. His senior-year address on "Prospects of the South American States" in May 1823 was not only indicative of the extent to which he embraced Rollin's cyclical view of history, but it was also suffused with the romantic nationalism and hemispheric pride that engulfed the United States after its narrow victory in the War of 1812. Hailing the recent advent of revolution in Spain's Latin American colonies as evidence of European decline and New World vigor, Fessenden blasted the tyrannical Spaniards' attempts to crush liberation struggles in Mexico. He contemplated with satisfaction the moment when the once mighty nations of Europe "shall at last reach the climax of their greatness, and then the fame of their deeds be obliterated from the calendar of time, or heard only in the song of their bards." "Then," he concluded bombastically, "will America rise & crush the serpents who would blast her infant liberty—& vie even with Athens in her glory."[33]

Although the young orator's colorful use of language identified him as his father's son, his interest in hemispheric events and enthusiastic embrace of Latin American revolutions showed that a Federalist upbringing was not a guarantee of conservative thought in all things. It is true that Fessenden's first major public speech after leaving Bowdoin, an address to the Portland Benevolent Society in October 1825, reflected his father's influence. His assertion that American society was composed of a hierarchy of mutually dependent classes "so nearly balanced, that no order has reason to apprehend the attacks of another," was pure Federalism (not to mention wishful thinking).[34] However, his nationalism, much more confident and expansive than that of his anxious father, was evident in another oration that he delivered to the Young Men of Portland two years later. In this speech he lauded the improving virtues of "free individual enterprize," manufactures, and education. The celebrated French supporter of the American Revolution, the Marquis de Lafayette, he said, had recently returned to find the United States "a mighty and powerful nation" blessed with vast natural resources, a magnificent climate, and entrepreneurial talent. There were clouds on the horizon, he admitted, none darker than southern slavery. However, he was hopeful that the republic would eventually declare this "disgraceful solecism . . . a sound hateful to her ear" and "pollution to her eye . . . at variance with every liberal emotion in the hearts of her children." Given America's boundless resources, the day would surely come when Great Britain, now risen to global predominance after the defeat of Napoleon, must yield to "young and vigorous America."[35]

Pitt Fessenden's youthful, optimistic nationalism was in stark contrast to the foreboding of his fellow Portlander, John Neal. A year older than Fessenden's father, Neal was sojourning in Great Britain, where he had become attracted to the utilitarian ideas of Jeremy Bentham.[36] From London he predicted the eventual breakup of the Union in the wake of the Missouri crisis of 1819–21. That disturbing crisis had pitted northern and southern politicians against one another in ferocious congressional debates over slavery expansion. Thomas Jefferson himself had confessed his fears for the republic despite the forging of a compromise solution that admitted Missouri and Maine as slave and free states respectively and prohibited slavery in

American-held territory north of the line 36° 30'. Neal did not despair entirely of a perpetual union of states but he observed "a natural tendency to separation, which is augmenting every hour" and which would be followed by war prompting "great mischief, principalities, powers, and varied forms of government."[37]

As the United States entered an era of dramatic economic change that would make a global impact, Fessenden prepared to follow his father into the law.[38] He was better equipped than most of his peers to join this elite profession. A silhouette cut in his twenties shows him sporting a cravat and smart jacket or frock coat.[39] With an aquiline nose, soft, feminine mouth and his hair worn short, he has the purposeful pose of an ambitious, well-to-do Yankee. But looks are not everything. Like most males on the verge of adulthood, he was not free from insecurities. Would he succeed in life? Could he forge an identity of his own separate from that of his strong-willed father? Would he find a woman whom he could love and who could love him?

After leaving Bowdoin, he removed to Portland, the principal port on Maine's rocky Atlantic coast. His father had settled there in 1822, doubtless concluding that New Gloucester would never be large or wealthy enough to support his law business. Portland had benefited greatly from the growth of New England commerce since the late eighteenth century. Taking advantage of the town's ice-free harbor, its merchants first grew rich from the carrying trade in the Napoleonic Wars and subsequently, when the war boom was curtailed by Jefferson's embargo on intercourse with Europe, they increased their fortunes by exporting backcountry products like lumber and live cattle in return for domestic and foreign manufactures and molasses from the slave island of Cuba. Back from the wharves along Casco Bay, nabobs like Hugh McLellan and his brother Stephen built grand homes in the Federal style. A growing middle class of professionals and upwardly mobile artisans and a laboring population of whites and blacks contributed to an increasingly diverse citizenry, nearly nine thousand strong in 1820.[40]

It was in this forward-looking city, swept continually by ocean breezes, that Pitt Fessenden embarked upon his career in the law. Living at home with his father, stepmother, and assorted half-brothers and sisters must have been a confining experience after the relative independence of college life. However, he was expertly tutored in equity by Samuel's friend Charles S. Daveis, one of the most respected lawyers in the new state of Maine, and applied himself diligently to the formidable task of preparing for the state bar. He read an array of statutes and commentaries and frequently attended sessions of the county court to watch how professional lawyers conducted their business. Admiring the clarity, simplicity, and conciseness of the arguments propounded by one particular attorney, Fessenden concentrated on making his presentations accessible not only to educated judges but also to the plain-speaking jurymen of New England.[41] He also honed his command of the English language and his ability to influence others by teaching school (mainly to supplement his meager income) and writing articles for local newspapers.

Eager for social standing and companionship outside the family, Fessenden joined prominent voluntary groups such as the Benevolent Society and the Young Men's Club, which also provided useful platforms for his oratory and his developing leadership skills. It seems likely too that he still had time to read for pleasure and self-improvement—histories of classical Greece and Rome and early modern and modern England, certainly, but also contemporary British journals like the *Westminster Review* and *Blackwood's Edinburgh Review* (he was always a keen student of British politics and jurisprudence), novels, and poetry.[42] As this increasingly democratic age progressed, Pitt Fessenden learned to wear his knowledge lightly. In a deliberate act of self-fashioning intended to enhance his powers as a lawyer and a legislator, he spoke publicly in the language of plain common sense. In private, however, friends found him "hospitable, cordial, and wonderfully fascinating in manner and conversation." He was, one recalled, "a brilliant talker, often speaking with humor, and far more ready to unload his memory and display his learning, love of poetry, anecdote, and literary resources at his own fireside than in any public theater."[43]

In the summer of 1826 Fessenden prevailed on his father to allow him to go to New York to pursue his training with Samuel's younger brother, Thomas, a partner in a flourishing law firm on Wall Street. Although he was excited by the prospect of spreading his wings in the republic's most cosmopolitan city, his expectations were not fulfilled. Living costs in Manhattan were much higher than those in Portland and Fessenden had to work like an errand-boy simply to pay for his board and lodging. So tiring were these duties that he had no time for study in the evening. With his hopes "blasted," he was left with the prospect of either returning home or venturing farther afield, perhaps the South.[44] For the first time in his life, Pitt Fessenden evinced a keen desire to visit a slave society. Appalled, his father refused his request and by the start of October the chastened law student was back under the parental roof.[45]

Samuel Fessenden's decision not to allow his talented boy to go below the Mason-Dixon line signaled his growing opposition to slavery. As a hard-line New England Federalist he had long been a foe of Virginia's influence in the corridors of national

power. The irreversible decline of his own party caused by its opposition to the War
of 1812 merely strengthened his conviction that southern influence was a corrupting force in the republic. Samuel was one of many northern Federalists (and Republicans) to name slavery as the source of this pollution, specifically the three-fifths
clause of the U.S. Constitution that artificially inflated southern power in the
House of Representatives by allowing slaves to be part counted for the purposes of
taxation and representation.[46] How "to break down" what his brother Thomas called
"that cursed southern ascendancy, which oppresses us all" was the burning question. At the time of the Missouri crisis, Thomas argued that encouraging northern
manufactures was the best way to undermine the South's political power. "Destroy
the masters," he wrote in September 1820, "& the slaves would . . . sink into their
proper insignificance."[47]

Although Samuel was not averse to supporting industry, he preferred to attack
southern influence more directly. During the 1820s he embraced the colonization
movement, which proposed to rid the country of slavery by transporting freed blacks
to the American Colonization Society's Liberian outpost on the west coast of Africa.
Colonization, however, was a blunt instrument for assailing slavery and southern
power. Some southerners actually supported the movement, either because they regarded it as a means of gradually eradicating slavery or because they saw it as a way
of expelling troublesome free blacks from their region. In 1832, Samuel renounced
colonization and endorsed the radical abolitionism of the crusading Massachusetts
printer, William Lloyd Garrison.[48] His refusal to allow his son to venture south can
thus be seen as a by-product of his evolving opposition to slavery and white racism.
A young man short on self-discipline at college for whom slavery was no more than
an abstract blot on the national escutcheon could only be corrupted by contact with
the South's "peculiar institution." Better he came home to breathe the free air of
New England.

Pitt Fessenden's decision to obey his father's call testified not only to his respect
for parental authority but also to the fact that he had not yet attained manhood. In
October 1827, however, he turned 21. At this symbolic moment of his life he received
an unsettling letter. It was from his mother. After the untimely death of her first husband in 1810, Ruth Green had married a shoemaker, Moses Bailey, borne him five
children (three of whom were still living), and was now residing in Hopkinton, New
Hampshire.[49] There is no record of what Fessenden had been told about his mother
before reading this communication. His father may have explained that she had
died in childbirth. Stunned by the humiliating revelation of his illegitimate birth,

he penned an emotional letter to Samuel requesting the facts of the case. "Will you have the goodness to remember . . ." he wrote angrily, "that this is *my* secret, and, as such I do not wish it communicated even to your wife—my mind not being exactly cool enough to bear the consciousness of her acquaintance with what concerns *myself*, in this particular."[50]

Biographer Charles Jellison contended that "[t]he blight of bastardy" hung heavy on his subject for the rest of his life. Fessenden's "bristling pride," he argued, "his quickness to take affront, his intolerance of human weakness in himself as well as in others, and his frequent displays of pettiness and petulance, all of these were at least in some degree mechanisms of defense or compensation for the ego of a man who was always painfully mindful of the fact that he was not quite respectable and never could be, either in his own eyes or in the eyes of others."[51] The argument is unconvincing. While some of the characteristics that Jellison attributed to Fessenden—his pride and irritability, for example—were real enough, they were clearly manifest during Pitt's student days and were primarily a product of his singular upbringing, not the belated discovery of his illegitimate birth. Bastardy, moreover, was not quite the sin in 1827 that it had been in the previous century. No matter how ashamed Fessenden felt initially about the revelation, it did not stop him later from visiting his mother or promoting the careers of his maternal relatives. Crucially, he already possessed the self-worth needed to limit the psychological damage done by the discovery. The knowledge that he had been born illegitimate did not prevent him from attaining high office—any more than it had held back one of his political heroes, Alexander Hamilton. Nor, in truth, did it render him any more sensitive to criticism than most contemporary politicians.

The primary import of Ruth's startling revelation lies in its effect on the relationship between Fessenden and his father. Although children in early nineteenth-century New England were instructed to obey their parents, the latter were required, in the words of one Maine preacher, to "enforce their instructions by their own example."[52] Learning that Samuel had sinned in the past was bound to affect the way the son related to his father. While it did not cause a breach in the relationship, the discovery contributed to Fessenden's growing independence. He would continue to respect his pushy, whole-souled parent but he was bound hereafter to be more critical, wary even, of his father's counsel on a range of issues and to rely principally on his own inner voice. As he moved from boyhood to manhood, this was perhaps no bad thing.

After being admitted to the state bar at his maturity, Pitt Fessenden practiced law in Bridgton, a village near the old family home in Fryeburg. The place proved too small to support a decent living and he returned to the coast in late 1829 to open a law office on Portland's bustling Middle Street. He worked hard to promote the new business yet found time for such improving pursuits as oratory and boxing. He particularly enjoyed sparring with Joseph Carr, a student in John Neal's law office.[53] Carr recalled that Fessenden was an effective left-arm fighter. On one occasion Fessenden delivered a knock-out punch, leaving Carr with a bloody nose and black eye. "I can see now in my mind's eye," Carr told the senator's son, Frank, half a century later, "the tall straight slim face of your father with lips compressed and eye contracted looking sternly at me and giving the straight out blow."[54]

Such an energetic, assured, determined, and well-mannered young gentleman must have been attractive to the belles of Portland even if his angular face made his appearance striking rather than conventionally handsome. At some point in 1828 he became romantically attached to 20-year-old Elizabeth Wadsworth Longfellow, eldest daughter of his father's colleague Stephen (a staunch Federalist lawyer who had attended the Hartford convention as a delegate from Massachusetts) and sister of the poet Henry W. Longfellow. In November the latter, traveling in Italy, declared himself "highly gratified" by news of the couple's engagement. Fessenden's romantic dreams of lifelong companionship, however, were cruelly dashed when his fiancée died from tuberculosis the following May.[55] He was probably devastated by the tragedy and responded by throwing himself into his work in an effort to suppress his grief. He entered his father's law office in 1830 and became a partner two years later.

Ambition drove him on. By his own admission William Pitt Fessenden was, in his mid-twenties, "a sober moralizing man, with little care for anything but to win prosperity, deriving absolute enjoyment from nothing but a new 'suit' and a long account of fees with a balance in my favor."[56] But it was not just the prospect of wealth that motivated him. Involvement in politics as well as the law assisted his recovery during 1829 and 1830. Reared by a parent convinced that political activism was the only way to save the country, Fessenden rejected the notion held by many of his compatriots that formal political organizations were dangerous, divisive entities. Party disputes, he told the Young Men's Club in 1827, were "incident to every state, in which flourishes a single shoot from the tree of liberty." "Nowhere, but in the dead sea of despotism," he added, "will you find a perfect calm."[57] While his attachment to party was always tempered by his fierce independence (a product of his relatively high social status and untypical upbringing), Fessenden engaged readily in political combat for the rest of his life. Politics attracted him for many reasons. It presented an alternative to personal unhappiness and an antidote to boredom and licentiousness; it made him feel virtuous as an active citizen of the American republic; and of course it offered a driven young man a pathway to fame and power. Two problems confronted him at the dawn of his political career. The first was that he had been raised by a staunch Federalist whose party no longer existed. The second was that he was a wealthy and socially conservative politician in an increasingly democratic age. Maine was on the verge of becoming a predominantly Jacksonian state where privileged men like him would be regarded with suspicion by many ordinary voters. He spent the next two decades seeking a solution to this second problem. Only when the sectional crisis between North and South entered its final phase in the mid-1850s did he find a secure route to high office. The first problem, the absence of a political home, was more easily solved.

Pitt Fessenden began his political life as a National Republican. For many a halfway house between the Federalist and Whig parties, National Republicanism was the political vehicle for the devotees of John Quincy Adams, scion of the celebrated Boston family that had played a central role in the Revolution. Adams, a committed nationalist, had broken controversially with the Federalists over their sectional opposition to Jefferson's foreign policy. Party disintegration after the War of 1812, however, produced a partial realignment of factions, resulting in his elevation to the presidency in 1824. His supporters were most numerous in the northern states where they included many ex-Federalists willing to forgive his apostasy because of his Hamiltonian embrace of positive government, notably in the realm of science and manufactures.

Fessenden's attachment to Adams was clear in a speech he delivered at Bowdoin shortly before the president's bitter election contest against Andrew Jackson in 1828. America had great advantages, he said. "But the great question here occurs, whether it is wise for us to let things take their course, and creep on to greatness by the mere force of time & circumstances, or whether we may not, by proper effort, greatly accelerate our progress; and again, whether by the enlightened direction of our physical and moral power, we may not attain a far greater height, than by a slow and toilsome march, in the beaten track of our ancestors." Only if the national government actively assisted America's qualitative advancement, through the promotion of science and education, was he confident that the United States would take the lead in extending "liberal" principles such as the rights of man and freedom of inquiry.[58]

Although Adams carried Maine in 1828 with nearly 60 percent of the popular vote, he lost the presidential battle. Worryingly for the state's National Republicans more and more new voters were coming to the polls (as they were across America). Democrats would control Maine for the next decade, their primacy rooted in Andrew Jackson's popularity as an authentic war hero; the president's outspoken opposition to monopoly, aristocracy, and nullification; and the party's support for free trade over protection and for agriculture over manufactures. During Adams's abortive campaign Fessenden's godfather, U.S. Senator Daniel Webster, observed that in New Hampshire the Jacksonians were strongest "in the remote parts of the state, farthest from the sources of intelligence, & out of the way of much intercourse with other quarters." The same was true in Maine. In the early 1830s backcountry farmers, many of them Baptists and Methodists operating beyond the reach of the market, remained stubbornly immune to National Republican calls for high tariffs to promote domestic manufactures. In coalition with pro-free trade merchants on the coast and many workingmen on the wharves, they represented a powerful obstacle to the federally supported and diversified capitalist economy favored by Webster, Fessenden, and other National Republicans.

The latter, however, were not despondent for long after Adams's defeat. In Maine they appealed to merchants sympathetic to industry and competed with the new Anti-Masonic Party for the votes of evangelical Protestants opposed to elite rule and perturbed by the way vices like intemperance were sapping the moral foundations of the republic. During the state election campaign of 1831, aware that Jackson's rhetorical opposition to Great Britain played well in remoter portions of Maine, Portland's National Republicans moved to shed their image as crypto-Federalists and Anglophiles by denouncing free trade as "the British System." Astutely blending local and national concerns, they contended that economic diversification was the only way to prevent their city from remaining a mere entrepot for goods headed elsewhere. The "American System" of banks, tariffs, and federally funded transportation development ("internal improvements" in contemporary parlance) favored by Kentucky's National Republican hero, Henry Clay, was the only way to stop Portland from falling behind its competitors. "Without it," insisted an editorial in the *Portland Advertiser,* "we may continue where we are—the humble servant of Boston, Providence, or New York, or the bobtail of some British work shop."[59] Even though the National Republicans were culturally more Anglophile than their opponents, the message, stiffened by attacks on Jacksonian officeholders, hit home among job-conscious workingmen in the town. The Democrats easily won the statewide contest for governor but three of Portland's four delegates to Maine's lower house elected that September were National Republicans. One of them was 24-year-old William

Pitt Fessenden. "This result is unusually brilliant," noted the fiercely partisan *Adver-tiser,* "because it is carried in the teeth of official influence, and after Jacksonism has been triumphant in other parts of the State."[60]

Politicking in the Age of Jackson

When Fessenden arrived at the new Augusta statehouse overlooking the Kennebec River in early January 1832 he found himself "in a decided minority."[61] Jacksonian Democrats outnumbered National Republicans by well over two to one. Among his first duties was having to listen to the message of Governor Samuel E. Smith. A Democrat in his second term of office, Smith gave notice that he expected little action from the assembly. "[W]e shall . . .," he said, emphasizing his party's defin-ing policy of limited government, "find but few laws that require alteration, and not many cases in which the public interest can be promoted by the aid of the Legisla-ture."[62] Aside from expounding on the primacy of agriculture and the importance of literary institutions, the governor's main aim was to urge legislators to cooperate with the Jackson administration's efforts to settle a dangerous boundary dispute be-tween Great Britain and the United States. The dispute, dating back to the 1780s, involved the precise location of the northeastern border between the United States and Canada. Reluctant to go to war over the issue, the two countries had sought mediation from a neutral power. In 1831 the arbitrator, William I, king of the Neth-erlands, had advanced a solution that would have split the contested region into two, with roughly two-thirds of the land going to the United States.[63] Although President Jackson was ready to accept the decision, Governor Smith did not fully endorse it because many local people were angered by its abandonment of the remote Mada-waska settlements claimed by Maine. However, in praising the administration's pa-cific foreign policy and advising that the national authorities be allowed to guard the state's interests in the disputed area, he indicated his preference for compromise.

Outnumbered though they were, National Republicans in the House quickly moved to advertise themselves as the only true defenders of the state's territorial claims in the boundary dispute. Their new recruit, William Pitt Fessenden, led a preliminary assault on what his party regarded as the Jackson administration's at-tempts to make the legislature its cats-paw ahead of a settlement adjudged to be injurious to the rights of Maine. His first legislative motion was an order instructing the Committee on Contested Elections to inquire whether any of the delegates were federal officeholders at the time of their election and therefore occupying their seats illegally under the Maine constitution. Although the Democrats thwarted this and subsequent attempts by Fessenden to probe the issue, the National Republicans had at least signaled their opposition to federal intrusion at a critical moment.

On January 13, 1832, boundary matters were referred to a committee for secret deliberation. Fessenden was not a member but he told his likeminded former tutor, Charles Daveis, that National Republicans on the committee would press the state's interests as forcefully as possible."[64] Fessenden's opposition to the arbitrator's decision was politically motivated for it was widely reviled in Maine. Many of the state's literate urban dwellers, particularly those from a Federalist background like himself, harbored a deep respect for British culture. Most Down Easters, however, had no love for the old enemy (Portland itself had been destroyed by the British during the Revolution) and politicians of all stripes could draw on a deep reservoir of popular Anglophobia. Fessenden knew that an issue calculated to drive a wedge between the Democrat-controlled state and national governments could benefit his own party ahead of the forthcoming presidential contest. As one shrewd National Republican put it, "Jackson would lose the electoral vote of Maine, if it could be clearly proved that his influence had caused the ratification of the award. It is therefore very important that our friends should go in solid columns against the division [of the border region], and that proofs of a different course of conduct on the part of the administration & its friends should be carefully noted."[65]

When the issue came up for debate Fessenden was in the vanguard of attempts to involve Massachusetts in the affair. Residents of Maine's parent state had land interests in the disputed territory and its National Republican government would be a counterweight to the power of local Jacksonians. Arguing that Maine needed all the support it could get, he asked if the House could "hesitate for a moment in adopting any course which can promote a cause of such vital importance to the State, a cause in which we are contending for our territory, for State rights, and constitutional principles."[66] Recognizing that they were in danger of being ensnared on the wrong side of a popular issue, Nathan Clifford, a York County lawyer and future U.S. Supreme Court justice, and other sage Democrats reluctantly backed the attempt to involve Massachusetts. Within days a Jacksonian agent of the state had been appointed to go to Boston. It was Pitt Fessenden's first significant political victory—of a sort.

Debate rumbled on in closed session during the early weeks of 1832 with the ardent young Portland representative continuing to play a leading role. At the end of February a joint committee of the House and Senate reported resolutions broadly supportive of the arbiter's compromise, now endorsed by the Jackson administration and by Maine's congressional delegation, under which Maine would cede territory in return for ample indemnity. The National Republicans derided the sacrifice of state interests to the federal government's free-trade policy. In late February Fessenden tried to secure Massachusetts's assent to the appointment of a commissioner with whom state negotiators would contrive a final settlement. One of his co-partisans moved that any deal should be ratified by the people of Maine rather than the state legislature. Both motions failed and the pro-compromise resolves were passed over National Republican opposition. Two weeks later the *Portland Advertiser* printed the names of those members of "the *British Party* who voted in *secret session* to SELL THEIR COUNTRY, for *money* or *land*."[67]

Fessenden's close involvement in his party's attempts to make political capital out of a difficult international dispute does not reflect particularly well on him. The dispute dragged on for another decade after the U.S. Senate finally rejected the arbiter's decision in June 1832 and later he would acquiesce to a less favorable compromise brokered by Daniel Webster. However, it reveals his early competence as a politician, assured in his use of wedge issues, brazen in his disregard of the risks attached to cynical politicking, more sensitive than many of his co-partisans of the need to adapt to an expanding electorate, and keenly aware of the importance of countervailing power to an embattled minority. At the end of the session he dispatched correspondence about the boundary issue to National Republicans in Boston. He hoped, he wrote, that Massachusetts would "take such steps as will much avail to expose the villainy of those among us who have manifested a willingness to sacrifice the interests of the State . . . Whether we shall be able to make as much of the business here as we wish, & as would seem to be reasonably anticipated, I cannot say. We shall make the attempt and do the best that we are able."[68]

Pitt Fessenden's rhetorical performances also revealed remarkable self-assurance as a first-time legislator. That boldness was particularly evident on February 9, 1832, when he delivered what one of his peers described as "a flaming speech" against Jacksonian resolves opposed to rechartering the Bank of the United States.[69] Deemed essential to the smooth working of the American economy by National Republicans and a hideous monopoly that threatened popular liberties by Andrew Jackson and his supporters, the Bank was destined to play a central role in the forthcoming presidential election. One witness reported how, responding to an anti-Bank tirade by Nathan Clifford, "A young man, the youngest in the House, rose up, a sarcastic smile playing upon his lips, and commenced his firing upon the resolutions and the authors of them."[70]

The ensuing speech was characterized by Fessenden's trademark logic, clarity, and pungency. He began by puncturing Clifford's balloon, observing pointedly that his ideas were purloined from an oration delivered by Senator Thomas Hart Benton of Missouri, and commenting sarcastically that if Clifford expected his remarks to envelop the chamber "in a flood of radiance . . . I must confess myself still in darkness." The Bank, he insisted, was not a threat to the people (in whom he professed to have more faith than the caucus-ridden Democrats). Rather, it was an essential tool for the promotion of a healthy and growing national economy. His comments marked him out as an effective supporter of Portland's dominant commercial interests and of global capitalist development in general. So what, he asked, if some of the Bank's investors were foreigners? Foreign investment was essential "for the advantage of a new country." So what if the charter's renewal raised the value of stockholders' assets? "[I]f a benefit is to accrue to the country, why should we refuse to accept that benefit, because others are to participate in it? . . . I abhor that littleness of soul, which cannot bear another's prosperity. I care not how rich other men may become—if they acquire that wealth by such a course as is consistant [sic] with the welfare of others."[71] By the close Clifford was allegedly "whittled down to a small compass." "Mr. Fessenden," concluded the admittedly partisan observer, "is decidedly one of the best speakers in the House."[72]

While much of the politicking in the assembly was pure theatrics ahead of the November presidential election, there was plenty of serious business to conduct. Here, Fessenden was often frustrated by his party's minority status. Everything proposed by the National Republicans, he complained, "is voted down, for fear that there may be some trick in it."[73] He was thwarted, therefore, in his attempts to pass a $3,000 public appropriation for Bowdoin College. The move laid Fessenden open to Jacksonian charges that he was attempting to gain favors for the rich, a charge that the Bowdoin graduate rebutted by asserting that he favored extending the advantages of a liberal education to all classes.[74] Even his efforts to procure a charter for Portland that would allow the city to increase its governance over residents were obstructed by Democrats like Clifford, who denounced the move as calculated to create a "creature" that was "ten thousand times more dangerous than the U.S. Bank."[75]

Exasperated by what he regarded as the demagogic maneuvers of his adversaries, Fessenden returned home from Augusta with his political reputation enhanced and eager to contribute to the National Republicans' evolving campaign to unseat Andrew Jackson. He was probably present at a meeting of young National Republicans in Portland on March 20. This gathering backed the presidential candidacy of Henry Clay and attacked the Democrats for their mishandling of state and national issues, principally their alleged sell-out on the boundary question and irresponsible opposition to the Bank of the United States and protective tariffs. It also appointed five delegates from Cumberland County to the party's Young Men's convention in Washington, DC, among them William Pitt Fessenden.[76]

Before leaving for the convention Fessenden got married. His bride, Ellen, was the youngest daughter of James Deering, a local ship-owner who had survived Jefferson's embargo to become one of the wealthiest merchants in Portland. He owned a two-story mansion built in 1804 on two hundred acres of improved farmland, woods, and meadows at Westbrook—where the marriage took place on April 23—on the western side of the city.[77] While there is no reason to suppose that this was anything other than a love-match, it was clearly a union of considerable material advantage to a professional man. Fessenden had long admired the innovative merchant class that had played such an instrumental role in Portland's development. In a public address of 1827, he had lavished praise on the merchants as "a race of [American] nobles;—not hereditary,—not depending upon the testimonials of worm-eaten statues, and rusty armor;—but self-created—and showing in support of their claims to the distinction, a splendid income,—a lordly palace,—and a magnificent expenditure;—all attained by their own industry and intelligence."[78] An enthusiastic proponent of economic progress along meritocratic, capitalist lines, he was now a fully paid-up member of New England's commercial elite.

Apart from homemaking, Fessenden spent the summer of 1832 campaigning on behalf of the National Republicans. As well as participating in the Washington convention, he attended a lavish function in Portland in early August in support of Maine's anti-Jackson U.S. senators.[79] A long procession snaked its way along Congress Street to City Hall, where guests were entertained by a band playing patriotic airs and listened to speeches and toasts from the politicians. Surrounding them were arches festooned with national symbols and slogans: a transparency of George Washington; the Stars and Stripes; the phrase "Liberty and Union, Now and Forever, One and Inseparable" from Daniel Webster's recent, ringing response to the South Carolina nullifier, Robert Y. Hayne; and, more prosaically, "The American System" and "The US Bank."[80]

The state election in September delivered another victory for the Democrats and a narrow defeat for Fessenden in his bid for reelection to the state House of Representatives.[81] He declared himself unfazed and generally satisfied with the party's showing. The Jacksonians, he reported, "are most thoroughly frightened—and I think that if we do our duty, and can *raise the wind*, Mr. Clay *may* carry Maine."[82] The tension mounted as the day of the November general election approached. In late October Fessenden signed an anti-Jackson address to the voters with his father, Stephen Longfellow, and, significantly, the local Anti-Masonic leader, Neal Dow, who had conceded that his own candidate, William Wirt, could not carry Maine. Pitched to a broad constituency, it claimed to be written not by politicians but concerned citizens anxious for the welfare of a republic in which the executive had betrayed his principles and set himself above the other branches of government.[83] The no-party ruse failed. Clay carried Portland but lost Maine (where the number of voters going to the polls had nearly doubled in four years) by more than six thousand votes. Jackson, benefiting from his popular stance on the Bank, was reelected by a crushing majority in the electoral college. National Republicans were left to lick their wounds and regroup with the majority of Anti-Masons in the embryonic Whig Party coalition.

Fessenden would be a loyal Whig for two decades. The party, however, did not coalesce immediately in the wake of Jackson's reelection nor did Fessenden, still a novice, initially play a leading role in fashioning the anti-Democratic coalition in Maine. The chief barrier to the development of a new political organization was the nullification crisis. In November 1832 a special convention in South Carolina formally nullified two protective federal tariffs, declaring them injurious to the interests of the state. Jackson, a staunch Unionist, responded decisively. He issued a forthright condemnation of separatism, warning that he would use force to uphold federal power. National Republican leaders in New England were invigorated not only by the president's no-nonsense riposte to southern nullifiers but also by the administration's endorsement of a "force bill" authorizing the president to suppress any resistance to federal authority. Lacking support from its fellow slave states, wavering at the prospect of invasion by federal troops, and mollified by a compromise on the tariff brokered in Congress by Henry Clay, South Carolina backed away from the brink. But during the first half of 1833 the president, mercilessly attacked by National Republicans during the fall election campaign, was regarded in a more positive light by his former opponents. For a time even Webster considered the possibility of aligning himself with his fellow nationalist in the White House.[84]

Pitt Fessenden spent most of 1833 applying himself to the business of earning a reputation in his father's Portland law office. He retained a keen interest in politics, however, and delivered a nationalistic address on Independence Day. It was a strong speech and one that illustrated clearly how nullification allowed post-Federalist New Englanders to emerge from the shadow of the Hartford convention and transfer the stain of disunion onto slaveholding southerners. In it he ignored his recent states' rights stance on the Maine boundary and gave thanks that during the recent crisis America had a president "with patriotism to abhor, and firmness vigorously to oppose, the designs of our misguided brethren." With memories of the Revolution fading, he went on, it was essential to nurture "the love of our national union" and to "[d]o no act that can injure it." To this end, said Fessenden, all subjects threatening the health of the body politic should be eradicated: "Of these great questions of national politics upon which parties are so much divided, I have at present only to remark that it were far better to adopt an unwise national policy than to endanger our harmony as a people."

While this last statement looked to be a grudging endorsement of Clay's compromise, Fessenden was at pains to emphasize that northerners should not roll over to appease the South. The most serious problem threatening the United States, he contended, was slavery, "a gross absurdity" in a republic and one that had an "injurious effect" on America's prosperity. Pursuing his central theme to its logical conclusion, he avowed that it was the non-slaveholding states' responsibility to eradicate an "evil" and "a curse" that had resisted reform and weakened the love of some of his countrymen for the Union. Although he confessed that immediate abolition was "impracticable," he insisted that it was time for men to speak their minds freely on the subject, thereby forcing slavery to yield before the moral power of public opinion. If this were not done, he could foresee a time when the Union would be convulsed by slave insurrections (presumably, though he did not mention the event by name, along the lines of Nat Turner's 1831 revolt in Virginia). "Not much longer," he warned, "will the slave writhe contentedly in his fetters—and such are the feelings of the non-slaveholding States that they will never aid in rivetting those chains which even now they cannot contemplate without a shudder."[85]

Fessenden's contention that slavery was an incubus around the neck of the republic as well as the enslaved, one that he had first articulated publicly in 1827, was not original to him. The same theme had been aired in more outspoken terms by northern politicians—wary of the political power that slavery gave to southerners and anxious about the damaging impact of bondholding on American liberties—since the late eighteenth century. However, he would soon retreat from his belief that northerners should continue to agitate the issue. Over the next two years, Garrisonian abolitionists like his father, a founding member of the Maine Antislavery

Society, employed moral suasion to induce slaveholders to give up their sinful practice.[86] Instead of yielding to religious appeals for emancipation, southerners came
out fighting. They defended slavery aggressively, deeming it a positive good for all
(the slaves included) and insisting that northerners must cease agitating the subject
if they wished to preserve national peace. The fiercely patriotic Jacksonians quickly
rallied to oppose the abolitionists who, in their view, threatened the republic's stability for the sake of unloved blacks. The Whig opposition, which began to coalesce
in late 1833 and 1834 around support for Clay's American System and, in the South,
around opposition to Jackson's uncompromising stance on nullification, also opposed agitation of the slavery question for the same patriotic reasons. However, the
situation was complicated by the fact that in the North a minority of Whigs (many of
them New England Protestants) regarded slavery as a moral evil, worse than drunkenness and desecration of the Sabbath. Portland's outspoken temperance advocate
Neal Dow, a former Anti-Masonic leader, claimed he had refused to support Clay in
1832 because the Kentuckian owned slaves.[87] Nevertheless, he subsequently joined
the Whig Party along with many of his third-party peers because its endorsement
of positive government and broadly improving ethos provided the most effective
vehicle for his perfectionist aims.

Like Dow, Fessenden joined the Whig Party in the mid-1830s because he believed that government action was the most effective way to promote progress in
nineteenth-century America. Unlike Dow, a fervent evangelical, he felt little com-
punction to perfect a tainted world or micro-manage the social lives of his fellow
citizens. Reared in the tradition of New England orthodoxy, Fessenden believed in
the existence of divine providence but did not pretend to second-guess the Creator's
intentions. He did not doubt that man was sinful and knew his Bible as well as anyone. He was, however, a rational thinker who preferred to base his opinions on hard
evidence rather than blind faith and to spend his Sundays relaxing at home rather
than worshiping ostentatiously in church. While he inherited a strong core of moral
principles from his father, he disliked slavery as much for its corrupting effect on
the Union as its degrading impact on fellow human beings. When the ferocious
southern response to abolitionist campaigning undermined his contention that debate over slavery would be beneficial to the republic, he was placed on the horns of
a dilemma that was personal as well as political.

The seriousness of that dilemma was brought home to him in August 1835. Fessenden had returned to Portland the previous April after an abortive attempt to
set up a law office in the backwoods boom-town of Bangor. While he may have

abandoned the attempt partly because the competition was too stiff, the talented young attorney probably went back to the coast because, as his friend Joseph Carr recalled, "there was in the [frontierlike] social and business atmosphere something that did not exactly suit his temperament and he did not or could not adapt himself to it."[88] His wife Ellen, in poor health after the birth of the couple's first son, James, as well as his father and step-family remained in Portland and he moved back and forth between Bangor and the coast during 1834—an indication that he was never entirely committed to a career in the Maine interior. Having returned to Casco Bay, he formed what proved to be a long-lasting partnership with William Willis, an older man whose organizational abilities and studious, retiring temperament perfectly complemented Fessenden's penetrating, analytical mind and his impressive ability to master copious amounts of detailed information and develop a concise, compelling argument before judge and jury alike. There can be little doubt that Fessenden expected to apply his prodigious talents to politics as well as the law. Portland had just elected a Whig mayor and the city offered a useful base for his political advancement in a Jacksonian state. It was at this point, however, that his position on the slavery question was exposed.

In mid-August 1835, ninety-two leading citizens of Portland and vicinity composed a nonpartisan address calling for an anti-abolitionist meeting to be held at City Hall. It was signed by many of the town's leading merchants, including James Deering.[89] Days later a large public rally, addressed by several businessmen, drew up a series of resolves stating, first, that the constitutional compromises over slavery made at Philadelphia in 1787 had brought unparalleled prosperity to the United States and granted no power to the federal government over slavery in the states and, second, that antislavery agitation would undermine not only the relationship that existed between masters and slaves but also the Union itself. Those in attendance, John Neal among them, committed themselves to shun abolitionist gatherings and to use their "utmost endeavors to prevent our friends and families from attending all such meetings."[90] The assembly did acknowledge that slavery was morally wrong (though forced on America by Great Britain) and some of those present convened at the end of the month to register their support for colonization. Local abolitionists responded to both meetings by defending their right to free speech and to advocate emancipation in areas directly controlled by the federal government. Like many other communities across America in the summer of 1835, Portland was a city divided by the intensifying debate over slavery's place in the United States.

Here was a personal dilemma for Pitt Fessenden that mirrored the political dilemma that slavery posed to all thinking citizens of the republic. His father was one of the most prominent abolitionists in New England and now his wealthy father-in-law was weighing in on the other side of the contest. Local Whigs, moreover, were deeply divided by slavery. Many, like Neal Dow, were colonizationists; others, including John Neal, were either opposed to any agitation of the issue or, a small minority, were outright abolitionists. The crisis might have passed had Portland's antislavery radicals not nominated Pitt Fessenden for office in mid-September 1835. If he wanted a political career, he could not stay silent. He responded to the nomination with a public letter that represented a frank disavowal of his father's cause. He had, he told readers of the *Portland Advertiser*, thought it to be a well-known fact that "I am not, and never have been, a member of any abolition society, and have made no secret of my unqualified want of confidence in the expediency and beneficial effects of such associations." Although he acknowledged the abolitionists' "benevolent motives" and decried "the senseless" manner in which they were currently assailed, he was not "an abolition man," nor, he added, was he ambitious for any public office.[91]

In Fessenden's denial one sees the making of a classic centrist Republican—a northerner genuinely opposed to slavery for several reasons but a pragmatic young politician whose disavowal of abolitionism made political sense at a time when most northerners were prepared to repress their dislike of slavery for the welfare of the Union. Other ambitious and patriotic antislavery Whigs who later found themselves at the vital center of the Republican Party (Abraham Lincoln in Illinois among them) made a similar calculation. Fessenden's refusal to place black freedom over the safety of the white republic clearly illustrated the sometimes subtle differences that existed between father and son on the slavery question. Samuel was a passionate man with a searing hatred of slavery that had deep political roots in his Federalist past but one which, probably by dint of his expanding interaction with local black abolitionists, was now translating into genuine empathy for people of color, enslaved and free.[92] Pitt Fessenden was a more ardent figure than his historical reputation as a moderate suggests. However, his opposition to the peculiar institution in the 1830s was tempered by an absence of hostility toward southerners, by a realistic awareness that abolitionism posed a serious threat to national peace, by the paucity of his own contacts with black people, and by an astute realization that antislavery radicalism was not the best way to attract northern voters.

Sired by an extreme New England sectionalist but heavily influenced by the youthful, vigorous nationalism of the 1820s, William Pitt Fessenden was a natural supporter of National Republicanism and Whiggery. These were powerful creeds, engines of bourgeois improvement that envisioned government—state *and* national—as an essential facilitator of American progress in the nineteenth century. An aspiring politician, he was deeply desirous of fame and influence, but not at the expense of his principles. Had ambition been his only driver, he would have become a Democrat before the decade was out. To secure a position in which he could put his modernizing principles into practice, this urbane Yankee lawyer would have to immerse himself in the affairs of the Whig Party. In August 1836 Fessenden went up to Bangor on the steamer. He went fishing with friends on the Sabbath. "[T]ell it not among the orthodox," he joked to his wife. He drank too: a glass of Madeira with dinner that gave him a headache.[93] Three months later the Democrats gave him something else to think about. They elected their presidential candidate, Martin Van Buren of New York, by a comfortable margin over his opponents. The Whigs won a majority of new voters among the electorate but the number of those recruits was too small to secure the presidency. Depressingly for Fessenden and his co-partisans the Whig vote in Maine was more than 5 percentage points down from the combined anti-Jacksonian vote in 1832.[94] His labors were just beginning.

A Loyal Whig, 1837–1848

William Pitt Fessenden's path to national power was far from smooth. He possessed many weapons in his armory: a remarkable self-confidence born of his privileged upbringing; a piercing intellect and suave, dignified manner that commanded respect from his peers; a strong sense of conviction tempered by a pragmatic politician's understanding of the need for compromise; a plain, direct speaking style honed in the courtrooms of New England; and a realistic awareness that most significant decisions, even in a relatively democratic republic, were made by professional politicians behind closed doors. Though undeniably bourgeois, he was an astute judge of public opinion. On occasions he would sneer privately at "the sovereign people," but he was sage enough to realize that the popular will could not be flouted carelessly in "the Age of Jackson."[1]

Obstructing his progress was not only the majoritarian Democratic Party but also contingency—that relentless sequence of interconnected historical events that could not be predicted accurately even by shrewd politicians like himself. His Whiggery was passionately held, rooted in his belief that the party possessed the optimal solutions to the myriad problems bedeviling the American republic in the middle decades of the nineteenth century. Although sensitive to the dangers of concentrated power (how could Samuel Fessenden's son be unaware of them?), he shared John Quincy Adams's view that government must be used positively to unlock the republic's vast resources and guard against moral corruption. However, while historian Daniel Walker Howe rightly asserts the importance of the Whigs' modernizing, even civilizing, influence on antebellum America, Pitt Fessenden's allegiance to the party of Clay and Webster in a relatively remote Jacksonian state gained for him no more than local notability during a period book-ended by the election of two Whig presidents.[2] Only as the growing crisis over slavery expansion strengthened his (and others') commitment to a republic shorn of southern domination did the prospect of rapid political advancement begin to open up.

Hard Times

Although Fessenden was, broadly speaking, at ease with the changes remaking the antebellum North, his heavy dependence on, and attention to, family ties through-out his career illustrated the importance of older forms of kinship networks to the development of politics and capitalism in the antebellum period. In an era of rapid material growth and high rates of geographical mobility, it was no longer as easy as it once had been to trust those with whom one dealt on a regular basis. Yet trust was essential in business and formal politics—hence the continuing reliance in both of these male-dominated spheres on family members. Without his father's example and assistance, it is unlikely that the Portlander would have become either a lawyer or a politician. His Uncle Thomas, who had contributed to the young man's legal educa-tion in the 1820s, was a secondary but important influence. In March 1837, Hiram Ketchum, Thomas's law partner in New York, offered Fessenden a giant step up the political ladder: a tour of the trans-Appalachian West with Senator Daniel Webster of Massachusetts.

Webster was one of the most influential politicians of his day. The Whig grandee had abandoned thoughts of an alliance with Jackson after the president took the con-troversial decision to remove federal deposits from the Bank of the United States and distribute them in state banks.[3] Unsuccessful in his bid for the presidency in 1836, Webster was eager to launch his second attempt to reach the White House. A trip to the West would help to dispel his image as a sectional candidate and enable him to make valuable personal connections ahead of the forthcoming campaign. What Webster required was "a travelling companion," Ketchum told Fessenden toward the end of March 1837, "some young, ambitious, and highly talented man, in whom he could repose unlimited confidence, who could say things for him, or on his behalf, that it would not be proper for him to say directly." Here, he thought, was the perfect opportunity. Out west Fessenden would not only meet some of the most powerful men in the country but also have the chance of "fully measuring one of the great-est minds in the world." Uncle Thomas urged his nephew to accept the offer, help-fully suggesting that James Deering might be able to offset the costs and venturing the hope that the trip would make Webster president soon and Pitt the same "in due time."[4]

It is unlikely that Fessenden took long to consider the offer. Willis could look after the law firm and the Deerings would take care of Ellen and the couple's two young boys. He joined Webster's small party at Harrisburg on May 9, reaching the Pennsylvania capital from Philadelphia in four days largely by two forms of internal improvement: canal and railroad. Thenceforth he journeyed around the West on stages and steamboats for three months, visiting Pittsburgh, Cincinnati, Lexington, Louisville, St. Louis, Alton, Jacksonville, Chicago, and Detroit before returning home. He met many important politicians along the way, Henry Clay among them, just as Ketchum had promised. But he also encountered individuals of lesser renown. One in particular impressed him, an aspiring Cincinnati law- yer with Portland connections named Salmon P. Chase who showed him around the city, pointing out landmarks, driving him to Lyman Beecher's famous Lane Seminary, and talking at length on western affairs.[5] At Alton, on the Mississippi, Fessenden ran into one of his father's friends, Elijah Lovejoy, a Maine-born aboli- tionist who had migrated to Illinois after his eastern press had been destroyed and was now editing another antislavery newspaper having recently been run out of St. Louis by a mob. Lovejoy was also speculating in western lands and Fessenden joked that the transplanted Yankee seemed to enjoy his new speculation "better than the old one, tho' he cannot help holding forth occasionally on the old topic."[6] Later the young traveler may have had cause to reflect that his gibe was not so funny in hindsight. Lovejoy was murdered by anti-abolitionist assailants five months after their meeting.

The tour confirmed Fessenden's Whiggish enthusiasm for government-built transportation links. Traveling on Pennsylvania's state-backed canals and railroads sent him into "a perfect rage" because of the Jacksonian administration's "little, mean, [and] sordid" obstruction of infrastructural development back home.[7] Al- though northern Whigs generally supported higher tariffs to promote manufac- turing, there was more than a touch of parochialism about his observations on Pittsburgh, one of the North's leading industrial centers. "One continual cloud," he commented, "hangs perpetually over the city & almost shuts out from view the hills all around us . . . Bustle, noise, smoke, steam, and all the signs & symptoms of enter- prise are continually in your *eyes*, & what's worse, in your nose & mouth . . . Every thing looks gloomy & filthy . . . I wouldn't live in P. so long as I could live any where else—that's certain."[8]

Fessenden was as critical an observer of his godfather as he was of Pittsburgh. Ketchum had emphasized that the young man's main duty was to dispatch regu- lar reports of the tour that could be worked up into glowing newspaper accounts of Daniel Webster's fitness for the presidency. Unfortunately, Fessenden was far from star-struck. He rapidly concluded that the senator's manner was "decidedly bad." Possibly fearing that Webster's inordinate ambition had got the better of a politician who, in the recent presidential election, had only managed to win the electoral votes of his home state, he told Ellen that Webster must appear "repulsive" to strangers and that the senator would have been better advised to stay at home and leave "his public fame & public services to speak for him."[9] It was a characteristically perceptive observation. In spite of his spell-binding oratory the saturnine Webster lacked human warmth and charisma and was too closely associated with the Bank of the United States to render him popular.[10] Consequently, the boom he hoped to ignite by touring the West failed to materialize after his party returned home in the late summer of 1837. Fessenden understood the political utility of his personal connection with "Godlike Daniel" and belatedly supplied Ketchum with the material he needed. Indeed, he was sensible enough to maintain close relations with the powerful statesman until Webster lost much of his support when a member of the Tyler administration. However, though conscious of being "a sort of satellite" on the western trip, he was always too confident in his own abilities to become his godfather's creature.[11]

As well as allowing him to see the fastest growing region in the country and observe what he termed ironically "the movements of great men," Fessenden's journey gave him the opportunity of witnessing the effects of a serious economic panic on the country at large.[12] Mercantile houses and banks across the United States were badly hit by a sudden financial collapse in the spring of 1837. New York banks suspended specie payments the day after he arrived in Harrisburg. Money and credit quickly became scarce throughout the republic, prices fell precipitously, and domestic commerce stalled. The political fallout was visible all along the route of Webster's progress as ordinary people flocked to express their opposition to the Democrats' financial policies, which they held responsible for the crash. "I do believe that the minds of men are rapidly preparing for a change," Fessenden wrote from Lexington, Kentucky, at the end of May. "The effects of bad government are being *felt*, and from the numbers of Admn. or former Jackson men who throng to hear Mr. W. . . . it is fair to infer that the public mind is thoroughly awakened—or at least beginning to awake."[13]

For the first time in the Whigs' short history, party leaders sensed a dramatic shift in the popular mood. Even in the Jacksonian stronghold of Maine the tide seemed to be turning. Shortly after he returned home to assist the Whig candidate Edward Kent with his gubernatorial campaign, Fessenden assured Webster "that we have the strongest indications of a great & radical change in this State, such as will render our voice of more importance with reference to future events, than it has been hitherto."[14] In September 1837 Kent was elected as the first Whig governor of Maine by the narrowest of majorities.

Like its Democratic rival, the national Whig Party was a conscious creation of elite politicians—first at the congressional level, where Senators Henry Clay and Daniel Webster fashioned coherent responses to the decentralized, hard-money economic policies of the Jackson and Van Buren administrations, and then in the states, where their acolytes strove to mobilize voters primarily on the basis not only of opposition to executive tyranny and support for the growth-oriented American System of protective tariffs, manufactures, banks, and infrastructural development but also on the back of local issues of live importance to the grassroots. Creating a workable national coalition in a large and expanding republic was a difficult task, not least because the Whig coalition in 1836–37 was weakened, first, by anti-partyism— hostility to factional organization increased by the Democrats' emphasis on party discipline at the expense of individual initiative and the national welfare—and, sec- ond, by the lack of federal patronage that had helped the Jacksonians to cohere as a state and national force. Aspiring Whig politicians like William Pitt Fessenden in Maine were certainly helped by the impact of the economic panic during the spring and summer of 1837. However, they understood that if the new party was to become a genuinely competitive force before the 1840 presidential election, it would require careful planning as well as the right mix of national and local issues.

During the course of 1838 Fessenden, pressed again by Ketchum, exerted himself on behalf of Daniel Webster's presidential ambitions.[15] It was a thank- less task. Webster's rival Henry Clay demonstrated greater appeal to moderates above and below the Mason-Dixon line and the Kentucky statesman successfully contested Webster's attempts to set himself up as the leading opponent of Van Buren's hard-money policies in Congress. In March Fessenden did manage to pre- vent his co-partisans in Maine from backing Clay for president at their legisla- tive convention in Augusta. However, although he told a grateful Webster that he possessed "implicit faith" in their common cause, he expressed concerns that some Maine Whigs were evincing a worrying tendency to subordinate their prin- ciples in an effort to make themselves more appealing to the predominantly Jack- sonian electorate. "The leaven of Loco-focoism," he wrote, "is working somewhat among our own friends. Small politicians are acquiring too much power, & narrow views are obstructing . . . the course of broad and manly principles."[16] This trend portended ill for Webster's presidential ambitions. Kent's defeat that fall revealed that the Whigs had no grip on Maine. With the economy seeming to improve, a more "available" candidate than Webster would be required if they were to carry the state in 1840.

While his law business prospered, hard work, a sharp intellect, and a savvy political mind enabled Pitt Fessenden to establish himself as one of Maine's leading Whigs in the late 1830s. Arguably his most important contribution to party building during this period was his successful wooing of Francis O. J. Smith. The Portland attorney was one of many Conservative Democrats across the country who were potential recruits for the Whig Party because of their antipathy to Van Buren's policy of setting up an Independent Treasury as a repository of federal funds. Denied reelection to Congress as a Jacksonian, Smith made it known in early 1839 that he intended to set up a newspaper in Portland to rival the city's leading Democratic organ, the *Argus*. Acutely aware of the partisan press's influence and the Whigs' minority status in Maine, Fessenden sought partial funding for the enterprise in New York and Portland. His aim was to split the opposition at home and ensure that, in a powerful signal to wavering Democrats, Smith came out against President Van Buren ahead of the 1840 election. Although the plan went down badly with some local Whigs (who believed Smith was using them for his own ends), Fessenden believed the risk was worth taking. "Whatever he may *say*," he wrote of Smith, "we know that his great aim is restoration to power. He must not, therefore, be trusted too far. If his position & skill can be rendered serviceable, they ought not to be lost. It is a question how far, & in what way, he can be used, and what he is worth."[17]

Like their co-partisans throughout the northern states, Maine Whigs had a clear vision in the summer of 1839: "A sound credit system,—a good currency,— confidence among the business men of the State,—the developement [sic] of our resources,—the settlement of our Public Lands,—a diminution of Executive power— the protection of our soil,—the speedy adjustment of our border difficulties,—a good State Government,—one that will place the State of Maine side by side with the most prosperous of the States of the Union."[18] Troublingly, however, the party's fortunes remained uncertain. Much of the optimism accompanying Kent's gubernatorial election in 1837 had dissipated. Only around sixty delegates attended the Cumberland County Whig convention on August 21 compared with the "hundreds" present the year before. These hard-core Whigs nominated candidates for county office, passed resolves condemning the ruling Democratic administration, declared in favor of Clay's presidential candidacy, and elected Fessenden as a delegate to the party's forthcoming national nominating convention.[19]

While he continued to labor diligently at the grassroots, morale generally within the party remained low. Most Maine Whigs simply did not believe they could overturn the state's natural Jacksonian majority even when times were hard. To make matters worse, the party was also coming under pressure from abolitionists, some of whom—incensed by congressional backing for the peculiar institution and rising support across the country for American annexation of the proslavery republic of Texas—were becoming convinced that independent political action was the only way to relax slavery's grip on the two major parties. Samuel Fessenden would be a late convert to the idea of forming an abolitionist party but he publicly questioned his son about slavery in July, a request that, for the moment, appears to have elicited no response.[20] Although Pitt Fessenden was elected one of Portland's representatives to the legislature, the Whigs' gubernatorial nominee, Edward Kent, went down to an ignominious defeat for the second year running. The *Portland Advertiser* blamed the party's poor showing on voter apathy and dismal weather.[21]

Whatever the cause, Whig defeats in Maine and other northern states greatly reduced Clay's chances of being the party's standard-bearer in 1840.[22] Despite exhortations from Hiram Ketchum to back Webster, Fessenden now considered that General William Henry Harrison, the hero of the Battle of Tippecanoe in 1811, was the only man who could defeat Van Buren by reaching out to new voters and disillusioned Conservatives like Frank Smith.[23] Recent efforts by Henry Clay to conciliate the proslavery South, he believed, would cost the Kentuckian New York, where twenty thousand antislavery Whigs would vote against him.[24] Only a less orthodox Whig, it seemed, would be able to attract dissident Democrats and new voters into the fold. In early December Fessenden attended the Whigs' national convention in Harrisburg, Pennsylvania. Maine delegates voted for Harrison, who was nominated over Clay with the assistance of New York's Whig boss, Thaddeus Stevens.

After Christmas the busy Portland politician journeyed to the Augusta statehouse for his second term in the lower chamber. Again he found himself in a distinct minority. The Democrat, Hannibal Hamlin, a future vice president of the United States whom he adjudged to be "not a great man" on first sighting, was elected speaker over his Whig opponent by 108 votes to 57 on January 1, 1840.[25] But as a leading Whig from Maine's most important urban center, Fessenden went on to play an active role in proceedings, enunciating his support for public education, banks, and state-subsidized internal improvements, and sitting on a committee charged with revising local statutes to meet, in his words, the interests of "a great and growing State."[26]

Significantly, he also declared that the "gag rule," passed by the U.S. House of Representatives in May 1836 to counter the flow of abolitionist petitions, was "a gross and wanton outrage upon the Constitution of the United States," though he again made it clear that he did not belong to any abolitionist society.[27] His double-edged statement accurately reflected the ambivalent approach that many northern Whigs took to slavery at this time. They deplored its damaging impact on American liberties (the gag rule seriously infringed the right to free speech) and could ill afford to alienate those religiously motivated abolitionists who were generally more attracted to their party than to the more secular, southern-oriented Democrats. On the other hand, as members of a patriotic and bisectional organization bent on winning the 1840 election, they could not afford to be identified closely with a group of radicals widely regarded as a threat to the Union.

At this juncture of Fessenden's career the pursuit of power took precedence over his dislike of slavery. On March 4, 1840, he delivered a "frank & manly" address at the Whigs' legislative caucus in favor of the party's presidential election ticket of William Henry Harrison and the conservative Virginian, John Tyler.[28] The caucus then drew up a series of resolutions to mobilize the electorate. Amid references to the virtues of positive government, the need for retrenchment, and the importance of harmonizing commerce, agriculture, and manufactures, there was only one reference to slavery: a condemnation of the gag as "an outrage upon the natural and constitutional right of the citizen."[29]

Despite his readiness to engage in acrimonious partisan warfare Fessenden was able, as he was throughout his political career, to distance himself somewhat from party. This was a product of many factors, not just of his own independent nature but also of the affection he felt for his young family back home in Portland. Notwithstanding her poor health Ellen had given birth to three sons—James, William, and Francis—by the time he reentered the legislature. The absent breadwinner missed them all and wrote home regularly during the winter session, trusting the boys "to their mother, & all to other friends, & to God who is the Protector of all his creatures."[30] However, while his love of home was genuine, it was not so strong that it prevented him from leaving Ellen and the boys for long stretches of time. His desire to be busy, to be useful, and to exert influence on the public weal was always stronger than his craving for a domestic sphere whose gendered parameters were being laid down steadily by the advance of industrialization and the American middle class. Fessenden understood this defining, masculine aspect of his character well enough. Playful comments in a letter home from his boarding house in Hallowell indicate that Ellen knew it too. The more he thought about it, he told his wife in early March 1840, "the better satisfied I am that a man's first duty is to take care of his own household." If Ellen were not "so confounded ambitious," he added, tongue in cheek, "the State might . . . look out for itself. Why will you compel me to mingle so much in politics—knowing as you do that I am 'never so happy as when in the bosom of my family.' Oh, wife, wife, your aspiring nature will be the death of *me*."[31]

The election campaigns of 1840 seemed set to intensify Fessenden's thirst for politics. He was widely tipped as a contender for the Whig gubernatorial nomination but his father urged him to reject any overtures in this direction. No one, Samuel told his ambitious son in typically forthright terms, would thank him for being an abject party tool: "[N]o honest man will be buoyed up by the popular breath—& you will sink in that ocean whose waters cast up only mire and dirt—& you will die young in all senses of the *word. Die.*"[32] Although his Whiggery limited his receptivity to the anti-party counsel of his radical parent, Pitt Fessenden had apparently given up any idea of running for governor by late May.[33] He did so, likely as not, first, because the powerful Bangor Whig Edward Kent wanted another tilt at the office and, second, because he had his heart set on the congressional nomination from the Portland district. Securing a seat in the House of Representatives would give him a national platform for the first time in his life, perhaps even, as Webster's ally Hiram Ketchum intimated, enable him to offer sound advice to the inexperienced Harrison.[34] His reputation among Conservative Democrats as a "liberal" Whig (as opposed to those designated neo-Federalists such as Kent) would enhance the prospects for success. But so would greater visibility before the voters. When his friend Freeman H. Morse, a carpenter and prominent Whig activist, advised him to take to the stump to increase his popularity, he agreed to speak in several Maine towns that summer.[35]

Fessenden's Independence Day address in the shipbuilding center of Bath was one of the highlights of the Whig campaign which, as it did across the United States, benefited greatly from the burgeoning economic depression. Speaking to an audience of more than a thousand people packed into the Third Congregational Parish Church, Fessenden expounded expertly on the familiar theme of republican declension.[36] Whigs, he urged, must act immediately to stem "the corruption & imbecility" of Democratic rule before it was too late. General Jackson, he admitted (with an eye on Conservatives in the crowd), was a patriotic man, but "[p]opularity & power" had blinded him to his own deficiencies and led him to become the "dupe" of designing men. The Democrats had failed to keep their promises of good governance and had become mere spoilsmen instead. But what kind of alternative did the Whigs offer?

Here Fessenden abandoned negative politics for a close assessment of the virtues of banks and a reliable currency that testified to the impact of the crisis on the farmers and mechanics of New England. President Van Buren's economic policies (especially the Independent Treasury scheme), he claimed, were intended to ensure unlimited government control over the public money on an inflexible specie basis that had proved disastrous for the wages of workingmen and the smooth operation of a market economy. What was required was a central bank akin to the Bank of the United States, a well-organized public-private institution that would furnish credit to entrepreneurs, regulate the money supply, and provide a secure repository for federal funds. The all-important currency question, he concluded in an astute flurry of anti-party rhetoric designed to serve Whig interests, had obliterated old party lines. The gratitude of future generations "will rest upon that man who can nobly burst the fetters of party—throw off the chains that bind the limbs of a freeman—and stand boldly forth in defence of those principles which his forefathers shed their heart's best blood for to establish on the soil of America."[37]

The *Portland Advertiser* commended the Bath speech as "an argument to the reason and consciences of men, rather than to their passions."[38] And so it was, up to a point, being a compelling diagnosis of the country's current problems and a clear statement of the Whigs' prognosis for economic recovery. However, Fessenden knew his audience well and he played on deep-rooted concerns for the safety of the republic to masterful effect. After some stumbling signs of recovery, the depression was biting deep. The United States, moaned one disillusioned Conservative, "formerly prosperous and happy," had been "reduced to a most wretched state of embarrassment, distress and poverty—the currency deranged and depreciated—the stores of our cities tenantless and business every where paralyzed—the farmer receiving but poor compensation for the products of his farm & mechanics and laborers soliciting employment in vain even at reduced prices."[39] Yet the Van Buren administration had nothing to offer but a continuation of the discredited policies of laissez-faire and hard money.

During the fall of 1840 the electorate delivered its verdict on the Democrats' stewardship of the economy. Swelled by the ballots of hundreds of thousands of new voters, the Whigs seized control of the White House, both chambers of Congress, and many key states. Harrison and Kent won in Maine with narrow majorities and the local Whigs were victorious in four of the eight congressional races. Among the successful candidates was Pitt Fessenden, who was elected to the House of Representatives from the Cumberland district by a majority of just 135.[40] His defeated opponent Albert Smith charged that he had been beaten by the votes of abolitionists and blacks. Although the *Portland Advertiser* denied what it regarded as a slander, Smith was partially correct.[41] Only twenty-six votes were listed as scattered, an indication that the majority of abolitionists in the district had probably voted the Whig ticket for Congress. The local antislavery sheet, moreover, welcomed this result with the hope that the winning candidate might "partake deeply of the spirit of his illustrious namesake."[42] It is likely, however, that Fessenden's narrow majority was equally reliant on the ballots of Conservative Democrats like F. O. J. Smith as well as the bulk of new voters in the district. Whatever its cause, Henry Wadsworth Longfellow was "delighted" by the result. "It is very lucky for Pitt," he told his father, "for I think defeat has a very bad effect on young men; by destroying their confidence in themselves. I think he will now go on successfully, and triumphantly."[43]

It was not long before Fessenden discovered that political power was not all it was cracked up to be. After General Harrison's stunning electoral victory, Whigs across the country mobilized to claim the spoils. As a freshman congressman presumed to have influence with Daniel Webster, the new secretary of state, Fessenden was deluged with requests to use his influence to procure lucrative federal posts under the new administration. He found the constant press for jobs irksome because it required him to make difficult choices between Portland's squabbling Whigs.[44] His Conservative ally Frank Smith was another problem. Smith and his friends wanted offices in return for their electoral support.[45] Fessenden had half a mind to cut them loose now that the Whigs were triumphant. But his irritation at Smith's "customary impertinence" was countered by his awareness that the renegade Democrat might have his uses and that it would not be prudent to antagonize Conservatives when Whigs were competing for the support of the city's workingmen.[46]

Continuing as he did to value kinship and friendship as the most reliable bonds, it was only when friends and family members sought office that Fessenden intervened in patronage matters. He told Webster that he wanted his ex-tutor Charles Daveis appointed U.S. district attorney and even asked that his mother's brother, Nathaniel Greene, a Jacksonian, should be retained as Boston postmaster on the grounds that he was poor. "Politics aside," he wrote, Uncle Nat was "a good fellow."[47] When, spurred by George Evans, Maine's new Whig senator, Fessenden tried to act decisively, he did so with only limited success.[48] His brother-in-law Nathaniel Deering was passed over for surveyor (the position going to a man favored by Samuel Fessenden) and Smith was defeated for clerk of the House of Representatives.[49] Even Uncle Nat was ejected in the frenzied cleanout.

Congressman Fessenden

Any hopes that the congressman-elect might have had that political life could only improve once the offices had been distributed were dampened in April 1841 when President Harrison died after only a month in office. Edward Kent thought the loss of a northern-backed candidate at the helm would be keenly felt at the next elections in Maine.[50] Much would depend on whether the Whig majority in the special session of Congress (called by Harrison to raise "funds for carrying on the government") would be able to work effectively with the general's successor, John Tyler, to enact the party's economic recovery program.[51] Fessenden traveled down to Washington with his father at the end of May. They tarried in Boston to visit his mother, Ruth, who was now living with her oldest son, Edwin. "She is in fine health," he told Ellen, "having grown stout, tho' not fat. She is one of the finest looking women, of her age, I ever saw. It is quite easy, on seeing her now[,] to believe the story of her beauty when a girl."[52] By early June he was hard at work on his congressional duties amid the squalid slave pens of the country's half-built capital—rising at six, dealing with correspondence until eight, visiting government departments from nine, attending the House and participating in committee business until adjournment in the late afternoon, and then preparing for the next day's business and writing letters after dinner.[53] He was taking his duties as a national legislator in his stride. It was just as well, for those duties were about to drive him to distraction.

Like all northern Whigs Fessenden regarded the special session of May–September 1841 as an opportunity to revitalize the American economy. He made his maiden speech on July 8 in support of a new national loan and voted predictably to demolish the Independent Treasury. His principal goal, however, was to pass a bill establishing "a national bankruptcy system that would thwart dishonest debtors" and release "the economic energies of honest debtors through legal discharges from past debts."[54] The measure was demanded by persons of all classes at home and he believed, as did his party's leading strategists, that passage would secure Whig victories in several northeastern states, Maine included, in the fall elections. To this end he delivered a major speech in Congress on August 11.

Although Fessenden would soon come to shun long orations, he adjudged this one-hour performance necessary to show the House and his constituents that he meant to do his political duty. The speech marked him out as a staunch Whig supporter of economic growth and federal power. Noting the "highly commercial character" of the country, the cross-class appeal of the bankruptcy bill, and the damaging effects of Van Buren's economic policies, he flayed those Democrats who claimed the Constitution did not allow Congress to impair the obligation of contracts. Fessenden understood the importance of contract to a modern economy. However, he used a combination of English authorities (among them Samuel Johnson and a Tudor statute on bankruptcy), common sense, and broad construction to undermine the Jacksonian case against the bill. The Constitution, he observed, declared explicitly that no *state* could pass laws impairing the right of contract. It did not therefore prohibit *Congress* from doing the same. "Government, *ex vi termini*," he said, "implies dominion over all subjects which may become proper and necessary subjects of legislation. No one will pretend that this power is not possessed by the British Parliament. Our Constitution recognises its prior existence in the States, by the very fact of its inhibition by that instrument. It is, too, a necessary power, for it is by no means difficult to imagine a condition of things in which the safety and well being of the State would imperatively demand its exercise." That situation, mass insolvency, was now upon the country. "Can it be pretended," he asked, "that a power to apply a remedy to a disorder that is paralyzing and destroying the body politic exists no where?"[55]

The first-time congressman admitted the tyrannous potential of such a power in the sphere of individual rights. But those rights, he contended, "must yield to high considerations of public policy" and broad understanding of what was necessary to protect "the general weal" and "national objects." No good could come of the Jacksonian obsession with narrow construction. He personally was "disposed to be somewhat liberal" in his interpretation of the Constitution, "—a latitudinarian, if you please—for I had much rather enlarge than belittle it. I wish to see that Constitution what its framers designed it to be—powerful for good—effective, energetic, broad, and deep."[56] Despite the diverse motives behind his stance on the bankruptcy bill, this statement was an accurate summation of Fessenden's political philosophy.[57] It articulated an expansive Whig vision of government activism that was rooted in his Federalist upbringing and informed throughout by his immersion in British history and culture. It also encompassed a Hamiltonian reading of the Constitution and of his duties as a national legislator that would inform his actions during the Civil War.

Listening to this carefully crafted speech was ex-President John Quincy Adams, now a maverick Whig who had taken the unusual step of returning to Congress to continue his personal struggle to save the national government from proslavery Jacksonians who, he believed, were sapping its vitality. Describing his fellow New Englander as "a promising young man," he noted privately that Pitt Fessenden's "slender form and pallid face" revealed "a feeble constitution, ill suited to the latitude of Portland." "He speaks with great facility," wrote Adams, not one to lard his peers with high praise, "without elegance—plain, sound sense, but without striking thought or imagery, wit or humor—always grave, always calm, always moderate; never very impressive, never original in thought or sentiment."[58] The reaction of Fessenden's friend Longfellow was more concise. "It seems to be direct and forcible;" he wrote of the speech, "and I think will please his constituents."[59]

The Bankruptcy Act failed to deliver the anticipated political dividends. One of the main causes of what proved to be a precipitate reversal in Whig fortunes in the fall of 1841 was the congressional party's inability to execute in full its ambitious economic program. Even before the special session had opened, the Whigs' banking plans had encountered opposition on states' rights grounds from President Tyler, a man described by Adams on the day of Harrison's untimely death in April as "a political sectarian, of the slave-driving, Virginian, Jeffersonian school, principled against all improvement, with all the interests and passions and vices of slavery rooted in his moral and political constitution."[60] By late June Tyler had outlined his states' rights opposition to the cornerstone of Henry Clay's legislative program: a bill to create a national bank as the engine of economic recovery. Fessenden was agitated by the readiness of southern Whigs like Tyler's fellow Virginian, Henry A. Wise, to oppose the bank measure and struggled to restrain his anger. "The truth is," he told his father, "that we are cursed with a set of allies who are enough to ruin any party. I mean the Virginia Abstractionists & Conservatives, & a few others out of Virginia of the same stamp. They are selfish, hair-splitting, senseless animals, without consistency & destitute of reason. The President stands at their head, & is the weakest of the lot."[61]

The situation now confronting the Whigs was pregnant with danger. An open breach with the president would end all hopes of enacting the American System because the congressional party lacked the two-thirds majority necessary to pass legislation over his opposition. It might also divide the Whig coalition along sectional lines. Fessenden's initial response, probably influenced by the fact that Daniel Webster remained a member of Tyler's cabinet, was to back Secretary of the Treasury Thomas Ewing's plan for a public-private bank that would, in most circumstances, require state endorsement before any branches could be established outside Washington. The measure was drafted as a workable compromise between the positions of Tyler and Clay and Secretary of State Webster endorsed it strongly. Fessenden, the recipient of pro-compromise, pro-Webster letters from Hiram Ketchum, defended his support for the Treasury bill on the grounds of political strategy. Bemoaning his co-partisans' lack of discipline (largely a function of their residual anti-partyism), he told Portland Whig Josiah Little that the Whigs' greatest problem had "always been a want of ability to *secure* a victory. The moment a battle is over we disperse, like the Scottish clans of old days, to our several homes—having waited only for our share of the plunder." Passage of Ewing's measure would generate "the *excitement* necessary to bring out our strength," especially among those "who care nothing for party as party, and who thought every thing was done when Van Buren was defeated." Whereas Tyler was bound to veto any bill that did not require state consent for branch banks, the compromise bill "would go far to save us, for a Bank our folks want, & will have, if they can get it."[62]

Unhappily for the Whigs there was to be no compromise over the banking issue. On August 6 the House passed its own compromise bill (more pro-bank than protective of states' rights than the Ewing version) with Fessenden voting in favor along with the vast majority of northern Whigs.[63] Tyler, determined to exert both his authority and his conviction that there must be limits to federal power, delivered his veto after a five-hour cabinet meeting in which Webster and others had urged him to sign the bill to unite the party.[64] Fessenden had no hesitation in blaming Tyler for the Whigs' disarray. "[T]o see all our labors prove abortive," he lamented angrily, "by the folly of such an accidental ass as the present President is wearying to human patience." He told Ellen, however, that his co-partisans would press on: "If we pack up in disgust, effecting nothing, our party & our cause are lost—all by the consummate vanity & obstinacy of a poor, miserable, animal, who never was worth the snuff of a candle, or a cheese-pairing [*sic*], or a quid of tobacco, for any practical purpose."[65] Congressional Whigs passed another banking bill at the end of the special session but Tyler handed down a second veto. Several cabinet members resigned in protest but Webster, fearful of subordinating himself to Clay, fond of the trappings of office, and convinced that only he could settle the still-simmering Maine boundary dispute with Britain, stayed on.[66] The intra-party squabble was rapidly turning into internecine warfare.

The political fallout was disastrous. The Whigs suffered serious reverses in the off-year elections of 1841. In Maine Governor Edward Kent was ejected from office in favor of a Democrat. Fessenden was now confronted with a difficult choice. He could either join his godfather and the unpopular president or cut most of his ties with "Black Dan" and follow the lead of Henry Clay. Another talented New England Whig and close ally of Webster, Caleb Cushing of Massachusetts, chose the first path. He soon became a member of "the Corporal's Guard," a small yet influential group of national Whigs who became fierce defenders of Tyler against increasingly vociferous opposition from his own party. That decision would help to make Cushing a Democrat; indeed, by the time President Franklin Pierce appointed him attorney general in 1853 he was one of the most powerful proslavery politicians in Washington.

There was never any doubt, given his commitment to Whiggery, that Pitt Fessenden would choose the second route. When he returned to Congress in December 1841 he acknowledged that his connections to Webster rendered many Whigs suspicious of his loyalty to the party.[67] By late March 1842, however, Tyler was battling with congressional Whigs over a raft of measures, including his Exchequer Bill (lauded by Webster as a halfway house between Van Buren's Independent Treasury and a national bank) and a tariff that would replenish the depleted federal coffers on condition that the public lands should be distributed to the states to build internal improvements. Fessenden was now ready to show his hand. If possible, he told Ellen, he would obtain the floor and define his position: "that of hostility to Tyler & all connected with him—and thus shall be thrown out of all communion with my old friend." Webster, he said ruthlessly, "does not look very kindly upon me now, & this will finish the business—but I cannot help it."[68]

His decision to join the ranks of Clay's supporters in the House made no difference to the course of events. Tyler resisted the Whigs' attempts to link the tariff with distribution while Clay's men remained hostile to the Exchequer plan. For a brief moment in July 1842 Congressman Fessenden hoped the president's opposition to the Whigs' legislative program might unite the party. It did not. A minority of southern and northern Whigs helped to prevent the House from passing the so-called Permanent Tariff (which connected raised import duties to distribution) over Tyler's veto in August. The president signed a tariff-for-revenue measure but he continued to thwart two key planks of the American System: a national bank and land distribution. "I look upon the entire destruction of our party as certain," lamented Fessenden. "Shame & disgrace cover the Whig party, and I am in absolute despair."[69]

The congressman's relations with the Tyler administration were further impaired by its determination to sacrifice Maine's interests in the pursuit of peace with Great Britain. In July Daniel Webster invited his godson to dine with Lord Ashburton, who had been dispatched from Whitehall to end the Anglo-American boundary dispute. Fessenden accepted the invitation, which was part of Webster's ongoing efforts to secure Maine's approval of a final settlement. At this point he thought any settlement would fail because Lord Ashburton would surely demand more than the state's negotiating commissioners would allow.[70] Webster had been using a deft combination of propaganda and lobbying to soften up the legislators and people of Maine. Secret service funds had been used to employ Francis O. J. Smith to place pro-compromise articles in the local press and the legislature had been shown a bogus map that appeared to support the claims of Great Britain.[71] But during the summer of 1842 the Maine commissioners were still holding out for more territory than the British were willing to cede. Not until the Tyler administration induced the commissioners to abandon their hard-line stance in the national interest was a treaty finally drawn up. The deal, formally approved by the United States on August 20, induced Fessenden to conclude that the game was up. The boundary agreement concluded by Ashburton and Webster (both of whom were representatives of the London-based Baring Brothers bank, which had a direct stake in Anglo-American rapprochement) gave Maine 58 percent of the disputed territory.[72] Fessenden, who had once opposed any sellout of Maine's interests and may not have known of Webster's duplicitous activities, grudgingly assented. There had been "much difficulty" about the boundary issue, he told Ellen, "and I think the Commissioners & the State have been fooled. But I gave my opinion in favour of the arrangement, if it was the best that could be made."[73]

Daniel Webster's refusal to leave Tyler's discredited cabinet greatly damaged relations with his godson as it did his reputation among Whigs across the country. Fessenden dined with the Websters at the time the boundary question was resolved but he did so mainly because of his feelings for the secretary's wife. "I have no compassion for him, but a great deal for her," he told Ellen bluntly.[74] By early 1843 Fessenden was finding it difficult to contain his outrage at Webster's conduct. "The truth is," he confided, "my bad manners are invincible. It is hard work for me to do any thing disagreeable, and it is unpleasant for me to go where Daniel is."[75]

The conflict with John Tyler stiffened the young legislator's attachment to party. An unpleasant spat that winter with Caleb Cushing, the Speaker of the House, emphasized the gulf that had opened up between the majority of congressional Whigs and the White House. Cushing, loyal to Webster and Tyler, denounced the Clay

Whigs for their vicious attacks on the president. It was time, he urged, for members to apply themselves to their legislative duties, "trampling under foot party questions" that impeded business. Fessenden, realizing these remarks were calculated to assist the administration's embryonic plans to form its own party, blamed Cushing for his role in the Whigs' disarray and commented sharply on what he regarded as the speaker's disingenuous embrace of anti-party rhetoric. To support his point he read a quote from Jonathan Swift depicting no-party men in a negative light and criticized Cushing for threatening to use executive patronage to influence forthcoming elections on behalf of the president. On January 19, Cushing responded by insisting that Tyler had made every effort to compromise with his party in Congress and by claiming that Whigs were duty bound to support their leader. When Fessenden demanded the floor, the speaker refused to yield. Swift, he said acidly, was "the most factious and corrupt writer that ever existed."[76]

As well as underlining the divided state of American Whiggery during the Tyler administration, the exchange illustrated perfectly *how* two ostensibly similar New England co-partisans—both talented, well-educated lawyers born at the beginning of the century, both closely connected to Daniel Webster—could respond differently to the same events. What it did not show was *why* they took different routes to power. Cushing's modern biographer suggests that the Massachusetts congressman sided with Tyler in 1841–42 for three reasons: his loyalty to Webster, his belief that Tyler was willing to compromise over the crucial bank issue, and the existence of a modicum of support at home for his conduct.[77] Even after Webster, his principal goals achieved, signaled his determination to pursue his presidential ambitions as a member of the Whig Party by resigning from the cabinet in May 1843, Cushing adhered to the president. If he thought his loyalty to the executive would bring him domestic power and influence in the immediate future, he was mistaken. Tyler's signature policy of promoting American territorial and commercial expansion was not enough to build him a following in the country, leaving Cushing "a man without a party" during 1843–44.[78] The subsequent elevation of the proslavery expansionist James K. Polk to the White House, however, enabled Cushing to join the Democrats on the basis of his support for American empire building and by 1847 he was firmly ensconced in the ranks of the Whigs' mortal enemies.

In theory, Fessenden could have pursued a similar path. He did not do so for two main reasons. First, as he indicated in his clash with the opportunistic Cushing, he was an ideologically committed Whig. Tyler's refusal to give his full backing to the party's recovery program struck him, as it did the majority of northern Whigs, as nothing short of treacherous. It offended his deep sense of party loyalty as well as his conviction that Whigs must surrender power if they did not execute their policies. Second, there was a strong sectional basis for his opposition to the president. Whereas Cushing drifted into the orbit of proslavery nationalism, his opponent's Whiggery took on a distinctly sectional hue. Fessenden was convinced that southern Whigs, Tyler's Virginians in particular, were responsible for the collapse of the Whigs' legislative program. Here was proof from his own experience that what a generation of northern politicians had been saying was true: that the slaveholding South was a threat to national improvement. "The more I become acquainted with the course of things," he told his abolitionist father, "the nearer am I brought to your opinion, that the slave interest is the controlling interest in this country, and that Slaveholders are determined that northern industry & northern rights shall not have even a chance to be let alone."[79]

Tellingly, Fessenden's experiences of southern "domination" transformed him from a critic of John Quincy Adams into one of the latter's most prominent admirers. When he first arrived in Washington, the Portland congressman made no distinction between Adams, a fire-breathing defender of northern rights, and the opinionated states' rights Virginian and staunch Tyler supporter, Henry Wise. Both men, he told Ellen, were "rated *nuisances* by common consent."[80] At the start of the special session in June 1841 Fessenden had joined Adams and other antislavery northern Whigs in trying to rescind Rule 21, passed by the previous House to prevent receipt of abolitionist petitions. But when these efforts were thwarted by southerners of both parties as well as by significant numbers of northern Democrats, he had parted company with Adams by supporting a compromise proposal favored by the majority of northern and southern Whigs.[81] Representing a technical and temporary suspension of Rule 21, this measure prevented receipt of any petition not directly related to emergency economic legislation. His vote made clear his desire, shared by other antislavery Whigs like Joshua Giddings and William Slade, to organize the House so that the party could get on with the main job at hand: dealing with the economic depression.

On January 24, 1842, Adams introduced a disunionist petition from a group of Massachusetts abolitionists angered by the country's continuing support for slavery. The onetime Federalist was no disunionist but he was determined not to allow the defenders of slavery to infringe northerners' right to free speech. The result was, in Adams's own words, a "snarling debate" in which southerners from both parties and many northern Democrats attempted to censure the old man for his allegedly treasonous act.[82] Fessenden, who shared the former president's irascibility and independence of mind, was shocked by the venom of Adams's assailants and privately condemned the whole affair as "a miserable farce."[83] The attack brought to the surface his own neo-Federalist prejudices that had been heightened by the southern Whigs' attempts to defeat Clay's economic program. "Old Q.," he admitted, sometimes acted rashly and intemperately. But, he told Ellen, "a thousand excuses" could be made for him because of the abuse he received from his enemies: "I love the old man for his indomitable spirit, and the uprightness of his soul." Crucially, Fessenden was now beginning to consider the advantages of realigning parties along sectional lines. "I am every day getting more of the opinion," he mused, "that we must abandon all divisions at home except that between the northern & Southern parties. The South is determined to make northern industry subservient to its own fancied interests, & the Locos of the north are willing it should be so if they can come in for the spoils of office. I wish to God *the people* of the free States could witness the proceedings of Congress. They would soon see and understand the mean subserviency of these northern hirelings, and cast them back into their native insignificance. The day must come. It may be distant, but it must come."[84]

Fessenden could do little to assist the cause of northern rights in the second session of the Twenty-seventh Congress beyond voting to support Adams in the censure controversy, backing receipt of the disunionist petition in order to bolster the right of free speech, and introducing a resolution, no more than symbolic, to rescind Rule 21.[85] Yet he felt he had done enough to convince the antislavery men of his state that he could be relied upon to act in their interests. This was not the case. In the spring of 1843, against a background of growing opposition to President Tyler's plans for the annexation of the independent proslavery republic of Texas, he was criticized publicly by Maine's political abolitionists, now organized as third-party Liberty men, for failing to live up to their expectations. Pitt Fessenden and Democratic congressman Nathan Clifford, they averred, could "speak eloquently about Tariffs and Commerce—the monied interests of the State. But all are silent when the rights of the citizens are invaded—when the petitions of their constituents are rejected."[86]

Aggrieved at being yoked together with his old rival Clifford, who had joined his fellow Democrats in opposing repeal of the gag rule, and genuinely convinced that he had fought strongly for the right of petition, Fessenden came out fighting.[87] First, he secured testimony from antislavery Whigs to prove that he had done all he could within the rules of the House to repeal the gag.[88] John Quincy Adams concurred and stated categorically that "I well remember that your votes were always against the rule and in favour of the right."[89] The ex-president thought the charges against his correspondent "unjust" but considered the congressional struggle over the gag unlikely to accomplish anything as long as "the slave ascendancy" persisted "in the Government of this Union."[90] Fessenden then wrote a combative letter to the *Portland Advertiser*. In this communication he not only cited Adams in his defense but also detailed his efforts on behalf of northern rights, laying particular stress on the difficulty that northern Whigs faced in procuring a suspension of the rules (a necessary precondition to voting directly on the gag) and the pointlessness of debating an issue on which minds were already made up. He then took the offensive. While he entertained "the highest respect" for most abolitionists, he knew that some antislavery men sought political aims: either the destruction of the major parties (by rendering both as obnoxious as one another as in the attempt to connect his voting record to Clifford's) or, more nefariously, the total evisceration of the Whig Party for the benefit of the Democrats. Those men who sought the latter goal, he charged, were "wolves in sheep[']s clothing" and "Locofocos disguised as Abolitionists."[91]

Once again, Fessenden was proving an adept partisan. Recognizing that the majority of Maine abolitionists were ex-Whigs and that the votes of Liberty men might be crucial if the party were to carry the state in 1844, he turned defense into attack in an attempt to persuade independents that their criticism of free-soil Whigs like himself could only redound to the benefit of economically irresponsible and prosouthern Democrats. The letter had a mixed impact. Asa Walker, a leading Liberty man, accepted the explanation and acknowledged that Fessenden, while no abolitionist, was "a highminded, honorable man" who would never lend his support to so infamous an institution as slavery. Clifford, by contrast, had always voted "with the slaveholding interest."[92] The radical Hallowell *Liberty Standard* was less willing to back down. While the paper conceded that press accounts of the congressional debates might not have yielded the full story of Fessenden's resistance to the gag, it criticized "the acrimony" of the congressman's style and reminded readers that he had voted to organize the House in 1841 with the gag rule intact and always denied being an abolitionist. It also observed pointedly that the Whigs had possessed a majority in the late Congress yet still failed to abolish the rule.[93] The assault was harsh but not entirely unfair. While the congressman's vote to organize the House had represented, in his words, "a virtual abrogation" of the 21st rule for the special session, it had still prevented the receipt of antislavery petitions.[94] The best defense for his action lay in the fact that northern Democrats like Clifford had played a key role in preventing outright repeal of the gag rule. But few abolitionists were likely to be swayed by his insistence that because southern Whigs had not yielded on a southern question, the failure of repeal was "not chargeable upon the Whig party, as a party."[95]

This last comment, made in a letter to Edward Stanly of Virginia, highlighted the inability of northern Whigs to pose convincingly as opponents of slavery as long as they remained within a bisectional organization. Fessenden was deeply frustrated by the actions of his southern co-partisans during his term in Congress. Yet despite his apparent predilection for realignment along sectional lines, his letter to the *Advertiser* made it clear that he had recovered quickly from the gloom of 1841–42 and remained a loyal Whig. Unlike his father he had limited empathy for slaves or free blacks. He was not a racist demagogue in the sense that he was prepared to whip up racial prejudice in the manner of many antebellum politicians—the majority of them Democrats. Subsequent public comments and actions, moreover, revealed a man hostile to the notion that color discrimination should be given the sanction of law in America. (He did, after all, live in one of the few states where adult black males could vote and testify in court.) However, disparaging references to blacks in his private correspondence, though typical of the time, revealed that his interest in northern rights was not matched by his concern for the oppressed. In December 1842, he joked lamely that he had asked his black chambermaid in Washington to play a tune on his piano "but she only showed her ivory."[96] The next month he observed John Quincy Adams expounding in the House on "some *nigger* question."[97] Maine abolitionists were thus right to sense that while Fessenden regarded slavery as a curse to the republic, he was not a passionate crusader for racial justice. Only at the point where opposition to slavery intersected with a defense of northern rights did he and they occupy common ground.

Fessenden declined a renomination to Congress in August 1843. The reasons for this decision are unclear but they were probably twofold. First, he was somewhat disillusioned by his frustrating experiences in Washington. He wrote to his father from the capital that he had seen enough of congressional life and "would not come here again, on any terms."[98] Second, he was seriously considering the possibility of pursuing his legal career in Boston, a much larger city than Portland and one that offered a wider field for his professional talents.[99] Crucially, however, his refusal to run for another term did not reflect any waning of his partisanship. He remained a committed Whig throughout the 1840s, his frustrations in Congress insufficiently deep to disturb his conviction that the party offered Americans the best hope for progress and prosperity.

Even though Henry Clay was a border-state southerner, he was widely regarded by northern Whigs as their strongest candidate for the presidency. His popularity was due partly to his support for colonization (still seen by many Americans on both sides of the Mason-Dixon line as a practical solution to the divisive slavery issue), but primarily to his unwavering commitment to federal support for a diversified market economy. The general government, he told an audience in Raleigh, North Carolina, in the spring of 1844, should supply all necessary "national means of safety, convenience and prosperity."[100] This commitment had been underlined in the fierce intra-party battles with President Tyler, whose efforts to forge a political base of his own had begun to founder on the strength of the existing parties, notwithstanding his attempts to broaden that base with an expansionist foreign policy. Tyler's efforts to annex Texas elicited an ambiguous response from Clay but the Kentuckian retained his popularity with conservative and more radical free-soil Whigs in the North, even after Daniel Webster finally resigned from the cabinet in the spring of 1843.

An increasingly prominent member of the party's antislavery wing, Fessenden played an active role in the 1844 election campaign in which Maine Whigs launched a cross-class appeal by lauding protective tariffs as essential to the welfare of local workingmen.[101] He was elected president of a mass meeting of Cumberland County Whigs on August 7 and addressed his excited co-partisans in what the *Advertiser* described as "his usual excellent style." On the rostrum with him in an open lot in downtown Portland were the Whigs' own working-class spokesman, Freeman Morse (who made the most of his "mechanical" roots), and U.S. Senator George Evans. The ensuing nominating convention (attended only by elected delegates) named Josiah Little for Congress and, in a bid to limit defections to the Liberty Party, adopted resolutions repudiating "the evils" of "*Slavery* and the *Slave-trade* wherever they exist."[102]

Shortly afterward Fessenden accompanied other Whig leaders to a church in Otisfield, a small town thirty miles from Portland, to debate slavery and slavery-related issues with local Liberty men, including his father, Samuel. The debate, an initiative of the Whigs, represented another attempt to shore up abolitionist support for Clay and was, by all accounts, conducted amicably.[103] Fessenden went on to address mass meetings of Whigs in several localities that summer, paying particular attention to the controversial issue of Texas annexation, which was regarded by a majority of northern Whigs and abolitionists as a naked attempt to augment southern power within the Union.[104]

He made his most innovative contribution to the cause at a Congregational meeting house in Thomaston on August 20. Here he spent an exhausting nine hours debating contemporary issues with a Boston Democrat, Benjamin F. Hallett. Although he focused largely on economic issues (especially the importance of protective tariffs to workingmen) a discernible strain of sectionalism ran through his remarks. The forthcoming election contest, he said, would decide "whether this great 'American system,' was to be sustained by Mr. Clay, or overthrown and utterly abolished by Mr. Polk, who is emphatically the Southern candidate, opposed to the vital interests of the North." James Polk, a slaveholding Tennessean, had come out strongly in favor of Texas annexation. If this policy were instigated, claimed Fessenden, it would result not only in war with Mexico (the neighboring republic from which Texas had gained its freedom in 1836) but also "the extension and increase of slavery, and of the slave-power" and ultimately "the probably consequent destruction of our glorious Union."[105] His use of the term "Slave Power" was highly significant. Political abolitionists had been using it for years to signify what they regarded as a vast and growing conspiracy by slaveholding aristocrats to spread their pernicious institution into every nook and cranny of the republic. Fessenden's embrace of the term indicated both the extent to which he had been radicalized by his experience of southern bullying in Congress and the narrowing gap between himself and radical antislavery men.

Pitt Fessenden's efforts on the campaign trail bore only limited fruit. In September 1844 he was elected with two other Portland Whigs to the Maine legislature.[106] Henry Clay was less successful. Despite widespread optimism in his camp before the November poll, American territorial expansion was favored by many northerners. He lost to Polk by 170 electoral college votes to 105 and a popular margin of just 38,000 votes. Maine Whigs had carried their state for Harrison in 1840 but four years later their vote was down by over 12,000. Even Portland went for Polk. The Whigs' failure to hold on to support in upper New England and the decision of most new voters elsewhere to vote Democrat were important factors in Clay's defeat.[107] Like many of his co-partisans, however, Fessenden was more inclined to blame the disaster on antislavery Whig defections to the Liberty Party candidate, James G. Birney. Overall, votes for Birney were not decisive in Maine but they did prevent Clay from carrying New York as Fessenden had predicted. Had Clay carried the Empire State, he may have had enough electoral college votes to secure the presidency.[108]

Midlife Upheavals

Pitt Fessenden was 37 years old in the fall of 1844. He had already accomplished much as a successful politician and one of the most able attorneys in Maine. His law business took up a great deal of his time. In fact he was unable to peruse the depressing election results because he was engaged in arguing *Doggett v Emerson* (a complex and remunerative case involving a fraudulent land sale) before the Massachusetts Supreme Court. Although well-known and well-connected in Boston, he had decided not to go into business there with his cousin, Theophilus Chandler. James Deering, his wealthy father-in-law, appears to have talked him out of the idea, possibly by persuading him that Ellen could not look after a large family without the assistance of her parents.[109] In contrast to his own constitution, which remained robust despite the occasional bout of rheumatism, Ellen was often in poor health, having given birth to four boys in eight years. The couple had been close in the first years of their marriage but signs of stress in what was never less than a companionate marriage were increasingly apparent. Ellen, for example, complained about his preoccupation with professional pursuits at the expense of family affairs and was hardly likely to have been mollified by his sporadic protestations that he was "cured, I hope forever, of fondness for a public life."[110] She began taking to her bed before her husband returned home from business and for the first time the latter's thoughts began to stray to another woman.[111]

Fessenden had known his 23-year-old cousin Elizabeth since she was a girl when he used to visit her father, Uncle Thomas, in lower Manhattan.[112] From the late 1830s on, when he provided educational advice, they began corresponding with greater frequency and emotional intensity. As "Lizzy" moved into womanhood, Fessenden's role changed from elder counselor to fond protector. Feelings of loneliness, intensified by his absences from home and Ellen's infirmity, provided powerful impetus for this shift. In December 1842, alone in his rooms in Washington, he imagined his young kinswoman sitting on his rocking chair with her back to the fire to preserve her complexion. Write "*long, very long*, letters," he implored Lizzy, who had recently married a pious dry-goods merchant from the Berkshires named William Pitt Warriner, "—for I am lonesome & melancholy."[113] In January 1845 Fessenden arrived at his lodgings in Hallowell to attend another session of the state legislature. Responding to a playful communication in which Lizzy had intimated that he might find her letters annoying, he implored his "sweet cousin" not to think him "stupid, or short, or stiff." "Oh, Lizzy, Lizzy!" he wrote, caressing her name with his pen, "You must *not* 'flirt,' whatever Mr W. may do. *I* forbid it—absolutely." Instead she must occupy her spare hours writing to her "forlorn cousin" and assure him of a welcome when he was next in New York.[114] Seven months later Fessenden was lying on a sofa at home in Portland. He was gazing dreamily at a miniature of Lizzy and wondering if her heart matched her pretty features. "At times," he said, the tiny painting "looks so natural . . . that, were the act not too lover-like, I should kiss it, though not much given to such things."[115]

There is no evidence that Fessenden strayed in deed as well as thought. He was an affectionate, if strict, father to the boys, writing short stories for them when they were small, counseling against overindulging them, and striving always to foster their own sense of independence and personal responsibility. He had a gentleman's sense of duty, to his family as well as to the public weal, and would never have left Ellen. He continued to rely heavily on the companionate dimension of their relationship even when his regular correspondence and occasional meetings with Lizzy provided him with an outlet for his repressed emotions. Although the domestic sphere always held an allure for him, he checked his urge for bourgeois comfort and leisure by engaging with the male-dominated world outside the home. He remained a driven individual but, possibly because of encroaching domestic unhappiness, he was even more inclined now to channel his passions into public activity. He loved Lizzy, undoubtedly, and probably desired her sexually. But any extramarital affair would have disturbed his respectable middle-class life. He was a practical, disciplined man who prioritized order over romantic excitement. "By the way," he told Lizzy off-handedly in late 1846, "I burnt up all your letters the other day, in company with divers & sundry papers of all description—essays, orations, pictures, &c. &c. . . . Do not be angry. It was no proof that I love either you or myself any the less. I hope you will follow my example if your desk is as much crowded as mine was."[116]

Notwithstanding Clay's depressing defeat at the hands of Polk, Fessenden remained a committed Whig despite the fact that the party faced difficult challenges in the mid-1840s. The Democrats, reenergized by their embrace of western expansion, were formidable foes in Maine, where they seemed to enjoy a natural majority. Internally, the Whigs were buffeted by fissiparous tensions. Antislavery men operating beyond and inside the organization continued to press for tougher action against the South and its peculiar institution. A new threat, however, was beginning to loom. Moral reformers within the party had started to campaign for tougher state action against liquor sales. As the changes unleashed by industrial development quickened, social instability in the North began to increase. Evangelical Protestants located the source of the instability in a range of evils but targeted alcohol

as the principal enemy of family breakdown, social responsibility, and good governance. Often they linked it to the influx of immigrants, notably impoverished Irish
Catholics. As Maine's largest city, Portland was by no means free from the strains induced by economic development and urban growth in the mid-nineteenth century.
The establishment of a regular police force in 1849 was just one sign of concern over
rising crime.[117] Another was Neal Dow's aggressive crusade against drunkenness.

Neal Dow was two years older than Fessenden. His father was a Portland
Federalist, a tanner who had been read out of the pacifist Quaker church because he
supported the War of 1812. He and Fessenden had been members of the same debating society in the late 1820s but the two men were never close. Enriching himself
by investing heavily in Portland real estate, Dow became interested in suppressing
liquor drinking when he joined the city's Charitable Mechanics' Association, a company of local employers keen to promote self-discipline and family stability among
their workers. In 1837, by now a committed Whig, he helped found the Maine Temperance Union alongside other local notables working within the Congregational
tradition of oversight of community morality by the godly elite. At the beginning of
1845 the Temperance Union, whose founders also included Samuel Fessenden and
former governor Edward Kent, reversed a previous decision and called for a statewide ban on liquor sales after its members decided that voluntary efforts had failed
to eradicate the social problems associated with alcohol abuse.[118]

Pitt Fessenden first encountered the political power of prohibitionists after his
third stint in the Maine House in 1845. Although the Whigs were again in a minority
that session, they were vociferously opposed to Texas annexation. The admission of a
vast slave state to the Union was deeply unpopular in the North—even Maine Democrats were divided on the issue—but the U.S. Senate finally annexed Texas by treaty
that spring. Fessenden, however, had entered the state legislature again not primarily
as an opponent of slavery expansion but as an ally of local businessmen who wanted to
build a railroad linking Portland to Montreal. The route was seen by local merchants,
James Deering among them, as the optimal means of diverting Canadian trade from
Boston. So important was the project to the state's economy that the Atlantic & St.
Lawrence Railroad was chartered with overwhelming bipartisan support in February.

Prohibition proved a thornier issue. From the mid-1840s northern Whig leaders
were divided over how to deal with it. Those of an evangelical and nativist (anti-
immigrant) bent favored endorsing prohibition in order to galvanize the party's siz-
able Protestant wing, which tended to support moral causes of all descriptions. Liberal
Whigs, however, recognized that if they embraced the cause officially they risked,

first, being condemned as intolerant by Democrats opposed to government intrusion in private morality and, second, alienating the growing numbers of beer-swilling foreign immigrants who were thronging the cities of the Northeast. Fessenden found himself caught between these two positions. Unlike his moralistic father, he was a moderate drinker himself, had always prioritized economic development over social reform, and was concerned about the divisive impact of prohibition on party unity. No great supporter of unrestricted immigrant voting, he was nonetheless opposed to telling Americans how to run their lives: his eldest son, James, he believed, should decide for himself whether he should take the pledge to abstain from drinking alcohol.[119] On the other hand, he recognized that many Whigs regarded prohibition as a prime solution to the social ills of the day and understood the importance of individual responsibility and self-reliance to a well-ordered republic.

When the Maine Temperance Union called on the legislature to enact a stringent prohibitory liquor law in January 1845, Fessenden found himself—like many centrist northern Whigs—in a tricky position. Though willing to introduce temperance petitions and personally supportive of a reasonable and effective bill, he failed to support the coercive legislation framed by Neal Dow and his crusading allies, arguing that it had not been drafted effectively.[120] When he stood for reelection to the assembly the next autumn it was soon clear that he had incurred the wrath of the reformers. In September the Temperance Union ran its own candidates against Fessenden and his fellow representative Phineas Barnes (the editor of the *Advertiser* who had also opposed prohibition). Hundreds of angry Whigs refused to vote the regular ticket in order to punish the recreants for their alleged cowardice. Both men were still short of the required majority after two more ballots later in the month. At this juncture the prohibitionists issued a circular denouncing the two Whigs as the enemies of temperance, virtue, and religion and charging them with treating the people's wishes with "studied and marked contempt."[121] Fessenden and Barnes were finally elected after a fourth vote but only with the help of Democrats who supported them to defeat the rival anti-liquor candidates.[122] It was an early sign of the potential of prohibition and other "ethnocultural" issues to further destabilize the existing party system at a time when, after the return of prosperity following the depression of 1837–43 and the reinjection of the slavery issue into politics, Clay's American System was no longer enough to hold northern Whigs together.

Maine's temperance reformers redoubled their efforts to pass an effective prohibitory liquor law when the legislature met again in the summer of 1846. Frustrated by the previous year's failure and fearful that the assembly would pass a toothless bill, Neal Dow pressed his demands on Fessenden before his fellow townsman left Portland for the capital. He wanted higher fines for offenders in order to ensure that the state did not devolve responsibility for law enforcement onto vigilant citizens like himself.[123] Fessenden resented being painted as an opponent of sensible prohibitory legislation but, now aware more than ever of the crusaders' political influence, told Ellen that grog shops were "a nuisance which I would gladly aid in abating." Parties at Augusta, he said, "were fearing & hoping my return, under the idea that I should strenuously oppose any bill upon this subject. They will find themselves mistaken."[124] In the event, Fessenden again refused to support what he regarded as badly drafted legislation. A bill prohibiting the sale of wine and spirits in small quantities did pass at this session but, as he predicted, it proved ineffective and the rum dealers of Maine continued to trade with relatively little fear of intervention from the state.[125]

Neal Dow's strenuous efforts to secure a tough prohibitory liquor law continued to disrupt Whig unity in Maine at the same time as sectional issues began to dominate politics at every level of the federal system in the late 1840s. President Polk's decision to declare war against Mexico in early 1846 proved especially divisive. Although westward expansion was far from unpopular in the free states and the battlefield successes of Generals Zachary Taylor and Winfield Scott were greeted enthusiastically by patriots on both sides of the Mason-Dixon line, deep-rooted fears that any territorial acquisitions would empower the South gave a further boost to what historian Susan-Mary Grant has termed "northern nationalism."[126] The latter, a distinctively sectional form of "national construction" that branded slavery an imminent threat to the welfare of the republic and increasingly imagined the United States defined by northern free-labor capitalism and democracy, had its origins in the fierce intra-elite struggles for national power that had dogged the early republic.[127] Strengthened by rapid economic change in both sections and serious political crises over the gag rule and Texas, it now took on greater force as northern politicians like Fessenden mobilized popular opposition to the Mexican-American War.

While the slavery issue threatened to divide the Whig Party along sectional and intra-sectional lines, popular opposition to southern influence was strong enough in New England to render Maine Whigs, pressured continually by abolitionists, outspoken in their attacks on what they regarded as an iniquitous war launched by a proslavery Democratic president in the interests of the southern states. Fessenden attended the Whigs' Cumberland County nominating conventions in Portland on August 12, 1846. The party faithful denounced the war against Mexico as "one

designed for the ultimate subjugation of the free States" and heard their congressional nominee, Josiah Little, embrace the abolitionists' conviction that the nation's ills could be put down to a dastardly plot by the Slave Power to spread human
bondage across the expanding republic. All northerners, hoped Little, "*irrespective
of party* could be roused to act as unitedly against the grasping encroachments of
the Slave power, as the South does in its support."[128] Here was proof that Texas's
annexation as a slave state had enhanced public receptivity to the Slave Power
thesis. It was little wonder that many antislavery Whigs began to sense they could
rally northerners of all parties behind their leadership on the basis of opposition to
putative southern domination.

The following month, in partial fulfillment of that expectation, the vast majority of northern Whigs and Democrats in the U.S. House of Representatives, Maine's
congressmen among them, voted for the Wilmot Proviso, which aimed to prohibit
the expansion of slavery into any territory ceded by Mexico. Even though the Proviso
stood no chance of being passed by the Democrat-controlled Senate, it was regarded
by many proslavery leaders as proof of the North's hostility to southern honor and
political influence. John C. Calhoun of South Carolina initiated the counterattack,
hoping to unite the South behind his leadership and still northern assaults on slavery
ahead of the 1848 presidential election.

In fact, while the Wilmot Proviso was a serious manifestation of sectional po-
larization, the struggle for national political power unleashed equally potent cen-
tripetal forces. There was no consensus, for example, among northern Whigs over
who should be the party's presidential candidate. In states where they lagged seriously behind the Democrats, many Whigs evinced an understandable tendency to
support the most popular candidate—just as they had in 1839–40. One such group
met at Augusta in July 1847 and passed resolutions supporting Zachary Taylor for
president despite the fact that the popular Mexican War general was a southern
plantation owner who refused to endorse the Proviso.[129] William Pitt Fessenden
was not among them. In spite of devoting much of his time to his thriving law
business and bringing the Atlantic & St. Lawrence project to fruition, he par-
ticipated actively in the campaign. Unlike the more cautious, conservative Whigs
who backed Taylor and were reluctant to make the divisive Wilmot Proviso a test
of party loyalty, he favored a strong show of sectional defiance. On August 26
he helped to draft resolutions condemning the Mexican War at the Cumberland
County Whig convention in Portland. The resolves not only denounced what was,
militarily, a resoundingly successful conflict as either a "CRIME or BLUNDER"

but also declared that adherence to the Proviso, "both in Congress and out," was the surest way to prevent the acquisition of more slave territory.[130] While this position was consistent with Fessenden's longstanding views on slavery, it also reflected his persistent determination to limit abolitionist defections and his personal experience of arrogant southerners in Washington. The meeting elected him a delegate to the Whigs' national convention in Philadelphia but pointedly made no nomination for president.

In May 1848 Fessenden received a letter from Daniel Webster's ever-faithful supporter Hiram Ketchum. Webster, the New York lawyer contended, was highly regarded by southern Whigs and stood a good chance of securing the nomination. Pitt must prepare for the contest and ensure that his godfather finally achieved his political destiny.[131] Fessenden was less committed to Webster than Ketchum assumed, not least because the Massachusetts senator, like his old rival Clay (who was also a candidate), had never endorsed the Wilmot Proviso. Yet he was determined to do what he could to prevent the entry of another slaveholding politician to the White House. He therefore played a prominent role at the state Whig convention in Augusta later that month, helping to block attempts by the Taylorites who controlled the Whig state committee to pass a resolution in support of the general. He also joined his friend Freeman Morse in calling for "consistent adherence to true Whig principles—to the principles of liberty, and a decent regard and respect to Northern rights." According to the new editor of the *Portland Advertiser*, Henry Carter (a staunch ally of Fessenden), the two men "fearlessly and faithfully exposed the inconsistency and absurdity of the Whigs of Maine,—an extreme Northern state,—passing by all the known and tried statesmen of the Northern and Free States to take up a Southern man occupying the position of Gen. Taylor." These comments, warmly rebutted by Taylor's supporters, "came from the heart," gushed Carter. Fessenden and Morse were "true to the mass of the people, and the people will remember them, when trading, trafficking politicians are forgotten, or remembered only to be condemned."[132]

Harboring residual loyalty to his godfather, Fessenden dutifully reported his actions to Ketchum. The New Yorker welcomed his stand. The nomination of any slaveholder, be it Taylor or Clay, he said, would destroy the Whig Party and allow "the Abolition party" to "become the party of the north."[133] To ensure Webster's nomination, New England delegates must unite on the Massachusetts senator from the first ballot. Fessenden left for Philadelphia at the beginning of June unsure of success. He tarried in New York (where he saw Lizzy) and told Ellen that while Taylor would probably secure a plurality on the first ballot, the general would struggle to secure the necessary majority because no northern delegate unpledged to him would support him. "I find the feeling that we should have a free State Candidate is very strong & increasing," he wrote. "Of course I have done my best to help it on. If it prevails, we shall have Webster or [General Winfield S.] Scott—*which*, it is impossible to guess.[134] But the *chances* are in favour of Taylor." Fessenden anticipated "a most uncomfortable week. We shall maneuver & quarrel all the time, and it will, probably, be hot as fury."[135] After arriving in the City of Brotherly Love, where thousands of Whigs crammed into all available accommodations, he told his wife that it would be "farewell to Whiggery" if Taylor were elected because Ohio and Massachusetts, states in which antislavery Whigs were prevalent, would surely "bolt." Only if General Taylor agreed to support the Proviso would he vote for him.[136]

As the convention moved from organization to balloting Fessenden grew increasingly pessimistic. The Whigs, he moaned, were about to nominate "a man confessedly ignorant of civil affairs" and who, until recently, "never rose above the rank of Colonel in a Regiment of Infantry—all because no *other* Slaveholder can be elected, & Southern Aristocracy has made a corrupt bargain with northern moneybags." "Be it so," he said, "*I will [have] none of it.*"[137] Although he adhered to Webster until the end, strong southern backing for Taylor and an absence of unanimity among northern delegates resulted in the general's nomination on the fifth ballot. As Fessenden had predicted, Taylor's success prompted immediate opposition from northern antislavery Whigs. Shortly after returning home he received an invitation from the prominent Boston "Conscience Whig," Charles Sumner, to address a third-party gathering in Worcester, Massachusetts, at the end of June. "We presume," wrote Sumner, "that you will be ready to unite in efforts to oppose the election of Cass & Taylor, & to sustain the principles of Free Soil."[138]

That summer large numbers of political abolitionists previously affiliated with the Liberty Party united with a minority of antislavery Whigs and anti-southern Democrats to form a new sectional organization, the Free Soil Party, pledged to impose the Wilmot Proviso. Neither the Whig candidate Taylor nor the Democratic nominee, Lewis Cass of Michigan, was willing to support congressional prohibition of slavery extension and both major parties had dodged the Proviso in their platforms. The Free Soilers, therefore, constituted the only partisans willing to pledge themselves formally in favor of unremitting opposition to the alleged designs of the Slave Power.

Sumner's presumption that Pitt Fessenden would commit himself to the Free Soil cause like his father was misplaced. The Portland attorney was certainly pained by

Taylor's nomination and refused to join prominent local Whigs in signing a call for a popular Taylor ratification meeting in late June. Yet he did not attend the Worcester convention and rebuffed the efforts of the Maine abolitionist Jabez C. Woodman to entice him into the local Free Soil movement.

Fessenden's decision to remain aloof from the new third party was the result of careful deliberation. In mid-July he admitted privately that he had been "excessively disgusted" by Maine Whigs' support for Taylor's nomination and indicated that he could not, in all conscience, campaign for the general. It was clear, however, that he had already begun to come to terms with the action of the Philadelphia convention. He reasoned, first, that the Free Soil Party did not present him or his cause with a better alternative to his current partisan allegiance. Woodman, he observed, was "a very honest man . . . but a notional and unsafe politician" and few leading Whigs or Democrats had been drawn off by the Free Soil movement. Second, he began to see the positive side of the ticket. He now claimed to "admire the personal character of Gen. Taylor" and considered "him to be substantially a sound Whig" who was "infinitely preferable" to Lewis Cass. Besides, the party's vice presidential nominee, Millard Fillmore of New York, was reliable on the slavery extension issue. Third, it was "a question of alternatives." A vote for Free Soil would merely let in another pro-southern Democrat just, as he believed, a vote for Birney in 1844 had led to Clay's defeat at the hands of Polk. Having been a member of the national convention, he could not think of opposing "what a majority of my friends have determined to sustain; for meanly as I may think of the few, the great mass of the honest, patriotic, and wise men and statesmen of our party have yielded their assent, in view of the present, perilous condition of affairs. The principle of the 'free soil' movement has my respect. But I cannot see that it will lead to any practical result other than the election of General Cass, a calamity to be deprecated by all good men. In these things we are bound, I think, to look at results, rather than to principles alone."[139]

Fessenden's pragmatic reasoning concealed a good deal of self-interest. Abandoning the established Whig Party for the untried Free Soilers carried with it obvious risks at a juncture when party disintegration was at an early stage and the possibility of a Taylor victory carried with it the promise of federal patronage as well as the implementation of Whig policies. For the moment at least he decided, like a majority of northern Whigs and Democrats, to remain true to party.

It was a close run thing. Fessenden publicly reiterated his allegiance to the Whig standard in an address to the local party's nominating convention in August.

Declining a nomination for Congress for "reasons of a private and domestic character," he emphasized his "continued attachment to the Whig party and Whig principles."[140] Revealingly, however, he did not mention Zachary Taylor by name, and privately he denounced the general's nomination as "an outrage" upon both the party and its principles.[141] Three weeks before the presidential election he complained that "Old Rough and Ready" had not brought strength to the ticket and, even after the Whigs' crucial gubernatorial victory in Pennsylvania, he speculated that the Free Soilers could throw the election to Cass. He was wrong on the second count, right on the first. The Free Soil vote actually helped Maine Whigs elect two congressmen (and sapped Democratic strength in the state's gubernatorial election), and did not, as a national force, prevent Taylor from winning the presidency.[142] However, the general succeeded not because he was wildly popular among northern Whigs but because Cass was even less inspiring to Democrats and failed to prevent Taylor from securing the electoral college votes of key states that Clay had failed narrowly to win four years previously.

If Fessenden was pleased with the result, the sensation was only temporary. His youngest child, Mary, died of scarlet fever four weeks later. Although he tried to rationalize the tragedy in orthodox terms, his limited religious faith provided scant solace. "[I] shall never be reconciled to the event," he told Lizzy Warriner in an unusually emotional letter. Mary "was my treasure, my comfort & my blessing—the light and joy of our home . . . God has taken her, and, doubtless, the dispensation is just & wise, & merciful. I hope it will make me better. That she is the gainer I am well assured, and the thought is a sweet one—but it does not bring her back to me."[143] It was a depressing end to a difficult year and an object warning, if any was required, that earthly happiness was fleeting.

The Whigs' electoral triumph and the death of his daughter lowered the curtain on a critical phase of Fessenden's life. A staunch nationalist at the start of the decade, he had begun, through a combination of experience, conviction, and political opportunism, to embrace the political abolitionists' diagnosis of America's ills. Even though his continuing commitment to Whiggery and innate political caution prevented him from joining the Free Soilers' revolt, he was alert to the seismic shifts occurring in domestic politics. Over the next seven years those shifts would destroy the Whig coalition at both the national and local levels and forge a new northern-based organization, the Republican Party. Few politicians in the country were as well equipped to take advantage of fundamental political change as William Pitt Fessenden.

Union among Ourselves, 1849–1856

Zachary Taylor's election was a false dawn for America's Whigs. Although they remained wedded to economic growth, the issues that had once been so central to their identity—protective tariffs, banking, and internal improvements—had declined in salience owing to the country's returning prosperity (further boosted by the discovery of California gold in 1848). In Maine, as in other northern states, the Jacksonians had stolen their clothes by supporting developmental projects like the Atlantic & St Lawrence Railroad. After the election of yet another Democratic governor the *Portland Advertiser* described the Democrats' abandonment of their "old humbugs" and embrace of the Whigs' pro-market "doctrines" as a compliment.[1] However, there was precious little compensation in this. Maine Whigs still faced the seemingly intractable problem of how to destroy the opposition's grip on state power.

William Pitt Fessenden and many of his co-partisans would find a solution to this problem in the so-called realignment process that modern political scientists have adjudged responsible for the destruction of old parties and the making of new ones in American history. Whereas scholars once identified the issue of slavery expansion as the sole destroyer of the Whig Party and the rise of the Republicans, historians such as William Gienapp and Michael Holt have developed a more sophisticated explanation for these developments, one that incorporates nativism, temperance, and factionalism as at least secondary factors (secondary, that is, to slavery) in the demise of the second-party system.[2] Fessenden secured national power in February 1854 by winning election to the U.S. Senate as the representative of an embryonic Republican coalition straddling antislavery, temperance, and nativism. He would not have been successful, moreover, without a serious split in the ranks of the Maine Democracy. In this respect, his ascent to high office can help us make greater sense of what Gienapp aptly calls "the confusion of fusion," the labyrinthine changes that remade the political landscape of the United States in the early 1850s.[3] Though his path was fraught with danger, for himself and the republic, he negotiated those changes with great skill. Having secured the high office that he had long craved, he attached his rising star to the Republican Party, a determined opponent of southern power whose raison d'être was not prohibition or nativism but vigorous opposition to slavery expansion. Thereafter he would rank as one of the staunchest advocates of northern rights in Washington. Only when the Union was controlled by northern men committed to free-soil principles, he insisted, would the republic be safe from the corrupting influence of aristocratic southern slaveholders. As events unfolded in the mid 1850s this undeniably self-serving yet sincerely held remedy for national degeneration became ever more compelling for northern voters. In 1856 the Republicans cemented their position as the main opposition to the proslavery Democracy by challenging hard for the presidency. Southern politicians, who had begun to doubt whether the Union provided sufficient security for slavery and were equally adept at exploiting sectional issues for their own ends, had every reason to be afraid.

Carpe Diem

Because Fessenden had opposed Taylor's nomination, he did not expect to enjoy significant influence with the new administration. Nonetheless, he took the opportunity, while arguing a case before the U.S. Supreme Court during the winter of 1848–49, to press the appointment of his fellow Maine Whig, Senator George Evans, to the cabinet. Taylor's appointing policy, however, was designed to further the president's plan of building a new conservative party on an almost no-party basis and Evans, a Webster loyalist, was soon passed over. Fessenden, still a committed Whig, was unimpressed. "I have some fears that the Genl. will get none but second rate men about him," he informed Ellen from Washington. With useless advisers, the inexperienced Taylor was bound to "break down."[4] When not attending court, the Portland lawyer enjoyed monitoring debates in Congress. "This is, evidently, the day of small things, as any one can see with half an eye, on looking at the Senate," he observed witheringly.[5] After dining at four, he sat in his room and read, wrote, and ruminated contemplatively in the relaxing glow of a roaring fire. Lonely as he often was on these trips, he told his unavailable cousin Lizzy Warriner (with transparent yearning) that he wished "I had somebody with me to make the time pass more agreeably, & to whom I might express my thoughts, & see if they amounted to any thing—wish for many things I can't get, & hope that the time will come when I can."[6]

Fessenden was home by early March and spent an unremarkable spring and summer on legal business. Family concerns also occupied much of his time. Recalling,
perhaps, his own wayward college days he monitored closely the activities of his eldest son, James, at Bowdoin; mediated in a dispute between his father's business
partner, Thomas Deblois, and Daniel Webster; and assisted his half-brother Daniel's
plans to go to the California gold fields.[7] Pitt found the prospect of family breakup
occasioned by Daniel's impending departure unsettling. He had, he told Lizzy, "become nervously apprehensive of calamity" and felt continually "as if the cord by
which my own life, & the lives of my wife & children, is held, was every moment
giving way."[8] The gathering crisis of the Union and signs of social disorder in Portland, evident in sporadic mob attacks on the home of a black man rumored to be
running a brothel, may have contributed to his sense of instability.[9] However, it was
most likely triggered by his daughter's tragic death, his feelings for Lizzy, and the
unmistakable onset of middle age (a tireless worker, Fessenden was just starting to
go gray).[10]

An outside observer would have struggled to detect instability in the lawyer's
household. His family was cocooned from the most debilitating effects of rapid economic change by wealth, old as well as new. In 1846 Pitt Fessenden had moved his
dependants into a spacious Federal-style home on fashionable State Street. Built
by a chief justice of the state supreme court, the house was a gift from his elderly
father-in-law, James Deering. His partnership with William Willis was already bringing in $3,000 a year but the Deering connection was worth much more to him. This
was particularly the case after James died in September 1850 at the age of 84.[11] The
merchant had owned a substantial amount of land in the Portland area and much of
it was rising in value as railroad development and building construction increased.
Through his marriage to Ellen, who inherited a portion of the estate, Fessenden was
now a man of independent means. The windfall meant that if he wanted to pursue a
political career, he could afford to do so.[12] He now owned real estate worth around
$10,000, a substantial sum at mid-century, and was able to employ three white ser-
vant girls to help Ellen run the large house and look after the couple's four boys, Sam
(9), Francis (11), William (15), and James (16).[13]

Comfortably well off, William Pitt Fessenden yearned not for greater riches
but for political power. Yet 1849 offered only tantalizing glimpses of personal advancement. He was active in trying to forge the anti-Democratic majority that had
proved elusive since the decade opened. The Free Soil vote in the recent presidential election had narrowed the gap between local Whigs and Democrats from over

13 percentage points in 1844 to just 4.8 in 1848, opening up the alluring prospect of a winning coalition if cooperation could be achieved between the Whig Party and the Free Soilers (many of whom were old Liberty men like his father and antislavery Conscience Whigs).[14] Maine Whigs and Free Soilers adopted a joint ticket in several localities ahead of the fall elections, their aim being to win a majority in the legislature that would elect Samuel Fessenden to the U.S. Senate. "There is no *agreement,* or *understanding,* to that effect, of course," Pitt confided to Lizzy, "but still it is to be so, *if*—but the *if* is every thing."[15]

The Whigs' efforts were spearheaded by Fessenden's ally, James S. Pike, a hardheaded small businessman from Calais who spent much of his time in Washington, DC, as a political correspondent of the *Boston Courier* and, after 1850, the *New-York Tribune.* These endeavors bore very limited fruit. "Fusion" was achieved in only a handful of counties and the Free Soilers virtually guaranteed the success of Democrat John Hubbard by nominating their own gubernatorial candidate.[16] More encouragingly, however, there were signs of a permanent rending of Jacksonian forces in the state. Hubbard, a Wilmot Proviso supporter, had been nominated over fierce opposition from powerful "Wildcat" Democrats from the eastern half of Maine, which included the Calhounite wilderness of Aroostook County. Their considerable influence was grounded in the formidable patronage of the federal land office and residual popular opposition to the market and neither they nor their constituents exhibited an interest in the slavery extension issue that exercised their "Woolhead" foes in the more developed western portion of the state.[17]

Pitt Fessenden's hopes of building a permanent Whig—or Whiggish—majority with Free Soil help were complicated by angry debates in Washington over slavery extension. His brother Daniel was not the only American to be seduced by the California gold rush. Hundreds of thousands of people from across the eastern states, Latin America, western Europe, Australia, and China flocked to the goldfields in 1849, resulting almost immediately in local efforts to create a state government. Because the Wilmot Proviso had never passed the Senate, the new Taylor administration had the unenviable task of developing a viable policy on the status of slavery in the vast Mexican Cession of which California was a part. Despite Fessenden's initial doubts about the president's political skills and likely proslavery bias, Zachary Taylor was an uncompromising nationalist who believed the best way to curtail sectional discord over slavery expansion was to circumvent the controversial Proviso and admit California and the neighboring region of New Mexico as states as quickly as possible. Unhappily for the president, his plan was heavily criticized by northern

Free Soilers and proslavery southern Democrats who considered it a sell-out to the other side. Many Whigs, especially in the South, received it coolly. As a result, on arriving in Washington that winter, Henry Clay (no admirer of the president's un-orthodox patronage policy) developed his own policy response, which included: the creation of a territorial government for New Mexico without reference to slavery; the admission of California as a free state; and, to mollify the South, a new fugitive slave law facilitating the retrieval of runaway chattels from free states and a prohibi-tion against interference with the profitable domestic slave trade.

The resulting debates in Congress threatened, even more than those over the Wilmot Proviso, to polarize opinion in the country and to obliterate existing party lines. While some southern rights politicians advocated secession if California was lost, antislavery northern Whigs joined free-soil Democrats like Maine's Hannibal Hamlin and Ohio's Free Soil Senator Salmon Chase in denouncing any concessions to the Slave Power. The crisis highlighted the difference between Fessenden and the aging Whig grandees Clay and Webster. After Webster defended the compromise proposals in a patriotic speech on March 7, he was widely excoriated in New Eng-land for his alleged abandonment of northern interests. Though more understand-ing than his irate father, Pitt described the Massachusetts senator's performance as a "great calamity."[18] Significantly, after reading a press report of Hamlin's more forthright oration, he told the Bangor Democrat that he liked the speech "very much." It gave, he said, "much better satisfaction to men of all parties here than Mr. Webster's." He concluded his missive by asking Hamlin (who had once worked in Samuel Fessenden's Portland law office) for a copy and pointedly signed himself "Yr friend."[19]

Pitt Fessenden's collegial gesture betokened closer cooperation between the sup-porters of antislavery and northern rights in all parties. In June 1850, with the com-promise measures temporarily stalled in Congress, Hamlin's Wildcat opponents in the Maine legislature tried to block his reelection to the Senate. Recognizing that the score of Free Soilers at Augusta could decide the contest between the warring Democratic factions, Samuel Fessenden (the Free Soilers' senatorial candidate) urged his co-partisans to transfer their votes from him to Hamlin who, in the wake of his speech on the Compromise, was widely regarded as the state's new cham-pion of northern rights. Although the Whigs joined Hamlin's Woolhead supporters and Free Soilers in backing strong resolves opposing the extension of slavery into the Mexican Cession as well as attempts in Congress to link this issue with south-ern concerns over the security of slave property, they did not rally behind Hamlin's senatorial candidacy.[20] Pitt Fessenden, however, clandestinely approved his father's strategy, which finally resulted in Hamlin's election on July 25. His primary aim was not at this stage to form an entirely new political organization committed to the advancement of northern rights. His main goals were to assist both the breakdown of the divided Democrats and his own political advancement. Like the Whigs, the Free Soilers had originally intended simply to postpone an election in order to foster deeper divisions between the Democrats. But when Hamlin provided the desired pledges on slavery to secure their votes, they had opted to vote for him. Fessenden arrived at Augusta as the drama closed. "I had much talk with him," commented Orrin Blanchard, one of the leading Free Soilers at the capital: "he says we have done just the right thing."[21]

There was method in Fessenden's support for a Democratic senator. He was a Whig candidate for congressman that fall and needed Free Soil votes to win a majority. By approving the antislavery radicals' aims and sanctioning cross-party voting he was endeavoring, as he had done in the past, to attract Free Soil backing in his district. More significantly, he already had his eye on a place in the U.S. Senate. To secure that, as the member of a political minority, he would need the backing not only of Free Soilers and likeminded Whigs but also of dissident Democrats. The early signs were propitious. Blanchard went to Portland to urge local Free Soilers to support a man known to have a solid antislavery record and to be a staunch supporter of northern rights. "Our folks there have agreed to vote for Pitt for Congress," reported Blanchard, "and he will be elected."[22]

Fessenden's dalliance with Free Soilers set him apart from the majority of Maine Whigs who, at their state convention in July (over which he presided), not only mourned the recent death of President Taylor but condemned the Free Soilers for backing a Democrat.[23] It is unlikely that he was unduly concerned about committing what some of his co-partisans may have regarded as an act of party treason. He wanted high political office to slake his ambition, believed the Whigs could only benefit from Democratic divisions, and, like his father, understood the importance of Hamlin's reelection to the broader struggle against southern proslavery domination. Cumberland County Free Soilers recognized Fessenden's value to the cause and, as Blanchard had predicted, nominated him for Congress in mid-August. They had reason to do so. The younger Fessenden was ardently opposed to the extension of slavery because it inflated southern power and thereby threatened those "northern *national* principles" whose defense was essential to the future greatness of the American republic.[24] He may not have shared some political abolitionists' enthusiasm for blacks, enslaved or free, but, as one anonymous Free Soiler put it, "he agrees with us on the great principles of human freedom to come before Congress." He opposed the extension of slavery by any means as well as the annexation of Cuba or the admission of any other slave territory to the Union and held that Congress should divorce itself from slavery wherever it had the constitutional power so to do. As the only staunch northern rights man who could possibly be elected from the Portland district, he was thus deemed a fit beneficiary of the Free Soilers' tactical voting that was designed to leaven the major parties with "free principles."[25]

The deal, intended to be mutually beneficial, nearly worked. Assisted by Free Soil support and widespread opposition to most of the Compromise measures that passed Congress in the weeks leading up to the election, Fessenden lost the September election by only 39 votes out of a total of nearly 12,000—this despite being buffeted by Democratic charges that he was hostile to workingmen, had backed Webster's course in Congress, and was a drunkard.[26] He gained 49.8 percent of the vote compared with the modest 39.9 percent won by the Whig congressional candidate in the Cumberland district two years previously. His narrow defeat, commented one of the Whigs' two victorious congressional candidates, Israel Washburn, Jr., was "most provoking."[27] Although an elementary counting error in one township probably cost him the election, Fessenden did not bother to contest the result.[28] He had bigger fish to fry.

Possibly because he sensed that a majority of Maine voters were willing to suppress their sectional prejudices to maintain the Union, Fessenden was less outspoken in his response to the Compromise of 1850 than many antislavery northern Whigs. Backed by the new Whig president, Millard Fillmore, and piloted adroitly through Congress by the Democrats' rising star, Senator Stephen Douglas of Illinois, the package of measures constituted a modification of Clay's original proposals.[29] It represented an attempt by nationalists in both parties to settle the question of slavery expansion into the territory ceded by Mexico and thereby avert the imminent danger of southern secession. Under the Compromise, California was admitted as a free state; two new territories—New Mexico and Utah—were created in which local residents would be permitted to decide the status of slavery for themselves according to the principles of "popular sovereignty"; and a tougher fugitive slave act provided for the more effective capture of runaway blacks. As Webster had already discovered, the Fugitive Slave Law was deeply unpopular in the North because it ensnared ordinary citizens in the unsavory business of manhunting on behalf of southern slave masters. However, a majority of northerners, relieved at slavery's exclusion from California, suppressed their distaste in a genuine effort to perpetuate the Union.

Fessenden did not like the Compromise and privately told Fillmore not to align himself with Clay and Webster whom, he advised, "have been most decidedly reprobated by a vast majority of Whigs."[30] Once Fillmore had given his blessing to the sectional armistice, however, the Portlander saw reason to keep his powder dry. As Hiram Ketchum pointed out, "we have now, what you & I never saw before, a genuine Whig administration" headed by a New Yorker with a solid track record on slavery expansion.[31] Fessenden's congratulatory letter to Hamlin underlined his own distaste for further compromises with slavery but he did not immediately make public his opposition to the Compromise.

Bipartisan support for the Compromise from conservative Whigs on both sides of the Mason-Dixon line and from many northern Democrats made it difficult for free-soil politicians belonging to either of the major parties to campaign effectively on the slavery issue ahead of the 1852 presidential election. Fessenden was in Washington at the end of February 1851. He met Daniel Webster in the Senate and, to his relief, found him "cordial." He also went to the White House and conversed with President Fillmore. "He is in fine health," Fessenden told his wife, "and looks the Prest. very well." If this comment betokened a lack of personal animus toward Fillmore (the New Yorker had been criticized by many antislavery men for endorsing the Fugitive Slave Act), it did not indicate much confidence in the party as a whole. Politics, Fessenden remarked, were "in utter confusion." Fillmore and Webster were already preparing to cut one another's throats in their desire to gain the presidential nomination. The Democrats were also riven by factionalism. "I look upon both parties with utter disgust, and upon politics in the same way," he scoffed in what may, in part, have been an attempt to rationalize his own lack of political influence.[32]

Politics were about to become even more confused. In April the prohibitionist Neal Dow was elected mayor of Portland against the opposition of centrist Whigs who disliked his intolerance, crusading zeal, and contempt for regular party discipline but with the support of many dry (pro-temperance) Democrats.[33] Dow immediately seized his chance and traveled to Augusta to demand passage of an effective prohibitory liquor law for Maine. The measure obliterated existing party lines in the legislature. Democrats supported prohibition 56–35 while Whigs backed it by 34 votes to 15.[34] Only the vehemently pro-temperance Free Soilers were united in favor. Governor Hubbard, sensing that temperance reform had widespread support beyond the capitol, signed the bill into law. State Land Agent Anson Morrill, a fearsomely ambitious, charismatic, and powerfully built Bangor Democrat, commended the action. "I had supposed it might meet strong opposition in this city & vicinity," he wrote of the new Maine Law, which contained tough penalties for the manufacture and sale of spirits, "—but such is not the case."[35]

Widespread, though by no means unanimous, popular support for the statute probably convinced Fessenden that he could not afford to cross Dow and his allies again. While he had grown no fonder of Dow's belligerent tactics since his brushes with the intolerant crusader in the mid-1840s, he accepted the link between prohibition and maintenance of social order and had no intention of placing himself on the wrong side of a reform favored by many middle-class Yankees. What he did not know was that prohibition was, as Dow put it later, "the breaking-up plow" of Maine politics.[36]

There were no state elections in 1851. The nearest Pitt Fessenden came to personal advancement that year was a vain attempt to gain a seat on the U.S. Supreme Court after Justice Levi Woodbury's death in September. Although the bid was probably doomed from the start (Maine was hardly the most important state in the Union and Fessenden failed to secure the backing of Fillmore's new secretary of state Daniel Webster), the very fact that he was willing to work for such a prestigious position by asking for Webster's support and that his colleagues on the Maine bar believed him fit for it, testified to his restless ambition and his skills as a jurist.[37] But for the most part the year was a dull one. He attended court and worried about Lizzy, whose husband's business affairs were on the slide. He felt, he told his cousin, "the importance of money, as a requisite to independence—and to a man this is almost essential to happiness. It is not so with women, and ought not to be so. The comforts of life are pretty much all she wants."[38]

One of Fessenden's most important local duties was to serve as a director of the Atlantic & St. Lawrence Railroad, a position he had held since 1846. He had played an important role in the road's early days, journeying to Montreal to negotiate with Canadian capitalists like the Montreal financier Alexander Galt. Although Whigs like himself were natural backers for such an expensive, capital-intensive project, the road enjoyed strong cross-party and cross-class support in Portland. Construction was well under way by 1851 but in that year widespread doubts over the road's financial condition caused Fessenden, always a cautious investor, to unload his shares in the venture—precipitately as it turned out because the share price soon recovered and the road, renamed the Grand Trunk Railroad, became a prime source of Portland's prosperity by the end of the decade. While the experience did not erode his faith in capitalism as a system, it appears to have soured his views of private rail-road companies. Unlike many politicians of his generation who hailed railroads as the miracle of the modern age (not to mention a cash cow for themselves), he would view them with an increasingly critical eye—alert henceforth to their dangers as well as their benefits.[39]

Notwithstanding his preoccupation with business affairs, Fessenden retained a strong interest in politics. His best hope of achieving power lay with realignment. In Maine the process began in earnest in 1852, a crucial presidential election year, after Wildcat Democrats rejected the renomination of Governor Hubbard by the party's legislative caucus in January and named their own gubernatorial candidate, Anson G. Chandler. Whereas Hubbard and his Woolhead allies endorsed the Maine Law, the Wildcats denounced it as a departure from the Jacksonians' traditional op-position to government interference in private affairs. A taste of what was to come occurred in Portland in April. A Whig committee that included Fessenden nomi-nated Neal Dow for mayor.[40] Instead of harmonizing the party, significant numbers of anti-Dow Whigs assisted in securing the election of a Democrat for the first time in a decade. Fessenden, who had endorsed local enforcement of the law and was therefore identified with Dow, lost his post as city solicitor. "You need not conclude that I am either ultra-temperance or 'te[e]totaller'—only 'Maine law,'" he told Lizzy, adding humorously that "the loss of office does not deprive me of bread."[41]

The gubernatorial election in September was also a referendum on prohibition and the result was further political chaos. Cross-party voting was rife as many dry Whigs and Free Soilers joined pro-temperance Democrats in rallying to Hubbard as the defender of social order and Christian morality while hundreds of wet Whigs aligned with anti–Maine Law Democrats to back Chandler. The bitter contest also attracted around 24,000 new voters to the polls, contributing to the largest elec-toral turnout in the state's history. William Gienapp has calculated that 30 percent of the Whigs, 50 percent of the Democrats, and more than 80 percent of the Free Soilers who had voted in 1850 either failed to vote at all in 1852, or else supported a different party from the one they had endorsed two years earlier.[42] Hubbard failed to secure the required majority and under state law the election devolved upon the legislature.

Maine Whigs looked on expectantly as the Democrats tore themselves apart. Their chances, however, of exploiting their opponents' divisions were diminished not only by the absence of an internal consensus on prohibition but also a serious rift over national affairs. Many conservative Whigs in Portland, notably the enthusiastic railroad promoter, John A. Poor, supported the 1850 Compromise as a final solution to the slavery question and favored the nomination for president of Millard Fillmore or Daniel Webster (both staunch proponents of the sectional amnesty in part because they wanted southern support for their campaigns). Pitt Fessenden was not among them. He favored the candidacy of the Mexican War hero, Major General Winfield Scott, who, pressed by antislavery Whig leaders, had not publicly endorsed the Compromise as a finality. At the Whigs' state convention in Portland's city hall on June 3 he acclaimed Scott's ability, loyalty, and patriotism and said that, having consulted widely with "gentlemen" from all parts of the country, he knew the general was the right candidate. The gathering elected Fessenden an at-large delegate to the national convention in Baltimore, declared for Scott, pledged devotion to the Union and the Constitution, and, after discussion, tabled a potentially divisive resolution requesting the state's delegates to resist any attempt to incorporate a pro-Compromise plank into the Whig platform.[43]

Fessenden arrived at the Whigs' national convention on June 14. He had changed trains in Wilmington and journeyed down to Baltimore with Stephen Douglas, the principal architect of the Compromise. He was impressed and found the "Little Giant" a surprisingly "sociable fellow." Douglas was keen to learn what his fellow Yankee thought of the dough-faced Democratic nominee, Franklin Pierce, a Bowdoin graduate. "[I] told him all the good I knew of him," Fessenden joked to Ellen, "—as perhaps I may turn Democrat, and want an office." As he had done four years earlier in Philadelphia, he predicted "a pretty stormy time" at the convention.[44] On this occasion he was more hopeful about his candidate's chances, because Scott would only need a few votes from those initially committed to Fillmore to see him across the line. If the Fillmoreites required as a condition of their support a resolution declaring the Compromise an end to sectional debate over slavery, he assured Ellen, they would not get it with his vote. Fessenden was as good as his word. A member of the platform committee, he fought consistently against southern attempts to write a finality plank.[45] He was eventually defeated because of a one-state, one-vote rule that curbed the influence of Scott supporters on the committee but, as he had intimated to his wife, there was no love lost between the two pro-Compromise candidates.[46] After forty-six ineffectual ballots in which it became clear that the supporters of Fillmore and Webster would not coalesce, Fessenden grew confident of a Scott victory. The South was determined to nominate Fillmore, he told Ellen, "as their friend and tool" and had been cheating Webster all along. Scott's men "are firm as a rock, and will, I hope & trust, hold on to the end."[47] They did. The general was finally elected on the fifty-third ballot, resulting in an outpouring of joy among northern antislavery delegates.

Pitt Fessenden explained his actions at a Whig ratification meeting in Portland on June 30. Had it been in his power, he said (with limited conviction), he would have made Webster, "the great statesman of New England," president of the United States. But it was the people's wish, as manifested by the declaration of the state convention, to give that office to General Scott, "the great chieftain of the age." Although he had opposed the finality resolution, he had decided not to reduce Maine's influence at the convention by leaving. However, this did not signify his consent to the principle of finality. He made clear "that the resolution referred to was, in his judgment, applicable only to the existing state of things. It bound neither the north or south with reference to any future aggressions either on one side or the other . . . But he trusted that none such would ever arise to disturb the harmony which ought to exist between all sections of the country, and, that the peace now declared might prove eternal."[48] Fessenden chose his words carefully. While he regarded the pro-Compromise Scott as a more available and acceptable candidate than Webster (one who would not surrender northern rights on the altar of proslavery Unionism), he remained enough of a Unionist and a Whig to acquiesce to the Compromise on condition that there were no more southern "aggressions."

Fessenden was a successful candidate for state representative in the confused September elections. In Portland he ran nearly a thousand votes ahead of the Whigs' gubernatorial candidate, William G. Crosby, in the same election.[49] He had decided to contest the place in the hope that he might take advantage of the political turmoil engulfing the state. The next legislature was scheduled to elect a U.S. senator for the full term of six years. Vanity and boredom, he confessed to Lizzy, explained his decision to stand. "But it is always best to put oneself in the way of luck, so as to catch any that come[s] along. And if I can accomplish nothing else, the change of occupation will be a relief of itself."[50]

Initially, it seemed that luck had deserted Fessenden and his party. In November southerners' lack of enthusiasm for Scott resulted in his defeat at the hands of Franklin Pierce. Many northern Whigs shared the view of one of Israel Washburn's correspondents that the party was "now dead—dead—dead!"[51] But while Fessenden himself declared Whiggery "defunct" in a letter to Hannibal Hamlin, the statement lacked conviction, accompanied as it was by the humorous contention that all were Democrats now.[52] The truth was that with the Whigs in a minority at Augusta, he needed cross-party votes to send him to Washington. Currying favor with Hamlin, the most powerful Woolhead in Maine, made sound political sense. Henry Carter, Fessenden's ally at the *Portland Advertiser,* was certainly not in favor of disbanding the party. He urged his fellow Whigs to wait on events: "[T]he feeling of opposition to any new aggressions of pro-slavery was never stronger. Such an issue presents something practical and tangible. It presents something to be done or prevented; and around such an issue, if any should be again forced upon us, the people may be successfully rallied."[53]

The Democrats' internal struggle for control of the state intensified after Pierce's election. The warring factions knew that if they could win that struggle the new administration would have to treat them as the legitimate voice of the Maine Democracy and they could then claim the spoils of victory. Initially, Fessenden was fairly pessimistic about his chances of exploiting this fracture. A Scott victory would have given his senatorial bid a major boost because his support for the general would have translated into political influence. He judged therefore that the presidential debacle left his "Senatorial visions . . . dissipated." "[I] must content myself with remaining the nobody I am," he told Lizzy despondently in December 1852.[54]

Yet when the legislature assembled the following month, minority Wildcats aligned themselves with Whigs to elect Crosby as governor over the Woolhead, John Hubbard, in order to ensure that they were not left out in the patronage wilderness. This action greatly complicated the ensuing battle for the vacant U.S. Senate seat, which was to be filled jointly by the House and Senate. Fessenden remained certain he could not win but his friends urged him to stay in Augusta and fight for office.[55] In the balloting he consistently won a majority in the Whig-controlled Senate but in the House, where there was a Democratic majority, he was always just short of success. Israel Washburn believed that some Whigs, loyal to Crosby, were voting against him as part of an informal deal with the Wildcats, who had procured the election of a Whig governor.[56] Fessenden thought the problem lay primarily with the Democrats. They were toying with him, he told Lizzy: some voted for him "to show their spite" (against the other faction) but they made sure he did not secure enough votes to be elected. "I have taken no active interest in the matter because I knew it was of no use," he wrote. Probably, he supposed, he could buy the seat but an office obtained in that way was not worth having. "True, I *generally used* to succeed in my undertakings, but this was in bye-gone [sic] days, when I was younger & smarter. I have made so many failures in these later days, when I had the strongest desire to succeed, that, truly, my self confidence is most seriously diminished."[57] On March 3 the legislature postponed further balloting on the senatorship, ensuring that the seat would remain vacant for another year.[58]

Frustrated he may have been but lacking in self-confidence he was not. Fessenden knew that in order to be elected U.S. senator he would have to forge a majoritarian coalition in the legislature between Woolhead Democrats, antislavery Whigs, and Free Soilers. Even with the turmoil created by the Maine Law this would be no easy task. His political ambitions were assisted by a further widening of the Democrats' factional squabbles during 1853. Despite an attempt to unify the party with a bland platform making no mention of either the Maine Law or the Compromise, Woolheads refused to accept the gubernatorial nomination of Albert Pillsbury and backed one of their own leaders, Anson Morrill, for the position. They also came out strongly for social reform, including prohibition, and declared their allegiance to the Pierce administration despite its confused response to the dissemination of offices in Maine. (Personally the president did not support the Woolheads' social agenda and favored a "bold vigorous assault" on what he called "this conglomeration of *isms*—separately contemptible—collectively infamous.")[59] The September election provided further evidence of party disintegration. Pillsbury only managed to win a plurality, again devolving the selection of a governor onto the legislature. Nearly three-quarters of Hubbard's 1852 supporters either abstained or rejected Pillsbury for one of the pro–Maine Law candidates: Morrill, Crosby, or the Free Soiler, Ezekiel Holmes.[60] The fact that the anti-Pillsbury vote collectively exceeded the Wildcat total by roughly 11,000 was not lost on some observers but the extent of cross-party voting left even professional politicians befuddled. "What a fog-bank we are in politically," George Evans remarked to Fessenden shortly after the election.[61]

The latter was uncertain what the contest meant for his political aspirations. It was hard to say, he told Lizzy, whether he was any closer to the Senate. "It is sufficient, perhaps, that no reasonable calculations can be founded on the present state of parties. The Democrats will have a majority in both branches of the legislature, but they are wo[e]fully divided. They have, however, a wonderful faculty of uniting, and it is fairly to be presumed that they may agree *now*."[62] Here Fessenden drew on his experience of Jacksonian party discipline and, by implication, the Whigs' historic lack of it. Yet he cannot have failed to do his sums. A fusion of the anti-Wildcat forces at Augusta could bring him success. As one Free Soil sheet commented: "These parties must and will coalesce."[63]

That fall Fessenden, who had been reelected as a state representative, began to position himself for the forthcoming fight. In October 1853 he signed a collective statement rejecting the contention of Portland conservative John Neal that the Maine Law had actually increased drunkenness in the city. Support for the legislation, the document claimed, emanated from the solid middle classes: "the intelligent farmers, mechanics and native business men of the country."[64] He also appears to have opened up communications with the Morrill Democrats. By mid-November Governor Crosby, who had been elected with Wildcat votes the previous year and subsequently distributed offices to his Democratic supporters, heard rumors of an understanding between the Woolheads and Whigs loyal to Fessenden that was intended to send the latter to Washington as senator and elect Morrill governor. Such an agreement, Crosby told Fessenden (his old Bowdoin classmate), would be destructive of Whig harmony. "I am satisfied," he wrote, "that to preserve harmony you & I must stand or fall together." The agitated governor added menacingly that if he was defeated, his friends, disappointed in their hopes for patronage, were bound to take revenge on Fessenden. "I am afraid," he said, "that this suspicion of your integrity, if it finds any ground on which to stand, will operate to your prejudice; I fear that it is so operating now, & I beg leave to suggest to you the expediency of doing something to allay it." The governor concluded with an appeal to self-interest and party loyalty: "With the present state of feeling I see nothing ahead but trouble & perplexity for both of us in particular & the Whig party in general, to follow from any coalition which has for its object a division of the two principal offices."[65] Shortly before he left his home in Belfast for the capital, Crosby argued that the Democrats would combine to make Pillsbury governor and elect a Woolhead to the Senate. "I still think you & I should not assume the responsibility of making any bargains. If we do we may find that the ratifying power will refuse to sanction it."[66]

Fessenden was not intimidated. There was no reason, he replied, for the two Bowdoin alumni to be joined at the hip. Crosby's election as governor, he said, would be a good outcome for the party, regardless of his own fate. His contention that the Whigs' best strategy was to combine with all the opponents of the Wildcats, however, underlined his distance from Crosby, who had reason to fear that plots were going on behind his back. The anxious governor, certainly, could not have drawn comfort from Fessenden's ambiguous statement that personally he would not participate in any backstage deals and that he would labor to implement "the decrees of the Whig party to the best of my power."[67] In late December the ambitious Portlander asked Senator Hannibal Hamlin to do what he could to defeat Nathan Clifford's attempts to secure votes from both Democratic factions in the legislature. "I would suggest," Fessenden ventured boldly, "whether you should not have some shrewd confidential friend at Augusta—as if your personal friends, and a reasonable number of the Morrill men refuse to support him [Clifford], he cannot be elected. Ten stiff democrats added to the Whig & Free Soil strength will ensure his defeat."[68]

When the legislature convened at the beginning of January 1854, Fessenden emerged as a leading player in a bloc of more than eighty Morrill Democrats, anti-Crosby Whigs, and pro–Maine Law, antislavery Free Soilers in the lower house. "A most remarkable state of affairs exists," commented one journalist, "*Party is blotted out!*"[69] Although the coalitionists had the numbers to prevent Pillsbury's name from being sent up to the state Senate for election (Crosby and Morrill were forwarded instead), a Maine Supreme Court decision frustrated Fessenden's attempts to pack the upper chamber with his allies. He could not, therefore, guarantee that Anson Morrill would be chosen governor as part of any deal to make him U.S. senator. And so it proved. Wildcat senators and loyal Whigs managed to reelect Crosby by sixteen votes to fifteen in the first week of February. This decision could easily have scuppered Fessenden's chances of election. These seemed to be further reduced when his Democratic opponents nominated Anson's more conservative cousin, Lot Morrill, in a bid to secure Woolhead support. But luckily the coalition held strong, He was elected by joint convention of the House and Senate to represent Maine in the U.S. Senate by a combination of majority Whig, Morrill Democrat, and Free Soil votes on February 10.

Why did the coalition hold after Anson Morrill had failed to secure the governorship? The answer lies partly, perhaps primarily, in the Woolheads' deep hatred of the Wildcats. Sending a Whig senator to Washington would spite not only their local rivals but also the Pierce administration, which had failed to recognize them as the legitimate voice of the Maine Democracy. Anson Morrill may have gambled that Fessenden, in recognition of the Woolheads' support, was more likely than any conservative Democrat, even his own cousin, to deliver offices to his friends. But it was not just a question of the spoils. Hostility to slavery was also at the forefront of the coalitionists' minds. As the legislature deliberated over elections, American politics were being transformed by the introduction of Stephen Douglas's Kansas-Nebraska Bill, condemned by the Free Soilers' Washington, DC organ on January 12 as part of a "conspiracy of the Slavery Propagandists" to abrogate the Missouri Compromise and expand slavery into the West.[70] The Woolheads and their Free Soil and Whig allies were committed opponents of southern power and slavery expansion and knew that Fessenden shared their views. The Maine Law had contributed significantly to the breakdown of state-level parties and the Portland attorney's elevation to high office, but the critical importance of slavery was now evident. Local politicians from every party looked to Fessenden to stiffen the cause of the free North at Washington.

While antislavery Whigs urged him to hasten on to the capital, leading coalitionists, including Anson Morrill, signed a call for a mass anti-Nebraska meeting in Augusta.[71] Local Free Soilers, encouraged by the all-party outrage generated by the bill and eager to encourage the fusion process, decided not to hold a gathering of their own. Maine, commented their Portland organ enthusiastically, was now in "a state of political revolution."[72] The same was true elsewhere. Politicians throughout the free states struggled to deliver coherent policies on emotive issues such as prohibition, the naturalization of immigrants, Catholic schools, and the containment of slavery. More divided inter-sectionally than the Democrats on slavery issues, the once great national Whig Party was in particular disarray. William Pitt Fessenden, however, was not a man to look backward. He was on his way to Washington to fight the Slave Power.

The Nebraska Outrage

Thirteen days after his election, the new senator from Maine strolled up Pennsylvania Avenue from his room at the Willard Hotel and took his seat in the nation's highest legislative body. He found the chamber in a state of high excitement after what he called Charles Sumner's "splendid speech" against the Kansas-Nebraska Bill.[73] Sumner and his fellow Free Soiler, Salmon P. Chase (Fessenden's Cincinnati guide in 1837) importuned him to make his debut as quickly as possible, as did the powerful New York Whig, William Henry Seward, whom Fessenden thought "the great man of the Senate." All three politicians were fired by the attempt to void the Missouri Compromise prohibition on slavery expansion into the old Louisiana Purchase and determined to press home the political advantage offered to them inadvertently by Stephen Douglas. Fessenden had been too busy advancing his career to pay much notice to events in Congress, but, having gained his prize, he quickly realized that the Kansas-Nebraska Bill's unpopularity opened up the possibility of sweeping the proslavery Democracy from national power. "The thing is a terrible outrage," he told Ellen after conversing with likeminded peers in Washington, "and the more I look at it the more enraged I become. It needs but little to make me an out & out abolitionist. If the bill passes, the free States must unite in a sectional party on this subject, or Slavery has possession of the Government henceforth and forever."[74]

Although the bill was sure to pass the conservative Senate and Fessenden fretted that his antislavery allies had already dealt with the key issues in their remarks, he delivered his maiden Senate speech late in the evening of March 3. He spoke for about an hour "entirely without preparation" or notes of any kind. (The normal practice in the Senate was to deliver long orations from a written text but as a confident extemporaneous speaker he considered the practice "a bad one" that "never makes good debaters.")[75] While Fessenden talked frankly, honestly, and generally without malice, his remarks were consistent with his erstwhile responses to the gag rule and tinctured with the Federalism of his youth. He was not, he assured the chamber in the tell-tale language of an antislavery centrist, what the Georgia Whig Robert Toombs had called "a humanity-monger." However, he made it clear not only that he respected the views of abolitionists but also that he was "opposed to slavery in any form and shape in which it exists, or may exist." New Englanders, he said, had no truck with proslavery arguments. They regarded all men as politically equal: "Their social relations, and their social condition and position, they make for themselves." He bemoaned, as he must have heard his father bemoan on numerous occasions, the artificial unity of the Slave Power, grounded in the three-fifths clause of the Constitution, and compared it unhappily with the divided nature of the more heterogeneous North. Since the founding of the republic, he argued, northerners had yielded to the expansion of slavery: first, after the Louisiana Purchase and then, later, at the time of the Missouri Compromise. Although he stated that he never would have acquiesced to the admission of Missouri as a slave state and had not supported the Compromise of 1850, he described these sectional amnesties as "compacts," implying grudging personal assent to both measures. The problem now, he insisted, was that southerners (to whom Douglas had capitulated in order to secure passage of the Kansas-Nebraska Act) were demanding further concessions over slavery extension. "If you hear of cavilings at the North, coupled with denunciations of slavery at the South," he intoned, "recollect the state of quiet from which you brought it forth."[76]

Toward the close of his remarks Fessenden exchanged words with Lewis Cass, like Stephen Douglas a northern exponent of popular sovereignty, over the critical issue of whether the Constitution empowered Congress to ban slavery from the territories. Fessenden, in common with his antislavery colleagues, used the phrases "the general government shall have the power to make all needful rules and regulations" to govern "the territory or other property of the United States" to insist that it did. Cass, favoring a narrow interpretation of this wording, demurred. What, asked Fessenden, could "to make all needful rules and regulations" mean if not to make laws? Surely, he remarked with a sarcastic flourish, "it was contrary to southern doctrine ever to resort to mere implication, when you find a positive provision in the Constitution on the subject?" He ended with a sectional jibe. Northerners, he pronounced, regarded persistent southern threats to leave the Union to be a bluff designed to prompt further concessions. Such threats were "mere *brutum fulmen, noise.*" The South Carolina senator and slave master Andrew P. Butler was so irritated by this arrogant presumption that he rose and cried out, "No, sir; if your doctrine is carried out, if such sentiments as yours prevail, I want a dissolution right away." To which Fessenden replied sternly, "[D]o not delay it on my account." Butler was not quite finished. Southerners would not, he said, delay secession on the Yankee's account. This gave Fessenden the chance to repeat that northerners did not believe southern threats. Doubtless the inhabitants of the two sections loved the Union with equal strength. "But, sir," he continued, "if it has come to this, that whenever a question comes up between the free States and the slave States of this Union we are to be threatened with disunion, unless we yield, if that is the only alternative to be considered, it ceases to be a very grave question for honorable men and freemen to decide."[77]

Pitt Fessenden's defiant debut was greeted enthusiastically across the North. He was gratified by the response. Many people, he informed Ellen after the bill had passed the Senate, were asking when the speech would appear in pamphlet form. Yet even he was taken aback by the *New-York Tribune's* overblown account of his "manly" conduct in refusing to be intimidated by the violent response of Senator Butler. "Poor old Mr Butler," he commented, "cut very foolish flourishes, yet he had no more idea of assaulting or even insulting me than he had of flying—& probably didn't remember a word about it the next morning."[78] While Fessenden was too sensible to let fame go to his head, he made no secret of the general commendation. "I receive letters assuring me that I am the most popular man at the North," he told Lizzy Warriner from his new lodgings on Capitol Hill, "simply because I happened to say what every body wanted somebody to say, about disunion & all that nonsense."[79]

No one was more pleased with the speech than his own father. Fresh from attending the anti-Nebraska convention in Augusta, Samuel—now in his seventies—was reportedly grinning from ear to ear, having read a personal communication from Sumner extolling the virtues of his celebrated son.[80] Pitt was aware that Douglas's bill had brought him closer politically to Samuel than any previous legislation. While he had never shared his father's irrepressible zeal for the antislavery cause, the two men had seldom disagreed on the importance of protecting northern interests.

Despite their differences they knew one another well and were disinclined to engage in mutual or self-deception. "I did not come here with any strong anticipations of adding to my happiness . . .," Pitt told Samuel on March 6, "but because I had my eye on the position long ago, and was resolved to reach it, if it could be done honorably. I have long been convinced that the quiet pursuit of my profession would be much better for me in every point of view—but I am not of a quiet spirit as you well know, and must follow my fate."[81]

The strengthened political bond between father and son mirrored the broader fusion process now gathering pace because of the Kansas-Nebraska Bill. The unanswered question for the North's disparate coalitionists was: whither fusion? Whereas some antislavery Whigs like ex-Governor Edward Kent and Congressman Israel Washburn, both keen Taylorites in 1848, were ready to disband their organization and cooperate with likeminded men from other parties to form an entirely new political entity, others were reluctant to dismantle the handiwork of Clay and Webster so quickly. In New York Senator Seward and his Machiavellian associate, Thurlow Weed, sensed they could capitalize on Douglas's mistake to reenergize the Whig Party along antislavery lines in the North and render it strong enough to capture the presidency in 1856. Conservative Whigs were appalled by the prospect of destroying the party or, worse, of converting it into a vehicle for sectionalism and, in their parlance, abolition. In June Seward's confidant, the journalist Henry J. Raymond who had founded the *New York Times* in 1851, exhorted Fessenden not to abandon the party in Maine on the grounds that "[n]othing would more certainly ruin the general cause."[82] Hailing from a Democratic state and knowing that he owed his place to the coalition, Maine's junior senator was less inclined to adhere rigidly to outdated party labels. "I think," he had told Governor Crosby shortly after his election, "I see in the present state of things a fair opportunity yet to build up a strong independent party essentially Whig."[83]

While other leading Maine Whigs such as Israel Washburn were quick to help found the new Republican Party that sprang up in many areas of the North during 1854, Fessenden initially remained aloof from the movement. He considered himself a cautious man and was not entirely sympathetic to the reform agenda of enthusiastic fusionists like Dow (whose defeat in Portland's mayoral contest, he regarded with equanimity).[84] On the other hand he saw no prospect of, nor justification for, restoring the Whigs as a bisectional organization, and broadly sympathized with the Free Soilers' goal of creating "a Party of Freedom" that would assert the rights of his region.

His first experiences in Congress continued to fuel his sectional ire. Three weeks after the Kansas-Nebraska Act had passed the House without a single vote of support from northern Whigs and over fierce opposition from many northern Democrats, he denounced Congress as "slavish" and President Pierce as "a most miserable dog" who appeared "bent on destroying his country, as well as himself."[85] It was time, he told Ellen, for change. "These Slave holders have grown saucy because we have been content to keep quiet. The day of flunkeyism is, I trust over, and if so, there is hope for the future."[86]

Affronted though he was by what he saw as the arrogance of southern politicians (and the spinelessness of northern ones like Pierce), he did not automatically dislike all southerners. Class ties and a shared partisan past enabled many Republicans to maintain good relations with individual southern politicians or, at the very least, to appreciate their talents. Just as Abraham Lincoln admired his former Whig colleague, the Georgian Alexander H. Stephens, Fessenden was impressed with the New Orleans lawyer, Judah P. Benjamin, another southern Whig, whose oratory he praised in July as "far above the ordinary style of the Senate."[87] Many northern and southern political leaders in the 1850s shared a commitment to republican values and an expansive vision for the United States. The existence of slavery, however, made it increasingly hard for them to find common ground. Most southern politicians regarded human bondage as the fundamental source of white liberty and social peace as well as their section's political influence within the Union. Growing numbers of their northern counterparts, in contrast, resented slavery's vice-like grip on American institutions dedicated to freedom and resented its detrimental impact on the political power of the North, a region that was fast outstripping the predominantly agrarian South in population and industrial growth. The gathering contest for national power—part political and part ideological in origin—impelled both sets of elites to use slavery as a weapon of intra- and intersectional political warfare with devastating consequences for the nation's domestic peace.

A loyal Whig for most of his adult life, Pitt Fessenden was sympathetic to the fusion process in Maine, where Free Soilers, antislavery Whigs, and Morrill Democrats united to support Anson Morrill for governor. He also understood the force of the view propounded by Austin Willey, a local Free Soiler, that "This war with slavery is too radical, too difficult, too long, too big, for success without a power constructed especially for it."[88] On returning home from Congress in August he was angered by those orthodox Whigs who, unable to see that their best interest lay in leading the incipient antislavery front, favored separate nominees ahead of the forthcoming elections. "Is it not provoking," he complained to the energetic fusionist James Pike, "that with men enough to sweep the State clean we should be beaten by the utter folly of men calling themselves *Whigs!*"[89]

Despite Fessenden's irritation at the obduracy of his co-partisans these grassroots fusion efforts paid off. Anson Morrill was rewarded with a handsome plurality over his regular Democrat and Whig opponents and the election of a fusionist majority to the Augusta legislature guaranteed him the governorship that winter. Although, as Fessenden had feared, an independent Whig candidate cost the coalitionists victory in the sixth district, their candidates won the other five congressional contests. With James G. Blaine, one of the most promising young Whigs in the state, now urging his co-partisans to stop hugging "the fossil remains of dead issues," the revolutionaries appeared to be on the verge of a lasting triumph. Two factors, however, hindered the formation of a new political organization dedicated to the defense of northern liberties: the sudden rise of political nativism and the perceived extremism of the fusionists' policies.

Anson Morrill owed his election not only to the votes of antislavery Democrats, Whigs, and Free Soilers but also to thousands of citizens who had never voted before. While many of these new voters were mobilized by the general adverse northern re-action to the Kansas-Nebraska Act, the high turnout for Morrill was also affected by the creation of Know-Nothing lodges in the western counties of the state. Members of these lodges opposed the political, social, and cultural influence of Catholic im-migrants on their own localities and on the nominally Protestant American republic. Blaming the impoverished Irish in particular for rising crime and drunkenness in cities like Portland and fearing the immigrants' growing influence on the body poli-tic, they found the existing parties unresponsive to their demands and the fusionists' reform agenda correspondingly attractive. Hence their backing for Morrill, officially endorsed by the Know-Nothing order, in the fall elections.

The injection of nativism into politics further confused the murky process of re-alignment in Maine, as it did in other parts of the Northeast. Unlike some fusionist politicians, and contrary to William Gienapp's suggestion that he may have joined the Americans, Fessenden did not enter a Know-Nothing lodge to enhance his ca-reer.[90] He was not free from the prejudices of his class. He referred disparagingly to one of his domestics as "a regular Paddy, who is good for nothing" and privately endorsed the nativists' success in the Washington, DC municipal election.[91] Impor-tantly, however, the senator was politically attuned to the dangers of adopting too radical a stance on divisive social issues. His antennae could not fail to detect the negative popular response to the coalition's efforts at Augusta in early 1855. As well as electing Anson Morrill as governor, its members in the state legislature passed a series of uncompromising resolutions and laws. They not only condemned slavery as a moral wrong, attacked the Fugitive Slave Act as unconstitutional, and denounced the repeal of the Missouri Compromise as the betrayal of a sacred compact, but also passed laws to protect the legal rights of blacks accused of being fugitive slaves and to further undercut federal authority over naturalization policy. One act required prospective immigrant voters to present their naturalization papers to a state official three months before any election.[92]

Fessenden kept his distance from Maine's new Republican Party, founded at a convention in Augusta in February, until the early summer of 1855. One reason for his caution, his residual Whiggery aside, was his realistic conviction that focused opposition to southern domination remained the most effective way of uniting northerners of different classes and parties into a functioning political unit capable of winning elections. Whenever southerners, he told the Senate the day after the Augusta gathering, "show that our legislation is to be directed, at all times, with reference to this slave power which governs us—for govern us it does—I stand here to oppose them, to make my opposition and protestation against them on all occasions and I shall stand at home . . . ready to *agitate* upon this subject."[93] By contrast, extreme positions on race, liquor drinking, and immigrants seemed unlikely to foster the Republicans' efforts to develop a new party at the state level, especially when their opponents could plausibly represent their policies as socially disruptive—as was the case after a fierce anti-prohibition riot in Portland on June 2. Fortunately for Republican organizers, southerners and their northern allies continued to foster the conditions necessary to complete the fusion process.

At the end of March 1855 thousands of Missourians crossed into Kansas to elect a proslavery territorial government based in Lecompton. While the fraudulent result made a mockery of popular sovereignty, it provided ideal political ammunition for northern party builders. During late May Edward Kent, chairman of the Republican gathering in Augusta, moved decisively to draw one of his most influential fellow Whigs into the new party. Fessenden, he said, must write an address to the Whigs of Maine explaining why their party would not hold a formal convention later in the year. Conservative Whigs, he argued, intended to derail fusion by maintaining the old party's structure at a time when events were moving against them. "The Kansas outrages," he wrote, "give us a great opportunity to revive & keep alive the great issue of Slavery. This is the true rallying point & ought to be kept prominent & to be constantly kept before the people. Don't hesitate but do it. You know how."[94] Fessenden responded by intimating that antislavery Whigs could persist with the policy of cooperation rather than outright fusion. That is, they could hold their convention as scheduled and declare in favor of Morrill's reelection. Kent, determined to get his man, pushed harder. Northern Whigs agreed that their southern peers had dissolved the national party by supporting the Kansas-Nebraska Bill. It was now time to show the voters that they were ready to match words with deeds. Formal Whig backing for Morrill would only alienate Free Soilers (who would consider him the Whig not fusion candidate) while straight Whigs would simply damn him as the Democratic candidate. Write the document, Kent insisted: "[W]e must I think begin to act & to speak as having concluded that the old Whig party is defeated."[95]

The ex-governor was pushing at an open door. Fessenden composed an appeal "To the Whigs of Maine" on behalf of the Whig state committee. In it he reviewed the progress of realignment to illustrate how a majority of his co-partisans had come to support a Democrat, Anson Morrill, for governor. Downplaying the impact of the Maine Law and the recent intrusion of political nativism, he named Kansas-Nebraska as the "paramount" issue in 1854 when only 14,000 Whigs had supported the party's official candidate. "Men's minds were full of it," he wrote of the Act: "It was the vital issue." That contest, he contended, "proved that a distinct Whig organization in this State, separate from, and outside of, the Republican party, can be productive of no practical benefit, but must tend, rather, to defeat all the professed objects and principles of the ruling [Republican] party." Fessenden did not try to hide the sectional nature of the new organization. Indeed, he consciously exploited northern nationalism to promote realignment. How, he asked, could northern Whigs go on cooperating with their southern peers "when it is manifest that by so doing we are placing the Southern foot upon northern necks, and retarding, if not preventing, that union of sentiment in the free States which alone can rescue them from entire subjugation to the Slave power?" Although Fessenden did inject criticism of the fusionists' recent legislation, he sought to excuse its rashness. If the Republican Party had erred, he wrote, "it has been from no defect of character, and no want of an anxious desire to promote the public good." Whigs, he intimated, could be justly proud of their past achievements but could not be "blind, or deaf to the calls of that crisis which is now close at hand."[96] The appeal was effective. Only four hundred delegates attended the Whig convention, which normally would have attracted twice that number.[97]

The senator followed up this initiative with a strong Independence Day speech in the coastal town of Damariscotta. It was America's "peculiar fortune," he told his audience, to possess "an authentic history" in which the deeds of the Founding Fathers remained alive to contemporaries. He was no more inclined to be uncritical of the Founders than he was of other so-called great men like William Allen or Daniel Webster. Though great, he said, "they were men after all, subject to infirmity of judgment, and liable to error." Time had shown that much was still left to be done by their successors. Here he alluded to the Founders' willingness to compromise over slavery, an institution that was a negation of everything he took the republic to stand for. Any system, he proclaimed, that gave one man absolute power over another, that condemned individuals to incessant toil, ignorance, and poverty forever, that sundered marriage ties and parental bonds, and that blasted all hope of social improvement, was "but a miserable commentary upon the high sounding phraze [sic] of our great charter of government."

Fessenden then embarked on a detailed analysis of constant northern surrenders to southern aggression that drew on Federalist and abolitionist interpretations of American history. That aggression, he claimed, had been instrumented by "a mere handful of men," the 350,000-strong slaveholding aristocracy of the South whose "united concentrated power dominates over the land, controls nominations for President, makes and unmakes laws, settles questions of policy, and claims to hold the Union in its grasp." Sectional peace, he said, had been destroyed by Kansas-Nebraska for the territory above the Missouri Compromise line had been "reserved for free labour—a place where the swelling millions of freemen in search of land would go, and not be placed on a level with the African servant, and pointed at & sneered at as no higher than a slave."

Keener to document slavery's detrimental impact on white men rather than blacks, Fessenden called for "union among ourselves." Northerners would find the remedy for their ills at the ballot box, where they should register "political death to every northern *doughface*" by voting Republican. He was, he insisted, "an ardent and enthusiastic friend" of the Constitution. However, it was time that plantocrats ceased trampling on northern interests. If the only way to protect free labor was to dispense with the Union, he declared himself willing to part with the latter "and trust to Him who made man free for another and a better." But, he added reassuringly (reiterating the view he had expressed in his Kansas-Nebraska speech), this would not be necessary because the southern threat of disunion was an empty one.[98]

This pellucid exposition of the Republicans' core principles of free soil, free labor, and free men failed to secure the party's success at the polls. Reacting after the Portland riot to the fusionists' perceived extremism, Maine voters dealt the co-alition a serious blow at the autumn elections. Morrill managed to secure a plurality in the gubernatorial contest but his opponents won a majority in the legislature, thereby sealing his fate in the winter. The regular Democratic vote was up by more than 20,000, proof that hard-line nativism and prohibitionism could endanger the Republicans' advance.[99] Fessenden was disappointed by the result, which he blamed on the 11,000 Whigs (roughly two-fifths of the total who had backed Scott in 1852) who refused to abandon their party organization.[100] Yet he remained upbeat. "I did hope that Maine would have placed herself in the front rank of that great northern movement which I believe to be essential to the future welfare of this country, and which lies, therefore, nearest my heart," he informed Lizzy Warriner, "Our miser-able local divisions have destroyed that hope for the present. But I shall renew the contest from year to year until the battle is finally lost, and all hope gone. As it is, the end is not yet."[101]

Free Soil, Free Men, Frémont

While ethnocultural issues contributed significantly to the destruction of the Whig Party, it was opposition to slavery and the South that fueled the expansion of the new Republican Party. Fessenden was keenly aware that as many Know-Nothings as possible should be incorporated into the expanding Republican coali-tion and was by no means unsympathetic to their goals. However, he remained convinced that the nascent anti-Democratic coalition should be organized primar-ily around opposition to putative southern aggression. His motives for favoring the creation of a popular front against slavery expansion were as mixed as those of the other leading Republican Party builders of the day. While his Federalist upbringing and personal experience of southern arrogance predisposed him to forge a coalition based around opposition to the Slave Power, that predisposition was enhanced by his awareness (confirmed by the Portland riot and its political fallout) that nativism lacked the power of sectionalism to unite northern voters across class lines. He did not doubt the superiority of free labor over slavery and put free-labor rhetoric to good use in some of his speeches. But free-labor ideology was not his only spur to action. For Pitt Fessenden the events of the 1850s were preeminently an extension of the long-running power struggle between northern and southern elites that he had first encountered as a freshman congressman. Now in a position of genuine influence, he saw the Republican Party as the perfect vehicle for thwarting southern ambitions, for fulfilling his own, and for permanently cementing northern supremacy within the Union.

The election result in Maine underlined local Democrats' ability to capitalize on grassroots opposition to the fusionists' zeal for social control. "The Republican party, in this State . . .," commented one observer in November 1855, "has been too much under the control of *ultra* and *extreme* men. Its late *temporary* defeat, is attributable to that fact alone."[102] Despite acting as Mayor Dow's legal defense after the Portland riot, Fessenden was as aware as this correspondent of U.S. Senator Hannibal Hamlin (who remained aloof from the coalition) that commitment to free-soil principles rather than to abolitionism or nativism or prohibition would be the key to success in the upcoming presidential contest.

Kansas events continued to generate sectional tension, exacerbating northerners' fears about the effects of slavery expansion and enabling Republicans to campaign effectively as the defenders of freedom. In October antislavery forces in the troubled territory formed a rival government to the proslavery Lecompton regime, which had been recognized as the legitimate voice of Kansans by the pro-southern Pierce administration. Sucking in arms and men from both sections of the Union, the opposing factions prepared to defend themselves against attack. By the time Fessenden returned to Washington in December for the first session of the Thirty-fourth Congress, Pierce's representative in Kansas, Governor Andrew Reeder, was struggling to keep the peace. In common with his fellow Republicans, Fessenden was in no mood to pour oil on troubled waters. He resented efforts by the Senate's Democratic majority to marginalize the Republicans as sectional extremists and looked forward to a union of Republicans and northern Know-Nothings on essentially Republican terms. Events, he told his son Frank, were rapidly bringing the two groups together: "The Slaveholders will be satisfied with nothing from their allies but an unconditional surrender—and this they will not obtain except from the Democrats—who have yielded long ago."[103] Publicly he was at pains to defend the right of northerners to go to Kansas and to defend themselves if necessary.

Although Senate Republicans voted together on most slavery-related issues, they were hardly a band of brothers. Fessenden was buoyed that winter by the arrival of more Republican senators in Washington. He considered Lyman Trumbull of Illinois, Lafayette Foster of Connecticut, and Jacob Collamer of Vermont all "fine men."[104] However, he was deprived of the company of Salmon Chase, one of the leading architects of the Republican Party who had returned to Ohio to become governor (in the process leaving Fessenden a bookcase as a token of remembrance from "one

who learned in a little while to like you very much").[105] And he was far from enamored with two of the chamber's leading Republicans, William Seward and Charles
Sumner. Seward, he remarked privately, was "very able" but regarded as "intensely
selfish, and not over honest" and therefore ill-fitted to be the leader that Republicans needed.[106] In the interests of the party Fessenden boldly informed the clubbable
New Yorker what he and his fellow Republicans thought of him. "This will do me no
good," he remarked privately, "but it may benefit him."[107]

While Fessenden was closer to the learned Sumner, he regarded him as "nothing
but a great boy," pompous and full of his own self-importance.[108] Again, he did not
hide his feelings. At a dinner party in Washington during the summer of 1854 he
intervened to stop Sumner boring the celebrated western explorer, Colonel John C.
Frémont, "with long talks about science and philosophy." Sumner, he related,
responded warmly "but I laughed, & Fremont laughed too, & the matter dropped."[109]
Fessenden was generally well regarded by his co-partisans at this stage of his career.
Sumner, for example, who subsequently remembered that his fellow New Englander
"was never more brilliant or kindly" than in his early Senate career, lauded him as
"the best debater on the floor of the Senate" and predicted "We shall be proud of
you."[110] Yet even at this time, Republican chieftains could be harsh judges of one
another and not all were as open about their views as Fessenden: Horace Greeley,
editor of the New-York Tribune, called him "a conspicuous bastard" in a letter to his
reporter, James Pike.[111]

Whatever Greeley thought about Fessenden in private, he could not deny that
the latter had become a major force in the new party. This was confirmed in February 1856 when a group of leading Whigs and Republicans met at the Washington
home of New York's patrician senator, Hamilton Fish. Fessenden argued strongly
against holding a national Whig convention on the grounds that the party of Clay
and Webster (both now deceased) had been rendered defunct by the activities of
Know-Nothings in the East and Republicans in the West.[112] While his trenchant comments did not persuade conservative listeners, they represented the majority view.
Even though many old-line Whigs would remain aloof from the overtly sectional
Republican organization throughout the decade, their party would hold no more
national conventions.

That same month Republicans and northern Know-Nothings combined forces in
the House of Representatives to elect as Speaker the antislavery nativist, Nathaniel
Banks. It was an important step on the road to uniting the anti-Democratic opposition in the North and Fessenden was delighted by an event that gave "the North

a character which it much needed."[113] With the rhetoric emanating from Kansas more inflamed than ever and the Pierce administration seemingly intent on making the territory a slave state, he was prepared for the final showdown with the Slave Power. As he told his son William, violence could erupt in Kansas any day. If the parties there finally came to blows, he wrote, "there is no knowing where the strife will end—but, let it come. The battle between freedom & Slavery must be fought some day, and this generation may as well meet it as the next."[114] His plans to make a speech on Kansas affairs, however, were disrupted by illness and he was back in Portland before the situation in the territory turned even uglier. The day after pro-slavery forces "sacked" the free-state town of Lawrence, John Brown—a violent foe of American slavery—led his small band of guerrillas to a homestead on Pottawattomie Creek and murdered three southern settlers in cold blood. The crime sparked a flurry of killings in the region, polarizing sentiment across the Union and rendering sectional issues of paramount importance in the 1856 election campaign.

The seriousness of the Kansas crisis was highlighted for Fessenden by two events. In early May, at home tending to his invalided wife as well as recovering his own strength, he dispatched a letter to his youngest son, Sam, at school in New Hampshire. Sam was a wayward boy who lacked the self-discipline of his brothers. Fessenden had been "almost discouraged" by the lad's poor class rank the previous term and moved to correct his character before it was too late. If this behavior continued, he iterated sternly, Sam's college career would "evidently be a failure." As always he mixed admonishment with genuine affection and some well-meaning emotional blackmail. "You must conquer, my dear boy, at any cost," he wrote, "your strong love of pleasure, and dislike of study," adding, "Both your mother and I have been quite sick pretty much all the time since you left us. She is now much better. I am about the same."[115] The warning backfired. On June 16, fired by exaggerated press accounts of the situation in Kansas, Sam ran away from college in Andover and struck out for the territory. His father heard the news shortly after he returned to Washington and was immediately "in great distress," not only out of concern for his headstrong boy but also because of fears about what Sam's rash departure might do to Ellen.[116] Sam was eventually tracked down in Illinois with the help of his older brother, James, other family members and friends, and the political contacts of Lyman Trumbull, but the distressing incident gave "Bleeding Kansas" an immediate personal resonance for the senator from Maine.[117]

The same was true of South Carolina congressman Preston Brooks's caning of Charles Sumner in May. Brooks, resentful of Sumner's verbal attack on his kinsman,

Andrew Butler, in a combative speech entitled "The Crime Against Kansas," administered his brutal revenge while the outspoken abolitionist was trapped at his desk. Popular responses divided along partisan and sectional lines. Northern Republicans denounced the outrage as evidence of proslavery barbarism while southerners defended Brooks's action as an honorable response to the conduct of a cowardly blackguard. Although Fessenden was rarely impressed by Sumner's studied orations, he was appalled by Brooks's action and visited his injured colleague when he returned to Washington in June. Sumner, he reported "was very much hurt. The shock to his nervous system was very severe, and some days he is utterly prostrated."[118] The wounded Yankee, now a martyr to the antislavery cause, was no better three weeks later: "He gains little in strength, has lost much flesh, and staggers as he walks. May God confound the villains."[119]

"Bleeding Kansas" and "Bleeding Sumner" signaled that conflict over slavery had now become violent in deed as well as in debate. Both events radicalized the North, enabling the young Republican Party to coalesce around opposition to Slave Power aggression. As Fessenden had predicted in the winter, it did so by absorbing the majority of northern Know-Nothings on broadly antislavery terms. Long attentive to free-state interests, he was genuinely disturbed by what he read of proslavery atrocities in Kansas (the Republican press was full of them), by what he saw of the invalided Sumner, and by what he regarded as despicable attempts by the Pierce administration to ram slavery down the throats of an unwilling people. His reaction to these shocking developments revealed their radicalizing effect on Republican centrists. Conditions in Kansas, he wrote angrily in July shortly after the Senate had passed an administration bill to admit the troubled territory as a slave state, were "truly horrible, and I, for one, am ready for civil war, if nothing else will do." The forthcoming presidential contest, he thought, "must decide whether we are to have civil war and consequent dissolution. I believe that if this state of things is to be forced on us yet further, the western people will retaliate upon Missouri the horrors which have been inflicted on Kansas—and that will be the beginning of the end. It is a mystery how any man in the free States can hesitate as to his proper course."[120]

Despite being regarded by some Republicans as presidential timber himself, Pitt Fessenden regarded John C. Frémont as the front-runner for the Republican presidential nomination. "The Pathfinder" was popular and well connected, just the man to attract support not only from the various elements inside the antislavery coalition but also from new voters mobilized by the sensational events of 1856. Fessenden did not travel to the Republicans' national convention in Philadelphia in June.

However, his law partner William Willis attended as a delegate from Maine and the senator was not slow to proffer advice. As long as the Know-Nothings present were willing to take Frémont, he said, the colonel would be nominated. Frémont, he emphasized, "would be the best Prest., if we can elect one . . . but I am content, let who will be the nominee. I hope Maine will vote as a unit."[121] The dispatch typified Fessenden's modus operandi: work through trusted friends or kin if possible, avoid clumsy attempts to control independent-minded men, yet state one's views clearly to influential individuals likely to respect them and therefore implement them. As he predicted, Frémont received the convention's backing—an action with which, he thought, "all conservative men ought to be satisfied."[122]

During the early summer Fessenden was optimistic about the election. "Frémont's prospects are growing brighter every day," he confided to Ellen in July.[123] Congressional Republicans strove to keep Kansas issues before the public, rightly calculating that sectional tensions played into their hands. So intent were they to retard action on any Kansas bill that Stephen Douglas publicly charged them with seeking to delay the legislation of the country for political gain.[124] Fessenden denied the accusation heatedly on July 23, prompting Douglas to inform him that he was "the most pugnacious man in the Senate." This, thought the Portlander, was "all a very great mistake" but he noted with republican pride, "that the impression prevails that I am not easily bullied or driven."[125]

By mid-August Fessenden's initial optimism about Frémont's chances of success had begun to dissipate. From Boston, on his way home from Washington, he told the candidate that he was "nervous" about the party's prospects in Maine, where the September state elections could prove crucial for the Republicans' chances in November.[126] Desiring repose after an exhausting session and reluctant to accept out-of-state speaking invitations, Fessenden still managed to play an active role in the campaign.[127] He used his contacts with Massachusetts businessmen to procure funding for what was bound to be an expensive contest; the shoe manufacturers Alley, Choate & Cummings, for example, sent a check for $500.[128] He also gave a limited number of speeches in Cumberland County. His efforts paid off. The popular ex-Democrat Hannibal Hamlin, who had belatedly joined the Republicans in June and whose friendship Fessenden wisely continued to cultivate, was elected governor with a "smashing" majority of nearly 18,000 votes over his Democrat and old-line Whig opponents.[129] Maine voters also elected a Republican legislature, a sure sign that the state party's decision to soft-pedal prohibition and focus on sectional issues had been a shrewd one.

But while the Republicans' takeover of a longtime Jacksonian stronghold indicated that realignment was nearing its end in Maine, it did not herald a Frémont
victory. Optimism engendered by the coup was dampened by narrow defeats in the
critical northern states of Indiana and Pennsylvania. The new party performed im-
pressively in the November general election, carrying a majority of northern states,
including Maine, where disillusioned Democrats stayed away from the polls in
droves. However, the Democratic nominee, James Buchanan, was (as Fessenden
had foreseen in the summer) a strong candidate and he won the presidency with
the backing of an almost-solid South and five non-slaveholding states, California,
Illinois, Indiana, New Jersey, and Pennsylvania. The Republicans had all-but seized
control of their section. The battle ahead was for control of the fractured American
Union.

The Road to Civil War, 1857–1861

Historians used to refer to the mid-nineteenth-century politicians who failed to prevent the American Civil War as "the blundering generation." They had a point. No one set out to spark a conflagration that would cost more than half a million American lives. However, the phrase conveyed at best a half truth. Mainstream politicians on both sides of the Mason-Dixon line were embroiled in a deepening sectional crisis that led them they knew not where. But this was not an accidental or, for that matter, an artificial crisis. It was one of their own making, raised to advance conflicting sectional ideologies, different party agendas, and the careers of leading politicians. In blackening their opponents as abolitionists or hirelings of the Slave Power, in threatening to tear down the Union if a Republican president was elected, or in dismissing talk of secession as hot air, they were all, to varying degrees, responsible for the carnage that followed.

William Pitt Fessenden believed that by engaging in political combat with proslavery Democrats he was helping to build a better republic—one that would be guided by northern not southern precepts. Even though his hostility to slavery was prompted less by humanitarian concern for the slave than a broader commitment to the well-being of the American republic, it was deep and it was genuine. During the late 1850s he continued to lay the foundations for the election of an antislavery Republican president, piling on the sectional rhetoric in order to alert northern voters to the growing menace of the Slave Power while all the time recognizing that excessive radicalism, especially in the wake of John Brown's abortive raid on Harpers Ferry, would endanger his party's claim to be acting as conservators of the Founding Fathers' policy of containing slavery. Convinced that southern talk of secession in the event of a Republican victory in 1860 was mere bluster intended to demoralize his party, he saw no reason to capitulate after the cotton states responded to Abraham Lincoln's election by leaving the Union. Steadfastness on the part of northerners would surely force a peaceful resolution to the sectional crisis by convincing southern leaders that their power in national counsels was ebbing away. He retained this understandable yet erroneous conviction until the secession crisis neared its violent denouement. But when civil war broke out in April 1861, the stern senator from Maine stood firmly by his promises that he was ready to defend the U.S. government against its foes.

Battling Buchanan

Pitt Fessenden cemented his reputation as one of the most combative Republicans in Washington on returning to the Senate less than a month after Frémont's narrow defeat. On December 4, 1856, he responded vigorously to Franklin Pierce's final message to Congress in which the doughface president blamed irresponsible Republicans for inflaming sectional tensions and endangering the Union. Aware that his party must appeal to northern conservatives if they were to capture the presidency in 1860, Fessenden moved quickly to rebut the president's charge that Republicans and abolitionists were one and the same thing. There was, he insisted, a clear distinction between the North's "very powerless class" of abolitionists who sought to meddle with slavery in the states where it had a constitutional right to exist, and the Republicans, whose commitment to containing slavery expansion was "entirely at war" with the abolitionists' principles. If, as southern senators claimed, some abolitionists had voted for Frémont, surely the Republicans could not be blamed for everyone who voted for them. It was not the Republicans, he averred, who were responsible for increasing agitation over slavery but proslavery northerners like Pierce, "an unworthy son" of New Hampshire whose message was designed for political effect. Southern Democrats were the true sectional extremists for trying to spread slavery into the territories where they had no right to carry it. Republicans, he said, opposed slavery expansion "not on the ground of humanity, not on the question, whether slavery is right or wrong in itself—with that, here, I do not choose to deal— but on the question of political power." Southerners were using slavery expansion to bolster their influence over national policy. It was a zero-sum game. The political power of "the slave interest" in America was "a direct encroachment on the political power of the free people of the free States. It may be constitutional—it may be legal; but it is none the less an encroachment. What tends to increase the one tends also to diminish the other."

The Union, Fessenden continued, was a "political partnership." Because slavery was, as Chief Justice John Marshall had admitted in 1832, economically inefficient and ruinous to whites, southerners should cease their attempts to force this "black wave" (here he quoted Marshall directly) onto territories held in common. "[W]e are States, but we are a nation; we are a people, yet a united people. What is interesting to one ought to be interesting to all. What strengthens a part of this great country strengthens the whole. What diminishes the power of one section diminishes the power of the whole country, directly, necessarily, inevitably." In order to deflect the obvious retort that the Republicans' antislavery policies damaged the South, Fessenden distinguished between slave masters and non-slaveholding southerners. The former, he maintained correctly, were a minority in the South: "There are other men than those who own slaves, or are interested in slaves; and for their benefit, as well as ours, I would open these Territories to freedom, and hold them consecrated to freedom forever."[1]

The senator modestly described his speech as "a sudden affair."[2] However, his extemporaneous remarks merited the praise that they elicited from his colleague Sumner, still recovering in Boston from Brooks's assault. In them he laid down a blueprint for electoral success in 1860. The Republicans must distance themselves from abolitionists, resist Democratic charges of sectionalism, and defend the rights of free white Americans in all parts of the country. They should insist that they were not "sickly sentimentalists" but hard-nosed patriots who had set their faces against slavery expansion for the common good. Although his co-partisans remained a minority in the Democrat-controlled Senate, Fessenden was in no mood to pander to the opposition—even after being placed on two unimportant committees at the beginning of the session. "We are a power, now," he assured Sumner confidently.[3]

More praise came from his cousin Lizzy Warriner. The speech, he admitted, had given him "a great increase of reputation perhaps because it was an off-hand affair, and not a studied oration." In this instance, however, he was more interested in telling Lizzy how much he missed her company. "I am wishing that my head was at this moment under your hands," he confided. At twilight the celebrated senator liked nothing more than to don his dressing gown and slippers and think wistfully of absent friends. "[Y]ou always come with them," he confessed. "Strange fancies these for a man over fifty. Do you ever get one? It seems to me at this moment as if I were talking, instead of writing, to you, and that you were actually present though invisible. I have already looked to see if I had not your ring on my finger."[4]

Reading the newspapers at his India Street home in Portland, Samuel Fessenden followed his son's "signal" contributions to debate. Although the old Federalist rejoiced in Pitt's ability to stand up to southern "overseerism," he feared that the Democrats' control of federal institutions would "enable them to consummate whatever they may design," namely, "[t]he extension and permanency of Slavery throughout the length and breadth of the Country." The slaveocracy, he wrote anxiously, meant to make slave states of Kansas, New Mexico, southern California, and Oregon, and to add Cuba and Nicaragua (where the proslavery mercenary William Walker had been active) to the republic's possessions. "You will call me a Croaker," he predicted: "I pray GOD I may not as heretofore in my political predictions turn out a true prophet."[5]

Family matters were much on Pitt Fessenden's mind that winter, none more so than the activities of his sons. Frank, now training to be a lawyer, took a keen interest in politics. His turn would "come soon enough," counseled the senator, "for if I leave my sons nothing else, I shall bequeath them the legacy of eternal warfare upon this infamous slave system, in all its parts and aspects. It is to be a contest of years, and I shall not live to see the end."[6] The senator had not given up on his youngest son. Having ascertained that Sam was safe in Illinois, he secretly provided funds for his maintenance while awaiting a change of heart. It came in January 1857. The youth expressed his sorrow for causing so much worry to his parents and asked for their forgiveness.[7] His father was overjoyed but took care to ensure that the prodigal had learned his lesson. "I am warned . . .," he said, "that, probably, before many years, there will be nothing left to you of your earthly parents but their memory. When they are gone you will realize how truly they loved you, and think of them with pleasure or grief, according as your future conduct may entitle you to think. That future is all your own. I entreat you not to rob yourself of all the good it may have in store."[8]

Fessenden had more counsel to give. Lizzy (increasingly concerned by Mr. Warriner's troubled mental state) had been told by a female acquaintance to exhibit more religious devotion. Fessenden, never much of a churchgoer himself, dismissed the self-righteous communication. Yet he added revealingly, "*I* have wished many times that I was truly, sincerely, religious—governed by a sense of religious duty." One spiritual virtue, he did possess, he thought, was "to make personal sacrifices where they are demanded by our duty to others."[9] Pitt Fessenden was no hypocrite and could spot religious cant faster than most of his contemporaries. He was also a reasonably good judge of his own character. A strong sense of civic responsibility and self-restraint in the service of friends, family, and the wider community had long been central to his makeup. Some of the old Congregational and republican virtues of New England were with him yet and they would be sorely tested in the gathering contest against the South.

Whatever Fessenden may have thought about his father's shrill indictment of his opponents, the notion of a villainous proslavery conspiracy acquired added plausibility in March 1857, when the Democratic majority on the U.S. Supreme Court ruled in the case of *Dred Scott v. Sandford*. During the winter Fessenden had clashed again with Lewis Cass on the question of whether the Constitution empowered Congress to prevent slavery from expanding into the territories.[10] Chief Justice Roger B. Taney upheld the proslavery interpretation of the territorial clause and in the process declared that blacks were not U.S. citizens within the meaning of the Constitution. Taney and the new president, James Buchanan, were conservative Unionists who hoped the decision would end the divisive debate over the territorial issue and damage the Republicans by removing legal sanction for their core policy of nonextension. The ruling also seemed fashioned to derail the political career of Stephen Douglas. The powerful northern Democrat remained wedded to popular sovereignty as a middle way between the positions staked out by southern Democrats and his Republican opponents in the North. Taney's defense of slaveholders' property rights rendered it difficult for Douglas to argue that the inhabitants of a territory could bar slavery if they so desired.

Dred Scott was by no means a disaster for the Republicans. As one of Fessenden's correspondents put it, it was in many ways "the best thing that could happen for the Republican party" precisely because it was so "thoroughly proslavery."[11] The senator from Maine was in no fit state to capitalize immediately on this latest outrage. In early February he was afflicted with serious diarrhea—probably a symptom of dysentery caused by poor sanitary conditions at the National Hotel where he was staying.[12] (The same conditions occasioned another outbreak the following month that killed two people and debilitated President James Buchanan shortly after his inauguration.)[13] Fessenden had already been suffering from his customary Washington headaches (occasioned most likely by extensive reading after dusk) and a sore throat but he now found himself in what he delicately termed "a pretty bad plight." His doctor ordered him to drink only boiled milk and tea and eat bland food such as toast and tapioca.[14]

Shortly after Taney handed down his *Dred Scott* ruling Fessenden returned to Portland in some distress. He did not enjoy robust health in later middle age, suffering constantly from digestive problems and sporadic bouts of diarrhea. The biographer Charles Jellison speculated that his subject may have suffered from malaria as a result of his lengthy stays in Washington.[15] While this is plausible, many of the senator's maladies, notably his rheumatism and periodic headaches, appear unsurprising for an unusually busy middle-class male in the Civil War era. His steadily worsen-ing intestinal problems may have been caused by some undiagnosed and untreated digestive disease, exacerbated by contracting dysentery in 1857. Crucially, his noto-rious "dyspepsia" (which contemporaries often used to explain his flurries of bad temper in the Senate) failed to prevent him from undertaking effectively his increas-ingly onerous civic duties. His irascible behavior, arguably no worse than that of many other senators, stemmed as much from his unwavering confidence in his own abilities and his dim view of the motives of other politicians as it did from bodily infirmity.

Even on sick leave in Portland after his unpleasant experience at the National, he was able to respond to a group of New York Republicans who had requested his views on the *Dred Scott* case. He penned a judiciously worded statement that re-flected a fairly general conviction among Republican leaders that the decision was overtly political but that it would be risky ahead of a presidential election to disavow flagrantly a verdict of the highest court in the land. Nevertheless, he was at pains to condemn the ruling as "subversive of individual rights, and at war with freedom and humanity." Vigilance was his central watchword. "[N]o man," he wrote, "who would guard the liberties of his country should forget that there is no point from which they may not be assailed, and that assaults are all the more dangerous when made from quarters least liable to suspicion."[16]

The summer was a traumatic one for Fessenden. Uncle Thomas, for whom he had always felt genuine affection, died at the beginning of July. More upsetting still was his wife's death later that month. Ellen had been in poor health for years and Fessenden had taken her on a trip into the mountains to aid her constitution. He was at her bedside when she died and overcome with grief. "You know that, with all my errors and shortcomings, I loved her truly and dearly," he told Lizzy.[17] Although he had begun to recover from the initial shock by August, one observer reported how sad and thin he seemed.[18] Unsurprisingly, he took no part in the fall campaign, which the Republicans won with relative ease.[19]

As had been the case at previous moments of personal crisis, politics assisted Fessenden's emotional and physical recovery. He was restored to reasonably good health by late 1857 when he arrived at his new lodgings at Mrs. Carter's boarding house near Capitol Hill.[20] Politics, he reported, was in "somewhat of a tangle" after Stephen Douglas had opposed President Buchanan's plan to admit Kansas as a state under the proslavery Lecompton constitution drawn up without the input of free soilers, who were now in a clear majority in that divided territory. The Little Giant was firmly wedded to popular sovereignty as a solution to the growing national crisis over slavery, understanding correctly that most northern Democrats had no great love for the peculiar institution. Buchanan's desire to appease southern Democrats and his concomitant willingness to allow slavery to take root in Kansas posed a direct threat to popular sovereignty, leaving Douglas little alternative but to break with the president. Even though a serious faction fight ensued within the national Democratic Party, Fessenden had little sympathy for the Illinois senator who, he thought, was probably motivated by "his own personal interest." What the result of his apostasy to the South and to the administration might be, no one could tell. If "the game" was serious, he pondered, Douglas would have to "establish new relations," presumably with the Republicans who controlled the House of Representatives and had twenty seats in the Senate compared with the Democrats' thirty-seven.[21] Personally, he did not share the desire of some of his co-partisans, notably Horace Greeley, to draft Douglas for the 1860 election. The latter, he told Hamilton Fish later that year, was "a low, vulgar, demagogue," less preferable as a candidate than the southern radical, John Slidell.[22]

During early 1858 Fessenden led Republican efforts to obstruct passage of the administration's controversial Lecompton bill. The measure's only concession to free soilers was that Kansans would be permitted to vote on the entry of new slaves into the region; Kansas's position as a slave state, however, would not be altered. Outraged like most northerners, he drew some confidence from the likelihood that passage of the bill would further unite northerners. In that respect, he told his son William, it was probably "best that the free States should drain the cup of degradation to its last dregs," though, he added, "perhaps even that will not do it."[23] Unable to predict the future with any certainty, he could only resolve to do his duty "and leave the events to him who disposes of all things according to his own will, seeing not as man sees, but overruling all for good."[24]

Pitt Fessenden's apparent willingness to leave the fate of the country in the hands of divine providence concealed his own agency. In January 1858 he opposed plans to increase the size of the U.S. Army. Supporters of the administration, including Mississippi Democrat Jefferson Davis, claimed the additional troops were needed to fight Indians and Mormons and defend the Pacific Northwest against the British. Trust, however, was a thing of the past. Most Republicans believed the soldiers would be sent to Kansas to cow the free soilers (federal dragoons had been used for this purpose in 1856). Fessenden not only made this point clearly but also denied that President Pierce had had any constitutional right to deploy American troops as a *posse comitatus* in order to enforce territorial law. When Democrats assailed his efforts to defend the free-soil Topeka movement, he moved effortlessly onto the offensive. If the administration tried to impose slavery on Kansas, he retorted, "then, sir, I justify their exhibiting the spirit that was exhibited by their ancestors; and I trust in God that spirit is not yet extinct in this country of ours." He added fiercely:

> I do not shrink from the accusation of being in favor of civil war, if it must come, whenever the necessity arises that calls for it. There is a point beyond which forbearance ceases to be a virtue in nations as well as in men; and when the time comes in this country that we cannot speak on certain things without being met with the accusation of desiring civil war, I, for one, tell you just when I am ready to meet it. Not that I desire or would call for it, or would not do everything that an honest man or a patriot could do to avoid it, but I should be unworthy the name of American citizen if I said that there could be no occasion when I should not be ready to meet the consequences.[25]

Fessenden's tone was equally bellicose on February 8 when he delivered one of his rare set speeches to the Senate. Denouncing the imposition of an arbitrary "test oath" (demanding fidelity to the hated Fugitive Slave Law) on the voters of Kansas, he labeled the proslavery Lecompton constitution "an outrage, deliberately planned, followed up remorselessly, and, perhaps, from the indications we have had, designed to be carried through and imposed on the people of Kansas." If slavery were imposed on the territory, he said, he would "agitate so long as a single hope remains that slavery may be driven from the Territory thus stolen, robbed from freedom." The senator did not confine his barbs to Buchanan's policy. He also condemned popular sovereignty for failing to keep the territories free, thereby signaling his opposition to any alliance with Stephen Douglas. He repeated his familiar assertion that he regarded southern threats to secede "without a particle of apprehension." Northerners, he insisted, would "not be driven" from their position of non-extension by blackmail but would "stand by the Union of this country so long as it is worth standing by."[26]

Fessenden's militant rhetoric, laced as it was with more frightening talk of civil war and Federalist tones of disunion, was too radical for at least one of his colleagues. William Seward of New York, a friend of Jefferson Davis, expressed regret that any American senator would intimate that the Union might cease to have value for them, a clear sign that his colleague had overreached himself. Davis tried to capitalize on the Republicans' discomfort by alluding to the Yankee senator's

readiness to "perpetrate a joke on the hazard" of national dissolution and condemning his criticism of southern institutions as "moral leprosy" in order to fulfill his
"malignant purposes." Fessenden immediately disavowed any intent to destroy the
Union and asked Davis if he could say the same. A petty exchange between two of
America's most intelligent politicians then ensued. Davis denied being a disunionist and retorted that Fessenden's stance on slavery would produce a dissolution. His
antagonist retaliated by denying that northerners were aggressors and, in another
neo-Federalist outburst, complained that southerners had done their utmost to undermine northern economic interests.

Although Seward blanched at this uncompromising rhetoric, Republicans outside Congress harbored few reservations. Fessenden sent copies to co-partisans
across the North. William Willis, knowing his friend's love of English history
and law, said the speech was "worthy of the British Parliament in any stage of its
history" and commended him for its "calm, dignified[,] fearless" tone.[27] Edward
Kent liked its "clear argument, conclusive reasonings & its manly (not impudent)
tone & language." Everywhere, he said, it was "highly spoken of & sought for and
read."[28] Governor Salmon Chase of Ohio commended his attacks on Douglas. The
"notion of a popular sovereignty," he wrote, "incapable during the whole period
of territorial existence of freeing itself from slavery & then, at the initiation of
state existence indifferent whether slave or free, but only asking the privilege of
saying which, will never do to found a party upon."[29] Fessenden's assertion that
Lecompton was part of an insidious Democratic design to spread slavery across
the United States went down especially well with another radicalized centrist,
Abraham Lincoln of Illinois, who drew on the same theme for his famous "House
Divided" speech in June.[30]

Apart from Seward the only major intra-party criticism of Fessenden's outspoken
remarks came from the St. Louis *Missouri Democrat*. The paper was owned by the
city's powerful Blair family, who had been fighting for years to build a solid base of
free-soil support in Missouri. Predictably, the *Democrat* assailed Fessenden for ig-
noring the difficult position of Republicans in the border slave states. The senator,
always sensitive to adverse press comment, was annoyed by the article, particularly
by its reappearance in the widely disseminated *New-York Tribune*. All he had done,
he told his friend, the *Tribune* journalist, James Pike, was stand four-square on the
Republican platform of non-extension.[31]

Fessenden did not lose any sleep over his outspoken attacks on the Lecompton
Bill. He was seldom consumed with self-doubt and the praise lavished on the speech

indicated that he spoke for a majority of Republicans. Historians might reasonably ask if it was an act of statesmanship at this dangerous point of the sectional crisis to speak so freely of civil war and disunion. The problem, as far as the maintenance of national peace was concerned, was that southerners had often talked menacingly about their right to hold slaves and their readiness to secede if that right was infringed, but had never followed through on their threats. Fessenden was deadly earnest when he talked about meeting proslavery expansionism with force if necessary but he did not believe, and had cause not to believe, that southerners' talk of secession was anything more than political theater designed to intimidate the elected representatives of the free North. His Lecompton speech and accompanying exchange with Jefferson Davis indicated that by the time of the Lecompton crisis Republicans and southern Democrats were not only talking past one another but prepared to up the ante regardless of the political consequences. The presidential election of 1860 would determine which section controlled the Union. What happened after that was anyone's guess.

The Lecompton Bill passed the Senate on March 23. Fessenden and his co-partisans opposed passage alongside a handful of northern Democrats (Douglas included) and border-state Know-Nothings.[32] Hopeful that the northern-dominated House would defeat "the villainy," he was far from despondent. Indeed, he was more put out that spring by two photographs that he had taken of himself in Washington. "Both look awful savage," he told Lizzy. "The truth is, no pleasant picture will be had of me, unless my friends are present when it is taken."[33]

Pitt Fessenden was not a cold man. He loved his kin, male and female, and was loved by them. He also had a number of close friends beyond his family circle, notably Republican senators James Grimes of Iowa, Jacob Collamer and Solomon Foot of Vermont, and his fellow Down Easter James Pike of the *Tribune* (with whom he enjoyed fishing trips in Maine). He was not, intellectually or temperamentally, a natural organization man like the artful James G. Blaine, but he was alert to the need to maintain a power base at home in order to bolster his position in the Senate. Here he benefited from the assistance of client-politicians such as Freeman Morse, Rufus Dwinel, Elijah Hamlin, and John Lynch, who liked him personally, admired his integrity, respected his political skills, and, of course, expected to benefit personally from their allegiance to one of New England's leading men. These allies communicated frequently with him, allowing him not only to monitor the popular pulse in Maine but also to watch the activities of opponents, actual and potential, among the state's ambitious Republicans.

Fessenden's mostly ex-Whig supporters constituted a loose yet identifiable faction within Maine's young Republican organization. They possessed an identity of their own and a strong sense of loyalty to their leader, which he consistently encouraged. At the end of April Dwinel, a Bangor lumber merchant, reported that moves were afoot to unseat the senator in 1859. Fessenden replied that although he had heard of the "scheme," it was only embryonic. "Perhaps it will be as well to have an eye upon the State Convention," he counseled prudently, "and see that the Republican State Committee is not packed against us." He did not, he added, "design to meddle much with the matter, but self defence is justifiable. As I was elected by the Whigs, as a Whig, the Republican party has never yet had a chance to give me a mark of its confidence."[34]

Fessenden's aloof reputation was only partially deserved. He was formal in his public dealings; found it hard to conceal his dislike for those he regarded as devoid of principle or gentlemanly virtues; and always preferred the company of a few friends, the New Englanders in his mess, for example, to large social gatherings. When he sought company in Washington it was normally to play cards—bezique, cribbage, euchre, or whist—in small groups that included women as well as men. There, however, he liked to swap political gossip and stories, smoke the occasional cigar, and drink in moderation. One Yankee who returned home with a sore head after a night spent in this convivial company recorded that his malady might have been caused by "Mr. Fessenden's jokes and stories."[35] Aware that powerful politicians must be seen in public in order to exert influence, the senator was not entirely disengaged from the social whirl of the American capital. In March 1858 he attended one of James Buchanan's famous levees hosted as usual by the bachelor-president's niece, Harriet Lane. Buchanan, for whom he had little respect after the Lecompton crisis, struck him as "a large fine looking man" while Miss Lane had the appearance of "a buxom good looking girl." The crowd in attendance, he commented snobbishly, "was a curious mixture of the elite and the great unwashed."[36]

Fessenden's sense of loneliness, a feature of all his stays in Washington, had several sources. He missed his family and friends as well as the State Street house, especially its fine garden (tended in his absence by an Irishman named Powers) and extensive library stocked mainly with books on classical and British history, political thought, poetry, and the law. His solitude was also accentuated by Ellen's death in 1857. Fessenden mourned her passing—as much one suspects as the mother of his sons and a dear friend and companion as the occupant of the marital bed. Even though, as the recent daguerreotypes revealed, he was aging fast, he enjoyed the company of good-looking women. His sex drive, perhaps reenergized by Ellen's death, remained strong. A Freudian reading of his account of an idealized fishing trip would suggest that Lizzy remained the primary focus of his desires. "How pleasant" it would be, he wrote dreamily to his cousin in the Berkshires,

> to saunter along the borders of a shaded stream, pausing now and then to admire some sweet spot, occasionally drawing your line gently along the surface, until you arrive at a dark deep pool, where all is still and quiet. There you softly steal along, and gently thrusting your rod between an opening in the bushes, touch the surface lightly with your tempting fly, gently moving it to and fro. In a moment all is life and animation. The pool is stirred to its lowest depths. The fly disappears from the surface, and the rod vibrates like a reed. Soon, however, the contest is over. The fish is in the basket, and the sportsman's eye glistens with satisfaction . . . I should like much to connect Pittsfield with just such a reminiscence.[37]

Although Lizzy, still hitched to the importunate and unstable Mr. Warriner, remained out of reach, her younger sister Kate was unattached. For a brief period before the Civil War, Fessenden pondered the possibility of a liaison. Nothing came of the relationship, such as it was, partly because of the age gap that he felt sorely, partly because it was Lizzy whom he truly loved.[38] He remained a relatively solitary individual, envious of his friend Grimes's close relationship with his pious, redheaded wife, Elizabeth, a staunch opponent of slavery whom he described as "quite a pretty and interesting little woman."[39]

In the Shadow of John Brown

Politics, rather than affairs of the heart, demanded Fessenden's attention in the late spring of 1858. Unable to pass the Lecompton bill through the House, the Democrats cobbled together a compromise solution that offered Kansans a substantial land grant if they supported the proslavery constitution in an August referendum. Pitt Fessenden had mixed feelings about Congressman William English's bill (which passed the Senate over Republican opposition on April 30). Though it consummated "[t]he Kansas iniquity," he considered the measure no more than a Pyrrhic victory for the administration, always providing that the Kansans had "virtue enough to spurn the bribe offered them—which I trust they will have."[40]

With Kansas issues declining in salience (the territory's free soil majority repaid Fessenden's faith and decisively rejected entry into the Union in the August poll) the Republicans cast around for other issues to mobilize voters ahead of the 1858 elections. "Retrenchment" was one of their principal watchwords. The Buchanan administration was notoriously corrupt and Americans were growing concerned about wasteful expenditure in the aftermath of a serious economic panic the previous year. Fessenden spoke out against unnecessary spending on military telegraphs, congressional franking privileges, and dubious army contracts. However, his willingness to reduce federal spending was tempered by sectional loyalty and a Whiggish attachment to positive government. Working on the presumption that federal revenues were beginning to rise, he supported a $55,000 appropriation for an internal improvement project in Michigan and argued strongly in favor of retaining bounties for New England fishermen.[41]

Partisan considerations weighed heavily on Fessenden's mind. He joined other Republicans in opposing the admission of Oregon as a state, ostensibly because its draft constitution forbade blacks from voting. This stance enabled him to denounce the racist content of the *Dred Scott* decision. He did not, he informed the Senate, "hold, either in substance or in form, to any extent whatever" to the racial doctrines announced by Chief Justice Taney, which he castigated as "a perversion of all law, of all fact, and of all history." Under Maine law, he reminded senators, blacks were citizens and voters. He could not therefore acquiesce to the admission of any state that attempted to deprive them of their rights under the comity clause of the U.S. Constitution.[42]

At first glance this defense of black rights seems at odds with Fessenden's normally cautious attitude to racial issues. He did not empathize any more with people of color in 1858 than he had done in the 1840s, nor did he think about them often. He knew too that Republicans were vulnerable on matters of race because of widespread color prejudice in the North and the readiness of anti-black Democrats to capitalize on voters' most basic fears. Slavery for him, as it was for most northern whites, was a problem primarily because it fostered southern power at the expense of his own section. Intellectually and morally he had always known that slavery was wrong—that blacks were persons, not things to be commodified. But this awareness seems not to have impelled him to complain privately about the slave pens of Washington, let alone crusade publicly for black rights like unrepresentative figures such as Sumner or his father. He was too aware of his own weaknesses (more self-aware than many leading politicians of his day), too much the pragmatist and the realist, too little the perfectionist and the zealot, to become a social reformer. Unlike Sumner and a few other antislavery Republicans he had no black friends. The only black people he encountered on a daily basis were the individuals he employed as servants. He probably treated them as he treated his other domestics—sternly, kindly, and rather patronizingly.

It would be wrong, however, to overplay Fessenden's racism. Despite being a centrist, he did not obsess about blacks' racial characteristics like his radical colleague, Benjamin Wade, nor did he exploit popular racism to garner votes. Stephen Douglas, who would spend the summer of 1858 inflaming the racial prejudices of Illinois voters in debates with Abraham Lincoln, was convinced that the Portlander's defense of black rights was symptomatic of the Republicans' hypocrisy on racial issues. Free staters in Kansas, he said, had voted to exclude blacks from the territory.[43] The point had force. Senate Republicans had not berated the Topeka movement for its racism and the main reason they opposed the admission of Oregon was that they feared it would be a Democratic state. But Fessenden did not have to use a racial argument to oppose the entry of Oregon. His colleague Lyman Trumbull rejected any suggestion that the federal Constitution required blacks to be placed on an equal footing with whites, yet argued against the admission of Oregon on the technical grounds that Congress had neither been presented with evidence concerning the size of the local population nor legislated for the formation of a state government in the Pacific Northwest.[44] Pitt Fessenden's relatively progressive stance over Oregon and his public commitment to the civic equality of free blacks reflected his own distaste as an old-style New England republican for the use of color prejudice as a tool of political oppression.

Fessenden returned to Portland in June 1858 having established his reputation as one of the leading northern politicians in Washington. (Senate Republicans had confirmed this by making him their candidate for president *pro tempore* during the spring.) Despite his new-found prestige he knew the fall elections would determine whether he would be reelected to the Senate. Worried that some of his allies were insufficiently active, he urged greater zest. "You must lay aside all squeamishness and set your friends at work," he told Freeman Morse, "Go to Augusta and make a speech."[45] He also contributed significant amounts of his own money—at least $1,500—to the Republican cause in the state elections.[46]

The administration's heavy use of money and patronage failed to deny Maine Republicans a comfortable victory. Their co-partisans outside the state were impressed and sought advice. Fessenden told John Bigelow of the *New York Evening Post* that "our great secret was unity of action—thinking nothing of men or cliques, and work-ing for success."[47] Notwithstanding the existence of certain intra-party tensions, this analysis was broadly accurate. Fessenden had cultivated good relations with his Sen-ate colleague, Hannibal Hamlin, the acknowledged leader of Maine's ex-Democrat Republicans. Despite those rumors of the previous spring, there was no opposition to his reelection to the Senate in January 1859.

Fessenden was relieved by his success and deeply gratified by the absence of a preliminary caucus—the first such instance, he thought, in the state's history.[48] In words dripping with Federalist paranoia his proud father congratulated him on gain-ing the prize without "any sinister *Caucus* influence." However, Samuel was more concerned to issue another of his familiar jeremiads. The Slave Power, he told the senator, was still plotting to seize Cuba and, what was worse, many Portlanders favored the acquisition on economic grounds. "All the curses of Slavery" and "the Curse of Offended Heaven," he wailed, would fall upon "such a corrupt and sin-loving people."[49] Pitt was skeptical that Cuba represented an imminent threat to the republic. Privately he regarded renewed Democratic talk of acquiring the Spanish sugar island as "a humbug"—a false issue, raised up by the opposition "for political effect."[50] This view reflected not only his natural cynicism but also his conviction that the northern "masses" were better informed than they had been during previous crises over slavery expansion. While New England merchants (the model Americans of his youth) might be ensnared by material inducements, the "mercantile mind," he reassured his father, no longer controlled "the Country."[51] Southern plans to spread slavery beyond the existing boundaries of the United States were real enough and some Republicans wanted to debate the issue at length. Yet Fessenden was so con-vinced that the administration's Cuba purchase bill was "a farce" that he opposed efforts to discuss the measure in the Senate on February 9 on the grounds that there were more important matters to legislate upon.[52] The whole thing, he announced, was got up "to enable gentlemen to make speeches on it" ahead of the forthcoming elections.[53]

Having recently been appointed to the Senate Finance Committee, one of the most important policymaking bodies in the chamber, Fessenden was keen to take up a number of essential appropriation bills. His co-partisan John P. Hale of New Hampshire objected on the grounds that acquiring more slave territory would be "fatal to our progress and even to our existence." Hale was especially frustrated at his colleague's determination to suppress debate over Cuba. If Fessenden would guar-antee, he said sarcastically, to "bring his gigantic intellect and his great powers of scrutiny and analysis to bear upon this question, I would willingly sit and listen."[54] Although Hale was a frequent irritant to his fellow Republicans, the intervention was an early sign that Fessenden's forthright debating style, with its overtones of intellectual superiority and relentless emphasis on the practical, could divide his friends as well as smite his political opponents. On this occasion he probably had the better of the argument. How, he asked, could such evils be inflicted on the country if the measure—which was eventually lost in the press of business—never came up for debate?

This spat did not betoken any weakening of Fessenden's position on slavery expansion. Later in the short second session of the Thirty-fifth Congress, he attacked Buchanan's request for authority to deploy U.S. military forces to Central America in order to protect American citizens in that war-ravaged region. Aware that proslavery filibusters were intent upon taking slavery into "sister republics" like Nicaragua, he had no intention of giving Buchanan power to spread slavery into Latin America any more than he had been willing to let the doughface president impose the peculiar institution on Kansas. The power to make war, he averred, was lodged in Congress not the president. Besides, added Fessenden, it was a matter of trust: Buchanan had shown he was "little fitted" to wield power. He hoped "the time will never come when we shall have a man at the head of this Republic who has so much the confidence of the people that we shall be willing to invest in him powers, and trust them to his discretion, which the Constitution has vested in us."[55] These were fine words. When civil war came, Fessenden would have to eat them.

Although Senate Republicans tended to act as a unit on slavery questions in the late 1850s, intra-party tensions were often evident. Pitt Fessenden was reluctant to accede to the incessant demands of many western Republicans for cheap homesteads and federal protection against hostile Indians.[56] He not only regarded these measures as damaging to the nation's finances but also lacked sympathy for those Americans who were disposed "to push into the wilderness," thereby exposing themselves "to all manner of depredations in the pursuit of . . . business or fancy" and prompting demands for the government to guarantee their losses.[57] Fessenden was not averse to western expansion. He knew there was strong public support for a transcontinental railroad and said he was willing to investigate the possibility of private companies taking on the grandiose project. However, he stated his preference for a central route through the western "desert" built by the federal government with federal funds.[58] Like many eastern Whig-Republicans he did not fully embrace the old Jacksonian vision of the United States as a white settler nation even in the Republicans' updated free-soil form. Americans would not, he believed, meet with expensive losses if they stayed "within the bounds of civilization."[59] His opposition to what he regarded as unjustified calls on the public treasury testified to his independence of thought and his lack of interest in playing the role of party leader.

By the spring of 1859 leadership was an increasingly salient topic in Republican circles. Party strategists knew the presidency was theirs if they found the right blend of issues and a candidate who could carry some or all of the four northern states—Pennsylvania, Illinois, Indiana, and New Jersey—which Frémont had lost in 1856. James Pike was keen to throw Fessenden's hat into the ring, partly because Horace Greeley, his boss at the *New-York Tribune,* wanted to prevent the nomination of William Seward (the Republican frontrunner), partly out of respect for his friend's political talents. He started the ball rolling by requesting autobiographical information from the senator when the latter returned to Portland. Fessenden's duties on the Finance Committee had been onerous. Hours spent poring over appropriation bills had done nothing to improve his health and he was relieved to return to State Street even if the large house was lonely with "no females but servants."[60] While he harbored no presidential ambitions, he was sufficiently protective of his public image to respond positively to news that the *Tribune* was planning an encyclopedia of American biography.[61] Any hope that Pike had of producing an eye-catching account of Fessenden's political career were dashed by Greeley's deputy, Charles A. Dana, who toned it down to ensure that other candidates remained in the vanguard of public consciousness.[62] Personally, Dana thought Salmon Chase the man to beat Seward. "The Fessenden movement is good," he told Pike, "but it can't come to any thing directly. Indirectly it may be very useful."[63]

The senator's pride meant that he provided scant assistance to Pike's president-making efforts in 1859 and even repulsed a favorite-son resolution at the state Republican convention, which he attended in July.[64] Such a move would only embarrass him in the upper chamber, he told Pike. "This consideration decided me. It was a sacrifice I am not bound to make for the good of any body, or every body, under the circumstances."[65] This action did not entirely quash efforts to draft him for the 1860 campaign. Ohio Know-Nothings and anti-Chase Republicans, impressed by another election victory for Maine Republicans in September, wanted him on a sectionally balanced ticket that would also include conservative Edward Bates of Missouri.[66] Fessenden, however, gave no encouragement to his backers, even declining a chance to showcase his talents before Massachusetts Republicans. "A quiet hour in my library," he confessed to Lizzy, "the world shut out, with a friend to keep me company, is worth all the honor I could gain by a dinner speech at Plymouth."[67]

Fessenden's refusal to join the presidential scrum at a time when many Republican politicians, some less able than himself, were already campaigning hard for the nomination, was a product of several factors. First, there were genuine limits to his ambition. He did not want the place, preferring legislative to executive duties and valuing the recuperation time that congressional service allowed him. Second, he lacked the will to fight a long campaign that would require constant networking among the party faithful and frequent engagement with the voters. Fessenden had always understood the importance of popular opinion in a mass democracy but, unlike other presidential hopefuls such as Seward or Abraham Lincoln of Illinois, he preferred to keep his distance from "the dear public" (the ironic phrase was Ellen's) whose verdicts he knew from experience to be capricious and unpredictable.[68] Scrapping for political office, besides, was unseemly for a dignified, gentleman-politician like himself. Much better, he calculated, to retain his honor and self-respect by remaining above the fray. Third, as a political realist he realized that location was against him. No New Englander was likely to secure the nomination as long as the Republicans needed to win the votes of conservatives in the mid-Atlantic and western states.

Not running for president did not mean disengaging from the nomination struggle. In August 1859 he journeyed into the mountains to confer with prominent Republicans in the fashionable resort town of Saratoga Springs and spend time with his Senate colleague Solomon Foot who had invited him to visit Vermont where there were men "with whom Republicanism is something else & something more than Sewardism."[69] There was much talk of the presidency at both venues and some speculation that neither Seward nor Chase had "a living chance" for the nomination.[70]

Republican plans to capture the White House were thrown into confusion after John Brown's sensational raid on the federal arsenal at Harpers Ferry, Virginia, in October 1859. Although the revolutionary abolitionist failed to trigger a slave insurrection across the South, his subsequent imprisonment, trial, and execution garnered substantial northern sympathy for both the man and his cause. The extent of that sympathy did not prevent Democrats from trying to make political capital out of the raid. With an eye on the 1860 election they condemned hypocritical Republicans for supporting Brown's treasonous attempts to interfere with slavery in the states and sought to connect the Republican candidate for Speaker of the House, John Sherman, to the raid. Along with many other Republican congressmen,

Sherman had endorsed an abridgment of Hinton Rowan Helper's *Impending Crisis of the South,* which Republican strategists were planning to distribute as a campaign tract. Helper, a white southerner, argued that slavery damaged the interests of non-slaveholders and should be abolished. Sherman's support for his allegedly incendiary text allowed Democrats to connect the Ohioan's candidacy with Harpers Ferry as part of their broader political assault on the "black Republicans" as disunionists and abolitionists—an attack calculated to undermine the Republicans' claims to be conservative defenders of the Union.[71]

If some of Fessenden's wilder talk of civil war marked him out as one of the most combative Republicans in the Senate, his cautious response to John Brown's raid revealed his continuing suspicion of radical abolitionism. Initially he was inclined to think the party would "lose nothing" by the event "in the end."[72] However, the extent of northern support for Brown, evident in his son Sam's enthusiastic response back home, took him by surprise. He was disinclined to join in the general clamor of sympathy, commenting privately on the "impropriety" of pro-Brown meetings "in the present state of public feeling." By this he meant that the South was bound to regard such gatherings as indicating sympathy for the raid. "It would be much better," he thought, "if our people would stay away from them." Fessenden was no more supportive of those Republicans who had endorsed Helper's book. Their action, he thought, had been "unwise"—"the first great mistake our friends have made." It would delay Sherman's election and "create some embarrassment hereafter."[73]

The senator from Maine worked hard to limit the political fallout from Harpers Ferry. He endorsed the formation of a special investigating committee to draw the sting from Democratic charges of Republican complicity. Subsequently, when one of Brown's co-conspirators, Thaddeus Hyatt, refused to testify before it, he defended Congress's right to direct Hyatt's imprisonment—a move condemned by John Hale as despotic.[74] But Pitt Fessenden was not a man to remain on the defensive. When, on January 23, 1860, Stephen Douglas assailed Seward for alluding to an "irrepressible conflict" between slavery and freedom and described Harpers Ferry as "the natural, logical, inevitable result of the doctrines and teachings of the Republican party," Fessenden tore into Douglas, who was now bidding for the Democratic presidential nomination.[75] There was no evidence, he retorted, of any Republican involvement in the raid. The aggression had come from the other side—notably from Douglas himself when he repealed the Missouri Compromise as a prelude to making Kansas a slave state. While Seward's phraseology had been "unfortunate," Fessenden had no qualms in stating his belief that if the New Yorker had diffused his idea "over half a page" instead of compressing it into two incendiary words, "nothing would ever have come of it." Slave and free states could coexist, he thought, but if their respective labor systems mingled on the same soil "they [would] necessarily antagonize" because free labor elevated the laborer by promoting his "comfort," "happiness," "wealth," and "manliness," while slavery inevitably degraded him.[76]

Although he repeated his loathing of slavery, Fessenden insisted that he did not hate slaveholders. He reserved most of his wrath for Douglas Democrats who, he claimed, were inciting southern hostility to the Republican Party to secure power for themselves. Unlike Douglas, who claimed to have no feeling on the relative merits of free and slave institutions, Fessenden made clear his "love" for the former. Lincoln had made the same point in his debates with the Little Giant in 1858. The senator from Maine, however, added a humanitarian twist that signaled his refusal to be intimidated by Democratic racism. Though no more desirous of interfering with slavery in the states than Douglas, he could not be "entirely indifferent to the question whether a portion of my fellow—yes, I was about to say of my fellow-citizens, but the Supreme Court has decided that blacks are not citizens—whether a portion of the human race are held in bondage." He concluded with a familiar warning to southerners. Their threats of secession, he said, were "a mere electioneering trick." If the election of a Republican president was to be regarded as a genuine excuse for dissolving the Union "the sooner the question is settled the better; because . . . the sooner we know it the sooner shall we be prepared to meet the consequences."[77]

Fessenden's response to Douglas, made at the behest of his Republican colleagues, testified again to his considerable powers of debate for it was, he told Lizzy, "wholly unpremeditated."[78] Underlying the effort was his unwavering conviction, shared by other Republicans like his friend Grimes, that the party must hold firm on slavery. "[M]oderation is always a virtue," he contended privately, "but that moderation which sacrifices the great end to temporary expediency is both a blunder and a crime."[79] While Fessenden continued to discourage any attempts to float his presidential balloon (Blaine dutifully suppressed a supportive resolution at the Republican state convention in March), contemporaries continued to talk of him as executive timber.[80] Pike's Iowa correspondent, Fitz Henry Warren, agreed to "take apartments . . . in the Pitti Palace" on the grounds that "a stiff backbone is worth all the rest of the human anatomy."[81] George Talbot, a Maine Republican delegate to the party's Chicago convention, expressed his admiration for Fessenden and assured Blaine that he would "feel honored in aiding his nomination if things look that way."[82]

The senator himself was under no illusions. He was, he assured Lizzy, "too far east" and declared his readiness to see the blunt-speaking Ohio radical Benjamin Wade gain the nomination (in hindsight a richly ironic statement given his efforts to prevent Wade from becoming president during the impeachment crisis of 1868). He felt ambivalent about Seward—suspicious of his burning desire for the presidency, sympathetic to him because he was a lightning rod for Democratic abuse, and in-clined to think he carried too much baggage to win in Chicago. "I shall pity him if he loses," Fessenden commented in early March, "for his heart is set upon it, and the disappointment will kill him—but it is better to kill him than the cause."[83] Later that month he scotched what little chance he had of securing the nomination himself by prohibiting the use of his name on the first ballot by the Maine delegation.[84]

The Crisis of Our Fate

William Pitt Fessenden did not leave his Senate place to attend the Chicago conven-tion in May. Maine Republicans present at the overcrowded Wigwam had not given up hope that the Portlander could be nominated as a dark-horse candidate even though they were divided on paper between Lincoln and Seward supporters. James Blaine told the senator that Seward delegates were assuming "an air of dictation" but predicted that their candidate would not succeed. At that point, he ventured, "the game lies between Lincoln and yourself."[85] Fessenden received a similar dispatch from another Maine delegate, Lot Morrill. Once Seward was disposed of, thought Morrill, Lincoln would take the lead. However, if he could not win over the Penn-sylvania and New Jersey delegations, leading Pennsylvanians would try to break the deadlock by presenting Fessenden's name if the opportunity arose. At that point the Maine delegation would second the nomination and trigger a stampede in his favor.[86] It did not happen. Although Seward failed to secure a majority as predicted, Abraham Lincoln—like Fessenden a hard-headed antislavery Whig-Republican but one who hailed from a crucial battleground state in the West—soon emerged as the front-runner. Fessenden's name never came to the floor. "The Railsplitter" was elected on the third ballot and Maine's senior U.S. senator, ex-Democrat Hannibal Hamlin, was nominated for vice president to balance the ticket. Fessenden was sur-prised by Lincoln's success but not disappointed by it. He told Lizzy Warriner that the convention's work gave "general satisfaction to the Republicans, & frightened the democrats." The choice of Hamlin, a potential rival in the party organization at home, was an added bonus. It was, he informed his cousin, "capital for Maine, & will save me a good deal of hard work, & some money—besides making room for several ambitious gentlemen, who are tired of waiting their turn for promotion."[87]

Before returning home for the campaign season, the senator completed his duties at the capital. In late May he joined fellow Republicans in opposing a set of pro-slavery resolutions introduced by the Mississippi Democrat Jefferson Davis. These included a resolve in favor of protecting slaveholders' rights in the territories. Fessenden, always impatient when colleagues failed to concentrate on the business before them, condemned Davis's attempt to "make a party platform" on the grounds that the Senate was a place for legislation.[88] Southern demands for a federal slave code for the territories had already split the Democrats sharply along sectional lines at their convention in Charleston. In June two Democratic challengers emerged from the resulting internal struggle: Stephen Douglas, who remained committed to popular sovereignty, and the pro-southern candidate, John C. Breckinridge. Constitutional Unionists (mostly old-line Whigs and Know-Nothings) nominated John Bell of Tennessee in a desperate bid to avert national disaster.

Discomfited by headaches after a long Senate session and needing rest, Fessenden had no choice but to immerse himself in politics when he returned to Portland in July. Maine's state elections would be regarded as a litmus-test for Republican fortunes in November. Any sign of weakness might lower morale at a critical moment in the party's short history. His efforts to promote unity were not assisted by his friend Freeman Morse's failure to secure reelection to Congress. He tried first to mollify Morse by assuring him that more elevated positions were open to him and then strove to galvanize the angry carpenter by advising him to work for the election of the Republicans' gubernatorial candidate, Israel Washburn, Jr. "There are those among us," he confided, "who would like nothing better than to get cause of complaint against either you or me."[89] Hearing that Charles Sumner was to deliver a campaign speech in Portland on September 4, Fessenden was quick to offer hospitality. "[M]y house will be yours while you stay," he told the Bostonian, "as at all other times when you will make me happy by taking it for your home."[90]

Although the senator gave James Pike $100 to use for political purposes in the eastern part of the state, his greatest sacrifice was time and energy.[91] Shortly before the elections he journeyed up the Penobscot River to Bucksport, where Pike's brother Fred was campaigning for Congress and facing opposition not only from Democrats but also disgruntled Republicans. There he coaxed and cajoled local party members to support the regular nominee. Subsequently he went on to Bangor, where he was taken sick and treated by a physician. He made it back to Portland in time to vote and then took to his bed. "The truth is," he reported, "I was not in a condition to take any part in the campaign, but nobody would believe it." Fortunately, the Republicans won a resounding victory, electing Washburn and all six congressmen and securing handsome majorities in the legislature. "Our great success must cure me . . .," wrote Fessenden. "Now, let other States do their duty, & the rascals are wiped out."[92]

By early November, after further victories in critical northern states, Fessenden was certain of Lincoln's election. Discounting southern talk of secession as most Republicans did, he was already looking ahead to the 1862 midterm contests without any thought of civil war. Though the Democrats might still control Congress, he believed the Republicans would soon be able to build a better Union. "We shall have the power to prevent Evil, without the responsibility of a failure to effect what we desire," he told Frank. "If things are well conducted, this will aid us—and in the next Congress after, we shall have the power we need."[93] Lincoln won only a plurality of the popular vote in the presidential election on November 6, but he carried every northern state to secure a comfortable majority in the electoral college. Cotton-state secessionists immediately denounced the Republican triumph as narrowly sectional and therefore illegitimate. Fessenden's longstanding views on the emptiness of southern disunion threats were about to be put to the test.

Initially, he saw no reason to change his opinions. His only worry about the secession movement, he informed Freeman Morse after the election, was "that it will not stand up long enough to be knocked down. It is a bold farce, & will prove so in a few weeks."[94] But by the time he reached Washington to attend the winter session of Congress, a serious secession movement was already underway in several Deep South states. Signs immediately appeared of a breach in Republican ranks. Some Republican organs, including Thurlow Weed's *Albany Evening Journal* which advocated extension of the Missouri Compromise line as a solution to the crisis, were swift to counsel concessions. From his mess on Pennsylvania Avenue, Fessenden rejected such responses as "silly." Most of his colleagues, he told his son William, were "firm" and opposed to abandoning the Chicago Platform. Firm they may have been but congressional Republicans lacked a clear and constructive policy on secession in December 1860. "What is to come I know not," added the senator, "We must 'watch and pray.'"[95]

The initial absence of a policy was caused partly by the fact that most Republicans shared Fessenden's dismissive attitude toward disunion. Lincoln, moreover, would not be inaugurated until March, meaning that the immediate responsibility for responding to secessionist moves devolved upon the Buchanan administration which, torn between maintaining the Union and empathy for the South, seemed content to wring its hands while proslavery forces burrowed away at the national edifice.

The pervasive atmosphere of uncertainty, punctuated by evidence and rumors of Republican backsliding, proved disturbing to antislavery radicals who, overjoyed by the Slave Power's defeat at the ballot box, now feared the prospect of another humiliating compromise over slavery. Samuel Fessenden moved swiftly to stiffen the backbone of his son and his party. Bemoaning again northerners' historic inability to resist southern aggression against the rights of their section and those of blacks, he urged Pitt to rebuff all compromise efforts, especially spineless calls for repeal of the personal liberty laws that many northern states, Maine included, had passed to weaken the Fugitive Slave Act. Manhood, self-respect, and party survival were all at stake. "Shall the Free States," asked the old Federalist, "who have achieved the late victory now be frightened from reaping its fruits by the threats of the slave holders? Then meet you Republicans in some room dark and pestilential as the Black Hole of Calcutta and . . . there write in a petition to Abraham Lincoln and Hannibal Hamlin that they will modestly decline the positions you have chosen them to occupy."[96]

Samuel need not have worried. Pitt Fessenden had no intention of surrendering the fruits of electoral victory. He remained convinced that southerners were bluffing. His miscalculation was partly the product of his own political cynicism. He knew that politics was not just about principles; that to outmaneuver opponents one sometimes had to raise false issues in order to frighten the enemy and mobilize the masses. He knew some of the southern leaders well. Surely they were rational men engaging in political sport for their own ends? Jefferson Davis, he told his friend Hamilton Fish in mid-December, "is not sincere. His whole action convinces me that he has no faith that any thing is to come of all this uproar. His object and hope are to demoralize the Republican party, by destroying the confidence of our people in our capacity & firmness." The correct response, he thought, was "to watch coolly, the enemy's game—for it is a game—" and wait for "conservative men in the South to arrest this tide of madness." Although he hoped the crisis would blow over peacefully, Fessenden was true to his promises and did not shrink from the possibility of violence. Southern politicians must know, he told Fish, "that secession is war, and the consequences must be on the heads of those who provoke it."[97] He therefore received his father's warning missive with "pride and pleasure." Republicans would remain silent for now out of respect for southern Unionists who feared that any pronouncements from the party of the North would hinder their efforts to prevent secession. But make no mistake, he added, they would not "throw away our game, either by servility or rashness."[98]

The senator's preference for remaining firm and silent in the hope that this approach would foster southern Unionism accorded with that of President-elect Abraham Lincoln, who worked hard behind the scenes to ensure that congressional Republicans did not barter away their central policy of opposing slavery expansion. The stance of both men, however, was less conciliatory than that of their influential colleague William Seward. The New Yorker's numerous Unionist contacts in the South assured him that any attempt by the government to coerce seceding states would result in the loss of key Upper South states like Virginia which, for the present, rejected secession. Seward used his influence to try and soften inflammatory Republican rhetoric, foster compromise efforts in Washington, and prevent the few remaining southern forts in federal hands—especially the garrison at Fort Sumter in Charleston harbor—from becoming flashpoints for war.

By December 17, three days before South Carolina seceded from the Union, Fessenden had begun to realize that southern Democratic leaders were in danger of surrendering power to "the rabble" and increasingly fearful that "the brute" they had unleashed would "turn upon them."[99] When, shortly afterward, Ben Wade broke ranks with the Republican minority in the Senate to deliver a menacing warning to southern rebels, Fessenden was not displeased. The hard-line speech, he thought, "has done good, and [I] am glad he made it."[100] While this comment revealed how difficult it was for Fessenden and most other Republicans in Washington to repress their anger at events below the Mason-Dixon line, it did not, in his case, signal a final acknowledgment that civil war was inevitable.

Although he had previously decried the notion of peaceable secession, his mind was not entirely fixed on this topic. Privately he was willing to speculate along lines informed by his memory of the nullification crisis and his Federalist upbringing. If South Carolina alone seceded, he told Lizzy, secession would be still-born, for the state was "of no consequence, and can hardly stand up long enough to be knocked down." If, in contrast to the events of 1832–33, South Carolina was joined by the other cotton states, the effect would still be "puny." A secession of all the slave states, however, would result in dissolution. He would not, he wrote,

yield one iota of the principles for which we have been contending even to avoid this catastrophe—for it is a question for all time. And I would far rather see a final separation between the free and Slave States than engraft upon the Constitution the idea that Slavery is a national institution and to be protected as such. The free States, by themselves, would make a great and powerful people, free from an element of weakness and division. New England by herself has elements of happiness and power, and I would rather belong to a small and free nation than be subject to the will of an oligarchy so overbearing and tyrannical as the Slave power has shown itself to be.[101]

In the immediate wake of South Carolina's decision to secede Pitt Fessenden's main priority, grounded in his belief that any surrender of the Republicans' electoral victory would be to the detriment of American liberty, was to stave off major concessions to the South. This was, he wrote, "the crisis of our fate. Concession, under menace, would be fatal to us as a party, and what is vastly more & worse, it would prostrate the north forever, at the feet of Slavery."[102] The secession of five other Deep South states in January did nothing to weaken his resolve. Although some conservative and centrist Republicans were prepared at this time to proffer olive branches to the South—at least the Upper South—Senate Republicans scotched the one plan that might have stopped secession in its tracks.

Kentucky senator John J. Crittenden had proposed that the Missouri Compromise line should be extended to the Pacific coast, that slavery should be protected south of the line in territory currently and in the future owned by the United States, and that existing constitutional safeguards around slave property should be strengthened. During the second week of January 1861 Fessenden joined his colleagues in stymieing debate on Crittenden's plan and then substituting hard-line Unionist resolves in its place.[103] When Seward delivered a strong compromise speech of his own, the senator from Maine observed cruelly that the New Yorker's effort had pleased only the women in the galleries. The truth was, he told Lizzy, Seward was "a poor creature— utterly selfish, false and mean. I am getting fairly to detest him."[104] Support for compromise was strong and growing, particularly among Democrats and conservative ex-Whigs in the commercial cities of the Northeast. But Fessenden, rightly confident that most rank-and-file Republicans opposed significant concessions, remained determined not to back down in the face of intense political pressure. "Nothing which we can do, short of absolute dishonor," he wrote privately, "would avail any thing—and we must save our honor—for, in yielding that, we not only disgrace ourselves, but destroy our institutions—or the principles which support them."[105]

Fessenden was not entirely preoccupied that winter with developing a party line on secession for there was a government to make. Although influential party strategists like Samuel Bowles, editor of the *Springfield Republican,* considered him well qualified for a place in Lincoln's cabinet, Fessenden did not want an executive role. This did not mean, however, that he played no part in cabinet making. At the turn of the New Year he was consulted on appointments by Lincoln's ally, Leonard Swett, who found him guardedly supportive of Gideon Welles's elevation to secretary of the navy despite the Connecticut Republican's prior attachment to the Democratic Party.[106]

When rumors began to circulate that the president-elect was planning to appoint Pennsylvania's political boss Simon Cameron to a top post, he intervened quickly. Cameron had a deserved reputation for corruption and Fessenden feared his appointment would have a detrimental impact on public confidence (not least because honest government had been one of the Republicans' chief campaign issues). Cameron, he told Lincoln candidly, had been a colleague on the Senate Finance Committee and was "utterly incompetent to discharge the duties of a Cabinet officer, in any position."[107] Fessenden failed to achieve his objective. Lincoln did, at one point, rescind an appointment to Cameron but the latter was a wily politician who refused to back away silently. Recognizing the Keystone State's political importance to the party and unable to find an alternative Pennsylvanian for the office, he finally appointed Cameron secretary of war.

This decision did not indicate any lack of respect for the senator from Maine. Fessenden was besieged with requests for government jobs from Republicans at home. He rebuffed some of these claimants, among them his old law partner William Willis, but was determined to secure the plum position of London consul for Freeman Morse—partly because the disaffected Morse was a friend as well as a loose cannon, partly because the appointment would confirm his own political influence to Republicans in Maine. Although there was intense competition for the post, Lincoln reserved the position for Morse.[108] He also made Fessenden's ally, James Pike, American minister to the Netherlands. At his father's behest, Senator Fessenden used his influence to secure two lesser posts for his half-brothers, Charles and Joseph.[109] While these last actions laid him open to charges of nepotism and sparked friction among Maine Republicans, Fessenden had few qualms in helping his closest kin. For him, blood was always thicker than water. Yet he had his pride. When Lincoln mistook a request from James Grimes to give Frank Fessenden a minor diplomatic post as having come from Frank's father, the latter stepped in promptly to deny that he desired the favor.[110]

On February 4, 1861, Deep South secessionists created a proslavery Confederate government in Montgomery, Alabama. Many Americans responded by redoubling their efforts to find a compromise solution to avert national calamity. While Crittenden's plan was debated at a hastily convened peace conference in Washington, William Seward persisted in decrying Republican talk of coercing the seceded states back into the Union, still hopeful that time would allow southern Unionists to assert control in the Upper South. Many northerners now favored offering concessions to save the Union but most Republicans remained adamant that the Chicago Platform should not be abandoned at the expense of the party and its antislavery principles.

While Pitt Fessenden was not an enthusiastic coercionist, he was rightly regarded as one of the most obdurate foes of compromise in the ranks of the Republican Party. "[I] say most distinctly," he told the Senate on February 11, "if the time ever does come . . . when it will be necessary to use force in order to execute the laws of the United States under the Constitution anywhere and everywhere within what is properly the United States, I am perfectly ready to do it, but I trust we shall have no such necessity." If war did come, he concluded, "I trust we shall be ready to meet all our responsibilities like men."[111] Privately, he told his father what the latter yearned to hear. The peace conference would amount to nothing, he wrote, adding that he would not "yield one particle of that great idea of human liberty, which lies at the foundation of our institutions, and without which they must inevitably fail."[112]

On the evening of March 3, the night before Lincoln's inauguration, senators prepared to debate compromise resolutions that had been submitted to Congress by the Washington peace conference. The chamber was stiflingly hot and the galleries were packed with noisy, excited spectators. Senator Crittenden prefaced discussion with a long speech in which he pleaded with Republicans to prevent civil war. His appeal fell on deaf ears. Fessenden joined his co-partisans in voting decisively against the peace conference resolves and the revived Crittenden plan.[113] Unlike a minority of Republicans he also refused to vote for a constitutional amendment to prohibit the federal government from interfering with slavery in the states—probably because he opposed introducing the word "slavery" into the nation's founding document.[114] The only compromise proposal he did support was one emanating from the Republican minority on a select committee set up to consider the peace convention's proposals. It invited state legislatures to inform Congress whether they wished to call a convention to recommend any amendments thought necessary to safeguard the nation's welfare. Inadequate to the peril now facing the country, it was defeated 25–14 with only Fessenden

and 13 of his co-partisans voting for it.[115] It was now up to the new Republican administration to determine the government's response to secession.

Even after Lincoln had made it clear in his inaugural address that he would not
permit the breakup of the Union, the senator from Maine retained some hope that
peace might be preserved. If the government could develop a policy, he surmised,
it might still be possible to "get the Country over this crisis without a war." Conceding that ardent Republicans like Wade were ready to suppress treason with military
force but encouraged by the fact that secessionists had failed to take control of the
Upper South, he believed "that while we yield no inch, we shall yet, if possible, let
time do its inevitable work—as it is doing, daily." He feared, however, that Seward's
peace policy might yet "disgust the Country, and dishearten those who are its true
reliance."[116]

His residual optimism—still shared by some of his colleagues—was misplaced.
Even as he wrote, federal troops in Charleston harbor were running out of provisions. At a crucial cabinet meeting at the end of March, President Lincoln—hoping
like Fessenden for peace but prepared for war if necessary to save the Union—found
increased support for his preferred option of resupplying Fort Sumter as the best
alternative to coercion or surrender. A relief expedition left New York on April 10.
Determined to exert its authority before the fleet arrived, the Confederate government ordered the fort to be bombarded. Backed by an outpouring of national outrage, Lincoln responded with a call for volunteers to suppress the rebellion—a move
that triggered the secession of the Upper South. Fessenden, home again in Portland,
had no alternative but to consider civil war "inevitable."[117] He greeted the event with
less fervor than many northerners, including his radical colleague Charles Sumner who rejoiced that "The day of insincerity & duplicity is now passed, & *all* the
cabinet is united in energetic action."[118] Yet even the sober Portlander was inclined
to regard the prospect of chastising rebels with a degree of equanimity. "My heart
aches, sometimes," he declared privately, "when I think of all the horrors that are
coming—but I am consoled with the belief that much good is to come out of it all.
The Country needs some such experience—especially the South, and with my consent there shall be no peace until all these disturbing questions are definitely and
properly settled."[119]

The *rage militaire* that took hold of the North after the attack on Fort Sumter
showed that the vast majority of northerners, regardless of party affiliation and their
views on compromise during the secession crisis, would not tolerate the destruction
of their beloved country. Because of the flawed nature of the antebellum Union,

William Pitt Fessenden was less given in late middle age to emotional displays of sentimental nationalism than he had been in his youth. But his patriotism ran deep and he would not allow the American republic to be destroyed by designing men. "Republics," he told Lizzy Warriner, "can only stand when based on honest principles, and should fall when perverted from their true purposes, as ours has long been."[120] While Fessenden did not hate southerners, not even those who claimed ownership of slaves, he knew the Republicans had bested them in a fair political fight and that any surrender of that victory portended greater evil for his party and the United States than armed defense of the lawfully elected government. The result would be civil war. But better that, he believed, than the negative peace that had prevailed for so long.

Saving the Republic, 1861–1864

Union victory in the American Civil War was not inevitable, for Confederate resistance was tenacious. It required an enormous collective effort by northerners
to defeat the enemy. While Abraham Lincoln and the mostly volunteer soldiers of
the North played a leading role in the dearly won triumph, so did Congress in its
near-ceaseless attempts to bring the country's superior resources to bear on the
Confederacy. The Republican legislators' Whiggish predilection for positive government action combined with necessity to produce results that were discernibly
modernizing: the growth of the federal bureaucracy, the strengthening of American
national identity, the destruction of slavery, and the tightening of links between the
central state and private capitalists. As chairman of the Senate Finance Committee, William Pitt Fessenden was at the center of all these developments. After the
departure of most southern congressmen from Washington, he was one of the most
powerful men in the country. Wholly committed to the Union cause, he devoted
his energies to generating the vast sums of money that would eventually help to
destroy the breakaway Confederacy and the system of human bondage that gave it
life and vigor.

In partnership with Secretary of the Treasury Salmon P. Chase and the House
Ways and Means Committee, which was mandated by the Constitution to initiate fiscal measures, Fessenden's hard-pressed committee strove to develop a viable financial structure for the North's wartime economy and raise the huge funds needed to
keep Federal troops in the field. He spent much of his time honing revenue-raising
bills and then piloting those same detailed measures through the Senate (and often
on into conference committees of the two houses). Yet, crucial though it was, this
was not his only function in the wartime Senate. As one of the most talented and
respected Republicans in Congress, he was widely regarded as a spokesman for party
policy on a wide range of war-related issues, including not only economic measures
but also the abolition of slavery. This placed him in a sensitive position within the

party, for Republicans were divided on means even as they agreed on the end of defeating the Confederacy. Although he used his influence constructively, liaising between the fractious Congress and a president whose conduct of the war was the cause of much concern among his fellow partisans, the senator was an imperfect broker. He had never suffered fools gladly and he soon discovered more fools within the ranks of the Republican Party than he had previously suspected. By the time he reluctantly accepted a post in Lincoln's cabinet, he was a controversial figure in abolitionist circles, wrongly suspected of being a conservative at a moment when, in the summer of 1864, the war against slavery and the South was still not won.

First Blows

Between April and December 1861 the government and people of the United States struggled in vain to subdue the slaveholders' rebellion. Complacent assumptions about an easy victory faded as the strength of Confederate will and arms became apparent to all. Throughout this frustrating period Fessenden devoted himself tirelessly to the government service, using his formidable political talents to develop a robust response to the treasonous action now imperiling the republic of the Fathers.

He had no doubt that the government must respond vigorously to the Confederate aggression against Fort Sumter. Writing to Secretary of War Simon Cameron shortly after President Lincoln had called for volunteers to suppress the revolt against national authority, he observed "the resolute determination existing among all classes of people in the free States to put down at once and forever this monstrous rebellion." The country's only fear, he said, was that the administration would "stop short of its whole duty; that when the work is half done . . . parties will spring up among us urging a compromise or something short of entire subjugation, and that we shall yield to the clamor." Northerners were "full of enthusiasm and wrath. Take advantage of it, and relax no effort until the cause of Government is vindicated and the traitors doomed." Fessenden's desire for action was tempered initially by a certain caution. "While mere invasion is to be avoided," he added, "I hold that . . . wherever rebels appear in arms to resist the laws they should be dispersed." A short, sharp shock—"some decided blow"—he wrote, might be enough to end the insurrection.[1] At this early stage of the war, even a politician as sage as William Pitt Fessenden could not foresee how long or how sanguinary the conflict would become.

The senator's attachment to the classical republican values of civic duty, keen-eyed vigilance, and sturdy independence, mediated by sectional loyalty and the meritocratic, free-labor ideas generated by economic change, had conditioned his responses to the political events of the 1850s. Bolstered by another essential republican trait, self-control, they would play an equally significant role in his policymaking efforts during the first three years of the Civil War, though the principal mediating force now would be the urgency of the national crisis. Desperate times required superhuman effort from every Unionist and a flexible approach to problems that might previously have elicited more dogmatic responses. Normally Fessenden would have spent the early summer tending his garden in Portland. President Lincoln, however, had other plans for him and, when summoned to Washington to discuss financial policy ahead of a special session of Congress, he willingly complied. With three of his four sons bent on joining the army, he was lonelier than ever. Though he craved female company, he was much too busy and still too fond of Elizabeth Warriner to pursue any other woman seriously. Lizzy, he confided shortly before leaving for Washington in the second week of June, was the only person capable of assuaging both his loneliness and his inner doubts. "I love you because you give me a better opinion of myself," he wrote with feeling.[2]

The Yankee senator found the shabby capital swarming with troops. For a few days at the beginning of the war, secessionists had threatened to sever communications between Washington and the Northeast. By June, however, Union forces controlled the city as well as its northern approaches through the slave state of Maryland. Hot-headed patriots quickly began calling for an immediate attack on the Confederates in northern Virginia. Favoring an energetic prosecution of the war himself, Fessenden was as perturbed as many other Republicans by General Winfield Scott's preference for strangling the Confederacy gradually rather than killing it quickly at birth.[3] Yet he was perceptive enough to note the poor discipline of the soldiers massing in and around Washington as well as the "great deficiency in field artillery." He was, he told Lizzy shortly before finding accommodation in the home of Secretary Chase, "willing to wait provided we can hold the people up to fighting pitch." This, of course, was partly Congress's job. Fessenden predicted a short but important session in which much of the labor would devolve upon the chairman of the Finance Committee. "I shall do it as well as I can," he said, "but shall be all the time wishing myself at home."[4]

During the last week of June the senator deliberated with Lincoln, Chase, and other leading Republicans over how to procure the funds necessary to subdue the rebellion. Fessenden thought the money would have to be obtained by a combination of loans (domestic and foreign) and excise taxes. If the war continued for any length of time, a tax on incomes might even be necessary for the first time in American history. And it would last, he now thought, unless a slave insurrection came to the aid of the Federals. Here he was responding to press reports that blacks in Virginia had begun fleeing to Union lines at Fortress Monroe where they had been received as "contrabands." "Very genteel and appropriate, isn't it?" he joked of the label to his friend James Pike who was now safely installed at The Hague.[5]

Just before Congress convened, Chase's attractive daughter Kate returned home unexpectedly. The treasury secretary urged him to stay but Fessenden soon found alternative living quarters close to the capitol. Shortly after the move he was visited by "a little brown child" who was probably owned by one of the senator's many white visitors. The urchin rolled around on the carpet and chattered for an hour. It was evidently very bright, he told Lizzy, "and the thought that it was owned, like a dog, by one of its fellow creatures, made me utter fresh maledictions on an institution which upholds such an atrocity."[6] While Fessenden's unguarded comment about contrabands confirmed his ambivalent attitude to people of color, he was perfectly capable of recognizing the humanity of individual blacks and remained as hostile to the peculiar institution as he had always been.

On July 5 Secretary Chase issued his first Treasury report. Hopeful of a relatively short war, Chase calculated the government's needs for the coming fiscal year to be just under $320 million. He reckoned that one-quarter of this sum should be raised from taxation and the remainder from loans. Congress, he urged, must find the lion's share of the taxation through a judicious mix of increased or altered tariff schedules, excise duties, and direct taxes on land.[7] Although Chase's arithmetic was hopelessly optimistic, his seemingly modest target represented, on past form, a very substantial amount of money for Congress to raise.

Pitt Fessenden was appointed chairman of the Finance Committee on July 6. He was one of eleven New Englanders, mostly centrists rather than antislavery Radicals, to be named chairman of a committee, an illustration of the dramatic power-shift occasioned by secession. Like all such bodies during the war it contained a majority of Republicans, among them the highly competent Ohio senator John Sherman. The seven members' duties were onerous because the committee had responsibility for appropriating as well as raising revenue.[8] They spent the next two weeks considering the details of a loan bill empowering the government to borrow up to $250 million through the issue of long-term bonds and short-term Treasury notes. Although Fessenden was broadly in favor of the loan, he was ready to consider amendments. Before leaving Portland he had expressed a willingness to accept suggested revisions from John Murray Forbes, a prominent Boston businessman who enjoyed a close relationship with many leading Republicans.[9] Forbes disliked the bill's pledge of import duties to bolster the loan. Fessenden, who took a dim view of any signal of national impotence, had the pledge struck out in committee.[10] Both men shared an unswerving devotion not only to the northern cause but also to what they regarded as morally responsible finance. The Portlander would heed Forbes's counsel on economic policy, as he would advice from other northeastern businessmen like the Bostonians William Gray and Samuel Hooper, throughout the war—a sign of his personal respect for these individuals as well as his shrewd understanding that capitalists and the government had a common interest in suppressing the rebellion.

While Fessenden busied himself with revenue-raising measures, clamor for an early offensive against the Confederate capital at Richmond continued to grow. Skeptical that Brigadier General Irvin McDowell's Army of Virginia was ready to move and unconvinced that politicians were the best judges of military strategy, Fessenden thwarted attempts by impatient Republicans in caucus to precipitate an advance by congressional resolve.[11] By the middle of the month, however, intense pressure from leading opinion-makers like Horace Greeley of the *New-York Tribune* and the looming end to the volunteers' ninety-day term of service induced the Union high command to throw McDowell's raw troops against a Confederate army massed on the Warrenton turnpike near Washington. Confident of victory, General Scott sent passes to members of Congress allowing them to watch the battle. Unlike his friend James Grimes, Fessenden chose not to pay $40 for a carriage to witness scenes of carnage that he had "no curiosity" to see and which, he thought, "should be avoided, unless at the imperative call of duty."[12] Even as he wrote these words Union regiments were being cut to pieces by a ferocious Confederate counterattack on the battlefield of First Bull Run. Discipline collapsed as terrified soldiers and spectators streamed back to Washington. The capital itself was only saved by the enemy's caution and fatigue. In spite of having had the wisdom not to venture out to Manassas, the senator was bombarded by shocking images in the days after the battle as McDowell's "demoralized" troops staggered around the capital. He longed to forget all he had seen: a man, for example, whose legs had been shattered in the fight begging another to shoot him. "I have felt at times during the week," he remarked, "as if I should be glad to have somebody do me the same favor—so intense has been my shame & disappointment."[13]

Although Bull Run was a military disaster for the Union, it showed northerners that the war would not be over soon. Resolve in Congress hardened. Most

Republicans, Fessenden included, did vote for a resolution introduced by Andrew Johnson of Tennessee, stating that the government did not seek to subjugate the southern states or interfere with slavery.[14] The measure was intended to allay the fears of southern Unionists and northern Democrats that the Republicans wanted to fight an abolition war. However, he made it clear that his purpose was to defend the Constitution and the laws "at whatever hazard" even if temporary subjugation was necessary to accomplish this objective.[15] Predictably, his father regarded Bull Run as a sign from a righteous God that the North must cease its temporizing over slavery. The indomitable abolitionist avowed that he would invade the slave states "with arms for the enslaved in one hand and a proclamation of liberty for the enslaved in the other, and cry, Havoc!"[16]

Pitt Fessenden's commitment to the Constitution and property rights, his long-standing caution over the legal status of slavery in the states, and his understandable reluctance to antagonize loyal southerners like Andrew Johnson made him a more hesitant warrior than his father but, like all his Republican colleagues, he understood the importance of slavery to grand strategy. The day after Bull Run he voted with his co-partisans for a confiscation act decreeing that any bondsman employed in the service of the Confederacy was "discharged" from his employment.[17] Northerners, he was convinced, would support any reasonable measures drafted by patriotic legislators to preserve the Union.

Fessenden's pragmatic response to the crisis was similarly evident in his approach to President Lincoln's extraordinary actions during the spring. After Sumter, Lincoln had taken it upon himself as commander-in-chief to call out state militias, suspend habeas corpus in certain areas, and proclaim a blockade of the southern coast. Before Congress convened Fessenden dismissed James Grimes's conservative fears about executive tyranny by indicating that "were I in Lincoln's place a small scruple would not detain me from doing what was needful."[18] He did not agree with his friend Jacob Collamer of Vermont that "the power to prosecute war and the manner of carrying on that war is entirely executive," but endorsed a controversial joint resolution legitimizing Lincoln's conduct after the event.[19] For the most part his ardent patriotism and Whiggish belief in active government impelled him to believe that the Constitution must be construed as broadly as possible if both it and the country were to survive the rebellion.

The senator's chief contribution to the war effort in the summer of 1861 was his painstaking work on behalf of the revenue-raising bills emanating from the House of Representatives. These included not only a measure authorizing Secretary Chase to borrow up to $250 million but also a detailed tariff act designed primarily to maximize government income.[20] The proposal to raise duties on most goods by an additional 10 percent did not please all Republicans. Charles Sumner claimed the move would "kill the bird that lays the golden egg" as well as antagonize foreign governments and hurt European workers.[21] This latter comment provoked an angry response from Fessenden, whose frustration with the egotistical Sumner (a fervent Anglophile at this early stage of the Civil War) would increase steadily over time. Insisting that the country was prosperous enough to go on buying foreign goods even at increased prices, he described the Massachusetts senator's reference to European concerns as "nothing less than an insult." He was, he said sarcastically, "willing to take all the risk of the righteous indignation of people abroad who think they do not make quite so much money out of us as they ought."[22]

Even at this early stage of the conflict Fessenden regarded the Civil War as a great patriotic struggle in which everyone, regardless of their station in northern society, had a part to play. He made this point clear when supporting his colleague James Simmons's proposal for an innovative national income tax as a substitute for the House's more modest proposal. Simmons, a Rhode Island Republican, based his amendment on British precedent from the Napoleonic Wars. Fessenden, aware like Simmons that western Republicans were keen to shift the tax burden from land to more liquid assets, asserted that an income tax would ensure that "the burdens will be more equalized on all classes of the community, more especially on those who are able to bear them." Battlefield defeats would not sway his underlying confidence in northerners' commitment to Union victory. "I believe all this nation is disposed to do its duty—," he iterated soberly just four days after Bull Run, "the Congress, the Executive, the members of the executive government, the Army, the Navy, the people . . . [I]f we keep on in that line, although we may make mistakes and commit errors and fall short of our duty, as human nature always must, from its imperfections; yet, bearing with each other, making proper allowances for each other, retaining the same spirit with which we began, I have no question that we shall come to a fortunate and successful issue."[23]

By the time Congress adjourned in early August 1861, Fessenden was exhausted from his labors yet convinced that he had helped to lay the foundations for future success. "Gen. Greeley and other fools," he told Lizzy, "are now content to hold their tongues and permit military matters to be managed by military men." However, while he was certain that "every provision for the Govt. that can be made by legislation" had been made, he had doubts about the quality of the president and his cabinet. These concerns increased in late summer when Lincoln, wary of alienating opinion in the loyal border slave states and determined to prevent military officers from asserting powers vested in him as commander-in-chief, rescinded a military order issued by Major General John C. Frémont emancipating the slaves of Missouri Rebels. Eager for tougher action against traitors, the senator from Maine considered Frémont's action statesmanlike. He fired off a supporting letter to the self-promoting commander and privately described the president's countermand as "very foolish"— "a most weak and unjustifiable concession to the Union men of the border States . . . who are haunted by this Slavery demon, night and day."[24]

By November, Fessenden's conviction that Congress had done all it could to prepare the ground for victory had begun to evaporate. Major General George B. McClellan's Army of the Potomac, the North's chief fighting force east of the Appalachians, had made no forward movement beyond a botched attempt to cross the Potomac at Ball's Bluff. Salmon Chase's insistence that the country's commercial banks must cooperate with the administration on a hard-money basis contributed to their suspension of specie payments at the end of the year, an action that threatened to plunge the country into economic crisis as well as deprive the government of essential funds. James Grimes, appalled by Lincoln's recent decision to remove Frémont from command, urged his friend to play a decisive role in the upcoming session of Congress. "If you determine," he told Fessenden, "to probe the sore spots to the bottom, and that right shall be done, we can inaugurate a new order of things, and the country can be saved. You have followers—you can control the Senate. The wicked fear you, and will flee before you. But, if you rest quietly in your seat, we shall go on from one enormity to another."[25] The ensuing session, likely to be "a session of Congress as the world never saw before," would test Pitt Fessenden's political skills to the limit.[26]

The Broker Politician

Prominent among those skills was Fessenden's ability to maintain a functioning relationship between congressional Republicans and their leader, Abraham Lincoln. Drawing strength from his position as one of the most prominent centrists in Washington, his brokerage efforts were never entirely successful—partly because he was less disciplined in his dealings with Senate colleagues than he was in his public comments on the administration. Despite his private lack of enthusiasm for the latter, however, he saw no alternative except to back the president, hoping against hope that executive action and congressional backing for tougher measures against the Rebels would deliver that elusive final victory.

Fessenden left Portland in late November, traveling to Washington via Boston, where he interrupted his journey to consult with John Murray Forbes. Chase and he needed the advice of "practical men," he told Forbes before setting off.[27] By December 1 he was installed in Mrs. Chipman's boarding house on Seventh Street with like-minded Republicans, including Grimes and Senators Collamer and Solomon Foot of Vermont. Moses, his black messenger, apprised him of the latest gossip on Mrs. Lincoln's notorious overspending. Though fond of Moses, he was less impressed with the elderly chambermaid who, he informed Lizzy, was "not only coloured, but particularly disagreeable both in looks & odor."[28]

Business in the second session of the Thirty-seventh Congress was dominated by Republican attempts to press for a more vigorous prosecution of the war. The limited actions of the summer's special session had failed to yield significant military progress and Republicans of all stripes were thirsting to get tough with traitors. Fessenden shared this objective but he differed from some of his more outspoken colleagues in considering it unwise "to tell the Country in advance that we have lost all confidence in everybody."[29] Though his efforts throughout the war were characterized by patriotic self-restraint, he acquiesced to the creation of the Joint Committee on the Conduct of the War. Prompted by the disaster at Ball's Bluff as well as the broader drift in Union military affairs, the committee was seen by some congressmen as a means of influencing operational strategy. Fessenden had no desire to do this; wars, in his view, should be fought by soldiers not politicians. Nevertheless, he saw no harm in warning executive officers that Congress was on their case.[30] It was "our bounden duty," he told senators on December 9, "to keep an anxious, watchful eye over all the executive agents who are carrying on the war at the direction of the people, whom we represent." This opinion was occasioned by his conviction that while the president (as commander-in-chief) and his generals must plan campaigns and direct battles, civilian legislators had a constitutional right and responsibility as the people's representatives to oversee the war. "Sir," he announced gravely, "we are not under the command of the military of this country. They are under ours as a Congress; and I stand here to maintain it."[31]

Despite his Whiggish belief in Congress's primacy over the president (a conviction grounded in his reading of the Constitution as well as his appreciation of Parliament's dominant role in modern British history) and his dim view of the administration, Fessenden did not want to endanger the Union war effort by indulging in public criticism of executive policy. This was evident in his refusal to join some of his peers in requiring Secretary of State William H. Seward to explain the arbitrary arrest of civilians in the loyal border states. Although no law existed to support these actions, he was willing to justify them because they were necessary to protect the government, even while agreeing with Lyman Trumbull and other colleagues fearful of encroaching despotism that legislators must be vigilant of "the first approach to any exercise of illegal power that is not fully justified by the pressing exigency of the hour."[32]

Fessenden's pragmatism in the service of the national interest was plain throughout the session. This was especially true with regard to his conduct on financial measures. In early December, just weeks before the banks suspended specie payments, Secretary Chase had reported that spending on the war was running out of control. The amount of revenue collected would be 30 percent below the figure anticipated the previous summer while expenditures would exceed the original estimate by nearly 70 percent.[33] Urgent action was essential if the government was to pay soldiers and contractors and thereby continue the war. Wedded now to the so-called Dutch System of deficit finance used successfully by the British since the late seventeenth century, Chase called on Congress to increase domestic taxes and import duties on coffee, tea, and sugar in order to make government loans more attractive to investors.[34] The chairman of the Senate Finance Committee had already developed a good working relationship with Chase and understood the Ohioan's desperate need for funds. Indeed, much of his energy during the session was expended on fashioning and then securing passage of complex tariff and internal revenue measures.

Before he could grapple with the complexities of taxation, Fessenden was greatly exercised by a controversial bill originating in the House Ways and Means Committee. The measure not only authorized Chase to market $500 million of government five-twenty bonds but also provided for a substantial issue of legal-tender Treasury notes (popularly known as "greenbacks") that were to be irredeemable in specie. As it came before the Senate, the new loan bill authorized Chase to issue $150 million in greenbacks as government-backed currency. Fessenden placed the measure in the hands of his deputy, John Sherman of Ohio, knowing that he could not personally advocate an innovation that he, like several members of his own committee, regarded as inflationary and therefore inimical to sound finance.

Although Chase, a reluctant convert to greenbacks, asked Fessenden not to remove the legal-tender clause from the House loan bill after passage on February 6, the senator's conscience prevented him from complying fully with this request.[35]

"Tormented . . . day and night for weeks" by the prospect of flooding the economy with inflationary scrip and with leading financial experts divided and uncertain in their responses, Fessenden made public his concerns on February 12. Acknowledging that he would use "the strong arm of the Government to any extent in order to accomplish the purpose in which we are engaged," he nevertheless told his colleagues that the legal-tender measure would encourage "bad morality" by promoting inflation and thereby privileging debtors over creditors. More than that it would allow the English, the country's principal foreign investors, to accuse the United States of "bad faith," a contention which, he said, "touches my pride."[36]

Predictably, the senator voted against the greenback clause on February 13.[37] However, he did not ignore Chase's counsel entirely. After ensuring that the interest on government bonds must be paid in coin not paper, he swallowed his doubts and supported the bill on final passage.[38] The insertion of this crucial provision was intended to demonstrate the good faith of the government in the eyes of domestic investors and foreign observers. Because Chase now saw bond sales as the chief means of financing the war, it meant that Americans would go on paying heavily for the war long after it had ended. Fessenden was untroubled by this unnerving prospect. The United States, he observed, was "one of the richest, one of the most favored [countries], in all particulars, on the globe."[39] Its robust, elastic economy could bear the expense of paying off its debt in gold. The servicing process would be burdensome but the pain induced was necessary to counteract the harm done by the greenbacks to the country's reputation and to the moral health of the community. The addition of the specie clause, the urgency of the situation, and his desire to preserve a united front thus enabled Fessenden to endorse a measure of dubious financial probity. The legal-tender clause had been "odious" to him, he confided to Pike. "I voted against it, but sustained the bill. The specie for interest saved it, people say, and *that* was mine."

One of Pitt Fessenden's chief complaints at the beginning of 1862 was that Lincoln's cabinet lacked zeal and ability. "Everybody is grumbling because nothing is done, and there are no symptoms that anything will be done," he reported, "The truth is that no man can be found who is equal to this crisis in any branch of the government."[40] Although pleased by Lincoln's decision to dismiss Simon Cameron in December, he was skeptical when the president named Edwin M. Stanton to replace him as secretary of war. Although Stanton had helped to energize the Buchanan administration after joining the cabinet for a brief term during the secession crisis, Fessenden was concerned that the Pennsylvania-born lawyer was a War Democrat rather than a sound Republican. He immediately delayed Senate confirmation of the appointment in order to seek further information. Secretary Chase, a keen supporter of Stanton like his cabinet colleague William Seward, immediately invited the powerful senator to vet the new appointee. After a long interview at which Chase was also present, Fessenden was relieved to discover that Stanton was as earnest and energetic a patriot as himself. "We agreed on every point—," he told Lizzy after his report to Senate Republicans had helped to secure Stanton's confirmation, "the duties of a Secretary of War—the conduct of the war—the negro question—and everything else." He talked at length to Lincoln about the appointment on the same day and found the president well meaning but "sadly deficient in the same qualities essential for a ruler in times like these. Stanton will, I hope, be of great benefit in *stiffening* the Cabinet—a thing which it much needs."[41]

Fessenden and Lincoln would never develop a close working relationship. The president's informal style masked a clear-sighted intelligence that Fessenden, reserved in his dealings with most people and perhaps too stiff himself to appreciate Lincoln's unrefined western manners and love of popular satire, was slow to appreciate. The commander-in-chief's readiness to propitiate loyal slaveholders and northern Democrats in order to build the broadest possible Union-saving coalition also hindered their relations, the more so as Fessenden became convinced that tough measures were necessary to defeat the rebellion. But it would be wrong to suggest that the two politicians were far apart on most matters of war policy. They had much in common. Both men were centrist Republicans with a shared Whig past, a preference for what they regarded as practical over utopian measures, and a conviction that the law of war empowered the government to take any reasonable action to defend itself. They were agreed too that slavery was a national evil and that the war presented an opportune moment to destroy it. Both recognized the relevance of emancipation to grand strategy, even if they differed subtly over the means to destroy it.

Among Edwin Stanton's private reassurances in the interview with Fessenden was a promise that he would court-martial any officer who returned fugitive slaves.[42] In the spring of 1861 most northerners had backed a war to save the Union, not to abolish slavery. Nearly a year after Fort Sumter growing numbers of them were concluding that military victory required vigorous action against the Confederacy and the peculiar institution that underpinned it. Some were even speculating that the old Constitution was unfit for purpose and should be abandoned in the desperate struggle for national survival. Fessenden's typically Whiggish (and neo-Federalist) preference for broad construction as well as the innate respect for the Constitution that he shared with most of the lawyer-politicians in Congress dissuaded him from cutting loose entirely from the republic's founding charter. "We are contending, fighting to restore the Constitution and the laws of the country," he reminded senators at the end of January 1862. "Let us be careful not to violate them ourselves."[43]

However, in contrast to northern conservatives, Fessenden was ready to use federal power against slavery—the root cause of the rebellion as well as a central prop of the Confederate war effort. In supporting a landmark bill to abolish slavery in Washington, he averred that Republicans "would rejoice to see slavery abolished everywhere, that they would rejoice if it no longer existed, that they feel it to be a blot upon our fair institutions and a curse to the country," and that this had always been his own personal opinion.[44]

Where he agreed with Lincoln and differed from abolitionists like his father was his reluctance to use what he saw as unconstitutional means to destroy the peculiar institution. Adhering to an antislavery interpretation of the Constitution, Samuel Fessenden told him that every slave should be discharged upon a writ of habeas corpus. "If you would save your name from the curses of coming generations," he exhorted, "and receive the blessing of all the good and virtuous of the present[,] vote Slavery out of existence wherever it is found to exist within the jurisdiction of the U States."[45] Though sympathetic to the antislavery crusade, Pitt Fessenden was disinclined to play fast and loose with the protection afforded to property rights in the country's fundamental law. Abolition was bound to come, he advised Samuel, but he doubted that Congress possessed "any power of legislation in time of war that it does not possess in time of peace," and held that emancipation would result inevitably from slave unrest and military action.[46] The result of these convictions was that Fessenden found himself increasingly at odds with Senate Radicals. Charged with piloting vital but prosaic revenue-raising measures through the Senate, he struggled to keep his temper in check when colleagues tried to secure precious debating time for what he regarded as pointless antislavery measures.

On occasions during the first seven months of 1862 Fessenden appeared perfectly capable of voting like a Radical. Urged on by antislavery men like Governor John A. Andrew of Massachusetts as well as his insistent parent, he supported not only abolition in the District of Columbia and the western territories but also U.S. recognition of the black republics of Haiti and Liberia.[47] He also opposed attempts to attach amendments to the District Emancipation Bill that provided for the colonization or apprenticeship of blacks emancipated in the capital.[48] His actions on the Militia Bill were similarly progressive, at least insofar as they aimed to provide for black military service and liberate enlisted runaway slaves (and their relations) whose ownership was claimed by Rebel slave masters.[49]

Unlike the more ardent abolitionists in the party, however, he balked at this relatively early stage of the war at interfering with the human property of loyal slaveholders, endorsed the use of slave labor in federal installations such as forts and dockyards, and opposed Charles Sumner's attempt to end the prohibition against black testimony in U.S. courts.[50] He seemed reluctant, too, to take excessively harsh measures against secessionists. In late February he and the majority of centrist Republican senators joined Democrats and border-state Unionists in the chamber to defeat an attempt by Sumner to prevent Benjamin Stark, the newly appointed senator from Oregon, from taking his seat.[51] There was abundant evidence that Stark was a secessionist sympathizer and a majority of Republicans, including centrists like Trumbull and Grimes, believed he should not be seated. Fessenden initially called for the matter to be investigated by the Judiciary Committee, an unprecedented act in itself that he defended on the grounds that "the times are those when we are compelled to make precedents."[52] When the committee concluded that Stark's comments should not prevent him from taking his seat, he grudgingly counseled compliance. Though Stark's language had been "very reprehensible," he said, the power of expelling senators was a dangerous one and should be used sparingly.[53]

Sumner took the ensuing defeat badly. The next day he expressed astonishment at the course of Stark's Republican defenders. Fessenden bridled at the attack and assailed the Massachusetts Radical for his constant "harangues" and claims that "the Senate would stultify itself by not following his lead." He did not appreciate this assault on his independence: "I do not like this style, sir. I am responsible for what I do."[54] On this occasion the two powerful New Englanders quickly buried the hatchet in public.[55] Such protestations of mutual friendship, however, were becoming increasingly hollow. "If I could cut the throats of about half a dozen Republican Senators, (figuratively speaking)," he confided, "I should use the knife as readily as I ever did upon an ugly looking shrub. Sumner would be the first victim, as by far the greatest fool in the lot."[56]

Fessenden's differences with the Radicals over punitive measures were most apparent during protracted debates over confiscation measures during the spring and summer of 1862. Property confiscation was conceived as much as an instrument for punishing traitors as it was for emancipating slaves. Lyman Trumbull's bill, introduced at the start of the session, confiscated Rebel property by *in rem* proceedings and liberated all slaves captured or fleeing from their masters.[57] While Fessenden had voted for the largely ineffectual First Confiscation Act the previous August, he seriously doubted whether Congress or indeed the president possessed the legal power to seize the property of southern civilians on such a vast scale. If any agency had such authority it was the army. "The war power," in his view, was "competent to dispose of all such questions, as they arise in the progress of our armies." He simply did not see "how our laws are to travel any faster than our armies—for where we have no foothold our laws have no force, having no aid from judicial power."[58]

When debate resumed later in the spring, Fessenden, like most of his fellow centrists, continued to exhibit little enthusiasm for confiscation and made more than one attempt to thwart Lyman Trumbull's revised bill. On May 6 the Illinoisan bitterly accused Fessenden of opposing confiscation. The latter, aware that punishing traitors was popular at home, denied the charge but his contention that he favored confiscating Rebel property "under the Constitution" made it clear where his allegiances lay.[59] The Radicals' irritation at his preference for a watered-down bill was often palpable. On May 19 Fessenden asked his colleagues to support one of the limited measures recently reported by a select committee. The committee contained a majority of pro-confiscation Republicans, he said, and there was a duty on all to compromise on what was really "a stringent bill." Irked, Ben Wade retorted that he was "not in a mood to stand very much lecturing in the Senate or anywhere else." Fessenden spoke of conciliation. "Where," he added bitterly, "did he [the senator from Maine] ever concede anything?"[60]

While Pitt Fessenden did vote for a select committee bill on June 28, this relatively weak confiscation measure failed to satisfy the House, where Radical and conservative influences were stronger. A subsequent conference committee report was then amended by the lower chamber and finally passed by the Senate on July 12 with the backing of most Republicans, including centrists like himself. Because the new act allowed *in rem* proceedings in all cases, it was more sweeping than Fessenden wanted. However, the recent failure of McClellan's drive on Richmond in the Peninsula Campaign had strengthened popular support for confiscation and, though he privately considered congressional confiscation nothing less than "a humbug," he believed "something must pass" in order to satisfy the public's growing clamor for hard-war policies against the Confederacy.[61] Though the bill contained no effective enforcement mechanism, its provisions for the emancipation of all slaves belonging to Rebels found within Union lines and for the enrollment of blacks in the armed forces of the United States sent out a powerful signal to the loyal and disloyal alike.

At this juncture President Lincoln made known his opposition to the new confiscation bill. Unbeknown to congressional Republicans, he was already on the verge of issuing an executive edict emancipating the slaves in Rebel-held territory. However, no Radical himself, he considered elements of the confiscation statute unlawful. Fessenden, perhaps recalling John Tyler's mistakes, knew that a veto would be disastrous for the party. Confiscation was popular in the North and had the support of congressional Republicans. "I fear that the Prest. will be mad enough to veto the Confiscation bill," he wrote confidentially. "Such an act will disappoint, & I fear will dishearten, the country."[62]

Although Fessenden was exhausted at the end of a laborious session, he agreed to visit the White House on the night of July 15 to ascertain the president's views, having been solicited to do so by "several members." Discovering that Lincoln would sign the bill if it did not work a forfeiture on property beyond the life of the individuals attainted, he returned to the upper chamber to watch Senator Daniel Clark of New Hampshire (who had accompanied him to the White House) introduce two explanatory amendments designed to obviate the president's objections. Ben Wade, pugnacious as ever, implied that Fessenden had dishonored the Senate by his interview but the Portlander, understandably irritated, was unbowed. Fessenden said he had his own reservations about legislating on confiscation and that the president had every right to express his misgivings about the bill. In a powerful statement he then appealed to Republicans to avoid the political damage likely to ensue from having to pass the measure over Lincoln's veto. "If all the essential features of the bill can be retained, or if the greater number of the most essential features can be secured by yielding one, . . . what is the objection, as a matter of common sense and common prudence, to taking the best we can and the most we can under such circumstances?"[63] While Radicals knew the amended bill would have little practical impact, Fessenden had won an important political battle—brokering a workable compromise over confiscation in order to prevent a potentially disastrous split between congressional Republicans and the president. The explanatory resolutions were attached and Lincoln signed the resulting bill into law on July 17.

Wade's criticism highlighted the personal cost of Fessenden's bridge leadership in the wartime Congress. By the middle of 1862 many Republicans were convinced that the administration was soft on traitors. The war was going badly yet Lincoln continued to employ incompetent generals, appease border-state slaveholders, appoint inordinate numbers of Democrats to high office, and shun abolition as a war measure. Fessenden harbored similar misgivings. "I am, at times, almost in despair," he told Lizzy Warriner, shortly after McClellan (a Democrat) had belatedly sallied forth from Washington in March 1862 only to find wooden guns arrayed against him in the abandoned Confederate lines at Centerville. "McClellan's every movement," he wrote bitterly, "has been a failure. And yet the President will keep him in command, and leave our destiny in his hands. I am, at times, almost in despair. Well—it cannot be helped. We went in for a rail-splitter, and we have got one."[64] Despite his lack of enthusiasm for Lincoln, Fessenden conceded the president's extraordinary authority as commander-in-chief even while insisting on the legislature's powers of oversight. Crucially, therefore, most of his criticism of the president was limited to private correspondence. Throughout the difficult middle years of the war, he not only defended Lincoln's actions in public but also voted to increase his powers—all in the belief that the day-to-day running of the conflict could be accomplished most efficiently by the executive branch.

While Fessenden's efforts to prevent a breach with the president testified to his skills as a mediator, he was never, as the historian Allan Bogue has astutely observed, "the complete broker."[65] The senator's tendency to berate colleagues for their failure to comprehend the primary importance of financial measures and his lack of enthusiasm for the Radicals' crusade against slavery offended many Republicans. So did his growing irritation with colleagues who, not unlike the crusading Portland prohibitionist Neal Dow, appeared "to think that they are the representatives of all righteousness."[66] When angry, he found it hard to curb his notoriously sharp tongue, a fearsome weapon of debate. In December 1861 he clashed briefly with the blunt-spoken Wade. "The difference between my friend from Ohio and myself," he snapped, "is that my acts may be important, and my words never are; but his words are always more important than his acts." The deflating comment elicited a ripple of laughter in the chamber but it was hardly calculated to foster intra-party unity.

Regional tensions between western and eastern Republicans also impaired Fessenden's effectiveness as a Senate leader. Despite his growing friendship with the gruff Iowan James Grimes, a fellow son of New Hampshire, most western Republicans regarded him not only as an inveterate promoter of New England interests but also as an opponent of their own rapidly developing section. There was substance to this perception. Fessenden voted for some of the important developmental legislation passed by the Republican-controlled Congress in 1862, notably the Homestead Act and the Land-Grant Colleges Act.[67] However, he supported this statist legislation not primarily because of its impact on the West but because he believed that it would strengthen the republic in time of war and that Republican unity required his assent. Personally, he had no great love for a region he had not visited since his trip with Webster and which, in a sarcastic aside on the hyperbolic rhetoric of western politicians, he once referred to as "the great West, the almighty West, the all-pervading West, the without-which-nothing-else-lives-in-the-world . . . West."[68]

Keenly aware of the region's political power, Fessenden was far too proud to yield automatically to its needy representatives in Congress. This was particularly apparent in his critical responses to westerners demanding money for Indian treaties. He rightly regarded these treaties as expensive land-grabbing exercises. On May 13, he refused to support a recommendation from the Indian Affairs Committee that $50,000 should be appropriated to fund negotiations with the Nez Perce on the Pacific coast. Instead of allowing whites to encroach on Indian reservations, he said, "I would drive them off at the point of the bayonet, and with powder and ball, whatever might be the expense." His sympathies, he added, were "with the Indians in such a question, because they have the right of it; they are human beings, and have a right to their soil."[69] It was a characteristically bold remark but not one that was calculated to win over western Republicans heavily dependent on the votes of Indian-hating settlers. Fessenden's subsequent failure to vote for the Pacific Railroad Bill on June 20 had more to do with his astute conviction that the project was a recipe for corruption than any feelings he might have had for Native Americans, but it was similarly unlikely to win him friends among his western colleagues.[70]

Despite his limitations as a party unifier, Fessenden was a remarkably effective legislator. His success rate, in terms of motions made and carried, was one of the best in the wartime Senate.[71] His views, especially those on financial and constitutional matters, were regarded as authoritative by many Republicans, especially by the large body of New Englanders with whom he associated closely—men like Henry B. Anthony and James Simmons of Rhode Island, Jacob Collamer and Solomon Foot of Vermont, and James Dixon and Lafayette Foster of Connecticut—and the crotchety James Grimes, who readily admitted the "magnetic" power Fessenden exercised over his own "wayward nature."[72] These men were centrist-oriented Republicans who prioritized saving the Union over eradicating slavery and racial prejudice and who were keen to find constitutional justifications for action even in time of war. Although they did not constitute an organized grouping, they were far more respectful of Fessenden's extensive knowledge of parliamentary rules and what they saw as his sound judgment on public policy than they were of outspoken antislavery politicians like Sumner.[73]

This did not make Fessenden "the Senate Republican leader," as one historian has described him."[74] There were too many egos in the upper chamber for any one individual to assume this role. Nor, because voting records shifted frequently during the war, can Fessenden simply be described as the leader of a loosely defined moderate bloc. (His support for hard-war measures actually made him look like a Radical at the conflict's midpoint.) There is no doubt, however, that he was generally regarded as one of the Senate's leading minds, that his debating skills were peerless, and that none of his Republican colleagues exerted a greater influence over policy-making than he did. Although other senators, even the abolitionist Sumner, maintained closer involvement with President Lincoln, the high degree of respect with which Fessenden was held among executive officers and his congressional peers gave him the edge when it came to intra-party brokerage. The senator from Maine was one of the most powerful Republicans in wartime Washington, the ire he sometimes elicited among his co-partisans as much a reflection of that power as it was of its limits.

It was on the Internal Revenue Bill—"this infernal tax bill" he called it—that Fessenden performed some of his most unsung labor during the late spring of 1862.[75] Secretary Chase and the bankers on whom he depended for funds were insistent that taxes must be increased to help pay for the war. The chairman of the Senate Finance Committee broadly concurred. The trick was to raise sufficient revenue without further alienating a public starved of morale-boosting victories in the field. Passed by the House in April, the measure was exceedingly cumbersome. Intended to maximize revenue and spread the resulting burden as widely as possible, it imposed a new income tax and levied new or higher taxes on a broad range of consumer goods, corporate activities, and occupations. Fessenden confronted a range of views in committee. Some members favored drafting an entirely new bill, a potentially futile strategy that he fought successfully.[76] He spent much undocumented time with lobbyists who inundated the Capitol—railroad managers and steamboat owners, for example—hearing their views on the proposed legislation.[77] After canvassing a spectrum of opinion, he threw his weight behind a bill that combined a vast expansion of excise taxes with a graduated income tax.

The Senate debated the measure every day for two weeks in late May and early June 1862.[78] Fessenden doggedly defended the revised bill against Republicans who opposed taxes on farmers, who viewed taxation as a weapon of emancipation in the border states, or who regarded any increase in taxes as political suicide.[79] Against these objections he wielded a battery of arguments, none more potent than his contention that the government needed the money, that northerners of every class were willing to suffer in pursuit of victory, and that Republicans should have the courage to do their duty.[80] The bill was far from perfect. He was under no illusions about that. It did not come close to yielding the $120 to $130 million that he predicted. Yet it did pass, almost unanimously, on June 6 with a total of 315 amendments.[81] It was a commonplace achievement but an important one nonetheless—not least because, in creating an Internal Revenue Bureau, it further increased the reach and powers of the central state.

By the summer of 1862 Pitt Fessenden was worn out with his efforts during one of the most momentous sessions of Congress in American history. Though still remarkably trim, he was now in his late fifties. His hair was thin and streaked with silver, his whiskers completely gray. The tax bill had been "an enormous labor" and he remained deeply concerned about the condition of the Union cause.[82] Like most of his co-partisans—Lincoln among them—he was becoming radicalized by Confederate resistance. On July 9, one week after McClellan's army had finally fallen back from Richmond on the Peninsula, he made his strongest pitch yet in support of arming and liberating the slaves. "Why," he asked, "should men who come to our camps in the enemy's country tendering service, tendering information, tendering their hands, their arms, their lives to aid us, be repelled and driven out, and our own soldiers sacrificed in performing the duties that they are so ready to perform? It is contrary to every principle of warfare." He was, he admitted, a "conservative" man, "that is, I am a tolerably prudent, cautious man; I do not say things here in my place except on deliberation." But, he added, "I say this upon full reflection, deliberately, because I think it ought to be said, and to be said in public, that this mode of white kid-glove warfare will not do."[83] Privately, Fessenden was even more critical of the administration's conduct of the war. General McClellan, he confided to Pike at The Hague, had "well nigh ruined one of the noblest armies in the world." The secretary of state, he thought, was primarily to blame for "[o]ur miserable policy of tenderness & conciliation, the maggot in Seward's brain."[84]

Stiffening Abe

Fessenden's lack of enthusiasm for the president, his secretary of state, and the army high command was shared by many of his Republican peers. The war was not going well for the North in the second half of 1862 and the administration was widely seen as inept. Matters were about to get even worse and the senator from Maine soon found himself taking an active role in congressional efforts to inject more steel into the country's floundering war effort. His frustration at the government's conduct of the war would induce him to build one of the more radical voting records in the third session of the Thirty-seventh Congress, the most active legislative gathering yet in American history.

The Confederates took the offensive in the wake of McClellan's abject display on the Peninsula. Raiding north in August to relieve the pressure on Richmond, Robert E. Lee's Army of Northern Virginia crushed a newly organized Federal army at Manassas at the end of the month. Among the Union dead at Second Bull Run was Fessenden's youngest son, Sam. Despite running away again after his adventures in Kansas in 1856, Sam had found enough self-discipline to graduate from Bowdoin five years later. His death came only months after his older brother Frank had been wounded at Shiloh. Another brother, James, was in service on the Carolina coast. Fessenden had loved Sam despite his rebellious streak. He was hardly consoled by the fact that he had died a patriot's death yet bore the news as stoically as anyone belonging to the rising tide of grieving northerners. "His loss has afflicted me severely," he wrote Grimes from Portland, "and the fact that two others of my sons are exposed to the same fate renders me unquiet and unhappy—but I have nothing for it but patience & submission."[85]

Pitt Fessenden's faith in McClellan was not enhanced by the general's inability to trap and defeat Lee at the bloody Battle of Antietam. This brutal engagement, however, represented a strategic success for the North because the Confederates were forced to retreat. Reluctant to exhibit any sign of desperation, Abraham Lincoln had held back his preliminary Emancipation Proclamation until the country received word of a military victory. Antietam gave him what he wanted and on September 22 he used the justification of military necessity to issue a judiciously worded edict declaring free all slaves in enemy territory on January 1, 1863. Fessenden failed to be impressed by this breath-taking maneuver. Believing that the slaves could only be liberated by the advancing Union army, he regarded the proclamation as a cynical move to satisfy the demands of antislavery radicals.[86] He even used one of his characteristically dismissive phrases, "brutum fulmen"—the same term he had used to dismiss southern talk of secession—to describe what he saw as the document's lack of practical significance.[87] The senator, it is clear, ignored the edict's unprecedented recognition of slaves as human beings and the portentous fact that it crushed the hopes of conservative Democrats who hoped to restore the antebellum Union. Regardless of what Fessenden thought about Lincoln's action, Republicans were now visibly united on the imperative need to destroy slavery in order to save the country. If the North emerged victorious, slavery was doomed.

Fessenden continued to take a bleak view of the canny president, partly because he was genuinely perplexed by Lincoln's refusal to dismiss McClellan after he failed to destroy Lee's invading army. In a ringing phrase, he privately condemned the president as "the Slave of McLellan [sic]," a reference to what he saw as Lincoln's fear of the general's popularity within the army.[88] "In truth," he told Chase, "I see nothing ahead but disaster. At Antietam we had the rebellion in our power. All accounts agree . . . that an advance the next day would have been decisive. It was not made, and today the enemy is again strong. Yet, McLellan [sic], in spite of his treachery, or cowardice, or imbecility, is still in command, and we, with all our troops, are daily snubbed & insulted. What is the Govt. thinking of?" Fessenden's patience was wearing thin. "I was silent during all the last session," he recalled, "upon the pig-headed obstinacy and stupidity which kept incompetent generals in command, and was destroying our armies to no purpose. May God forgive me! If I live to take my seat once more, and this horrible abuse continues, I will try to redeem my errors."[89]

Lincoln finally dismissed McClellan after what, for the administration, were the disappointing midterm elections of autumn 1862. Although the Republicans retained control of most free-state governorships and legislatures, the Democrats won morale-boosting victories in New York, New Jersey, Illinois, and Indiana and secured a net gain of thirty-four in the House of Representatives.[90] McClellan's sacking was "a great step," Fessenden told John Murray Forbes, but one that should have been taken before the ill-fated Peninsula Campaign. Fear of offending the Democrats, he thought, was to blame for Union disasters on the battlefield. He hoped the party's recent losses would teach Lincoln there was nothing to be gained from appeasing the Republicans' political enemies at home. "The only way to get the support of the Democracy," he commented, "is to show that you don't fear them."[91]

In mid-December the new Union commander Ambrose Burnside directed the Army of the Potomac in a futile assault on strong Confederate positions south of the Rappahannock River at Fredericksburg. Federal casualties (12,600) were more than twice as heavy as those of the Rebels. This morale-sapping defeat marked a low point of the war for northerners. Leading Republicans had already been discussing the urgent need for a shake-up of department heads to revive the cause. Forbes wanted Fessenden to join Lincoln's cabinet. Even Chase, he believed, lacked the senator's "uncompromising directness of will."[92] Fessenden dreaded such a prospect. No counsel could be effective, he feared, as long as Lincoln, surrounded as he had been by "toadies and office-seekers" since his election, remained convinced that he had been "specially chosen by the Almighty for this crisis."[93] Fredericksburg, however, transformed the situation. Desperate times required desperate remedies. Three days after the battle Fessenden was one of the ringleaders in an attempted senatorial coup against Seward, having been assured by Chase that the latter's rival grandee exercised an unhealthy influence over the president. Seward was widely regarded by northern Republicans as the chief opponent of tough measures against the Confederacy—the president's "evil genius" in the words of one leading newspaper editor.[94] Fessenden suspected that Lincoln was too dependent on Seward to remove him but now decided that he must act promptly to stave off impending national disaster.

The putsch began with a caucus of Republican senators on December 16. From the start Fessenden assumed the role of a patriotic mediator bent on galvanizing Lincoln but determined also not to humiliate him and to limit the immediate damage to the Republican-led wartime coalition, now relabeled (to attract pro-war Democrats) as the Union Party.[95] The first senators to speak at this closed gathering made it clear they wanted Seward dismissed and, presuming Chase's widely disseminated allegations about the lack of collective government to be accurate, insisted the president should consult regularly on important matters with his full cabinet. Fessenden's ally James Grimes actually called for a vote of no-confidence in the secretary of state, a motion which, if carried through, would have resulted in the Senate assuming the same powers as the British Parliament. Fessenden, primed by Chase, confirmed the existence of "a back-stairs influence which often controlled the apparent conclusions of the Cabinet itself" and acknowledged that it was time for senators to step beyond their customary sphere to save the nation. Yet he counseled caution. Rash action, he said, would not only alarm the country but also weaken the hands of the commander-in-chief. Probably out of deference to the minority of senators present who were unconvinced of Seward's guilt, he reported that "a secret influence" was controlling the president without actually naming its source. Apparently concurring with Fessenden that "without entire unanimity our action would not only be without force but productive of evil," the lawmakers adjourned to "give time for reflection."[96]

The Republican senators reconvened the next day unaware that Seward had been apprised of developments and that he had sent his resignation to the president. There were more harsh words in caucus. John Sherman blamed the president for the mess in which the country found itself after Fredericksburg. Lincoln, said the Ohioan, "had neither dignity, order, nor firmness."[97] Although Fessenden shared this

SAVING THE REPUBLIC, 1861–1864

view, it was not one he chose to articulate at the meeting. After much discussion the caucus resolved to appoint a committee to wait upon the president and secure a more vigorous prosecution of the war "by a change in and partial reconstruction of the Cabinet."[98] The senators also accepted, with modifications, a paper written by Jacob Collamer of Vermont that delineated their belief that Lincoln should make important decisions after obtaining the agreement of a majority of cabinet members.

The nine-man committee visited the White House on the evening of December 18. Collamer set the agenda by reading his paper and a frank discussion ensued. Fessenden spoke bluntly but without anger or malice. Senate Republicans, he attested, had confidence in the patriotism and integrity of the president but believed they had the right as his "constitutional advisers" to tender their advice in a time of emergency.[99] They held, he said, that it would be best for the country if major decisions were discussed thoroughly in cabinet. He stated frankly that Secretary Seward was widely regarded as an incubus on the war effort and that the administration must give military power to antislavery Republicans rather than conservative Democrats like McClellan. The president responded to these and other senators' comments by defending both Seward and the way his cabinet operated. Military victory was what the country wanted, he argued, and a change in the cabinet would not, by itself, secure this end. Lincoln ended the meeting on a conciliatory note by promising that he would examine Collamer's paper carefully. The senators left the White House at around 10:00 p.m. under the impression that he would take their counsel seriously.

Lincoln handled the crisis adroitly. Having no intention of surrendering his secretary of state, he summoned the cabinet, all bar Seward, to meet the following morning. Around the table at the White House he informed cabinet members of recent proceedings and told them that he "could not afford to lose" any of them.[100] Calculating that no one in the room, Chase included, would break ranks when publicly confronted with the accusations about Seward, he asked the cabinet to meet with the legislators later in the day. Chase squirmed but had to toe the line.

That evening the senators returned to the White House for what historian Allan Nevins described as "one of the most momentous meetings in the nation's history."[101] Ushered into an anteroom they were surprised to find cabinet members (Seward excepted) milling around and had little choice but to accept the president's request that the two groups should enter his office together. When Lincoln offered a vigorous defense of existing cabinet relations and invited department heads to comment on the legislators' concerns, Chase—having been maneuvered into the spotlight—confessed that major issues were normally discussed in collectivity and that unanimity usually prevailed. Although Fessenden was irritated by Chase's retreat, he pressed ahead. Recalling an incident when President John Quincy Adams had been overruled by his cabinet, he expressed his support for the principle of collective government while conceding significantly that the president should not be bound by cabinet members.[102] Postmaster General Montgomery Blair, scion of a Jacksonian family, was determined to thwart the designs of Radical Republicans. He responded with defiance, heatedly attacking the Whiggish notion of a plural executive—a position sustained by Attorney General Edward Bates and Secretary of the Navy Gideon Welles. Lincoln then asked the senators if they and their constituents believed Seward should resign, whereupon Fessenden grasped the nettle once again. He could not speak for his constituents, he said, because the issue had not been debated openly. However, he declared that many of Seward's former friends had lost confidence in the secretary and said that if the president was prepared to take the senators' advice he would ascertain their wishes.[103]

At this point the cabinet withdrew. Senator Fessenden then asked Lincoln if Seward had already resigned and, on being told that he had, inquired if the question now was whether he should be asked to withdraw that resignation. When Lincoln replied in the affirmative Fessenden made his boldest move of the evening, indeed of the entire war. Senator Ira Harris of New York had claimed the resignation would divide the party back home. Fessenden argued that any damage likely to accrue had already been done and that the withdrawal of Seward's resignation would not heal any divisions. He thus advised that Lincoln should accept the resignation and expressed his disappointment that the president had not consulted with senators before making cabinet appointments. When Lincoln voiced his fear that the cabinet would break up—that Chase and Stanton would also resign—the senators responded that this was not their aim. The meeting adjourned in the early hours of the morning without a final resolution.[104]

Fessenden's attempts to broker a consensual solution to the deep national and intra-party crisis induced by the Fredericksburg debacle exhibited his well-honed political skills to good effect. He worked carefully to maintain unity of purpose among Senate Republicans (to minimize dissent and maximize leverage) while aiming simultaneously to stiffen the executive arm of government without unduly wounding or antagonizing the commander-in-chief. Ultimately, of course, the failed coup served to demonstrate Lincoln's impressive leadership skills: the harassed Chase offered to leave the cabinet, famously allowing his exultant chief to reject both his resignation and that of Seward. However, even though the crisis proved that the president and not Congress controlled the government, it would be wrong to belittle the actions of his critics.[105] Fessenden exaggerated Seward's influence over Lincoln and had been far too willing to believe Chase's self-serving diagnosis of national ills, yet he acted from the best of motives and was far from delusional. He told his father the day after the second White House gathering that Lincoln, "an earnest and true man" lacking "dignity, order, and vigor," was unlikely to accept Seward's resignation because he could not get by without him. Yet, continued the senator, the very act of trying to get rid of Seward would be "productive of good."[106] Even though Fessenden hoped that pressure from New York might still unseat "the Svengali-like" secretary of state, he seemed content to have administered a lesson to the embattled administration—one intended to reduce Seward's putatively conservative influence on the president and thereby speed the onset of hard-war policies.[107] While some commentators were critical of Fessenden and his colleagues for their involvement in "the conspiracy" against Seward, the coup may not have been a complete failure.[108] According to historian David Donald, Lincoln made greater efforts that winter to consult with cabinet members, even requesting them to submit written opinions on whether he should veto a bill to admit the Unionist rump of Virginia as a state.[109] Attorney General Edward Bates, moreover, observed that in the wake of the senators' action, Seward and Stanton appeared more inclined to support what he regarded as radical measures.[110]

Convinced that an energized executive branch held the key to defeating the Confederacy and that "the safety of the Republic" was "the supreme law," Fessenden spent the winter helping to augment the president's war-making capacity—notably by indemnifying Lincoln for his suspension of habeas corpus and approving a bill that directed the government to draft able-bodied men into the armed forces of the United States.[111] The Conscription Act of February 1863 greatly expanded the reach of what, before the war, had been a relatively weak national state that had impinged directly on American citizens in only limited areas of their lives. Although Fessenden was a less enthusiastic state builder than some of his more radical colleagues (witness his opposition to the formation of a new Department of Agriculture the previous spring), his attachment to Whiggery had always led him to favor the creation of an effective national government.[112] In his view, the parlous condition of the Union after Fredericksburg merely underlined the case for a significant increase in federal power.

The senator's sometimes grudging support for centralizing and nationalizing legislation was most apparent in his willingness to endorse bold financial measures that he would not have accepted in peacetime. On February 13 he reported a Finance Committee amendment taxing the notes of state banks. The aim was to promote Chase's plan for a national banking system that would facilitate operations of the bond market on which the northern cause was so heavily dependent. Taxing the issues of state banks would pave the way for national banks empowered to issue the new legal-tender U.S. notes. The ambitious program was deeply unpopular with many Republicans, including Fessenden's centrist allies Collamer and Grimes, who disliked its erosion of state institutions. Fessenden shared many of their reservations, partly because he came from a region with the most robust state banking system in the country. Nevertheless, he dismissed opposition to the committee's proposal. Secretary Chase, he said, considered the measure essential and besides, he added pointedly, "[W]e are obliged to do in times like these what we would not do in times of a different character."[113] Fessenden was not so enamored of the National Currency Bill that he was willing to shepherd it through the Senate. Most of that work, "full of difficulty and detail," was left to John Sherman.[114] Crucially, however, he suppressed his doubts and voted yea on the final roll call, knowing full well that his opposition could easily have defeated the bill.[115] His continuing self-restraint was the product of his profound conviction that the citizens of a republic must restrain their own passions in pursuit of the collective good. Although he seriously doubted the wisdom of the greenbacks, he knew the importance in wartime of deferring to the executive power and the view of the majority. "Chase's Bank scheme has been no favourite with me from the beginning," he later confided to James Pike. "I yielded to it because he demanded it as essential to his financial success, & without which he would be responsible for nothing, and the President seconded his demand."[116]

William Pitt Fessenden's pragmatic stance on financial policy was not determined solely by his perception of national necessity. Many sectors of the northern economy were now booming and Chase's bond sales had proved remarkably successful, owing to the efforts of his marketing agent, the Philadelphia banker Jay Cooke. Early in 1863 the hard-pressed Senate Finance Committee sanctioned another $150,000 issue of greenbacks as well as nearly $1.5 billion of borrowing on the public credit in the next fiscal year. Fessenden's belated endorsement of the legal-tenders signified his realization that the American economy had been strong enough to withstand the shock of war—that it had in some respects benefited from the experience. The greenbacks, he reflected, had done much less harm than he feared, the effects mitigated by the elasticity of the economy and the people's confidence in the new notes. "Its daily and rapid conversion into bonds," he wrote of the government's paper currency, "speaks volumes, and our financial system must be regarded as a success."[117]

The war continued to radicalize Fessenden's racial views just as it did his attitude to financial matters. His mailbag contained letters pointing to strong support on the homefront and in the army for Congress's policy, now endorsed by the administration, of creating black regiments to fight the Confederacy.[118] He not only sanctioned the enlistment of blacks into the armed forces of the United States, but also began to vote like an antislavery radical on other race-related motions. During the early months of 1863 he endorsed Charles Sumner's attempts to bring about emancipation in Union-occupied Missouri by July 4, 1864, and to prohibit the exclusion of blacks on the Alexandria & Washington Railroad.[119] Fessenden had never been at the forefront of the humanitarian crusade for equal justice for blacks. Even the war had not dispelled his suspicion of abolitionists and Radical Republicans, who championed their moral certainties at the expense of practical measures to save the Union, and these votes did not, certainly, herald the onset of closer personal relations between Fessenden and Sumner. But the Portlander had always been sympathetic to the idea of equal rights for northern free blacks and knew that slavery had blighted national development in a variety of different ways. He sensed correctly that the time was right for a change in the way that blacks were treated under federal law. Aligned with his backing for a raft of hard-war measures, his support for decisive attacks on slavery and racial prejudice gave him, according to Allan Bogue, the fourth most radical voting record in the upper chamber during the first half of 1863.[120] For a politician who normally operated at the vital center of his party and who was certainly not a member of the party's ill-defined Radical faction, it was a remarkable shift in political conduct—one that revealed not only his capacity to grow with the times but also the exceptional nature of the times themselves.

Fessenden returned to Portland in the early spring convinced, as he had been two years previously, that he had done everything possible to promote northern victory. The session, he told his friend Freeman Morse on April 5, had been exceedingly "arduous." He thought that this "most remarkable Congress" had "discharged its great responsibility, if not with the most consummate wisdom, yet with great vigor & devotion. If the Country is to be saved, (and it is to be) Congress will have saved it." Lincoln, he added hyperbolically, had been made "a Dictator in all but the name. No Govt. on earth, not absolute, ever wielded such a power."[121] His doubts about the administration's competence, however, had not evaporated. In a letter to Pike on the same day, he bemoaned Seward's baleful influence on the war effort and blamed Chase for allowing him to stay in post. "Let the Cabinet look to it that there are no more failures," he wrote. "They must succeed before Congress meets again, or give place to others. They have chosen to stay, with the opinion & feeling of the country against them. The coming campaigns must be decisive, or they must retire in disgrace."[122]

Digging Deep

The initial signs on the battlefield were not good. Union armies on both sides of the Appalachians continued to encounter ferocious resistance from their Confederate opponents and in early May the senator's favorite general, tough-talking Joseph Hooker, was defeated by the audacious Robert E. Lee at Chancellorsville in yet another crushing setback for the Army of the Potomac.[123] Although Fessenden was preoccupied with family matters—Lizzy's husband had died in Pittsfield on May 25 while she was on a visit to Portland and he continued to fret about the safety of Frank and James in the army—his Washington contacts kept him informed on military developments and political gossip.[124] The journalist John W. Forney, a close ally of the president, told him at the start of June that Lincoln retained confidence in Hooker and the western general, Ulysses S. Grant, but that "the great want of men & approach of the warm season occasions much solicitude."[125] Forney wrote just days before Lee launched his second great raid into the North. Hooker lost his nerve as the Army of Northern Virginia advanced rapidly and was immediately replaced by George Meade, a competent commander whose steadiness in the face of Lee's assaults at Gettysburg resulted in a hard-fought Union victory on July 3. Grant took Vicksburg, the Rebel stronghold on the Mississippi, the next day. Although Meade's caution enabled Lee to retreat safely into Virginia, the two Union successes generated fresh optimism that the war's end was in sight at last.

Fessenden reckoned that the government could now safely delay the draft in Maine in order to maximize support for the ruling Union Party coalition in the September elections. He wrote to Secretary of War Stanton to this effect in late July. Stanton disagreed and replied that the draftees were needed to reinforce the Army of the Potomac, which had been depleted by its losses at Gettysburg. Although the secretary concurred that political requirements must not be overlooked, he reminded Fessenden that "military necessities will sometimes require a hazard to be run."[126] Although the Portlander remained on good terms with Stanton, it is unlikely that this response, matched as it was by Gideon Welles's refusal to act against antiwar

Democrats in the U.S. Navy Yard at Kittery, bolstered his faith in the effectiveness of the cabinet.[127] Fortunately for local Republicans their fears of a Copperhead surge in the polls proved groundless. The Union ticket was victorious by a majority of around twenty thousand.[128] Despite entrenched Peace Democrat opposition to the war, businessmen, lumbermen, and skilled workers in the shipyards were beneficiaries of the prosperity that was a by-product of rising government expenditures. "Such flourishing operations you never saw as now," commented one Maine Republican. "Abundance of money everywhere."[129]

Fessenden journeyed back to Washington at the beginning of December. The military situation was much improved after the summer's triumphs but the Confederates remained a stubborn foe. He boarded in more spacious quarters at a house on F Street, where he was waited upon by "a little negro boy."[130] Most of his working hours in the early days of the new Congress were spent finalizing the membership of committees, an irksome duty that nevertheless testified to his influence in the Senate. He spent some of his evenings playing euchre and drinking whiskey punch with James Grimes, his wife, and two pretty women, Mrs. White and Mrs. Paulding. Moses was often in attendance, always useful as a courier when Fessenden needed one. This was not, clearly, a relationship of equals and there is no direct evidence of what the outwardly loyal black servant really thought about his well-to-do employer. However, Moses felt secure enough to proffer advice and insights beyond his station. At one point that winter he told Fessenden that he would never get married as long as Lizzy was around to look after him. "Shrewd isn't he?" the senator wrote to his cousin who was now living permanently under his protection in the State Street house in Portland.[131]

In early December 1863 President Lincoln set the agenda for the forthcoming session of Congress. In his Proclamation of Amnesty and Reconstruction he declared his support for a liberal policy of reintegrating the southern states into the national fold. As soon as 10 percent of the adult male population of a Confederate state took an oath of future loyalty to the republic, he would initiate the process of restoration by ordering the formation of a Unionist state government committed to emancipation and the withdrawal of secession ordinances. Although Lincoln's proclamation was well received in Washington, Fessenden was underwhelmed. It was, he confided, "a silly performance, but he is lucky, & I hope it may work well. Think of telling the rebels they may fight as long as they can, and take a pardon when they have had enough of it."[132] Within weeks Unionists in Louisiana and Arkansas had established 10 percent governments with White House backing. The initial consensus waned quickly as many congressional Republicans began to question both the wisdom of proceeding with Reconstruction on such a flimsy basis and Lincoln's authority to direct the process himself.

While Pitt Fessenden had his own ideas about these subjects, his mind during the early months of 1864 was on other matters. He devoted much of his time as usual to financial measures. Having collected only $37.6 million in internal revenue by the end of 1863, the administration was in dire need of more money to fund the war effort and help raise new loans.[133] With more than a million men in the field and victory still elusive, the situation remained perilous. Chase's Treasury report released before Christmas revealed that the national debt was increasing at an alarming rate, that government revenues were insufficient to support war expenditures or interest payments, and that spending for fiscal 1863–64 would total a staggering $749 million. Manifestly, the only solution was to issue more bonds and impose higher taxation.

Fessenden was under no illusions about the need to act quickly. Despite his reservations about Chase's spineless conduct during the failed cabinet coup, he moved to expedite Senate action on revenue-raising bills originating in the House. One of these measures, H.R. 405, followed British precedent in targeting selected consumer goods such as alcohol and tobacco for heavy taxation. Significantly, however, Fessenden announced his committee's opposition to placing inordinate burdens on property. In February, for example, he oversaw passage of an amendment striking out the House's attempt to tax liquor stored by distillers in warehouses. This amendment (which angered temperance advocates) stemmed partly from the chairman's continuing determination not to reduce government income or stimulate political opposition by suppressing trade. But there was more to his opposition to swingeing taxes than this. Like all Republicans he embraced a vision of America as a society committed to the quintessential free-labor values of hard work and meritocracy. Senators, he announced on May 24 when opposing increased (and in his view discriminatory) taxes on incomes above $25,000 a year, would understand the importance of property to the country:

> It is for the interest of the community that men should be incited in every possible way to accumulate, because as much as they accumulate by their industry they add to the national wealth; that all should be encouraged to accumulate; and the prosperity of our country in a very great part is owing to the fact that our institutions leave the path of wealth, as of honor, open to

all men, and encourage all men, whatever may be their situations in life and however they may start, to better their condition and to accumulate wealth, because the more they accumulate it the more the nation has of wealth.[134]

This statement not only underlines Fessenden's recurring commitment to the capitalist economy reshaping nineteenth-century America but also hints at the correctness of historian Heather Cox Richardson's judgment that the early Republicans' "tragic weakness" was their "self-righteous optimism" in the virtues of free-labor capitalism.[135] The exigencies of war, she argues, impelled them to develop national structures conducive to the growth of a modern, corporate economy—one that would quickly subvert their liberating conception of America as a prosperous community of independent farmers, small manufacturers, and upwardly mobile workers. Fessenden's underlying faith in the market and overriding commitment to Union victory certainly made him a witting architect of the new financial system, which fostered the development of closer links between the national government and businessmen of all kinds. However, somewhat ironically given his onetime devotion to Clay's American System, his own privileged class position and ingrained republicanism enabled him to glimpse the oppressive potential of large corporations. Once a booster for the Atlantic & St. Lawrence Railroad, he now shared with growing numbers of Americans an increasingly negative view of powerful railway companies. During the Civil War he was greatly exercised by the zealous attempts of the Portland & Kennebec Railroad to gain access across his family's land. Why, he wondered, "should the property, the comfort of private individuals, be sacrificed for the purpose of making a Rail road more profitable to its owners?" Was "legislation solely for the benefit of corporations?"[136] His irritation did not, at any stage, lead him to critique the Republicans' free-labor vision of the country's future. Why would it have done so given his own longstanding commitment to that vision? However, it is important to recognize that free-labor thought was evolving constantly during the mid-nineteenth century under the press of economic, social, and political change. Fessenden was never a supporter of the radical producerist version of free-labor ideology that would lead Radical Republicans to demand land for the emancipated slaves, but neither was he an unthinking advocate of what passed for progress in the nineteenth-century United States. Even the much vaunted speed of railway trains, he noted, could be a threat to the safety of the public.[137]

When Fessenden referred to "all men" in his paean to free labor, it is likely he meant blacks as well as whites. Yet the senator sometimes found it difficult to square his overriding commitment to winning the war with his views on what was just. This became evident early in the first session of the Thirty-eighth Congress when he was embroiled in an unpleasant spat over whether black troops who had been promised equal pay with white soldiers at the time of enlistment were entitled to back pay when Congress finally got around to debating an equalization bill. He supported the basic principle of equal pay for black soldiers but opposed the measure's retroactive feature because it would be too costly to the Treasury. His comment that "we ought to be a little careful in our expenditures" laid him wide open to abolitionist charges that he was placing expediency before justice.[138] Frederick Douglass and Wendell Phillips condemned his views in speeches in Portland.[139] William Lloyd Garrison opined that he wished "Senator Fessenden could understand that rectitude is good political economy" and compared his conduct unfavorably with that of "his venerable and liberty-loving father." Fessenden's "petty calculation of the sum that will be necessary to pay back dues," he added, "is worthy only of a trickster."[140] Pitt Fessenden was not slow to trace the origins of the criticism. "Sumner's newspapers & friends," he informed his son William, "have taken special pains to abuse me—I have little doubt at his suggestion. He is not a man but a malignant scoundrel, & is so considered by many besides myself."[141]

Although Fessenden insisted that his critics were wrong, the controversy highlighted his reluctance to make policy solely on the basis of humanitarian principles. As chairman of the Finance Committee, however, he was duty bound to protect the public treasury at a critical stage of the war when every cent was needed to keep the Union armies in the field. Moreover, while he demanded that "[t]he question of economy must enter into everything," he calibrated this utilitarian assertion by adding "in so far as it does not check the exercise of a proper humanity and the doing of that which is necessary to be done before the country and before God, in order to justify ourselves to the world and to the Ruler of the universe."[142]

The senator was not, as some of his critics seemed to think, totally opposed to retroactive pay. He thought it might be warranted in the case of two Massachusetts regiments that had reportedly been promised equal pay by Governor John A. Andrew and even expressed a willingness to fund back pay from the beginning of the year.[143] He also made it clear in his remarks of early February (which Wendell Phillips confessed not to having read fully) that in the future all U.S. soldiers belonging to the same service arm should receive the same pay.[144] No distinction on the grounds of color, he said, should be made: "These [black] soldiers are men. They render the same service as others, and perhaps as good service. Whether as a whole class they render as good service or not I do not know, but certainly a great many of them are much better than a great many of the white soldiers, if one may judge from the experience of the country."[145] His position was that of a stern patriot. Soldiers of whatever color, he proclaimed, would not want their pay increased if they knew it would injure the government for which they were fighting. Republicans, therefore, must act like statesmen not petty politicians. "A statesman," he added by way of clarification, "is not at liberty to try rash experiments and to make rash propositions when he has nothing to propose by way of meeting the difficulty that may follow."[146]

Pitt Fessenden's record on racial issues in the first half of 1864 was relatively progressive. He endorsed Sumner's anti-discrimination rider to a Washington, DC street railroad bill, initially supported the enfranchisement of blacks in Montana territory, and cast his vote in favor of the historic Thirteenth Amendment imparting legal substance to the Emancipation Proclamation.[147] Yet his relations with some of the Senate's more extreme Republicans continued to deteriorate—a fact that may have contributed to, and been influenced by, his relatively moderate voting record in the opening session of the Thirty-eighth Congress.[148]

This retreat to the center was partly a consequence of his position at the head of the Finance Committee. Antislavery ultras continued to resent his insistence on prioritizing revenue-raising measures over their attempts to promote equal rights for blacks, just as he remained impatient with their failure to perceive the preeminence of Finance Committee business. But the Radicals' hostility toward Fessenden was also a product of early deliberations over Reconstruction. The debates that occurred on this issue during the spring of 1864 were indicative of incipient tensions within the Republican Party over the extent to which the federal government could and should remake southern society during and after the Civil War. Grounded in personal rivalry as well as significant ideological differences, these tensions would seriously affect the outcome of congressional Reconstruction later in the decade.

Fessenden's views on Reconstruction evolved slowly during the session and had by no means cohered by the time he entered the cabinet in early July. His pragmatic conviction "that we can do anything that is necessary to be done" to save the Union seemed to render it likely that he would support an expansive view of the federal government's role in Reconstruction.[149] He certainly believed that "the question of reconstruction as it is called, the question of what is and what is not a State entitled to be represented here, should properly be settled by Congress, and cannot be settled by any other power than Congress in any possible way."[150] On these grounds he joined his fellow Republicans in opposing the admission of senators from Union-controlled Arkansas elected under the terms of Lincoln's Ten Percent Plan.[151] But he and other centrist Republicans differed with the likes of Sumner in their opposition to unduly coercive measures and their resistance to the centralizing drift of Radical policy toward the South.

Fessenden signaled his aversion to punitive action in January 1864 when he successfully opposed attempts to expel the garrulous Kentucky Unionist, Garrett Davis, for introducing allegedly treasonable resolutions into the Senate. In defending Davis's right under "parliamentary privilege"—"the great safeguard against corruption"—to express unpalatable views on the chamber floor, he could not resist a dig at puffed-up legislators of every political stripe. "Senators," he said coolly, "have different modes of gaining immortality, and each one selects the mode that he thinks best suited to himself. Some make speeches, interminable speeches, and some lay resolutions on the table almost equally interminable; some read orations, and some present bills, and some do the whole."[152]

Fessenden's unmatched ability to combine high-handed opinion in the service of what Radicals labeled conservatism with thinly disguised insults directed primarily at Charles Sumner contributed to the ongoing decline in relations between the two leading New England senators. Their most serious clash occurred on April 27. While the ostensible cause of the ruction was a debate over whether individual states should be allowed to tax any capital stock of Chase's new national banks invested in U.S. bonds, much of the bad blood was caused by the bearing that this abstruse subject had on Reconstruction.

Speaking the previous day in favor of his committee's proposal to reject the House's prohibition on state taxation of national bank stock, Fessenden had argued—like the good Whig he had once been—that the amendment would reduce class jealousies because the rich owned most of the stock and would therefore have to pay the state taxes. During the course of his remarks he could not resist passing sarcastic comment on Zachariah Chandler's claim to be a "practical banker." The Michigan senator was an aggressive Radical Republican hell-bent on punishing traitors and remaking southern institutions in the image of the North. "I have conversed," said Fessenden, "with several men, not perhaps so 'practical' as my friend, but still who claim to be 'practical bankers' and interested in this subject, and their opinions were entirely different from his." Angered, Chandler condemned the sneering barb. "The Senator from Maine," he retorted, "has lectured this body about enough, not only on practical knowledge, but about its business and general conduct. For my part I have got about enough of his lecturing, and I will thank him to lecture somebody else next time."[153]

This clash set the tone for discussion the following day. Determined, for reasons related primarily to Reconstruction policy, to scotch the snake of states' rights that he and other Radicals held responsible for the war, Charles Sumner bemoaned the fact that senators could still be found defending a disastrous and redundant constitutional doctrine. Chief Justice John Marshall, he claimed, had tried to protect the rights of the old Bank of the United States against hostile state action in *McCulloch v. Maryland*. When Sumner went on to quote Milton in his defense, Fessenden lost his temper. Sumner, he snapped, had treated the chamber to "a running commentary" on a case "with which those of us who are lawyers might be supposed to be tolerably familiar, in connection with a little poetry." He was, he snorted (perhaps forgetting that he had once cited Swift in his defense), delighted "that this dry subject of finance can occasionally be softened and illuminated by an admixture of that which makes it a little more interesting." After emphasizing that the national banks were actually private corporations and insisting that *McCulloch* had left Maryland with the power to tax the real estate of the Bank of the United States, Fessenden underlined his continuing attachment to the vital principle of American federalism—the country's main protection against tyranny. He was, he said (in what looked to be a marker for Reconstruction), "a believer in the States as institutions, and I should like to ask the Senate if those institutions cease to exist what becomes of the United States?" The discussion then descended into accusation and counter accusation. Sumner assailed Fessenden for dealing in personalities; the senator from Maine charged his nemesis with whining and attacking him through the press (a charge that Sumner denied). Only when John Sherman intervened to stop "this very pleasant episode" did the squabble end.[154]

Zachariah Chandler was not the only Republican to complain about Fessenden's readiness to lecture colleagues or resent his tendency to engage in personal animus. Minnesota Radical Morton S. Wilkinson accused the Finance Committee head of acting "sometimes a little like a dictator on this floor."[155] In truth, those wounded by Fessenden in debate, not all of them Radicals, gave almost as good as they got. Wilkinson chided him for being "the guardian of the Treasury" and denounced his "pettifogging."[156] Lyman Trumbull, a fellow centrist, actually ordered the Portlander to "keep his seat" in the middle of a long harangue against the use of "unparliamentary" language.[157]

So hostile was Trumbull's criticism that Reverdy Johnson, a Maryland Democrat, felt bound to step in and defend Fessenden. The latter, he confessed, was as impulsive as the next man, but, he added, exhibited a "countervailing quality which he ever exhibits . . . a generous nature . . . which gives to him as a member of this body a character of great firmness and eminent ability."[158] Johnson's defense indicated that Fessenden had his admirers as well as detractors in the Senate. His acid tongue did not undermine his effectiveness in the first session of the Thirty-eighth Congress any more than it had done in previous wartime sessions. It may even have assisted his cause when directed against Radicals like Chandler and Sumner. On May 6 a narrow majority of Republicans, including Grimes and all the New England centrists, defeated Sumner's efforts to subject national banks to virtually exclusive national taxation.[159] Four days later, however, most Republicans, Fessenden included, voted for the amended bill to create a national currency secured by a pledge of U.S. bonds.[160] A modicum of unity on fundamentals—the need for military victory, a recognition that increased federal power was the only way to achieve this end, and an expanded vision of American nationhood—enabled Fessenden (with the help of his many parliamentary skills and the assistance of his deputy, John Sherman) to pilot a series of critical revenue-raising bills through the Senate in the first half of 1864.

The rift with Sumner was so deep that it had an impact on the Union Party's national convention. Fessenden was too busy to be involved with presidential matters and frankly contemptuous of the wartime politicking engaged in by Lincoln and some of his main rivals, among them Salmon Chase. Though he did express private support for tough-talking Major General Benjamin F. Butler, what little spare capacity he possessed went on worrying about his oldest son Frank, who had been wounded at Monett's Bluff, an engagement in the Federals' ill-fated Red River Campaign in Louisiana.[161] Relieved to learn from an early press report that Frank's wound was superficial, he cruelly found out two weeks after the operation that his son's leg had been amputated below the knee. While his rival fretted, Sumner, stung by Fessenden's public jibes and fearful of his tormentor's influence, moved on his position. To the surprise of many observers, Massachusetts delegates at the Baltimore convention failed to support the renomination of Vice President Hannibal Hamlin, who lost his place on the ticket to the Unionist governor of Tennessee, Andrew Johnson, a War Democrat. Although Johnson's nomination suited those Republicans who wanted a balanced ticket, a member of the Bay State's delegation confessed that Sumner had wanted to dump Hamlin in order to free him up for a Senate race against Fessenden the following January.[162] The Pennsylvanian Simon Cameron assured Fessenden that, while he had done everything he could to renominate Hamlin "as well for his own sake, as for yours," he had failed because New England, notably Massachusetts, had not adhered to him.[163]

Immersed in finalizing the details of tax and tariff bills, Pitt Fessenden had little time in June to consider the implications of Hamlin's defeat for his own career. As forces commanded by Lincoln's new general-in-chief, Ulysses S. Grant, ground down the enemy in Virginia at a dispiriting cost in Union lives, he was so preoccupied with business that he played little role in the critical Reconstruction measures under discussion in late June and early July. However, he appears to have abstained purposefully on July 2, 1864, when a final vote was taken on the Wade-Davis Bill, Congress's stringent response to Lincoln's Ten Percent Plan, which was viewed as too lenient by a majority of congressional Republicans. Fessenden had implicitly criticized the president's policy on June 29, arguing that it was "not enough that a small portion or even a considerable portion of the people sustained by our military authority . . . declare themselves to be a State." But he had also refused to express his opinion on a bill that he claimed, probably truthfully, not to have studied. His failure to vote on the Wade-Davis Bill three days later resulted partly from an understandable wish to preserve his good offices with the White House (he had, as we will see, just received notification of his appointment to the cabinet).[164] Yet it may also have been the case that, after studying the bill more closely, he genuinely held the measure to be flawed. Shortly after Lincoln pocket-vetoed the bill (much to the consternation of Republicans in Washington), Fessenden informed the president that he concurred with his action because the bill had gone too far in its efforts to abolish slavery ahead of the pending Thirteenth Amendment.[165]

Between the spring of 1861 and the early summer of 1864 William Pitt Fessenden used his legislative power responsibly and constructively. He played a leading role in the Union war effort, not only by trying to inject verve into what many northerners regarded as a flaccid administration but also by helping to construct Chase's national financial system and honing a series of complex revenue-raising bills designed to keep the Union cause afloat. Although he did not always support the legislation under consideration, he suppressed many of his reservations in the service of effective policymaking. If his impressive self-restraint was sometimes forgotten in the heat of debate, it is worth recalling his longstanding belief that political controversy was the sign of a healthy republic. As he put it in February 1862, repeating a maxim he had last used publicly in his twenties, "Only in the dead sea of despotism is there a perfect calm."[166]

On the morning of July 1, Fessenden arrived at the White House to discover, much to his consternation, that President Lincoln had nominated him to succeed Salmon Chase as secretary of the treasury. A new and important chapter of his political career was about to open.

Secretary of the Treasury, 1864–1865

William Pitt Fessenden served eight difficult months as U.S. secretary of the treasury. Though short, his tenure covered the decisive final phase of the Civil War. Union victory was still far from guaranteed in the summer of 1864. The Army of the Potomac, its ranks seriously depleted after the bloody Overland Campaign, had crossed the James River three weeks before he took up office but Grant struggled to cut Lee's defenses at Petersburg near Richmond. In the western theater Sherman's hard-bitten troops advanced slowly through northern Georgia, winning a crucial victory at Kennesaw Mountain on June 27 before embarking upon extended operations to take the city of Atlanta. The success or failure of Fessenden's executive career, like that of his chief, would be determined primarily by military movements on both sides of the Appalachians. However, he was far from being a passive spectator at this time. Charged with the awesome responsibility of keeping the Union armies in the field when costs were spiraling out of control, he fulfilled his duties to the best of his ability without winning over those financial conservatives who had expected him to undo Salmon Chase's unorthodox economic policies or satisfying antislavery Radicals who wanted him to improve the lot of the emancipated slaves. Those slaves, however, could not have been liberated without Union military victory and, in the absence of a steady supply of funds, that triumph would have remained elusive. By the time he left his post in March 1865 to return to the Senate, the war was virtually won and Fessenden could congratulate himself on a job well done. Both he and the country at large could now prepare themselves to meet the coming questions of Reconstruction.

A Fine Mess

The appointment came as a great surprise. Salmon Chase had been intriguing against the president for months and had not yet given up hope of being placed at the head of an anti-Lincoln ticket by abolitionists, dissident Republicans, or pro-war Democrats. When the secretary provoked a dispute over a patronage appointment in New York, Lincoln—his renomination now secure—seized the chance to accept his resignation. Fessenden knew nothing of what was going on until he met Chase at the Capitol on June 30 to discuss an item of legislation. A messenger approached and told him that Chase had been dismissed. He asked the secretary if he had resigned. Chase replied that he had done so but had not received word until that moment that his offer had been accepted. The senator expressed "his surprise and disappointment" and the two men parted company.[1]

Lincoln had not yet decided to appoint Fessenden to the vacancy. His first choice was David "Pot Metal" Tod, a hard-money man and former Ohio governor whose appointment was likely to satisfy the conservative bankers of the Northeast. Only when Tod declined did the president turn to Fessenden. He knew the Finance Committee chairman was an advocate of responsible monetary measures, a man highly respected by the financial community, and a patriotic broker-politician whom he regarded astutely as "a radical—without the petulant and vicious fretfulness of many radicals."[2] Although Secretary of the Navy Gideon Welles interpreted Lincoln's abrupt shift from the conservative Tod to the man who had implemented Chase's currency reforms as evidence of his chief's inability to understand money matters, the turn made sense given the senator's prudent approach to the country's finances.[3] On July 1 Fessenden went to the White House for an interview. He was shocked to discover that Lincoln had already sent his nomination for treasury secretary to the Senate and immediately insisted that he could not accept the post. "If you decline, you must do it in open day," said the president, "for I shall not recall the nomination."[4]

Fessenden did not want the position. Desperate for a restorative summer at home with Lizzy, he drafted an urgent letter declining the post on the grounds that his health had never been strong and that he was "utterly exhausted by the labors of the session."[5] What he did not say was that he had no desire to join an administration for which he had little regard and that he, an untested administrator, doubted his ability to do the job. Lincoln, however, needed a treasury head whom the country would respect and would not be rebuffed again. When Fessenden returned to the White House to discuss the appointment, the president refused to accept the letter, "saying that Providence had pointed out the man for the crisis, none other could be found, and I had no right to decline."[6]

Other leading figures in Washington also appealed to the senator's vanity and patriotism to secure his compliance. One of the most persuasive arguments came from Secretary of War Stanton, who told him he could no more evade his duty than his disabled son Frank.[7] A conversation with Chase also contributed to his decision. In the process of encouraging him to accept, the outgoing department head assured Fessenden that "all the great work of the Department was now fairly blocked out and in progress" and that the senator would have the advantage of not having alienated so many powerful money men.[8] By July 3, Fessenden had decided to accept the post. "I go to it with all the feelings of a man being led to execution," he told one correspondent. "If my physical powers enable me to endure its labors and anxieties, I see in it the grave of all my comforts and all my hopes for the future."[9] Appalled by the prospect awaiting him, he was already planning an exit strategy. That same day he wrote to a friend in Maine to determine if he could be appointed chief justice of the state supreme court.[10]

At least Fessenden could be gratified by the broadly positive response to his appointment. Lincoln cleverly dispatched a group of New York bankers to urge his acceptance and forwarded laudatory telegrams, including one from the Cincinnati Chamber of Commerce.[11] Businessmen of all kinds welcomed the news. "The appointment is universally accepted as a good one—the best that could be made," reported Harris C. Fahnestock, one of Jay Cooke's deputies in Washington.[12] After a meeting with the new secretary, the Boston cotton manufacturer Edward Atkinson purred that "He despises gold bills and other tinkering, has common sense and courage and will not be a man of expediency and devices."[13] Fessenden's appointment was well received even by some conservatives who did not share his relatively progressive views on race. General Francis P. Blair, Jr., whose powerful border-state family was delighted to see the back of Chase, thought the country would "gain largely" from the cabinet change: "He is I suppose," wrote Blair from the front in northern Georgia, "a thorough Radical but that is no objection in my mind if a man is honest, brave and patriotic which I believe Fessenden to be and which Chase is not and besides Fessenden has more ability and some toleration for the opinions of others, which no damned hypocrite like Chase can afford to have or to express."[14]

The Portlander joined a fractious but functioning seven-member cabinet of which, though it included two especially talented and influential figures in Seward and Stanton, Abraham Lincoln was undeniably master. The president allowed most of his department heads free rein in their designated spheres. He reserved the right to interfere with appointments when he deemed it necessary but Fessenden could be reasonably sure that he would be left to run his own show because Lincoln was far more interested in military matters than financial policy. Although he was the

most radical member of the cabinet (which also included conservatives Edward
Bates, Montgomery Blair, John P. Usher, and Gideon Welles), he had no desire to
play a leading role within the administration. Executive matters held few charms
for him and, besides, there was business aplenty for him to attend to in his new
department.

Fessenden took charge of the Treasury on July 5. Chase accompanied him that
morning and introduced him to the officials, notably Hugh McCulloch and George
Harrington, who would be his most valuable advisers throughout his short tenure.
Fessenden was not a natural bureaucrat but his forensic mind, legal expertise, and
prodigious capacity for hard work soon impressed. "The department people like the
clear way in which he takes hold of and dispatches business," reported Fahnestock
(eager to foster close relations with the secretary in the hope of resuming Jay Cooke
& Company's highly remunerative agency work for the government).[15] Needing
larger private quarters in which to conduct business, Fessenden accepted an invitation from Congressman Samuel Hooper, a wealthy Massachusetts capitalist, to make
use of his spacious house (fully equipped with servants) at the corner of 15th and H
streets, close to the department.[16]

The financial crisis confronting the United States at the most dangerous point of
its existence was severe. Costs continued to soar as the war dragged on. Chase had
been forced to issue suspended requisitions and high-interest certificates of indebtedness as an emergency measure and there were more than $162 million of these ex-
pensive notes outstanding at the start of Fessenden's tenure. By this time, however,
contractors wanted payment in real money. Quartermaster General Montgomery
Meigs reported that the purchase of artillery horses had been delayed at several
points because sellers would no longer accept the government's promises to pay.[17]

The inexorable rise of the national debt was deeply troubling to northerners.
Estimated at $1.8 billion by the end of fiscal 1864, the U.S. wartime debt may have
been paltry by today's standards but it was a harbinger of tyranny for those fearful
that Lincoln and his allies were undermining the tree of liberty. Fessenden's determination to win the war, together with his faith in the resilience of the American
economy and his Whiggish preference for a stronger national state, had led him
to endorse Chase's policy of funding the war primarily by increasing the country's
bonded indebtedness. However, as treasury secretary, he was now confronted by the
urgent need not only to find money to keep the armed forces in the field but also to
service the mounting debt. Interest payments and military expenses were reckoned
to be $2.25 million a day. Worryingly, his sources of income were insufficient to

meet this figure. The tax bill he had just piloted through the Senate would probably yield only $750,000 per diem. Although congressional Republicans had raised taxes in response to belated appeals from Chase, they had no desire to antagonize voters in a presidential election year and were ideologically opposed to the oppressive levels of taxation favored by the monarchical governments of Europe in time of war.

Confronted with a disturbing balance sheet, the new secretary was forced to consider his options at speed. His first instinct was to use his connections with northeastern capitalists to secure a substantial loan from the commercial banks of New York. Despite his initial optimism, the negotiations in New York proved fruitless. The bankers had not yet come to terms with Chase's national banking system and tried to use Fessenden's request for money to place themselves on a par with the nationals as federal depositories. Finding the banks short of cash (much of it had gone west to finance the upcoming harvest) and that the law made it difficult for him to agree to their terms, he left Manhattan after "a most exhausting week" without the $50 million offered by the banks.[18] Although the bankers expressed satisfaction with Lincoln's decision to appoint a secretary with such "high moral integrity," Harris Fahnestock reported that Fessenden had been "*devilled* by the Dutchmen in New York" until he was "sick of them."[19]

Sick or not, the impoverished secretary was in a bind. He was left with four main options for revenue procurement, at least one of which had to be adopted immediately if the Union cause were to remain afloat: issue more greenbacks, increase taxation, negotiate a foreign loan, or sell more interest-bearing bonds. Vermont Congressman Justin Morrill, the leading mind on the House Ways and Means Committee, urged him to prioritize a long-term loan over greenbacks for political reasons. "Further inflation," wrote Morrill, "will inflate prices so much as to create great distress among the poor and swell the material from which copperhead votes will spawn at the elections."[20] He need not have worried. His fellow New Englander understood the political dangers of inflation and high taxes and, besides, had always regarded both the greenbacks and attacks on property as morally dubious and corrosive of republican virtue. He was also unprepared, at this early stage of his tenure, to go cap in hand to foreign bankers. Left with no other option, he ordered his officials to begin preparing a popular $300 million loan of seven-thirty bonds authorized by Congress in June.

In offering his new loan to the country, Fessenden relied more heavily on patriotism than appeals to the pocketbook. His circular, written to accompany the advertised loan of July 25, described the war as a people's conflict that could only be won with greater effort. "It is *your* war," asserted the document. "You proclaimed it, and you have sustained it against traitors everywhere, with a patriotic devotion unsurpassed in the world's history."[21] Not everyone agreed with Fessenden's conviction that northerners' commitment to the Union would sustain his initiative. "Patriotism weighed against profit generally kicks the beam," Harris Fahnestock opined.[22] It was a cynical yet realistic appraisal. There were simply too many more attractive investments available for the loan to take off.

By the end of the month Fessenden was disheartened by the public's unenthusiastic response to the seven-thirties.[23] The one man who might have made a difference was Jay Cooke, the banker whose innovative marketing techniques had made Chase's five-twenty loan such an outstanding success. Although many financial experts regarded Cooke as nothing more than "a good advertiser of patent medicines," Chase held him in high regard.[24] It was probably on the former secretary's advice that Fessenden met with Cooke in Washington just before the loan was floated.[25] However, he erred in confessing that adverse criticism of Cooke's agency role in 1862–63 made it impossible for him to make use of his services in an official capacity. Cooke, a pious man convinced of his worth to the Union cause, was deeply hurt by the secretary's comment. He returned home to tell Chase that Fessenden would not make a success of the new loan unless it was advertised effectively. One million dollars spent on engaging the services of diverse newspapers would, he thought, make all the difference.[26]

The exhausted secretary left Washington for a break in Maine on the same depressing day that hundreds of Union troops, many of them black, were slaughtered at the Battle of the Crater outside Petersburg. Although Fahnestock reckoned he was "[f]iddling while Rome burns," he was in desperate need of rest after an onerous last eight months.[27] He also had political matters to attend to. The Maine legislature would elect a new U.S. senator for a full term in January. Fessenden was now determined to return to the Senate, where he could deploy his talents to the full, in the process thwarting Hannibal Hamlin's efforts to succeed him. As well as politicking he sought relaxation by pottering in his garden, reading in the library, and talking about matters domestic and political with cousin Lizzy and second son William. Normally a spell at home would have revived his flagging spirits and tired body. Not on this occasion. He was, he told his deputy Harrington, "too uneasy" to gain much rest "while money affairs look so badly." The flat state of the loan preyed on his mind continually. "The people are not awake to the urgency of the case," he moaned, "and I see no way of opening their eyes. I cannot sell the bonds other than by public notice, for we should at once be accused of stealing. Every thing must be open as the day."[28]

Fessenden was back at the helm by August 22, working nine until five "and then indefinitely thereafter" in ninety-degree heat. Although the government's finances remained his primary concern, he had other business to deal with. Freedmen's affairs numbered among the most important. Toward the end of the last session Congress had transferred control over noncombatant blacks from the War Department to the Treasury. Although some freedmen had gained possession of land due to free-labor experiments on the Carolina coast and in the Davis Bend area of Mississippi, the majority of ex-slaves not enrolled in the armed forces were working for wages on plantations owned by northern lessees or, in Union-occupied Louisiana, laboring under the constraints of a controversial apprenticeship system implemented by one of Lincoln's favorite political generals, Nathaniel Banks. Shortly before leaving for Portland, Fessenden had promulgated regulations designed to breathe life into a statute passed by Congress in July to regulate trade in the occupied South. Among them was a set of measures for superintendence of the freedmen. Treasury officials were instructed to oversee labor contracts and mandate wage rates far more liberal than those operating in Louisiana. Blacks were to enjoy a first lien on the crop and no products could be shipped to market until the local treasury agent had certified that the workers had been properly paid.[29] An appreciative writer in the antislavery *Liberator* contended that the new regulations provided justice for the freedmen without the attendant incubus of a government bureau and, "in the absence of contradictory evidence," gave the credit to Fessenden.[30]

The new secretary was not the author of the regulations. They had been drawn up, on Chase's orders, by William P. Mellen, a close political ally of the scheming Ohioan. Because neither Chase nor Mellen had given up on the former's presidential chances, the rules were probably intended to effect what the *New-York Tribune* called "a practical repudiation" of the Banks system which enjoyed Lincoln's support.[31] Military officials entrusted with oversight of the freedmen took a dim view of Mellen's handiwork. Concerned that the regulations would cause administrative confusion and suffering for the ex-slaves, Colonel John Eaton, an unusually well-intentioned army officer, journeyed to Washington in early August to persuade Lincoln that only the military was in a position to assume practical care of the freedmen. The president gave him a sympathetic hearing and sent him to speak to the man in control of freedmen's affairs. Although Fessenden had left for Maine, George Harrington found Eaton as persuasive as the president and temporarily suspended the rules. When his superior returned to Washington the suspension was confirmed.[32]

Pitt Fessenden's decision to leave the freedmen under the control of the War Department ran counter to the wishes of Congress. It is likely he had mixed reasons for siding with Eaton. First, he had enough problems on his hands without having to assume responsibility for the tens of thousands of impoverished blacks freed from bondage by the Emancipation Proclamation, their own efforts, and the advance of the army. Second, as someone who considered himself a practical man, he was doubtless convinced by Eaton's contention that military officials were best placed to oversee the development of a free-labor society in the South in the absence of a specialized bureau. At the very least they had the personnel on the ground. Third, he knew that the commander-in-chief favored suspending the regulations and had probably come to a clear understanding of their relevance to the coming election. Even though Fessenden had never been Abraham Lincoln's greatest champion, he was certain by the late summer of 1864 that no one else should be the Union Party's standard-bearer. The president was tolerably popular and the Portlander was now willing to concede, a major concession this, that he was "an astute politician" who was "much more than a match for any of his Cabinet."[33]

The fourth, and perhaps most important, reason why Fessenden did not take control of the freedmen is that he did not share his predecessor's strong interest in their fate. This is not to say he had no concern for them at all. Several of his actions as secretary show that he was aware of the serious social problems caused by the continuing collapse of slavery in the South. He waived duties on foreign aid to the freedmen and set aside $10,000 per month from taxes on cotton produced by loyal lessees to pay for medical supplies.[34] He also granted an audience to prominent humanitarians, including Colonel Eaton and Josephine Griffing, a tireless promoter of the freedmen's welfare who wanted northern states to offer asylum to liberated slaves.[35]

What Fessenden lacked was a far-sighted vision of black people as property owners. Although he had endorsed preemption rights for freedmen at Port Royal, South Carolina, he had not joined Radical Republicans and abolitionists in their efforts to redistribute confiscated and abandoned land to southern blacks as remuneration for their years of bonded toil and an instrument for destroying the power of the disloyal planter class. By no means careless of the importance of securing justice for African Americans, he remained as reluctant as he had been during the debates over retroactive pay for black troops to decouple questions of right from matters of cost. Nor could he envisage the freedpeople—certainly not in wartime—as anything more than a race of paid plantation hands. The blacks, he wrote tellingly, were "best and most economically provided for by their employment as agracultural [sic] laborers."[36] Whereas Chase had always shown a keen interest in questions of land redistribution and black citizenship, Fessenden, preoccupied from the outset by the enormity of the financial crisis, exhibited no such enthusiasm. Shortly after leaving the cabinet, Chase reflected on how much he had hoped to achieve through Treasury oversight of the freedmen. "Will my successor do this work?" he wondered. "I fear not. He had not the same heart for this measure that I had."[37]

Fessenden's most serious mistake with regard to freedmen's policy in 1864 was his failure to communicate the abatement of the Mellen regulations effectively. Unaware that the rules had been suspended, Benjamin Flanders, a Chase loyalist in charge of Treasury affairs in New Orleans, tried to assume control of the freedmen in Louisiana in November, much to the consternation of army officers in the state. The ensuing bureaucratic wrangle and consequent black suffering indicated not only the dangers of a split jurisdiction between government departments but also the sobering truth that individual treasury agents had neither the organizational nous nor the manpower to oversee the chaotic wartime transition from slavery to freedom. It was fortunate, therefore, that Fessenden did not, at any stage, order his officials to assume supervision of blacks on a general basis. The creation of a specialized freedmen's bureau under the overall control of the War Department in March 1865 made sound practical sense in the light of experience during the final year of the conflict.

Soon after returning to Washington from his break in Portland, Fessenden was confronted with another policy headache. At his first cabinet meeting on July 5, he had listened to President Lincoln endorse Edward Atkinson's suggestion that the government should procure as much cotton grown outside Union lines as possible. Atkinson reasoned that high demand for cotton enabled southerners to make as much money from their dwindling stocks as they had done in the boom times before the war. Lincoln was unwilling to let the Confederates receive any payments in gold but, eager to promote intersectional trade as an instrument of reunion, gave the idea his backing. With Stanton vehemently opposing the idea of trading with the enemy, Fessenden dodged the issue by claiming to be ignorant of the subject.[38] By late summer Atkinson had persuaded the secretary that his idea was a sound one—at least insofar as it involved the importation of cotton from the Confederacy (Fessenden was unpersuaded that supplies should be traded back and forth between the lines).

It is likely that the president's enthusiasm and his own desperate need for money from any source were important factors in his decision to endorse this dubious commerce. The secretary may also have been attracted by Atkinson's conviction that, if the government could secure large amounts of cotton, it could flood the market, drain Britain of specie, and precipitate "a general crash" across the Atlantic.[39] Fessenden's natural Anglophilia was momentarily tempered by Britain's refusal to support the Union cause. "The English," he had blustered in 1863, were "the meanest people on earth," whom he regarded with "a compound of contempt & hate."[40] If cotton trading could be used to wreak revenge against perfidious Albion, perhaps its lack of moral luster could be overlooked.

At a cabinet meeting on September 9 Fessenden assented to the controversial plan by which treasury agents were authorized to purchase cotton and then sell it on the open market in return for specie. Two weeks later Lincoln issued an executive order authorizing persons claiming control of cotton beyond the lines to bring the staple to designated purchasing agents in the occupied South. Those agents would then buy it for two-thirds of the price listed in New York. Goods and supplies not declared contraband of war were allowed to be exported to, and imported from, the Confederacy.[41] Fessenden knew better than anyone the government's desperate need for revenue at this time. "The principal and most desirable" of these products, he told his new purchasing agent in New Orleans, "is cotton, to the purchase of which you will give your especial attention."[42]

The cabinet's decision to sanction trade with the enemy when Union troops were still dying in their thousands resulted in serious inter-departmental friction. Many Federal commanders considered the trade obstructive of efficient military operations. Even before the president's edict was released, Major General Edward R. S. Canby in the Gulf Department had issued a military order prohibiting all trade with the Confederacy. "It is of primary consequence to our success that rigid non intercourse should be kept," his deputy told Lincoln. No one could "deal in purchases of cotton without violating his allegiance to the Country & of necessity holding communication with and giving aid to the public enemy."[43] Widespread confusion on the ground resulted as military officials attempted to thwart the trade while cotton buyers and purchasing agents insisted on their legal right to engage in commerce across the lines. Fessenden wrote a terse note to Stanton in October complaining of the arrest of a treasury official in Natchez and noted circumspectly in his official report later in the year that "proper execution" of the new trade policy had "been attended with great embarrassment."[44] Ultimately, intense opposition to

inter-belligerent commerce from the Union high command engendered a cessation of the policy, but not before huge profits had been made by a small number of
favored companies and individuals.

Government officials were heavily engaged in cotton speculating during the Civil
War. Although Chase and Stanton were men of some integrity, many of their subor-
dinates were not. When Fessenden joined the cabinet James Grimes urged him to
clean out the department because many of Chase's appointees were regarded as corrupt.[45] The secretary did not act on this advice with the result that several treasury
officials—including two of his most valued assistants in Washington, Hanson A.
Risley (an associate of the New York boss, Thurlow Weed) and George Harrington
(a partner in a Memphis trading firm)—became involved in the rapacious activities
of northern cotton rings by dint of their influence over trading permits.[46]

William Pitt Fessenden was not corrupt by the standards of his or any age. Although he gave a clerkship to one of his half-brothers, the limited appointments he
made were mainly charity cases or geared toward fostering his reelection to the Senate. He was also aware of the dangers of graft in his department, acting positively at
one point to secure entry into the vulnerable currency room. However, his tendency
to regard allegations against the department as a slight on his own character made
him relatively impervious to criticism of the Treasury, particularly when these allegations emanated from military men whose own thirst for cotton was well known.
In another sharp letter to Stanton, written after Grant had alleged that treasury
agents were consciously or unconsciously assisting the enemy, he snapped: "Whatever cause of complaint there may be at City Point, I am persuaded is not chargeable
to either the ignorance or corruption of Treasury Agents."[47] The secretary's social
conservatism, moreover, prevented him from assuming the worst of gentlemen like
Harrington and Risley, whom he regarded as selfless public servants like himself.

In fairness to Fessenden he did not, as Grimes assumed, have total control over
patronage in his department. When, in late August 1864, the powerful Seward–
Weed wing of the New York Republican Party demanded that Hiram Barney, Chase's
New York collector, be replaced with its own candidate, Simeon Draper, the president obliged by sending his aide, John Hay, to New York to secure Barney's resignation. Even though Fessenden may have been consoled by Draper's standing in
the old Whig organization and persuaded by Senator William Evarts's contention
that the change was needed to attract ex-Whigs in the upcoming election (Barney
was an ex-Democrat), Lincoln did not consult him over one of the most important
treasury appointments in the country. The New York collectorship was notoriously

lucrative. When Fessenden subsequently designated Draper his cotton purchasing agent in Savannah, he was inadvertently placing a fox in charge of the chickens. Draper had already grown fat on auction fees selling captured southern property for the government and it is probable that he paid handsomely for his purchasing commission—$20,000 to Lincoln's wife, Mary, according to Supreme Court Justice David Davis.[48] Secretary of the Navy Gideon Welles was convinced that his cabinet colleague had been duped by another cotton ring. "Fessenden . . . knows as little of men as Chase," he wrote in his diary. "This mission of Draper will be a swindle, I can scarcely doubt."[49]

While the blame in this case attaches primarily to Lincoln, neither the president nor his secretary of the treasury wanted to undertake a purge of Chase's appointees, some of whom, as Grimes suspected, were clearly on the make. To do so would have been to exacerbate intra-party tensions before a critical election and risk undermining Treasury operations. Fessenden, additionally, remained heavily reliant on Chase for counsel and continued to voice his friendship for the Ohioan despite their cooled relations after the failed coup attempt against Seward.[50] Chase, certainly, does not appear to have blamed him for Barney's dismissal, for which the secretary took care to disclaim all responsibility.[51]

The Tide Turns

Although cotton trading and freedmen's affairs were much on his mind during the summer of 1864, Pitt Fessenden remained preoccupied by the perilous state of government finances. Popular confidence in ultimate victory ebbed away daily as Union armies struggled to break through the Confederate defenses around Atlanta and Petersburg. Northern morale was now so depressed that Abraham Lincoln was prepared to think the unthinkable. On August 23 he asked all his cabinet members to endorse, unread, a "blind memorandum" in which he stated his readiness to cooperate with a Democratic president-elect to save the Union before the inauguration, "as he will have secured his election on such ground that he cannot possibly secure it afterwards."[52] Weighed down with cares, Fessenden could offer little practical aid to the party's election efforts, though he did ask General Benjamin Butler in Virginia to allow the Portlander, General George F. Shepley, to campaign back home.[53] In reality, he was a prisoner of events. Shortly before the Democratic national convention in late August he wrote to Lizzy. Their relationship was more intimate than ever now that his cousin was liberated from her difficult marriage and a resident at State

Street. "How is the widow?" he inquired affectionately, "The one I become more in love with than ever, when at home." Practical as always, he wrote too of his despondency about the seven-thirty loan: "Money comes in very slowly, and not half so much as I need." Disconcertingly for a committed republican, he also admitted that he was not master of his own destiny. "Oh, for a great victory," he sighed. "What a financial operation it would be. If General Grant doesn't help me out of this scrape, I am a lost man."[54]

In fact it was Sherman who salvaged his reputation. At the end of August the Democrats nominated General George McClellan on a platform committing the party to a negotiated peace. On September 2, Sherman's forces entered Atlanta, having cut the last supply route into the city. It was the turning point of the war. With a Union victory virtually assured McClellan was forced to repudiate the controversial peace plank. Yet even this maneuver seemed unlikely to unseat President Lincoln when, later in the fall, General Philip H. Sheridan finally put paid to the Confederate threat in the Shenandoah Valley. Although these decisive military triumphs did not solve all of Fessenden's financial problems, they did—by bolstering the government's credit—make it easier for him to obtain money. In mid-September he floated a modest $30 million loan and was delighted to discover that it was a "great success," being hugely oversubscribed and attracting bids 4 percent above par.[55] Jay Cooke & Company took the majority of the bonds, partly because government securities were now a more attractive proposition and partly because the firm remained hopeful of resuming its profitable marketing activities for the administration.[56]

The secretary was not yet ready to use private bankers as government bond agents. Chase understood his reluctance to incur political opprobrium. "I hardly blame him for not being willing [to employ you]," he told Cooke self-pityingly, "What did I get—what can any body get for preferring [sic] country & duty to private interests & compliant favor?"[57] Fessenden did contemplate employing the Philadelphia banker in a more limited role and asked him to market U.S. bonds in Europe on a private basis. Cooke, however, was still hurt after being rebuffed earlier in the summer and initially refused the invitation.[58] Asking Chase to cross the Atlantic to negotiate a foreign loan remained a second and serious option but ultimately Fessenden decided not to pursue it seriously—probably because he expected Chase to be appointed chief justice of the Supreme Court after Taney's death on October 12. That month he managed to float a $40 million loan of five-twenty bonds to parties that included his acquaintance Morris Ketchum, a wealthy New York banker who was the brother of Webster loyalist, Hiram.[59] Yet money remained in short supply.

"It looks as if matters would go on from bad to worse," wrote Jay's brother Henry, "until government returns to its old policy of a *six per cent subscription loan.*"[60]

In mid-October Fessenden returned to the department after visiting the Union supply depot at City Point in Virginia. He was still uncertain whether to pursue the foreign loan option or to market a new popular loan through Jay Cooke. Several of his New York advisers were now counseling him against seeking a formal loan abroad on the grounds that foreigners were buying large quantities of U.S. bonds.[61] The secretary waited on the election result before making a final decision. He was far from passive ahead of the crucial poll, however, and sanctioned the sale of government-held specie to reduce the price of gold, which he and other treasury officials believed was being artificially inflated by Democrats to persuade voters that the war was unwinnable. By November 7, the day before the election, his chief officer in New York had parted with specie worth around $6 million to steady the gold price on the city's bullion market. Lincoln's victory, earned with the help of soldiers in the field, ensured that the war would be fought to a successful conclusion.

No longer so concerned about the effect of adverse political criticism, Fessenden now determined to employ Cooke & Co to sell bonds. To satisfy himself that the company would be able to deliver on its promises, he invited it to market at par, and on a commission basis, a large tranche of five-twenties immediately after the election.[62] The sale of the first $3 million option went well. Henry Cooke reported that Fessenden was "much gratified at the success of our operations, which, notwithstanding the large sales, are putting up the market."[63] On November 13 the banker took a pile of telegrams to the Treasury to illustrate the demand for the bonds and to show how the company strengthened the market by making occasional purchases of its own. Evidently the cash-starved secretary was prepared to accept such manipulations for the greater good. "He was *delighted*—," Henry Cooke told his brother, "and when I showed him the last quotations he said he was much gratified that we were working them off at such a good profit." Continued Cooke, "I told him *we* did not realise all the profit the outside quotations indicated: but that we gave the dealers to whom we sold, a part of the apparent profit thus insuring their zeal and activity. 'Well,' said he, 'you *earn* all you make and I don't begrudge it . . . Now . . . I want to continue sales of govts [sic] through you. If you can furnish me steadily one million, (in money) per day . . . I will not have to look elsewhere for money, and would greatly prefer to rely solely upon you folks for all I want.'"[64]

Fessenden spent the next few weeks preparing his annual report. It was a laborious task and he relied on Harrington to provide the necessary statistics. The tone of the resulting document, released on December 6, was characteristically frank. In it he attributed the rising gap between revenue and expenditures to democracy and war. It was, he thought, "impossible to apply fixed rules to a condition of affairs constantly changing, or to meet contingencies which no human wisdom can foresee by a steady application of general laws, especially in a Government, and with a people, where public opinion is the controlling element, and that opinion is not under the direction of those who may happen to administer public affairs."[65] While he intended this statement to explain the government's failure to support the war by high taxation, he did suggest that a graduated tax on all incomes, no matter how small, would help to make up the expected deficiency of $482 million for the next three quarters. Beyond this, he had few concrete revenue-raising ploys for Congress to discuss. The rest of the report was a dry account of the stop-gap measures he had taken since July to meet the drain on expenditure. While the analysis was reasonably thorough, he declined to mention his negotiations with Cooke's banking firm. Perhaps the secretary's most significant point was his suggestion that Congress should pass legislation securing the withdrawal of all non-national currency. His contention that the national banking system deserved "a fair trial" indicated that he had come to terms with Chase's financial revolution. He had little to say of the freedmen and cotton trading and ended on a downbeat note by thanking his staff for enabling him to sustain "the weight of a most onerous and embarrassing position."[66]

Conservatives who had placed faith in Fessenden were swift to criticize the report. The *New York Herald* described it as "a public disappointment" and "about the weakest and most evasive document that could possibly have been concocted," while the staid *Merchants' Magazine and Commercial Review* lambasted its author for failing to demand swingeing taxation.[67] "Oh, for a man brave enough to strike out boldly and swim against this current which is hurrying us on to bankruptcy!" lamented the *Review*.[68] While Fessenden tried to dismiss these attacks by remarking sarcastically that it was unfortunate he was legally required to report to Congress rather than the New York press, he remained sensitive to public criticism. He was particularly stung by suggestions in the city's *Post* and *Tribune*, both Radical, pro-Chase organs, that the report was "the work of a clerk, and not of a finance minister."[69] Determined to defend his reputation, he assured his son William that leading politicians like Chase were "perfectly satisfied" with the document. Enclosed in his letter were two positive articles from western journals that he asked William to have reprinted in the *Portland Press* with "appropriate remarks." Any comment, he ordered, should not be couched in a cautious tone: "It must be an affirmative article if any."[70]

One reason why Pitt Fessenden was so intent on answering his critics was his desire to return to the Senate. The race seemed tougher than he had anticipated. Hannibal Hamlin desired the nomination and was working hard to secure it. Fessenden was too busy to play a hands-on role in the campaign and left his trusted lieutenants, foremost among them Portland Congressman John Lynch, to work on his behalf. James G. Blaine, well-placed to influence the powerful Kennebec delegation's course at Augusta, was the kingmaker between the two Republican heavyweights. Although he joined in Hamlin's abortive efforts to persuade Lincoln to appoint Fessenden chief justice of the Supreme Court to succeed Taney, Blaine had no intention of alienating Maine's most powerful Republican. On October 17 he assured the secretary that if he wanted to return to the Senate the Kennebec men would favor his reelection.[71] Hamlin's best hope was for Lincoln to announce his wish for Fessenden to remain in the cabinet but the president, apparently sharing Blaine's view of the situation, made no such declaration.

Fessenden deployed a battery of arguments to make his case for reelection. Expecting his allies to use antebellum loyalties on his behalf, he informed Israel Washburn, Jr. that "If the Whigs of old think the old Democrats must have everything, let it be so."[72] In another communication intended for circulation among friendly legislators at Augusta, he emphasized that he had only accepted a cabinet post on the understanding that he wished to return to the Senate "when the public exigency which called upon me to leave it no longer existed." Although his Treasury report had failed to satisfy some New York journalists the country was, he avowed, "pretty well satisfied" with his tenure. Now, however, he wished to see through "this great struggle" as a legislator. Why, he asked, should he not receive the same proof of public approval as that received by peers such as Sumner and Wade? He had had some share in the war. As well as sacrificing his own best interests by joining the cabinet, "[o]ne son has fallen upon the field. Another has given a limb to his country. A third has exposed his life in many battles." Not to receive a token of public esteem, therefore, would be "rather mortifying." He ended by stating that his current job was "rapidly destroying my nervous system by its unceasing and unremitting bodily and mental labour."[73]

Not every Augusta legislator can have been persuaded by Fessenden's plea of poor health. (If he was that ill, was he really fit enough to take on any more Senate duties?) However, when aligned with his undoubted political influence and impressive record as a legislator, his claim to be *entitled* to reelection as a mark of respect for services rendered to the Union was a convincing one. Early in January 1865

Fessenden's Maine allies seized control of the Union Party caucus committee and rushed through orders to secure an early election. As soon as it became clear that Hamlin lacked the strength to win, the unseated vice president's name was withdrawn to avoid embarrassment.[74] Fessenden was speedily returned to the Senate for another six-year term. Irate at another humiliating defeat, Hamlin complained bitterly to his wife about his betrayal. His only solace was that many Republican senators in Washington expressed their disappointment that he had not secured the nomination. "I do not believe," he added, "that there are over half a dozen who did not sincerely desire it. Most of them I find dislike Mr Fessenden for his arrogance and ill temper, which he so often displays."[75]

The secretary sent in his resignation, effective March 3 or sooner if the president desired, in the first week of February.[76] His last major act as a member of Lincoln's cabinet was to give Jay Cooke's firm the job of selling U.S. bonds on a commission basis. Initially, he had wanted Cooke to cooperate with Morris Ketchum. However, when Jay reported that Ketchum was actually trying to depress the market for government securities, he prepared to make Cooke sole agent for the government. He drove a hard bargain. The Philadelphian was to receive three-quarters of 1 percent commission on the first $50 million of seven-thirties that he sold, five-eighths of 1 percent on the second $50 million, and the rate on sales above $100 million was to be fixed later.[77] The agent was to pay all expenses incurred in marketing the loan and the Treasury reserved the right to terminate the deal at any stage. Cooke was agitated by some of the terms but he signed up anyway. Assisted by the improving military situation, sales went well from the start. Cooke's brother Henry reported that a deposit of nearly $8 million into the Treasury in mid-February left Fessenden "delighted . . . but, if possible, even more puzzled, and *dumbfounded,* than delighted."[78] On the day of Fessenden's resignation, Congress assented, at his behest, to a second $300 million issue of seven-thirty notes. By July, after a third series of $230 million had been authorized, Jay Cooke and his efficient sales network had disposed of the best part of $830 million of U.S. securities.

The public's judgment on Fessenden's tenure was mixed. Conservatives blamed him for failing to control expenditure and impose high taxes in order to soak up inflation ahead of a swift return to specie payments. The New Englander Charles Francis Adams, Jr., grandson and great-grandson of presidents, thought Fessenden had done the country "great injury by doing nothing in the crisis of our fate"—a view that coincided with the *Commercial Review*'s opinion that the Treasury Department had been conducted along lines that were "[f]requently at variance with well

settled principles of economical science, and therefore entirely outside the calculations of the most sagacious."[79] Businessmen—generally manufacturers who had
welcomed the wartime trend toward nationalization of the financial system and a
greater volume of currency—were similarly unimpressed. Edward Atkinson thought
the outgoing secretary had erred in not supporting greenbacks to the hilt, while John
Williams, editor of an influential manufacturers' journal, agreed with the economist
Henry Carey that Fessenden "was a failure." "[B]etter for his own fame," he ventured, "had he never been Secretary."[80]

There was praise too, however. An Albany banker thanked him personally for
the "remarkably quiet & unpretending manner" in which he had saved the country
from the dangers of an inflated currency and for restoring confidence in government
securities.[81] Greeley's *New-York Tribune* commended his "qualities of simplicity and
integrity" for saving "his administration of the Treasury in the most critical epoch
of our Finances" and for protecting the republic "from new systems and untried
experiments." "A just History of the war of the Union," contended the *Tribune,* "will
give him a place beside the great Generals who have won the Union victories."[82]
For himself, Fessenden believed he had done a tolerably good job. The Treasury, he
confided to Freeman Morse, had been "a terribly hard place" but "the Country gives
me credit for managing affairs successfully. I entered the Department at its darkest
hour, and left my successor under a bright star. Much of this, undoubtedly, is to be
imputed to the improved aspect of [military] affairs, but people are beginning to
discover that tho' I did not deem it safe or prudent to reverse Mr Chase's action, and
thus throw the business of the country into confusion, yet that I had a policy which
time only allowed me to begin."[83]

Fessenden had performed respectably in a post he had never wanted. Even if his
tenure was not characterized by flair or originality, he had, with the help of Sherman
and Sheridan, kept the Treasury afloat and the armies of the republic in the field. Of
course, there was a downside to continuing existing policy. Conducting the war primarily on a credit basis—with long bonds payable in coin—meant that the country
would be servicing a mounting and very expensive debt for decades to come. Employing Jay Cooke to market the bonds as a patriotic as well as a financial investment, however, had democratized the once elite business of bondholding. During
the antebellum period U.S. bonds had always been purchased by a coterie of banks
and bankers. Now, thanks to Chase and Fessenden, the success of Cooke's marketing
drives, and the improving military position of the Union, "millions of Americans of
all classes" were stakeholders in the republic.[84] The outgoing secretary had always

envisaged the Civil War as a people's war. Nowhere, apart from the battlefield itself, was this hope more realized than in the altered sphere of wartime finance.

Storm Clouds

Fessenden left for Portland shortly after handing over control of the Treasury to his deputy Hugh McCulloch. He considered the Indiana banker and former Bowdoin student "a safe man" who would continue to promote responsible financial policies geared toward an eventual return to specie payments.[85] From home he dispatched a detailed letter full of advice to his successor. As well as outlining his deal with Jay Cooke, offering counsel on appointments, and urging cooperation with Stanton ("a true man, and worth all the rest of them"), he told McCulloch to teach Lincoln "not to interfere in matters connected with the Revenue."[86] Concerned that Hamlin and his friends might be preparing to exact their revenge, he also penned a note to George Harrington underlining his determination to retain the upper hand over state patronage. McCulloch, he wrote, should "be careful" with regard to offices: "[I] hope he will make no changes in Maine without consulting me, as there is some scheming which I do not like."[87]

Fessenden knew the war was nearly over. Just days after these communications reached Washington, Grant's besieging troops finally breached the Confederate lines at Petersburg. Lee surrendered in Virginia on April 9 and the only other Rebel army worthy of the name was soon cornered in North Carolina. But in the interim northerners' rejoicing at the war's successful conclusion was cruelly interrupted by the assassination of President Lincoln in Washington. There is no evidence that this shocking event plunged Fessenden into paroxysms of grief. Although he had left office with "great and increased respect" for Lincoln's personality and ability, he had never numbered among his greatest admirers.[88] What worried him more were early signs that Hamlin would try to capitalize on Vice President Andrew Johnson's promotion to claw his way back into power.

Just eight days after Lincoln's death, Fessenden dispatched a confidential letter to Hugh McCulloch. "I do not," he wrote, "much like to see that the old democrats (of a certain sort) are gathering about him [Johnson]. They are men to whom a back-stairs influence is always most agreeable, and who never do any thing in a straight forward manly way." Fessenden assured the conservative secretary that since Hamlin's "crushing and ignominious defeat in his contest with me, he has ceased to be of much account at home because all his power depended on patronage." He also warned McCulloch to be vigilant over Treasury posts in Maine and to prevent Hamlin or any other allegedly discredited ex-Democrat from being promoted to the cabinet, where they could circumvent his senatorial influence over appointments. "If Mr Johnson makes any change, let him select men of known ability, and not mere trading[,] selfish and broken down politicians."[89] In a follow-up letter the next day he told his successor that if Hamlin and ex-Governor Samuel Cony, another former Democrat, tried to have "Hamlin's bugle-man," George P. Sewall, made an internal revenue assessor, he must "shun him as you would pestilence." If Hamlin made claims that Lincoln had promised him any offices, they too should be rejected. The late president, he said, "told me he would make none—and he once told me that Mr H. claimed of him a promise which he was not able to remember."[90] The agitated, highly personal tone of these communications indicated an unusual degree of anxiety on Fessenden's part that the assassin John Wilkes Booth might have undermined his power base as well as killed a president. Patronage concerns remained high on his agenda in the coming years and subtly affected his stance on important policy issues.

Although Pitt Fessenden spent the spring of 1865 recuperating from his intensive labors of the past year, he followed political developments closely through the newspapers. When Stanton and Sherman fell out over the latter's generous surrender terms in North Carolina, he quickly proffered support to the secretary of war in terms that revealed his dislike not only of one of the country's most effective commanders but also one of his Republican colleagues on the Senate Finance Committee. He could never see, he observed disparagingly, "any extraordinary merit" in General Sherman's Atlanta campaign, "considering that he had three to one, and Joe Hooker did about all the fighting and his subsequent march was nothing but a march. I suspect that, after all, he is a brother of John [the senator from Ohio], and, like him, vain, ambitious, and selfish." The best thing now, Fessenden concluded, was to "[p]ay off Sherman's Army as soon as possible, and let every body understand that Mr Stanton is Secretary of War."[91]

His preference for rapid demobilization revealed that he had no conception in the immediate aftermath of the war of a sustained military occupation of the defeated South. By June, however, many Republicans were growing anxious that, despite his backing for the abolition of slavery, President Johnson was too eager to restore the defeated Rebels to power. They were especially disturbed by two proclamations at the end of May in which he not only declined to mandate black suffrage as an integral component of Reconstruction but also pardoned southerners willing to take an oath of future loyalty to the Union (excepting only the wealthiest and most influential Confederates) and enunciated a policy of creating provisional regimes that would restore "a republican form of government" in each of the late Rebel states ahead of recognizing their full rights under the Constitution. Coming as they did so soon after Lincoln's murder, the proclamations were regarded as too generous for traitors who had unleashed the deadliest conflict in American history. This was certainly the view of Radicals like Charles Sumner who regarded black suffrage primarily as an act that would promote justice and security for African Americans *and* of some non-Radicals who held, in the words of newspaper editor Joseph Medill, that "Without the black vote the loyal whites of no gulf state or coast state can begin to sustain themselves."[92]

While Fessenden continued to protect his back by paying close attention to appointments, he spent the summer tending the garden at State Street. Yet he was fully aware of the dangers of a magnanimous Reconstruction policy. One of his correspondents in Richmond reported that many large planters outside the former Confederate capital were determined "to hold on to the rule of the chivalry" if they could.[93] Senate colleague Lot Morrill told him that during the recess Washington was crowded with Rebels seeking pardons, offices, and control of the southern states.[94] In July he hosted Salmon Chase (who had just returned from a tour of the South) and was doubtless appraised of the blacks' need for land and the ballot.[95] "It strikes me that matters are getting complicated," Fessenden confided to James Grimes, "and that the rebels are having it all their own way."[96]

That summer Republicans engaged in diverse conversations—face-to-face and epistolary ones—about the president's policy. Although a few conservatives, notably Secretary of State Seward, the Wisconsin senator James Doolittle, and the virulently anti-Radical Blairs, embraced the idea of a speedy restoration of the southern states' normal constitutional relations, the majority of Republicans were deeply anxious about these developments. No consensus, however, existed about the right response. Party members differed on critical questions such as the degree to which states' rights should be infringed in the pursuit of a durable peace, the relative merits of limited, impartial (equal) and universal suffrage, and the wisdom of precipitating a break with the president.[97]

Convinced that any split between Johnson and the party would be disastrous for the country, Fessenden went down to Washington to find out what was going on. In early September he had a two-hour meeting about "public measures" with the president. The interview went well. Afterward he told Senator Henry Wilson of Massachusetts that Johnson was "right in sentiment and opinion on all matters pertaining to the negroes excepting suffrage." Although he said the president was "wrong" on this issue, he hoped "that time and firmness and prudence on our part will bring him right." "Fessenden goes home more confident of the future," Wilson told his colleague, Charles Sumner, adding that "[w]hile we stand firm as a rock for Suffrage for the negro, we must not weaken our cause . . . by saying or doing imprudent things."[98] Although some Radicals were spoiling for a fight, most Republican leaders concurred with Fessenden and agreed to give Andrew Johnson the benefit of the doubt at this early stage of Reconstruction.

Reluctant to endanger party unity before Congress reconvened, Maine's senator-elect did not make any major public policy statements during the fall of 1865. His silence did not betoken a lack of concern for events. Southerners' adoption of oppressive Black Codes (designed to maintain white supremacy) and the election to Congress of former Confederate leaders like Alexander H. Stephens made clear to all Unionists the looming possibility of a Rebel resurgence. In the North the refusal of Connecticut and Wisconsin voters to enfranchise local blacks underlined the constraints on policymaking imposed by the racism of many whites, conservative Republicans as well as Democrats. Fessenden shared the view propounded by his son James, a Union officer in the South, that neither the former Rebels nor the ex-slaves were fully prepared for the brave new world opened up by Confederate defeat and emancipation.[99] However, his comments to Henry Wilson revealed his readiness to adapt to changing circumstances. Some form of black suffrage, he believed, must play a central role in remaking the defeated South. He had no wish to break with Andrew Johnson but nor did he intend to let the ex-Confederates win the peace.

Fessenden was back in Washington again by the beginning of December. His ally, Congressman Fred Pike, predicted "an interesting session of Congress." Without the unifying pressure of the war, thought Pike, Congress and the president "will both be inclined to take the bits. The negro is hard to be got out of politics, & it is difficult to say what sort of a hoist he will give parties this time."[100] Fessenden seemed hopeful that all would be well. "Every body here is in good spirits upon the appearance of public affairs," he told Lizzy on December 3.[101] Other Republican senators were less sanguine, among them Sumner, who left a deeply unsatisfactory meeting with Johnson convinced that the Tennessean "does not understand the cause."[102] Few Republicans, certainly not Samuel Fessenden who continued to follow national politics closely despite his failing eyesight, were impressed with Johnson's message to Congress, which reiterated his commitment to a speedy restoration based upon emancipation, the recognition of states' rights, and liberal use of his pardoning power.[103] His son registered no opinion on the message, being more satisfied that his Finance Committee had been "made up" to suit him. "[I] look forward to a quiet time," he wrote.[104]

The senator could not have been more mistaken. Disturbed by signs of a Rebel resurgence Republicans in both houses supported the creation of a bicameral committee to investigate conditions in the southern states and formulate a coherent response to the president's controversial policies. Fessenden approved the creation of the Joint Committee on Reconstruction on the grounds that the question of southern readmission to Congress was an issue of "infinite importance, requiring calm and serious consideration."[105] Insistent on Congress's right to make Reconstruction policy, he displayed no animus toward Andrew Johnson. Indeed, he was at pains to state that he was "ready to support him to the best of my ability, as every gentleman around me is, in good faith and with kind feeling in all that he may desire that is consistent with my views of duty to the country." He also laid down as a marker "the principle which I intend shall guide my action, and I hope will guide the action of all of us. We have just gone through a state of war. While we were in it it became necessary all around to do certain things for which perhaps no strict warrant will be found . . . I upheld many things then that perhaps I would not uphold now because they are not necessary."[106]

While Fessenden did not speak for Radicals like Sumner, it soon became clear that he was the preferred choice of most Senate Republicans for the position of co-chair (with Congressman Thaddeus Stevens) of the new committee—a testimony to the high esteem in which his parliamentary skills were held by many of his colleagues. Hannibal Hamlin, still smarting from his defeat the previous winter despite his recent appointment to the lucrative post of Boston port collector, told Sumner that he hoped Fessenden would not get the office, "for he has no heart in the matter and I fear would fail just when he would be needed." Yet the disappointed politician had no more desire to confront Andrew Johnson than his old rival. "I hope our true friends will not fail to confer often with the President," wrote Hamlin.[107] Fessenden did not exactly want the chairmanship. It was, he told Lizzy Warriner, a "delicate" assignment "involving very great labour, & requiring great care & circumspection." Still, he could draw comfort from the fact that, while Sumner had wanted the job, "even his friends declined to support him, and almost to a man fixed upon me." "Luckily," he continued, "I had marked out my line, and every body understands where I am. I think I can see my way through, and if Sumner & Stevens & a few other rash men do not embroil us with the President, matters can be satisfactorily arranged—satisfactorily, I mean, to the great bulk of Union men throughout the States."[108]

The senator ended this revealing letter by telling his cousin how much he missed her when they were apart. Although definitive evidence is lacking, the two middle-aged kinsfolk were probably living together clandestinely as if they were man and wife. The couple may have wished to maintain a scrupulously respectable front—not least because Lizzy had spent so much time at State Street before the death of her late husband. Portlanders would have found nothing untoward in a wealthy states-man taking an impoverished widowed cousin under his protection but the reputa-tions of both parties would have suffered grievously had there been any hint of an affair before William Pitt Warriner's untimely demise. Behind closed doors and away from prying eyes their relationship was, in many respects, a model of mid-Victorian domestic bliss. "There are many things which none but a woman can do, and which you do better than any body," wrote the absent senator. "Nobody else sews a button on my shirt in the right place, as I found this morning—besides many other little things too numerous to be mentioned."[109]

Restored to "his empire" in the Senate, the place where, State Street aside, he felt most at home, Fessenden could reflect that he had spent more than a decade at the heart of American political life.[110] He had done everything in his power to save the republic from dishonor and destruction. True, his recent career at the Treasury had not been an unalloyed personal triumph but he had kept the government cause afloat at a time of acute national peril, aided crucially by the military genius of Wil-liam T. Sherman and the dynamic marketing techniques of Jay Cooke. Although he and the country had greeted the end of the war with understandable relief, Lincoln's successor, Andrew Johnson, was now inducing fresh anxieties by embarking on his own dangerous experiment in peacemaking. Pitt Fessenden remained guardedly op-timistic that matters would turn out right in the end, but he knew too much to rest on his senatorial laurels.

The Chief Tinker:
Congressional Reconstruction, 1866–1868

The twin tasks of reintegrating the defeated Rebel states into the Union and managing the South's transition from a slave to a free-labor society after one of the bloodiest wars in human history were daunting ones. William Pitt Fessenden would need to draw on all his prodigious talents to find a way through the political mire. Historians used to give him high marks for trying to thwart what they saw as the vindictive plans of the Radicals and for voting successfully to acquit President Andrew Johnson in the impeachment trial of 1868. But modern scholars regard him in a less positive light for his role, alongside that of other centrist Republicans, in applying a brake to federal policy at a critical moment in America's past. Fessenden was one of the most powerful policymakers in Washington and therefore contributed disproportionately to the making of congressional Reconstruction—that remarkable moment in American history that engendered black equality under the law even as it failed to impart lasting justice and security to the former slaves. Although he did not share the Radicals' vision of the postwar South as an interracial democracy, he played a decisive role in fashioning his party's response to President Andrew Johnson's white supremacist Reconstruction policy. Only when he felt that the Radicals posed an even greater threat to the general welfare than the discredited Johnson did he oppose their efforts to revolutionize a war-torn government and society in desperate need of peace and tranquility.

During the crucial years of congressional Reconstruction, Fessenden worked to achieve a durable peace settlement that guaranteed the future greatness of the American republic. This patriotic goal impelled him to ensure, first, that the fruits of northern victory were preserved by seeking adequate protection for southern Unionists (black and white), by eradicating oppressive distinctions of race and color enshrined in American law, and by promoting the continued success of the Republican Party, the political organization that, in his eyes, had saved the country from disaster. Second, it led him to oppose any attempt by Radicals to impose humiliating terms on the ex-Confederates. While Fessenden insisted that southern whites must face up to the consequences of their actions, he also held that they must be included in the peace process if that peace were to endure. Third, his concern for the nation's welfare made him determined to resist Radical attempts to further unbalance the relationship between Washington and the states. Federalism for him was the rock on which American liberty and national cohesion were based and he would not allow men for whom he had growing contempt to succeed in their efforts to destroy it.

1866: A Critical Year

Pitt Fessenden did not anticipate failure as 1865 drew to a close. Writing to his elderly and virtually blind father on New Year's Eve, he described Reconstruction as "a difficult subject to deal with" because of the steps already taken by President Johnson to create provisional governments and pardon former Confederates. "[Y]et," he added optimistically, "I think I see the way through it, if Congress stands firm, as I think it will."[1] Despite being concerned about the activities of those he regarded as political extremists on both sides of Reconstruction, he was confident that his Joint Committee could develop effective policies for the South. The group of three Radical Republicans, nine non-Radicals, and three Democrats contained "a large majority of thorough men, who are resolved that ample security shall attend any restoration of the insurgent States, come what will—while they desire to avoid, if possible, a division between Congress and the Executive which could only result in unmixed evil."[2]

Charged with the difficult task of fashioning an alternative plan of Reconstruction to the president's lenient restoration policy, the Joint Committee was the most important special committee raised by Congress in the nineteenth century. It included a number of highly talented legislators: Congressman Thaddeus Stevens, a racially progressive Pennsylvanian whose cynicism, pragmatism, and partisanship made him an ideal co-chair with Fessenden despite his position as one of the most vengeful Radicals in Washington; Elihu B. Washburne, well-known as the wartime patron of Ulysses S. Grant and another staunch Radical; Stevens's centrist colleague in the House, John A. Bingham, a devout Ohio Presbyterian and brilliant constitutional lawyer devoted to the idea of national citizenship; Fessenden's ally, James Grimes, who shared his belief that there must be limits to government activism now that the war was over; and the elderly Maryland Unionist, Reverdy Johnson, who was the most influential of the outnumbered Democrats on the committee.

On January 8, 1866, Senator Fessenden accompanied Washburne and Johnson to the White House to secure a commitment from the president that he would attempt no further initiatives on Reconstruction until the Joint Committee had acted. The delegation left the hour-long interview satisfied with Andrew Johnson's statement that, desiring harmony between the two branches of the government, he did not intend "to do more than had been done for the present."[3] Over the course of the next five months, the committee deliberated secretly and periodically over how to manage the southern states' return to the national fold without surrendering political power to ex-Confederates. While Fessenden took no part in the evidence-gathering operations (four subgroups were formed to collect testimony about conditions in the South), he was instrumental in helping to craft a new constitutional amendment—the Fourteenth—that would satisfy Republican demands for a coherent southern policy and thereby safeguard the North's recent military triumph.

Blocking southern political power was a critical objective. Emancipation had made the Constitution's three-fifths clause redundant and northerners were facing the gloomy prospect of southern whites returning to Washington with their influence enhanced if they were allowed to disfranchise blacks but count them for apportionment purposes. Eight months after the close of a rebellion that had cost the lives of 360,000 Union soldiers, this outcome was unacceptable to a majority of northerners. The obvious solution was to ensure that the loyal freedmen could vote. Republicans, however, were divided over whether the former slaves, impoverished and uneducated in the main, were fit to be given the same voting privileges as white males. (Even a Radical like Thaddeus Stevens took a dim view of blacks' capacity to vote independently of their former masters at this early stage of African American freedom.) Debates also raged over the relative merits of universal, limited, and impartial suffrage and the extent to which any suffrage qualifications could be imposed on states of the Union. Republicans understood too that southern whites were vehemently opposed to black voting and that the issue was hardly a vote-winner in the North. Something had to be done. The question before the Joint Committee was: what?

The preponderance of non-Radical Republicans on the committee did at least ensure that the president's charitable plan of Reconstruction would not be matched by what centrists regarded as an equally disastrous Radical program of territorialization, property confiscation, and land redistribution for the South outlined by Thaddeus Stevens in his "dead states" speech to the House in mid-December. On January 20 Fessenden reported two proposals for a new constitutional amendment to a full meeting of the committee. The first apportioned representation in Congress and direct taxes according to the number of U.S. citizens in each state and expressly voided any legal distinctions in "political or civil rights or privileges" that were made on the basis of "race, creed or color." The second excluded from the basis of representation any persons denied the vote on the grounds of race, creed, or color. Both options were coupled with a provision empowering Congress to secure to all U.S. citizens in every state "the same political rights and privileges; and to all persons in every State equal protection in the enjoyment of life, liberty and property."[4]

The first proposition was Fessenden's.[5] Thaddeus Stevens, however (ironically given his fear that "weak[-]kneed" and "trimming" Republicans like the senator from Maine would betray the cause), was unconvinced that such a direct prohibition of racial discrimination would find favor with the majority of congressional Republicans and supported the second proposal, which passed the committee by a vote of 11–3.[6] Neither proposition guaranteed African Americans the vote. States would still be free to disfranchise "citizens" (the term embraced native-born blacks as well as whites according to a civil rights bill then being drawn up in Congress) on bases other than race, creed, or color. But the second was intended primarily to protect northern influence in Congress: if the southern states refused to enfranchise loyal blacks their power in Washington would be reduced accordingly. Fessenden's proposal was a bolder, typically direct declaration that color prejudice had no further role to play in the governance of the republic at any level of the federal polity. He, like Stevens, held "caste exclusion" responsible for the war and "entirely contrary to the spirit of our Government, or of any republican form of Government."[7]

Fessenden's support for what he later called "a proposition which went to the root of the whole matter" was consistent with his longstanding attachment to the progressive free-labor view that all American citizens, regardless of color, should have an equal chance in the race of life.[8] It did not signify that he shared the Radicals' vision of the post-emancipation South as a true interracial democracy purged of the corrupting influence of the treasonous planter class. He assumed—because he knew slavery to have been an insidious institution—that the freedpeople would continue to be ruled by white southerners for the foreseeable future. He therefore took issue with reformers like Sumner in doubting publicly that "the great mass of those who were recently slaves, (undoubtedly there may be exceptions,) and who have been kept in ignorance all their lives, oppressed, more or less forbidden to acquire information, are fit at this day to exercise the right of suffrage, or could be trusted to do it, unless under such good advice as those better able might be prepared to give them."[9]

Convinced that most adult freedmen were no more fit to vote than women or children, he favored the broadening of the franchise on an equal or impartial basis. Southern states would be entitled to impose literacy qualifications that would affect illiterate whites as well as blacks, but this would provide a powerful incentive for southern elites to provide schools for their people and for ordinary men of both races to seek an education. Crucially, however, although he declared his "great hopes" for the whites below the Mason-Dixon line, he did not suggest that the ex-Rebels should be left to govern their former charges without federal oversight.[10] In common with all those Republicans affronted by the Black Codes, he insisted that the U.S. government was duty bound to ensure equitable treatment of its new black citizens. Fessenden's mistake was to assume that President Johnson, a former southern Democrat lacking empathy for the emancipated slaves, shared his view of that responsibility.

In early January 1866 Lyman Trumbull reported two important measures from his Judiciary Committee designed to supplement the work of Fessenden's group. While the Civil Rights Bill aimed to defend blacks in their capacity as American citizens against discriminatory action by individual states, the Freedmen's Bureau Bill extended the life of this innovative federal agency whose officers were now empowered to establish courts and build schools as part of their brief to protect the former slaves and manage the South's transition to a post-emancipation society. Congressional Republicans did not regard either measure as contentious for both were intended to nullify the unpopular Black Codes. When rumors began to circulate that Johnson was preparing to oppose congressional policy, Fessenden took it upon himself to resume his wartime role of broker between Congress and the White House.

On January 23, the day after he had reported a revised version of the constitutional amendment to the Senate, Fessenden endorsed the Freedmen's Bureau Bill, which passed two days later. Importantly, he dismissed the argument of conservative Democrats that the Constitution conferred no power to clothe and feed people in the states: "Whether you call it the war power or some other power, the power must necessarily exist, from the nature of the case, somewhere, and if anywhere, in us, to provide for what was one of the results of the contests in which we have been engaged. All the world would cry shame upon us if we did not."[11] He went out of his way, too, to dismiss talk of an impending collision between Johnson and Congress by describing it as "idle" and "ridiculous." In what he described to Lizzy Warriner as "a bow drawn at a venture" intended to alleviate fears of such a clash and to furnish Johnson with a guide for action, he insisted that the president was entirely respectful of the rights of Congress and that rumors of a split were the work of extremists in both parties.[12] The general wish among Republicans, he said, was to reunite the nation as soon as possible: "I seek not to impose nor shall I try to impose any conditions upon any people in this Union who are to make a part of us that either now or any future time shall have anything in them of the character of degradation."[13]

So keen was Fessenden to stop the president from falling captive to Democrats bent on regaining their lost influence that he began to attend Johnson's "stupid" levees—a major concession from a retiring man who normally shunned large social gatherings and who was, in early 1866, plagued by biliousness, a bad cold, and more of his perennial headaches.[14] Johnson, spurred by the senator's remarks, invited him to the White House for a meeting on Sunday, January 28. Fessenden came away assured that Johnson was ready to make common cause with Congress. Even when James Grimes showed him a newspaper account of the president's interview with Senator James Dixon of Connecticut on the same day—one that reported Johnson's belief that Congress should not meddle with black suffrage—he remained determined "to keep the peace, if possible, between the President and Congress." Though he admitted that "copperheads, ultra abolitionists and toadies" were intent on causing a breach, the president, he thought, meant "to stand by those who elected him, if it can be done consistently with the great interests of the country, as I think it can."[15]

No "ultra abolitionist" proved more troublesome than Sumner, who attacked the constitutional amendment (passed by House Republicans at the end of January) in a two-day oration. Marshalling authorities as diverse as James Madison, Abraham Lincoln, and Immanuel Kant, the learned Massachusetts senator assailed the Joint Committee's handiwork as yet "another Compromise of Human Rights."[16] Fessenden responded with extensive comments of his own on February 7. He admitted that the amendment was imperfect but stressed the need for, and virtues of, a pragmatic approach to Reconstruction. Noting the evidence of northern racial prejudice provided by the recent Wisconsin and Connecticut referenda in which majorities in both states had opposed local black suffrage, he argued that it was always better "to govern men by their own convictions of their own interests than by force." The amendment, he insisted, would induce southern whites to prepare the ex-slaves to vote, "thus bringing up an oppressed and downtrodden race to an equality, if capable of an equality, and I hope it may be, with their white brethren, children of the same father."[17]

Fessenden's paternalistic comments may have been prompted by a desire to promote dialogue with the president, whose doubts about the ex-slaves' fitness for voting far exceeded his own. Initial moves in the Joint Committee toward readmitting Johnson's home state of Tennessee were intended by non-Radicals to improve relations with the executive.[18] Fessenden thought Tennessee's admission "in some shape" (that is, possibly with conditions attached) would furnish "a valuable precedent" for the rest of the defunct Confederacy. Yet the senator was unsure whether Johnson would be "easy" if Tennessee were admitted and insisted that he would not "keep the peace" if it meant endangering "the safeguards necessary in the terrible condition of affairs." Privately, he remained deeply concerned too about the Radicals' intention to press on with the work of Reconstruction at any cost. "Mr Sumner," he confided, "with his impracticable notions, his vanity, his hatred of the President, coupled with his power over public opinion, is doing infinite harm. So are some others. All I can do is to act as if I was practical, swallow my wrath, and try to evoke something like order and safety out of the dangers around us."[19]

Fessenden's fears of an impending breach were realized when the president vetoed the Freedmen's Bureau Bill on February 19. In his message Johnson not only assailed the Bureau as an excessively powerful government agency whose activities would prevent the former slaves from working, but also averred that Congress had no right to take key policy decisions while the southern states remained unrepresented in it. Three days later, after the votes of five conservative Republicans had prevented the Senate from overriding his veto, an emboldened Johnson equated Radical leaders like Thaddeus Stevens with traitorous Confederates and—a clear sign that this onetime supporter of Andrew Jackson would brook no interference with his authority from legislators of any description—labeled the Joint Committee "an irresponsible central directory."[20]

This was a watershed in Reconstruction. The president of the United States had declared open warfare on the people's representatives, leaving congressional Republicans with a stark choice. They could either moderate their policies in order to keep the peace or press ahead and, less than a year after Appomattox, risk a potentially disastrous break with the conservative Tennessean. On February 23 the Senate debated its response to Johnson's action: a concurrent resolution proclaiming that Congress would not admit delegates from any ex-Confederate state until such state had been formally declared entitled to representation therein. The no-nonsense resolve drew on the legislature's constitutional power to seat its own members and was designed to thwart Johnson's efforts to restore the Union in hot haste. Ohio's influential centrist Republican, John Sherman, a more cautious and racially conservative man than Fessenden, feared the measure would further antagonize the president and urged restraint. But he carried only a minority of his party with him and debate ensued.[21]

William Pitt Fessenden now emerged as a prime mover in the simmering revolt against Johnson's policy. The president, he said, had been wrong to contend that *he* was empowered to say whether the late Rebel states had evinced sufficient evidence of renewed fealty to the nation. If senators yielded to that contention, "we should be yielding everything, we should have no power left, we should be less than children, we should hardly be entitled to call ourselves slaves."[22] The country had reached a crossroads. If Congress was to save it from ignominy, if it was to ensure that the Union dead had not died in vain, it must act without delay.

Fessenden took care in this landmark speech to deny Johnson's assertion that congressional Republicans were acting illegitimately. Embracing the "grasp of war" theory advocated by Boston lawyer Richard Henry Dana, he acknowledged that the Constitution made no specific mention of civil war. Republicans were thus acting as conquerors according to the international law of war set down by European authorities like Emmerich de Vattel and out of the necessity of the case. Though he disagreed with Stevens's theory that the ex-Confederate states had placed themselves at the government's mercy by committing suicide, he contended that they could not be "States of the Union" until Congress acknowledged that the old connection had been restored. After "an exhausting war," characterized by "savage hate" on the part of the country's enemies and involving enormous costs in men and treasure, it was entirely reasonable for Congress not to admit southern representatives too quickly. Though Fessenden emphasized that "the exercise of power is always dangerous" and that the southern states should be readmitted "just as soon as it can be done consistently with the safety of the people of this country," he confessed his displeasure at Johnson's denunciation of the Senate and the Joint Committee. The president, he reminded his colleagues, had told the southern states to make specific provisions in their constitutions for the abolition of slavery and nonpayment of Rebel debt. "If he had the right to do it," Fessenden asked, "have we not?"[23] The speech was one of the Portland Republican's most popular efforts: fifty thousand copies were ordered to be printed.[24]

The senator's trenchant comments indicated how deeply he felt let down by the administration. Although they left him "utterly exhausted," he was "much relieved" that the uncertainty over the president's course was over. Johnson, he thought, badly advised by clapped-out politicians like William Seward, had "broken his faith, betrayed his trust, and must sink from detestation into contempt." Any relief he felt at no longer having to tiptoe around the president was tempered by his awareness that the ending of civil war was not about to usher in the peace for which he and his compatriots yearned. "The consequences I cannot foresee," he told Lizzy, "but they must be terribly disastrous. I see nothing ahead but a long wearisome struggle for three years, and in the meantime great domestic convulsions, and an entire cessation of the work of reform—perhaps a return to power of the Country's worst enemies—northern Copperheads."[25]

The unpalatable prospect of surrendering power to seditious Democrats imposed a degree of unity on Senate Republicans. Leading non-Radicals like Grimes and Trumbull joined Fessenden in helping to pass the concurrent resolution on the readmission of southern delegates on March 2.[26] The constitutional amendment, however, represented a more difficult hurdle to climb because passage (ahead of submitting the amendment to the states for ratification) required a two-thirds majority in both houses. With the Senate having failed narrowly to pass the Freedmen's Bureau Bill over the veto by the same two-thirds majority, Fessenden glumly predicted that the amendment would fail. He was right. On March 9, Charles Sumner, believing half a loaf would not suffice if the loaf was "poisoned," joined with conservatives and seven other Republicans to defeat the measure 25–22 in the Senate.[27] Despite being prepared for this result, Fessenden was furious (as was Thaddeus Stevens). He responded with a two-hour speech in which he pitched into the Massachusetts senator for reading out yet another tedious printed oration (he contrasted this mode of rhetoric unfavorably with the extemporaneous form preferred in the British Parliament) and for destroying the amendment when neither he (Sumner) nor his long list of authorities were known to support universal suffrage. "I believe every body was gratified with the whipping I gave Sumner," he told Lizzy, "for his speech was atrocious . . . I regret exceedingly that the amendment was lost, for we can get nothing so good. If we carry any other through Congress, it will not be adopted by the States, and the blacks are left without hope."[28]

Notwithstanding the senator's pessimism, Andrew Johnson's opposition to the Freedmen's Bureau Bill had convinced most Republicans that there was no point trying to conciliate a president preoccupied with appealing to conservatives on both sides of the Mason-Dixon line. With rumors abounding that Johnson would veto the Civil Rights Bill, it was imperative to fashion an alternative Reconstruction policy if the Republicans were to win the crucial midterm elections later in the year.

Determined to secure the requisite majority needed to pass legislation over the president's opposition, Fessenden exerted his leadership by arguing, in defiance of

Trumbull's Judiciary Committee, that John P. Stockton, a Democrat whose credentials had not yet been affirmed, had been elected illegally by the New Jersey legislature. Stockton was thus ruthlessly expelled in a successful move to bolster the Republicans' political power in the Senate.[29] Fessenden was convinced the ends justified the means. "[T]he hope is that we may have a reliable party," he told his son William at the end of March. "It was a hard fight over Stockton but we killed him at last." It was, he added, "all important that we should have two thirds in each branch. I never will consent to take in a man from the Confederate States, until we have something for the future. Andy's conduct has rendered this course a necessity." On the same day the Senate narrowly dispatched Stockton, it received word that Johnson had vetoed the Civil Rights Bill on the grounds that blacks were not citizens. Privately, Fessenden declared his readiness to take bold action as head of the Joint Committee, but feared the consequences of continued political strife. "Perhaps another fight may grow out of it," he pondered bleakly, "but that will be a final one, and I don't know but it will be needed."[30] His decisive efforts to bolster the Senate's Republican majority did not end with his actions in the Stockton case. That spring he also wrote to local Republican leaders in Vermont and Connecticut to try to secure the election of senators likely to support congressional Reconstruction policy.[31]

The political dividend accruing from Stockton's exclusion quickly became apparent when centrist and Radical Republicans joined forces on April 6, 1866 to pass the Civil Rights Act over Johnson's veto, the first such action in American history. "God bless you all," commented one relieved Yankee, "heroes with those who fought at Gettysburg, Mission[ary] Ridge, and Five Forks."[32] Under the auspices of their mutual friends Anna and Samuel Hooper, Sumner and Fessenden shook hands on a temporary truce outside the latter's committee rooms. "I don't love him and never can—," Fessenden remarked coldly, "but the hatchet is buried, and I shall not dig it up again."[33]

The vexed question of the constitutional amendment torpedoed by Sumner remained. One intriguing proposal considered by the Joint Committee came from the Indiana reformer Robert Dale Owen. Sympathetic to the idea of black suffrage but convinced that the former slaves were not yet fit to vote, Owen arrived in Washington in late March with a draft amendment prohibiting the disfranchisement of any persons on the grounds of race, color, or previous condition of servitude after July 4, 1876. Gaining an enthusiastic response from Thaddeus Stevens, he then took the idea to Fessenden. Owen found the senator "[c]old, deliberate, dispassionate, cautious," but Fessenden listened to him patiently and asked him to leave the draft behind. "When he returned two days later, Fessenden told him, "in guarded and general terms, that he thought well of my proposal, as the best that had yet been presented to their committee."[34]

Frustratingly for Owen, Republicans outside the Joint Committee had no intention of fighting the fall elections on black suffrage and mobilized successfully to suppress the amendment. Fessenden was confined to his bed with a mild case of smallpox during the second half of April—an absence that Owen believed caused the draft's defeat.[35] Although the senator had been attracted to the proposal's deft combination of directness and delay, he missed early deliberations over the measure and only returned to his post in time to abstain on Stevens's April 28 motion to strike the ten-year suffrage deadline from the amendment.[36] In its place the committee drew up an alternative proposal, primarily the work of John A. Bingham, providing for a national guarantee of equality before the law. The measure also reduced the representation of states that disfranchised adult, male U.S. citizens, and excluded Confederates from voting in national elections until 1870. The amendment passed the House with little debate on May 10 but the Rebel disfranchisement clause elicited little support from non-Radicals in the upper chamber. Amid rumors of a rapprochement between Johnson and Congress, Senate Republicans empowered Fessenden, Grimes, and Howard—two centrists and a Radical—to moderate the amendment.[37] Howard presented the revised document on May 29. In its new form it declared all persons born in the country to be citizens of the United States and of the states in which they resided and barred former Rebels from officeholding rather than voting.

While the Republicans' opposition to presidential Reconstruction drove the Fourteenth Amendment debate toward a successful conclusion, important differences remained between Radical and centrist members of the ruling party in Washington. Crucially, the centrists had not completely given up on the president and his administration. Fessenden remained guardedly optimistic that Johnson would come to his senses now that Congress had shown its determination to act decisively. Personally he liked the Tennessean, finding him "always very cordial and kind" and apparently disposed to oblige his recommendations for office.[38] Partly out of a desire to consolidate his paramount influence over federal patronage in Maine, he also maintained close ties with his former deputy, Secretary of the Treasury Hugh McCulloch. Even though Fessenden considered McCulloch "a little too much under the influence of Jay Cooke," he consistently defended him in Congress against criticism from angry

Radicals who regarded the secretary as a tool of the president.[39] While Fessenden's course on Reconstruction was determined primarily by his desire to secure the fruits of victory and not by self-interest, patronage considerations as well as his strong brokerage instincts prevented him from joining the growing band of Johnson's public assailants.

Fessenden had been too weak after his smallpox attack to write the report of the Joint Committee, which should have been submitted to Congress with the constitutional amendment. However, as the committee's ranking Republican, he could not evade the responsibility once he had recovered. He told Lizzy in early June that the document would be "a very stupid affair, for it has been composed in weary hours, when I could find time, in which I should have rested."[40] His task was a difficult one. The report would frame the Republicans' agreed policy on Reconstruction—encapsulated in the proposed Fourteenth Amendment—ahead of the midterm elections. It had to be fit for public consumption (for journalists and politicians were bound to use it during the campaign) and acceptable to Radicals and non-Radicals alike. Despite his desire for repose, the result of Fessenden's endeavors was one of the finest state papers in American history, marked throughout by his familiar clarity of thought and expression, plain common sense, and sureness of political touch.

He began the fifteen-page report, presented officially on June 6, by justifying the work of the Joint Committee. Authorities agreed, he asserted, that at the end of "a civil war of the greatest magnitude" caused by the deliberate actions of malignant traitors, the Rebel states were exhausted and, in the words of the president, "deprived of all civil government." Andrew Johnson had been entirely within his constitutional rights as commander-in-chief to use his military power to appoint provisional governors when Congress was not sitting. However, though his motives were undoubtedly patriotic, the president had unwittingly rekindled southern defiance. He could not assume sole responsibility for making permanent civil governments for the South. The war had been won by the people of the United States "acting through all the co-ordinate branches of the government, and not by the executive department alone." It was Congress's duty to assess when southerners were entitled to enjoy all their rights under the Constitution and to ensure that each state of the Union had a republican government. Discussion about the constitutional standing of the defeated states revolved around a "profitless abstraction." Those states were "disorganized communities" that had voluntarily severed their normal ties to the government, and currently evinced "no evidence whatever of repentance for their crime." Under "the law of nations," the former Confederates were beaten enemies "at the mercy of the conquerors." To argue that they could now claim all their constitutional rights was plainly ridiculous: "If this is indeed true, then is the government of the United States powerless for its own protection, and flagrant rebellion, carried to the extreme of civil war, is a pastime which any State may play at, not only certain that it can lose nothing in any event, but may even be the gainer by defeat." Haughty Rebels would simply be able to "change their theatre of operations from the battle-field, where they were defeated and over-thrown, to the halls of Congress, and, through their representatives, seize upon the government which they fought to destroy."[41]

Fessenden was at pains to note the particular problem caused by the fact that the emancipation of the slaves made the three-fifths clause redundant. "It did not seem just or proper," he reasoned, "that all the political advantages derived from their be-coming free should be confined to their former masters, who had fought against the Union, and withheld from themselves, who had always been loyal." The proposed constitutional amendment was designed to obviate this difficulty. By providing "the advantage of increased political power as an inducement to allow all to participate in its exercise," it "would be in its nature gentle and persuasive, and would lead, it was hoped, at no distant day, to an equal participation of all, without distinction, in all the rights and privileges of citizenship." In the course of his carefully worded exposi-tion, Fessenden did not hesitate to draw the public's attention to white southerners' "deep-seated prejudice against color" by enunciating the committee's abhorrence of the "acts of cruelty, oppression, and murder" against blacks to which many witnesses had drawn its attention.[42]

Because it so ably exposed the fallacious basis of presidential Reconstruction and explained clearly the rationale behind congressional policy, the report was well received by the Republican press. It appeared in Greeley's *New-York Tribune* in the second week of June. The same paper editorialized that it would "occupy a conspicu-ous place in the history of the Republican party" and would "commend itself to the friends of the Union as a conclusive and admirable summary of the measures which the majority of the party regard as indispensable for securing the lasting restoration of the Union and the triumph of the principles of Justice and Freedom."[43]

The constitutional amendment finally passed the Senate on June 8. Fessenden mustered enough strength to correct the erroneous claim of James Doolittle, one of Johnson's few Republican supporters in Congress, that the measure's citizenship clause had been generated by fears that the Civil Rights Act was unconstitutional.

Debate, however, was exhausted. The House concurred with the Senate amendments a week later. Although Thaddeus Stevens was unimpressed with the product of six months' labor, he signaled his distance from the impractical Sumner by defending his decision to support the measure on the grounds that he lived "among men and not among angels."[44]

Pitt Fessenden was now eager to return to Maine—and not just because he was debilitated by work and illness. A devastating fire in Portland on the night of July 4 consumed more than one-third of the city, including his father's house and business properties owned by the family.[45] Although the properties were insured, he ordered Lizzy and William to make certain that the State Street house was "well guarded" against "roughs, fire &c."[46] Political developments in Maine were hardly less perturbing. His allies had failed to prevent the nomination of Colonel Joshua Chamberlain for governor. Chamberlain, a Union hero at Gettysburg, had no political track record and Fessenden considered his elevation, like the Whigs' nomination of General Zachary Taylor in 1848, "positively absurd." Although he professed confidence that Chamberlain's inexperience would soon use up "the military hero business" at home, his negative response to the wounded colonel's nomination betrayed a striking lack of understanding of the political power of Union veterans. The boys in blue had fought nobly for their country but Fessenden assumed it was in their interest to entrust the specialized business of politics to proven leaders like himself, not "false Gods" like Chamberlain.[47]

There was worrying news on the national front too. In late June the president's supporters issued a call for a National Union convention, confirmation that Johnsonites would contest the forthcoming elections by mobilizing conservatives opposed to congressional Reconstruction. The following month more than thirty black Unionists were murdered in political violence in New Orleans. Denounced by the northern press as evidence that the spirit of rebellion was still abroad, the bloodshed strengthened the Radicals' case against the president while highlighting the social and political instability of the former Confederacy.

Fessenden had to wait before he could fight fires at home. Reconstruction business had delayed action on a new tariff measure for which he, as chairman of the Finance Committee, had prime responsibility. Discussion on the bill highlighted tensions between eastern protectionists and low-tariff midwesterners within the Republican Party and Fessenden struggled hard to persuade the latter, Grimes among them, that the increased duties were not designed solely for the benefit of New England manufacturers.[48]

As far as Reconstruction measures were concerned the senator displayed a typically independent streak. He voted with the Republican majority to pass another Freedmen's Bureau Bill over Johnson's veto and joined his fellow centrists in sanctioning the admission of James Patterson, the new senator from Tennessee, despite the fact that Patterson was an ex-Confederate who could not swear the ironclad Unionist oath of 1862.[49] Significantly, however, he averred that he disagreed with the House of Representatives' contention that Tennessee delegates were being seated automatically because of that state's recent ratification of the Fourteenth Amendment. Tennessee was a distinctive case, he insisted. Its voters had ratified a genuinely republican constitution and exhibited their allegiance to the government. He added that it would be unsafe to admit southern delegates routinely until the constitutional amendment had been ratified by the requisite three-quarters majority of all the states.[50] In two more important votes he sided with non-Radicals in favor of a literacy qualification for District of Columbia voters (many of whom would be black) yet, genuinely committed to equal rights under the law and conscious of the hypocrisy involved in inviting southerners to enfranchise a people excluded from political rights in many northern states, he joined Sumner and only three other Republicans in an abortive bid to make the admission of Nebraska conditional upon the new state undertaking not to deny the vote or other rights to anyone on the grounds of race or color.[51]

Broadly speaking, though his opposition to Johnson's vetoes had contributed greatly to the radicalization of federal Reconstruction policy, he was reluctant to push the war-born revolution in government much further. In what looked like a conscious warning to Radicals he pointedly opposed a congressional appropriation, essentially a charitable gesture, to purchase the library of South Carolina Unionist James Pettigru on the grounds that "we are becoming exceedingly loose in our legislation."[52] His dissatisfaction with excessive statism was also reflected in his opposition to federal aid for private corporations like the Northern Pacific Railroad. He did not object to large public works per se, but feared the corrupting effect of such legislation on the country and on individuals. "It was," he told the Senate in tones that reflected his personal animus toward grasping railway companies, "getting to be the case under the legislation of Congress . . . that the country is to be controlled by great corporations and our legislation is to be controlled by them, so that we are no longer really to have any power left in relation to such subjects."[53]

Fessenden knew his words would be taken seriously for his influence in the chamber was now unsurpassed. In mid-June he made one of his periodic defenses of treasury head Hugh McCulloch, who had recently criticized congressional Republicans as "a set of Constitution tinkers." He confessed that he found McCulloch's remark in "bad taste" but put it down to the secretary's lack of experience as a public speaker. Besides, he said, if anyone should be offended it was himself, having "been placed in a position where I was considerable of a tinker." "The chief," piped up several of his colleagues in unison. "The chief tinker, if you please," he replied in unusual good humor.[54]

Declining a request from admiring Massachusetts Republicans that he give a public address at Fanueil Hall in Boston, Pitt Fessenden finally arrived home in mid-August.[55] Though fatigued and preoccupied with business matters arising out of the fire, he watched political developments unfold with growing alarm, especially the administration's attempts to bolster the new National Union Party with a purge of anti-Johnson officeholders. Working through McCulloch, he tried to protect his officeholding allies in Maine—men like the powerful Portland collector Israel Washburn, Jr.—and simultaneously alert the White House to the dangers of a patronage policy demanded only by "old democrats, & a very few flunkies of no political character."[56] "Turning our friends out of office any where," he warned the secretary, "only unties their tongues, and intensifies the activity of energetic and influential men. If the President will do it to gratify such flunkies as Doolittle & Cowan, he must take the consequences."[57]

Fessenden was not a disinterested counselor. He wrote partly to save his political clients and thereby shore up his power. Yet his political antennae were sound. The controversial patronage purge merely added to Johnson's woes. Republican resistance to presidential Reconstruction was further stiffened by a disastrous presidential speaking tour in which Johnson compared himself risibly to the suffering Christ, advocated the hanging of Thaddeus Stevens and Wendell Phillips, and blamed Congress for the New Orleans riot. In a reference to press reports of Johnson's drunkenness on tour, John Sherman, no longer an advocate of caution, thought Johnson had plunged the executive office "to the level of a grog-house."[58]

The Republicans carried Maine easily at the beginning of September, a result hailed by the *New-York Tribune* as "a regular Appomattox."[59] Fessenden told McCulloch that the victory had exceeded his expectations. "In my deliberate judgment," he wrote, "the people of the really loyal States would prefer another war to admitting the Confederates to an equal share of the government before we have some adequate security for their future good conduct, and an equal participation of all men in civil and political rights and privileges. He who stands in the way of this must inevitably go under."[60] While Fessenden blamed "Seward's evil counsels" for misleading the president into supposing he could take on the Republican majority, he criticized Johnson for attacking Congress on his embarrassing "swing around the circle" and contrasted this with his own restrained conduct during the state election campaign. "I think the President will find abundant occasion to regret that he has not followed my example," he wrote, "Personally, he has always treated me kindly, and I shall *try* not to forget it, however much we may differ, or however grieved I may feel."[61]

Not all Republicans were as generous in their assessment of Andrew Johnson. Radicals, outraged by the president's slurs and his opposition to the Fourteenth Amendment, were planning new Reconstruction measures: the disfranchisement of ex-Confederates, sweeping confiscation, and the redistribution of southern land. They also began calling seriously for the president's impeachment. Aware that these policies were backed by many beleaguered southern Unionists, Radical leaders like Stevens and Sumner interpreted the party's impressive election wins in the North as a popular mandate for revolutionizing southern society in the service of human freedom and national security and as just retribution for the crime of secession. Their hand was strengthened by the southern states' rejection of the constitutional amendment between October 1866 and January 1867. The measure had represented a political compromise, largely on the centrists' terms, between Radical and non-Radical Republicans in Congress. Southern resistance to congressional policy, encouraged by the president, gave the Radicals new leverage. Centrists now had little choice but to support black suffrage as an alternative to more extreme measures. The main issue was the extent to which they could hold the line on the Fourteenth Amendment program outlined in Fessenden's *Report of the Joint Committee.*

Initially, the senator from Maine was unsure about the meaning of the election results, which increased Republican strength in the House from 136 to 173 and in the Senate from 39 to 57. The struggle between Congress and Johnson would begin again soon, he told Freeman Morse. "What we are to meet, it is not easy to foresee." The president, surrounded by Copperheads and Rebels and counseled by cabinet members who, save Stanton, were "good for nothing," was "obstinate and self willed." Yet heartened by the retention of his "personal friends" (Morse, consul in London, among them), he thought the president might regain his senses after the Johnsonites' election drubbing and cease his patronage purges. At any rate, he added, "Your retention was promised me, and as matters stand, they don't like to offend me."[62]

Fessenden's own stock in the Republican Party remained gratifyingly high. In October Senator Edwin D. Morgan invited him, at the behest of New York's business elite, to attend a reception in his honor in Manhattan. Fessenden, said Morgan, had long been a towering figure in the upper chamber: "You are the acknowledged leader of that Body."[63] Though not every Republican in Congress would have agreed with this flattering sentiment, few could doubt Fessenden's enormous influence in national circles as he turned 60. He was fully aware of his power and exerted it to persuade Stanton to stay in the cabinet. "If I could see you in a position to make secretaries," he told the redoubtable Ohioan, "I should feel that the nation you have served so faithfully was safe."[64] He was less sanguine about Hugh McCulloch's assistance in the Reconstruction fight but he continued to exploit his friendship with the secretary in order to limit the president's reliance on patronage advice from Democrats and save valued allies and family members holding government office from the ax. At the beginning of November he described the newly appointed surveyor at Portland as "a man of no education, and totally incompetent." "I hope you had nothing to do with it," he wrote imperiously, adding that Washburn should remain as collector: "He is my friend, and I hope you will continue to protect him."[65]

The Leadership of Fools

Pitt Fessenden went to Washington for the second session of the Thirty-ninth Congress in an optimistic mood. His health had been restored after the break at home, he enjoyed dining with Sumner and his new wife Alice in Boston, he was duly feted at the Manhattan reception ("a great affair," he exulted), and on arriving in Washington he found time to flirt with young Katie Kearon, one of his favorite treasury clerks.[66] He had now reached the conclusion that the recent election victories were a triumph for moderation and would prevent "further serious trouble" with the White House as long as Congress kept cool and acted with "discretion" and "firmness."[67] On visiting the president, he found him "cordial as usual" but in poor spirits.[68] Johnson seemed to appreciate the courtesy call. "He hoped we should be able to work together for the good of the country," reported Fessenden, "and said he wanted to have a long interview with me, and talk it all over—adding, 'I am at one end of the line, and you at the other.' Of course, I expressed my readiness to meet him at any time. It is quite evident that there has been a disposition to avoid treading on my toes, which I impute to the fact that I have not seen occasion to indulge in personal abuse. I hope this feeling will give me some power to do good—at all events, to prevent some evil."[69]

Fessenden's continued willingness to act as a bridge leader exemplified the distance between himself and those Radicals who saw the president as a malign counter-revolutionary and the election results as a green light for their own program. Convinced, in the words of one anxious southern Unionist, that "[t]he Rebellion is now transfered [sic] from the Battlefield to the congress Halls," Radicals regarded the new session as a transformative moment in the life of the republic, a historic opportunity to render the United States true to what they saw as its founding commitment to human equality.[70] "If we succeed now, the victory will be for always," cried Sumner at the end of December.[71]

Fessenden did not share the Radicals' sense of urgency, let alone their desire to impeach the president and impose further measures on the post-emancipation South. Lacking their moral zeal, their determination to punish traitors, and their hatred of Johnson, he was prepared "to wait patiently" until the ex-Confederates grew "wiser" and ratified the Fourteenth Amendment. In truth, he saw little hope for effective policymaking until the general election in two years' time delivered a president and Congress "working to the same end."[72] Although he considered the amendment flawed, he believed it the only constitutional revision likely to be enacted in the short term. When the influential Massachusetts Republican, Richard H. Dana, asked him whether the Bay State should ratify the amendment, he replied affirmatively. He would, he said, regard its defeat as "a most severe blow" to the Republicans' retention of power upon which the country's future depended. The senator was not prepared to regard it as a conclusive settlement any more than he had been willing to accept the Compromise of 1850 as a complete finality. Congress still had the power to investigate the new constitutions of those southern states that did ratify the amendment before seating their representatives. The amendment was thus "a preliminary offer of terms looking to restoration," and he reserved his right "to vote for or against admission in such a case, according as I might or might not be satisfied with the provisions of any such State Constitution." In his view white southerners' willingness to accept the offer should determine whether Reconstruction went any further. The measure, he told Dana, "might make less probable any other amendment going further in the same direction."[73]

Fessenden's main concern at the opening of the session was the Radicals' eagerness to hurry the party and the country onto disaster. "Our great danger," he told Lizzy Warriner, "is from the hot heads of over-zealous men, who are in haste to immortalize themselves—but I am in hopes we may be able to act like men, & not like boys."[74] His refusal to make the readmission of any southern state automatic upon its ratification of the Fourteenth Amendment indicated that he was not a conservative on Reconstruction. So did his decision to vote for black suffrage in the District of Columbia without a literacy test requirement and his backing for anti-discrimination riders to bills providing for the admission of Nebraska and Colorado territories as states of the Union.[75] However, in common with other centrists, he was worried about the centralizing trend of Radical policy, reluctant to *impose* black suffrage on the southern states (where, unlike the capital or the territories, federal power appeared to be constitutionally limited), and wary of the ultras' readiness to attack Johnson. On February 27, 1867, he reminded colleagues of his attachment to the principle of federalism in studied remarks directed against the creation of a government department of education. "I am not much of a State rights man," he said, "and I never was, but I think our country differs very much from other countries in the fact that it is made up of States, a congregation of States, which have been in the habit of considering that they had some duties to perform under our system, which distinguishes us pretty much from all other nations."[76]

While Radical calls for Johnson's impeachment enjoyed only limited support among congressional Republicans that winter, there was broader agreement, in the wake of the ongoing patronage purges, on the need for legislation to reassert the Senate's constitutional power over federal appointments. In debates on the Tenure of Office Bill, a measure authorizing federal officeholders to stay in their posts until the Senate had approved their replacements and prohibiting the unauthorized dismissal of department heads during the term of office of the president who appointed them, Fessenden upheld the chamber's authority to stipulate its lawful power in appointment matters. However, he defended the president's right to name his own counselors and to remove a cabinet member in a recess "if he deems it necessary."[77] He also rejected as impractical Charles Sumner's attempt to sweep away large numbers of officeholders appointed by Johnson since July 1, 1866. In doing so, he revealed that his patience with the Bostonian was wearing thin. "[W]hen anything appears clear to his own mind," Fessenden snapped, "he [Sumner] cannot imagine that it is not perfectly clear to everybody else, both as to its propriety and its correctness, and therefore the man who doubts it either wants honesty or wants intelligence."[78] The senator from Maine eventually voted for the measure and later supported its passage over an executive veto, but he did so with serious reservations.[79]

Fessenden's mood had darkened considerably. Hard work trying to protect New England interests in the new tariff bill, an irritating cough, and "an attack of dyspepsia" that may have been a portent of the debilitating bowel condition that would eventually kill him further reduced his capacity to deal easily with the Radicals. "[W]e are doing all we can to destroy the confidence of the people in our discretion, and even in our integrity," he complained.[80] An article in the *New York World*, a Democratic sheet, highlighting the number of Fessenden family members on the government payroll, did nothing to improve his temper.[81] Nor did an appearance before the Supreme Court—his first in over a decade. Even though the Court was now headed by Salmon Chase and contained four other Lincoln appointees, he reported high-handedly that the justices "did not look to me like very big men" and that he "felt very much like telling them that though in a high place they were 'no great shakes,' after all."[82]

At least the senator's labors on the Joint Committee on Reconstruction were light. House Radicals wanted to bypass the centrist-controlled body and Fessenden, as chairman, had little desire, time, or energy to tout for business.[83] The principal Reconstruction measures before Congress in early 1867 were debated first in the lower chamber. Not until early February did the committee sanction a bill imposing military rule on the defeated Confederacy. Subsequent debate in the House centered on whether federal control should cease automatically once the southern states had ratified the Fourteenth Amendment and given blacks the vote. In a crucial roll call Radicals and Democrats joined forces to defeat Congressman James G. Blaine's attempt to recommit the Military Reconstruction Bill to the Joint Committee with a mandate that it should be reported back with provisions for readmitting southern delegates to Congress upon ratification of the Fourteenth Amendment.

On February 14, the Military Reconstruction Bill came before the Senate with a measure to reconstruct the state of Louisiana. Here was another important moment in American history. Pitt Fessenden's actions over the next few days would astonish his co-partisans but they reflected his continuing desire to forge a practical southern policy that sustained the North's wartime triumph without excluding the embittered ex-Confederates.

His relations with the Radicals had worsened in recent days. Both parties were opposed to the precipitate admission of southern delegates to Congress. But whereas the Radicals wanted to prolong Reconstruction in order to build a more perfect South, Fessenden rejected the idea of imposing further conditions on the defeated Rebels to achieve this objective. At the beginning of the month he had clashed again with Sumner—this time over Sumner's attempt to require southern judges to swear they had never aided the Confederacy. "Test oaths," said Fessenden, were always a necessary evil at best and should only be used to regulate political offices in the South. "[O]utside of that," he averred, "I am desirous, and I presume every Senator here is desirous, that at the earliest possible day all these [ex-Rebel] States of which we speak . . . may again be prosperous in every sense of the word."[84] Sumner, rightly convinced that blacks could expect little justice from southern courts, was appalled. Fessenden's course, he contended, would help to "invigorate that spirit of the rebellion which I know he hates as well as I."[85]

The Portlander also invited Radical criticism by defending Hugh McCulloch on the Senate floor. The treasury secretary had alienated many Republicans for supporting Johnson's patronage purge and even Fessenden conceded he was not much of a statesman. However, the senator greatly preferred McCulloch's commitment to financial orthodoxy over the Radicals' liking for inflationary policies and he described his former deputy as "an upright" and capable official.[86]

While these comments highlighted the distance between Fessenden and the Radicals, the former revealed that he was not wholly opposed to additional legislation for the South. Confronted by the two Reconstruction measures, he announced that he was willing to vote for both bills with unspecified amendments. But he preferred to prioritize the Military Reconstruction Bill (which he had supported in the Joint Committee) over the highly specific and somewhat "defective" Louisiana Bill.[87] Subjecting the southern states to federal military control was an idea, he said, "which I have always supposed to be the correct idea as applicable to those States until they become in a better condition."[88] Though he would have wished to authorize the executive to secure the lives and property of southern Unionists rather than have Congress take the initiative in this regard, he appears to have had no doubt that the federal government was duty bound to provide that protection.[89]

In a concerted effort to prevent Democrats from deciding close roll calls between Radicals and non-Radicals, Senate Republicans caucused and agreed to form a committee of seven, including Fessenden and Sumner, to coordinate a response to the House legislation. The group, chaired by Sherman, devised a composite bill that combined temporary military rule with the Blaine amendment. Federal commanders would oversee a process of new constitution making in the southern states, culminating in ratification of the Fourteenth Amendment and readmission of those reconstructed states to Congress. Importantly, while the committee stipulated that blacks should vote in the elections for delegates to the constitutional conventions, the majority rejected Sumner's call for universal suffrage to be embedded into the new constitutions. Fessenden spoke out vigorously against the latter proposal.

However, when the measure came before the full caucus Sumner renewed his plea to mandate black enfranchisement. This time he met with success. Senate Republicans supported him by seventeen votes to fifteen.

Fessenden opposed this revolutionary step for several reasons. First, aware of the critical importance of the 1868 presidential election, he feared that universal suffrage would increase the Democrats' political power because, in his view, the freedmen would be dominated by "the wealth and intelligence" of the South. The Radicals were thus fooling themselves in thinking they could control the South "through the aid of the negroes."[90] Second, he considered Sumner's proposal inconsistent with both the Constitution and the Fourteenth Amendment because it deprived states of their lawful authority over the franchise. Third, he feared that it would inject the controversial issue of black suffrage into northern state politics with damaging consequences for the Republican Party and therefore for the country. Fourth, he considered it unwise because it implied a guarantee that no further conditions would be required of the former Confederates. His reasoning was not entirely convincing, for he underestimated the freedmen's capacity to operate independently of their former masters. However, it was not without political acumen. He was right, for example, to note the extent of northern racial prejudice ahead of the presidential election and to predict that Republicans could not count on dominating every southern state with freedmen's votes.

Fessenden was exhausted and abed when the amended Military Reconstruction Bill passed on February 16. While the *New-York Tribune* greeted it as "a complete basis of Reconstruction," he was privately opposed to the measure.[91] "We are doing excessively silly things here," he informed his son William the following day, "—against my judgment and against my protest. Our strides towards destruction as a party are large and rapid."[92] Intent on defeating the bill, he took the unusual step of entering the lower chamber in an effort to persuade House Republicans to reject the Senate's handiwork.[93] Radicals there were outraged that the bill left Johnson's discredited provisional governments intact, authorized the president to appoint military commanders, and contained no provision for disfranchising ex-Confederates. With the assistance of Democrats aiming to defeat any Reconstruction measure they rejected the Senate's proposed amendments. The large Republican majority in the House then moved to make the bill more palatable to southern Unionists by prohibiting anyone barred from office under the Fourteenth Amendment from participating in the constitution-making process and severely restricting the authority of the provisional governments. When the bill returned to the Senate on February

19, Fessenden stunned his colleagues by refusing to support it. Instead, he called for a conference committee to fashion a bill agreeable to both chambers—a move that, ironically, placed him in the same camp as Sumner, who disliked the measure's conservative features. His preference, he said, had been for the Joint Committee's Military Reconstruction Bill, "pure and simple, without having anything else upon it, and leaving to other legislation, if it was judged expedient, what else might be done." "[T]rue statesmanship, he added, "requires that you should do no more than is absolutely demanded by the exigency of the case."[94]

Fessenden insisted that he did "not want to see this bill lost."[95] He opposed it in this form because its procedural nature meant that most southern states would probably be readmitted to Congress before the crucial 1868 election. Unconvinced that black suffrage would guarantee Republicans the electoral college votes of all those states, he regarded this prospect with genuine alarm. Whatever the rights and wrongs of this policy diagnosis, his parliamentary conduct was questionable. His co-partisans were angered by the revelation that he had gone behind their backs after a binding caucus to try and subvert the bill in the House. Fessenden's comment that his desire for greater safeguards for southern Unionists made him more radical than "gentlemen who glory in the name of radical" appeared lame in the light of his opposition to Sumner's universal suffrage proposal.[96] Ben Wade was quick to berate him for his lack of frankness. He would, he remarked sarcastically, be only too delighted if Fessenden "with his vast influence here, will throw it on the side of radicalism and aid such poor radicals as I am to get measures satisfactory to ourselves."[97]

Fessenden had overreached himself on this occasion. He was so convinced of the superior merit of his policy analysis and the weight of his influence that he had broken caucus discipline in an attempt to revise the bill after it had passed the Senate. Although his power inside the congressional Republican Party remained unbroken, the opposition to his covert action revealed its limitations. That spring, his colleagues passed him over for president of the Senate—a position he described as "very stupid" but one he would have been happy to accept—in favor of Wade.[98] Confronted with the alternatives of supporting Johnson, embracing the Radicals' un-palatable agenda, or aligning with the Republican majority behind temporary mili-tary oversight and the Fourteenth Amendment—a policy that did at least promise some return to normality—he chose the latter course. On March 2 he fell into line behind the Republican majority by voting to override President Johnson's vetoes of the Tenure of Office and Military Reconstruction Acts.[99]

Could Fessenden's policy of subjecting southern whites to the discipline of the political wilderness and federal military oversight have delivered a more equitable postwar settlement than the procedural solution enshrined in the Military Reconstruction Act? Keeping southerners out of Congress until Republican legislators had assured their bona fides (ideally until after the 1868 election) would have incentivized good behavior on the part of local elites. Southerners cozying up to Andrew Johnson would have been left in no doubt that the president was a lame duck. Some, especially those ex-Whig leaders with whom Fessenden had much in common, might have proceeded from this unpalatable realization to calculate that the only way to regain national influence and rid themselves of federal military rule was to acquiesce to the Republicans' demand for the safeguarding of Unionists' security and Fourteenth Amendment rights for African Americans. Had they responded thus, Fessenden's policy might conceivably have laid the groundwork for a more robust peace settlement between North and South than the Military Reconstruction Act seemed to promise.

A durable peace was certainly his fundamental objective and he articulated this aim clearly in the brief opening session of the Fortieth Congress. Fessenden vacated his laborious position as head of the Finance Committee in favor of less exhausting duties at the beginning of March 1867. He then took an active role in extended debates over a supplementary Reconstruction Bill intended to establish clear guidelines for the election of southern state constitutional conventions under federal military oversight. On March 15 he moved that Johnson's provisional governments should be required to call the conventions into being before the constitution-making process began.[100]

This was a controversial proposal. Though technically still legal, Johnson's satrapies were widely reviled in the North. The motion envisaged giving defeated Rebels a hold over Reconstruction that many Republicans were not prepared to allow them. Yet there was method in what looked to be Fessenden's madness. He defended his pithy statement that "the men who went out should be the men who should ask to come in" on the grounds of national security.[101] The ex-Confederates were now complaining that northerners wanted to impose readmission terms upon them. As long as their complaints carried weight the Union would never be safe. But if they called the new state conventions into being themselves—expressed in effect their wish to return to the Union—they would never be able to say that they were coerced back into the national fold. "I do not want to have that lie in their mouths," he said, "that they wished to continue independent, but were not only invited back, but forced back by our action."[102] Of course, it might take time for southern politicians to come to their senses and call the conventions. But Fessenden was in no hurry to readmit southern delegates to Congress before the presidential election because he feared that the Republicans could not count on the votes of the reconstructed states. To those Republican senators who contended that his motion would simply subject southern loyalists to an unspecified period of Rebel rule, Fessenden retorted that the Military Reconstruction Act provided them with government protection. Only by giving the late insurgents a stake in the process could the basis for a lasting peace between the two sections be laid. Although the motion was defeated 33–14 (only a minority of Republicans voted alongside him), it bore testimony not only to his statecraft—his continuing desire to find consensual solutions to the problems bedeviling a still-divided nation—but also to his political guile.[103]

While Fessenden's policy aimed at restoring the southern states without sacrificing either the safety of the region's black and white loyalists or Republican control of the country, it was less geared toward securing equality for the emancipated slaves than the Radicals' alternative plan. Whereas the latter sought to empower African Americans by providing them with the ballot, land, and government-funded education, Fessenden adhered to his conviction that such measures would only cause further instability in the South and were poorly tailored to assist impoverished, illiterate blacks. The freedmen, he believed, needed time to gain the education and labor discipline required of independent-minded U.S. citizens. Lest one mistakes Fessenden for a doctrinaire exponent of laissez-faire, it must be remembered that he was not entirely averse to federal aid for the emancipated slaves. He not only supported the Freedmen's Bureau, the legal protections of the Fourteenth Amendment, and military Reconstruction, but also acquiesced to a reduction in the government's cotton tax (which compounded the oppressive tax burden for poor farmers in the postwar South) and later gave his backing to the sale of government property at Harpers Ferry in aid of black Storer College.[104] However, he supported only restricted, temporary federal assistance for southern blacks—just enough to put them on their feet. In the medium and longer terms they would have to make their own way in the South's new free-labor society with the help of their former masters, well-intentioned northerners, and the state governments in which, after passage of the Military Reconstruction Act, they were bound to play a part.

Disagreement over the optimal level of federal support for African Americans lay at the heart of rapidly rising tensions between Radicals and non-Radicals in the spring of 1867. The intra-party fault-line was highlighted during the March session when Charles Sumner introduced, as "a declaration of principle and of purpose," a set of resolutions indicating Congress's backing for a range of southern reforms, including government homesteads and education for African Americans. Fessenden was quick to assail them. When Sumner argued that blacks should be given the land on which they currently resided, he retorted, "That is more than we do for white men." Sumner's response—that white men had never been enslaved—carried more weight with later historians than it did with his Senate peers who feared the demoralizing effects of excessive federal aid to blacks. Fessenden and other centrists successfully defeated Radical attempts to embed mandatory reforms—such as free schools—in the new southern state constitutions to be written under military rule. Sumner took the setbacks personally. "How few here sympathize with me!" he moaned. "I sometimes feel that I am alone in the Senate."[105]

Although he failed to secure an adjournment until the winter (Congress agreed to reconvene in July if the president misbehaved), Fessenden left Washington in April pleased to have thwarted attempts by "disorganizers" to ruin the party. "[A]lthough we have done much—very much—to make ourselves odious and contemptible, we are saved from absolute disgrace," he wrote to Lizzy shortly before bidding farewell to Moses. "The last five months have been on the whole the most wearying & unsatisfactory of my life."[106] Back home in Portland, he penned a letter to James Grimes in which he asserted that few Republicans thought there would be any need for a summer session of Congress. Yet the Radicals, he warned, had not given up hope of securing the presidency for Wade in 1868 and were busy "abusing every body—not excepting [General Ulysses S.] Grant. You know the nature of the animals."[107] His suspicion of the ultras mirrored their conviction that centrists wanted to subordinate Reconstruction issues to partisan expediency. At a meeting of the American Anti-Slavery Society in early May, Wendell Phillips condemned non-Radicals for their preoccupation with Grant as the most "available" presidential candidate and accused senators like Fessenden and Sherman of plotting to barter "principle for patronage" and "the leadership of their party for family advancement."[108] Fessenden was so aggravated by these comments that he dashed off a furious letter to the Yankee reformer demanding to know whether newspaper reports of the speech were accurate and, if so, the source of the allegation of "gross corruption."[109]

While Pitt Fessenden was deeply concerned about the Radicals' conduct, he continued to hold that southern whites should exhibit proof of their preparedness to rejoin the Union before their delegates were readmitted to Congress. In late April 1867 former North Carolina Whig, Kenneth Rayner, an opponent of secession during the winter of 1860–61, asked Fessenden to help secure the release or speedy trial of Confederate president Jefferson Davis, who had been incarcerated by the government for more than two years. Revealingly, he described Fessenden as a Republican who was "generally regarded by the Southern people as a man of humane, just, and moderate views."[110] The senator from Maine responded on May 9, shortly after Davis's release from prison, that he desired "a speedy adjustment of the unhappy difficulties growing out of the late terrible war." However, he emphasized that this outcome could not proceed simply from northern magnanimity. Southerners, he hoped, would "by their speedy adoption of the terms of Reconstruction demonstrate their intention to conform, in a right spirit, to the necessities of the situation, created by themselves."[111]

Fessenden had not planned to spend the summer in Portland. He had left the capital expecting to visit Europe. With his natural Anglophilia reawakened after the Civil War, he was looking forward to witnessing debates in Parliament. Among "the giants" of mid-Victorian politics he hoped to see was William Ewart Gladstone, a forceful and intelligent debater with whom Fessenden identified closely despite his public statement after Antietam that the Confederates had "made a nation."[112] "I have sympathy for & with Mr Gladstone," he told Freeman Morse who was still clinging on to the consular post in London, "as I see he is accused of bad temper— a charge Sumner and others are fond of making against me." Gladstone, he added, must be impatient "with the annoyances inevitable upon the leadership of fools. It is easy to deal with open adversaries—but it is hard to bear with the selfishness and vanity of political associates whose delight it is to increase your troubles."[113] However intriguing the possibility of a meeting between two of the principal statesmen of the Anglo-American world, Fessenden did not manage to get away. Rebuilding after the Portland fire cost time and money. And before long there was a return journey to Washington to consider.

In mid-June Attorney General Henry Stanbery issued a legal ruling intended to undo the recent work of congressional Republicans. In it he sought to restrict the political influence of military commanders in the South by opining that Johnson's provisional governments remained the paramount power until new state constitutions had been ratified. The chairman of the Republican executive congressional committee promptly summoned party members back to Washington to respond to the administration's challenge. Fessenden was uncertain whether to go. Although he thought the Radicals were "jumping at a pretence," feared the centrists would be weakened by absentees, and had some sympathy with Stanbery's interpretation of

THE CHIEF TINKER: CONGRESSIONAL RECONSTRUCTION, 1866–1868

the law, he admitted to being "disgusted with Johnson" for providing the ultras with yet another chance to promote their revolutionary agenda.[114] After a flurry of correspondence among themselves, non-Radical senators agreed to attend the session. "I don['] t see but we must go on," Fessenden told his Maine colleague Lot Morrill. "I am out of all patience with Johnson for being such a fool. Why couldn't he let matters take their course."[115]

Pitt Fessenden's determination to outwit his opponents was evident from the start of the adjourned session. In a Republican caucus on July 3 he took the lead in securing agreement on a resolution declaring that business should be confined largely to the issues raised by Stanbery's ruling. "Sumner died hard," he reported, "and swore like a trooper."[116] When, on the Senate floor, the aggrieved Bostonian compared the resolution to the infamous gag rule, Fessenden flayed him mercilessly for breaking with a caucus decision.[117] To Ben Wade, who asked the numerically superior centrists to recall how tyrannically the small band of Republican senators was treated by proslavery Democrats in the 1850s, he replied bluntly, "a minority does not like to be a minority."[118] Hemmed in, the Radicals achieved little in the next few weeks beyond another Reconstruction act explicitly empowering federal commanders in the South to dismiss civilian officials. (The bill received the assent of all Republicans and was easily passed over Johnson's predictable veto.) Thwarted in their efforts to assail the president and impose further reforms and conditions on the southern states, the Radicals proceeded to vent their frustration on their principal nemesis.

On the last day of the July session Zachariah Chandler delivered a furious personal attack on Fessenden, denouncing him repeatedly as "the Conservative Senator from Maine" for his alleged faith in Andrew Johnson and condemning like-minded Republicans as a contemptible set of "hybrids" whose days were numbered. Stung by what he labeled contemptuously "this prepared attack," Fessenden claimed that Chandler and other Radicals were deliberately attempting to injure his "standing and position" in the party. Perhaps unwisely, he drew the Senate's attention to an article in a Detroit newspaper (allegedly planted by Chandler) contending that he opposed impeachment to protect his friends and relations in office. He proceeded with a detailed defense of the charge, becoming unusually emotional when he referred to his three sons who had fought for the Union. "My youngest son fell upon his first field," he avowed. "Another had his arm shattered and his leg shot off. The third was not wounded, but served and fought in twenty battles. I never asked for the appointment of one of them to any office." He closed by denying that he had confidence in Johnson and asserting that if he were a conservative, he was in good company among Senate Republicans.

This defense may not have been the strongest speech of Fessenden's career, but Chandler's stinging assault revealed his opponent to be at the height of his power. Fessenden was certainly not responsible for holding back the Radicals on his own. The imposition of the "gag" at the start of the session revealed little support among Republican senators in July 1867 for what a majority of northerners regarded as extreme measures. However, there was some truth to Sumner's charge, delivered to a journalist at the end of the summer, that Fessenden was "the captain of the obstructives."[119] No other non-Radical Republican possessed his range or caliber of parliamentary skills or exercised as much influence as he did over the amorphous group of centrists in the upper chamber. While his perceived conservatism was one reason for the intense personal animosity directed against him, the Radicals' gathering animus—redolent of their criticism of Lincoln at the time of the Wade-Davis Bill—was surely induced in large part by their deep frustration at what they might have achieved with him on their side.[120] Although the differences between Fessenden and the ultras were no wider than those between Lincoln and the Radicals, they were large enough to prevent mutual cooperation in the summer of 1867. The senator from Maine had never been a social revolutionary, nor did he ascribe to Henry Wilson's view that the cause of the Republican Party was "the cause of the poor and the oppressed."[121] He despised the Radicals for what he saw as their intolerance and inattention to political realities. If the republic were to survive the current crisis, he knew he must set his face against them.

Third Bull Run: The Trial of Andrew Johnson

Pitt Fessenden returned home not only to relax and restore his equilibrium but also to correspond with Johnson's department heads on behalf of his political allies. He told Seward to keep "my friend" Morse in his post and reassured the worried consul that he was probably safe as long as the secretary remained in office and he (Fessenden) remained on good terms with Johnson.[122] In an exchange with Hugh McCulloch he successfully protested the dismissal of his pet, Katie Kearon, from the Treasury, explaining that her long absence from duty had been caused by illness. He took, he wrote, "a special interest" in the girl and her family, having known her father—a man with a mother, a wife, and eight children to support—when he worked in the congressional library.[123]

THE CHIEF TINKER: CONGRESSIONAL RECONSTRUCTION, 1866–1868   225

While the president seemed inclined to go on indulging Fessenden's patronage wishes, he showed few signs of reaching out positively to non-Radical Republicans in general as some of his wiser supporters advised.[124] In fact he was soon on the warpath again. In mid-August Johnson suspended Edwin Stanton from office, replacing him with Ulysses S. Grant as secretary of war ad interim. Stanton was the only supporter of congressional Reconstruction left in the cabinet and his suspension caused huge controversy, combined as it was with the reassignment of generals such as Philip H. Sheridan who were also sympathetic to congressional policy. Politics, Fessenden told Morse, were again "all in a muddle," with the Radicals intent on impeaching the president—an action he had always opposed "as a rock on which the Republican party must inevitably go to pieces."[125] Though concerned about what the Radicals might do next, he was again irritated with Johnson for providing more grist for their mill. "[T]he D——l," he told McCulloch, "will be to pay when Congress meets. The sentiment of New England was decidedly, almost unanimously adverse to the operations of Wade[,] Butler & Co, when we last adjourned. Now, I meet no man who is not in favour of impeachment if any decent pretence for it can be found. It does seem as if Johnson was resolved upon destruction."[126]

That fall Fessenden found himself in the unusual position of anticipating Republican losses in northern state elections with a degree of equanimity. Grimes's prediction that the Democrats would make gains in the Midwest would, if realized, leave the Radicals' hopes "somewhat clouded."[127] The Democrats did do well, winning important victories in New York, Pennsylvania, and Ohio partly by dint of their openly racist stance on black suffrage. Ben Wade, his hopes of reelection to the Senate dashed by the result in Ohio, exclaimed bluntly, "The nigger whipped us."[128] Although northern losses were accompanied by Republican successes in elections for delegates to southern constitutional conventions, Fessenden made no comment on the decisive role played by black Republican voters in these contests. Preoccupied with the party's northern base, he interpreted the results as a popular verdict on Radical schemes as well as a guarantee that the centrist-oriented military hero Grant would receive the Republican presidential nomination in the spring. However, he was not naïve enough to think that his enemies would take their beating lying down. There would be, he told Grimes, "crimination & recrimination" aplenty when Congress reconvened.[129]

In late October Fessenden penned a memorandum to accompany the latest version of his will. He was comfortably well off—his total estate was worth more than $40,000, half of it wrapped up in the State Street property.[130] One of the main purposes of this note was to bespeak protection from his sons for his "dear cousin" Lizzy. "She has been my true and dear friend from her childhood," he wrote, "and I hope they will not suffer her to want the comforts of life so long as they have power to supply them." Fessenden asked his half-brother Daniel to burn any items in his correspondence that he thought should be destroyed, "particularly all he may find from females, except such as are upon matters of business." He wished to be buried, he stated, between his late wife and daughter.[131] His affairs in hand, the senator returned to Washington without tarrying in Portland to hear a lecture by Charles Sumner. The latter was reportedly hurt that he did not attend, a response that prompted Fessenden to dismiss him as a "great baby."[132]

As the new session of Congress opened at the beginning of December, Fessenden worried that Johnson's recent actions would impel the House of Representatives to begin impeachment proceedings. Radicals had been pushing the idea for nearly two years but the measure had stalled in committee. Fessenden remained convinced, even after Stanton's suspension and Sheridan's removal, that impeachment would be "ruin to our party" ahead of the 1868 presidential election.[133] The nation's postwar economy, encumbered with debt and taxation, was in a parlous state. Republicans, he reasoned, could ill afford to alienate northern voters by ousting the president of the United States, thereby destabilizing the government and damaging the country's reputation abroad. Initially, many of his co-partisans agreed. In early December the House defeated an impeachment resolution with a narrow majority of Republicans voting against it.

Historians have noted the close correlation between opposition to impeachment and support for hard-money policies as a solution to America's economic woes.[134] For reasons of morality as well as financial orthodoxy, Fessenden was a staunch advocate of measures designed to achieve a relatively swift return to specie payments: robust taxation levels, the steady withdrawal of greenbacks from circulation, and the payment of interest on the country's war debt in gold. He therefore opposed the "Jeremy Diddler style of financiering" favored by many pro-inflation Radicals and welcomed the anti-impeachment vote as a signal for Congress to concentrate on the all-important task of devising responsible financial legislation to meet the needs of the hour.[135] Although he confessed that Johnson had been "guilty of very serious offences[,] the consequence, I think, of bad temper and self confidence," he did not believe the president had "committed any specific act" that would justify his impeachment under the Constitution for "high crimes and misdemeanors." Grant's nomination was now certain, he thought. "He has shown much ability in his management of the War Department, and well informed men express great confidence in him."[136]

Fessenden's optimism soon evaporated. Republican reverses in the autumn elections combined with the defeat of the impeachment resolution to further embolden the president. As December wore on, Johnson rashly dismissed more federal commanders sympathetic to congressional policy and encouraged southern whites to oppose the new state constitutions drawn up by Republican-dominated conventions. Adamant that impeachment was essential for their survival, hard-pressed southern Republicans clamored for action. One of Sumner's Texas correspondents reported that loyal men, most of them black, were being murdered on a regular basis. "To me," he wrote, "Congress appears responsible for the blood-shed it might easily have to a very considerable extent averted."[137] On January 13, 1868, the Senate moved to reinstate Stanton as secretary of war. Disturbed by the treatment of one of his political friends and affronted by the president's challenge to Senate authority, Fessenden delivered a forthright and impromptu speech in favor of voiding the suspension and voted with his colleagues for a resolution non-concurring in Stanton's removal. For a brief moment the party seemed united in its response. Even Zachariah Chandler told Fessenden that he forgave him all his "sins."[138] It was probably the last (backhanded) compliment he received from a Radical in his lifetime.

The Senate's action triggered a series of dramatic events. Grant, sensing that Johnson had overstepped the mark and aware that a presidential nomination was within his grasp, returned his cabinet post to Stanton—a response that won approval from Radical and centrist Republicans alike. Furious, Johnson formally dismissed Stanton on February 21 on the grounds that he was not protected by the Tenure of Office Act and replaced him as secretary of war ad interim by Adjutant General Lorenzo Thomas. This inflammatory move caused most Senate non-Radicals to shift their ground. Fessenden, however, doubted whether the president's action infringed the terms of the Tenure of Office statute and realized that passage of Henry Wilson's resolve denying Andrew Johnson's right "so to act, under the existing laws, without the consent of the Senate" would precipitate impeachment proceedings in the lower house.[139] But although he and a number of other non-Radicals voted against this declaration, twenty-eight of their peers secured its passage. Fessenden was appalled. "Madness has ruled the hour with the majority," he told Freeman Morse. "Passion has almost banished sense, and the power which we might have easily retained for many years is fast departing from us. You must not be surprised if we are beaten at the coming elections."[140] To Lizzy, he wrote that he was "utterly discouraged and out of spirits. Either I am very stupid, or my friends are acting like fools, and hurrying us to destruction."[141] On February 24 the House of Representatives finally approved articles of impeachment against the president and voted to try him before the Senate. America was plunged into a tumult. Charles Dickens, in Boston halfway through a highly profitable reading tour of the United States, predicted that the matter would, "for the time, probably over-ride and over-throw everything in this country. It instantly emptied our great gallery here last night, and paralyzed the Theatres in the midst of a rush of good business."[142]

It was immediately apparent that the pressure on senators to convict would be intense. Many Republicans assumed Johnson's guilt despite the fact that the Senate had yet to consider the legal case against him. The Maine legislature speedily recorded its "hearty approval" of the House's action while Portland Republicans, Neal Dow among them, ominously described impeachment as "a necessity and a duty."[143] Even Fessenden's son, William, insisted the president must go or "it is all over with us."[144] However, even before the impeachment trial began, Fessenden signaled to close friends and family that he took a dim view of those Republicans, southern as well as northern, who regarded Johnson's political execution as inevitable. "The country has so bad an opinion of him [Johnson], which he fully deserves," the senator told his father shortly before the trial began, "that it expects his condemnation and removal from office. This fact places those who are to try him, if they are conscientious men, in a possibly painful position, especially as a failure to convict may be attended with very disastrous consequences to the dominant party, & consequently to the great cause which depends upon its success." Senators had a duty to try the unpopular president "impartially," he wrote—adding significantly, "I still think that whatever may have been his misdemeanours, it would have been wiser to tolerate him to the end of his term, rather than to expose our party, and our country, to so great a hazard."[145]

The trial began in mid-March. Anticipating a swift verdict, House impeachment managers drew up a set of articles that aimed to convict on grounds that were as much political as legal. Conversely, the president's elite defense team strove from the outset to make the trial as formal as possible, recognizing that Johnson's best chance of acquittal lay in convincing non-Radical senators that the president had not committed an illegal act. They also sought to delay the proceedings as much as possible, aware that public interest in the trial was likely to diminish over time and that the wordier and more protracted their defense, the stronger the president's case would become. Much to the chagrin of the House managers, Johnson's attorneys succeeded. The trial dragged on through the second half of March, all through April, and on into the first two weeks of May. From the start and fairly consistently thereafter Fessenden voted to sustain the defense position on most questions, including motions intended to prolong the trial.[146] Within a few weeks public interest in the case was beginning to wane.

Although Fessenden was keen to furnish the impression that he would keep an open mind, his private comments during the trial as well as his relatively consistent voting record on procedural motions revealed that he was hostile to conviction from the beginning. At the end of March he told his son Frank that he "would give much to avoid the responsibility" of pronouncing judgment on the president, "for it may be that I shall feel compelled to disappoint all the expectations & wishes of our friends."[147] He informed Lizzy at the same juncture that if Johnson were to be impeached for "general cussedness" there would be no problem. This, however, was not the issue: "[W]hatever I may think and feel as a politician, I cannot and will not violate my oath, if I can avoid it."[148] Despite these comments Fessenden did join the Republican majority on a handful of occasions, for example, on April 2 when he voted against motions to sustain the president's counsel and to adjourn until noon the following day. These instances suggest that his mind was not completely made up even though he was clearly veering toward acquittal from the outset. "I have not yet conclusively determined how I shall vote—," he told Lizzy ten days later, "but I am determined to keep my oath, if my wishes & prejudices will permit me to do so, and to take all the consequences, whatever they may be." Keenly aware that he might have done more to oppose the previous year's Reconstruction legislation, he added, "Cowardice has led me to follow bad counsels, because the majority so determined, as far as I can go."[149]

Fessenden had little doubt that the consequences of an acquittal vote would be serious. As he had intimated to Frank, Maine Republicans were almost entirely in favor of impeachment. Neal Dow, never one to question his own rectitude, told Fessenden in early April how everyone at home was looking "*longingly* for the hour when that bold, bad man shall be dismissed from his high office."[150] "Hang Johnson up by the heels like a dead crow in a cornfield to frighten all his tribe," added Dow in a follow-up letter the following day.[151] By the middle of that month the *New-York Tribune* was naming Fessenden as one of ten Republicans who might break ranks and vote for acquittal with the Johnsonites and Democrats.[152] His political friends at home grew nervous. One of them, Rufus Dwinel, felt impelled to warn him that, rightly or wrongly, "the multitude" would hold him responsible if he voted to let Johnson off the hook.[153]

After seven weeks of interminable argument and counterargument, the prosecutors had become deeply frustrated with their opponents' delaying tactics. "The trial lags," reported Charles Sumner bitterly. "There are senators, calling themselves republicans, who are Johnsonite in sentiments. At the head of these is Fessenden, who has opposed every measure by which this country has been saved. Had he openly joined the enemy several years ago, it would have been better for us. He has sown trouble in our camp & been a constant ally to the enemy."[154] On May 3 the senator from Maine repeated his conviction that impeachment should never have been attempted. "Make up your mind, if need be," he told William, "to hear me denounced as a traitor, & perhaps hung in effigy. I have not yet formed a conclusive opinion, but my vote will be given according to my convictions, whatever they may be." He added that the result of the trial was "quite uncertain." Seven Republican votes were necessary to acquit. Three of his colleagues had already told him they intended to find the president not guilty, while another seven or eight were wavering.[155] Massachusetts Radicals clearly had reason to be wary of his intentions. Edward L. Pierce told Sumner on May 7 that Fessenden "would escape from an affirmative vote if he could do so with any chance of holding his place with the Republican party—and such a man is always doubtful and dangerous."[156] James Grimes, who probably knew his friend's mind better than anyone at this late stage of the trial, reported on same day that "I think that Fessenden, Trumbull, Henderson & myself will vote against conviction."[157]

Whatever lingering doubts remained in Fessenden's mind about how he would vote were induced by rational concern for his political position. Any worries about what Johnson might actually do in the event of an acquittal had probably been allayed by the beginning of May. As the trial neared its conclusion Grimes spoke to the president at a private dinner party. At this prearranged meeting the Iowan sought assurances that Johnson would do nothing rash if found not guilty. The president, who had ceased his operations against congressional policy on the advice of his counsel, was happy to provide those guarantees, which Grimes immediately passed on to wavering senators. Shortly afterward, Johnson backed up his comments by appointing the respected Union general John M. Schofield to the post of secretary of war. Fessenden, who may have had prior notice of Schofield's elevation, must have been reassured by this development.[158] His main concern at the close of proceedings was thus the political storm likely to descend upon him if he voted against impeachment. On May 11, he received encouraging word on this score from Horace White, the influential editor of the *Chicago Tribune*. White told him that he would not hold an acquittal vote against him and asked him to relay this information to Grimes.[159] That same day Fessenden joined the Iowan and two other Republicans in announcing, in secret session, that he would not sustain any of the charges leveled against the president.

A skilled constitutional lawyer, William Pitt Fessenden genuinely believed that there were sound legal reasons for opposing conviction. He had taken an oath at the start of the trial to "do impartial justice according to the Constitution and the laws." As he stated in his written opinion submitted at the end of the proceedings, he could not therefore treat the occasion as a political show-trial and was bound, as the Earl of Eldon had asserted while presiding over the British government's 1820 prosecution of George IV's estranged wife, Caroline of Brunswick, to "take no notice of what is passing out of doors, because I am supposed constitutionally not to be acquainted with it." Although he had never questioned the Tenure of Office Act's constitutionality, he did not believe that its provisions protected Stanton, who had been appointed by Lincoln in his first term and thus held his post at Johnson's pleasure. Thomas's interim appointment, moreover, he adjudged lawful under an obscure 1795 statute governing departmental vacancies. The managers' charge that Johnson had attempted to foster opposition to Congress, he dismissed as an infringement of the president's right to free speech. In a comment signifying the extent to which his Whiggish belief in the primacy of Congress had been tempered by months of factionalism and fears of rampant statism, Fessenden held too that the impeachment of a president was an inherently dangerous act likely to further destabilize a polity that had been dangerously unbalanced by the Civil War. Anything, he reasoned, which tended to undermine the executive—"one of the great coördinate branches of the Government"—"would be to shake the faith of the friends of constitutional liberty in the permanency of our free institutions and the capacity of man for self-government."[160]

Many Republicans received the news of Fessenden's stance in the secret session as they had responded to battlefield disasters during the war. "You had better put Trumbull, Fessenden & Co into the nearest lunatic asylum," wrote one agitated Pennsylvanian. "May the lord have mercy on their poor souls. The whole country feels this *third* Bull Run as much as the first or second."[161] Not everyone had abandoned hope. Poor Rufus Dwinel penned another desperate letter to Fessenden urging him not "to sacrifice yourself forever, & your friends without a word to say in extenuation . . . If for nothing else, to satisfy those who elected you, you are bound to vote for a conviction."[162] This argument for democratic accountability, tinged as it was with self-interest in Dwinel's case, cut no ice with his political patron. Fessenden had always held that an American senator should make up his own mind and not be unduly influenced by a public which, "when roused and excited by passion & prejudice, is little better than a wild beast."[163]

Saturday, May 16, dawned a beautiful spring day in Washington. The marble Capitol fairly glistened in the sunshine as the crowds made their way toward the most celebrated political theater in America. Although attendances at the trial had dropped since the opening weeks, the Senate galleries were soon crammed with excited onlookers, many of them still hopeful that Johnson would be found guilty by the required two-thirds vote of the chamber. Beneath them William Pitt Fessenden appeared unusually agitated but ready as always to do his duty as he saw it. One reporter observed how he "had banished all expression from his face and held his head erect, defiantly turning from side to side continually."[164] Chief Justice Chase entered the chamber at noon and senators then agreed to vote first on Article XI, the charge regarded as most likely to secure a conviction. Missing at this point was James Grimes, who had recently suffered a paralytic stroke. Fessenden moved to delay the verdict to give his friend time to enter the chamber. But at this moment Grimes was dramatically "half carried" into the Senate, whereupon the critical vote proceeded according to alphabetical order.[165] When asked if he found the president guilty under the eleventh article, Fessenden arose and responded "nay." Six other non-Radical Republicans, including Grimes and Trumbull, cast negative votes. The final tally was 35–19 in favor of conviction. Johnson had been acquitted by one vote.

What Fessenden did not say in his written opinion, but what most of his contemporaries well knew, was that by helping to acquit the president he was thwarting the Radicals' plans to take control of the government. If convicted Johnson would cede power to Ben Wade, one of the Portlander's fiercest critics within the Republican Party. Sumner, it was rumored, would be Wade's secretary of state. Fessenden's aversion to this unsavory prospect was prompted partly by his dislike of ultra policies such as confiscation, universal suffrage, and greenback inflation, all of which Wade supported. But he was motivated too by the fact that he disliked the Radicals as men as much as they personally disliked him. He had derived pleasure from defying them in the past and there is every reason to believe that his vote was influenced by a very human desire to deal his critics a crushing blow. In this respect the Radicals' attacks on him over the previous year were counterproductive. They strengthened his republican pride and stubborn resolve to act independently of what he saw as party dictation. His desire to thwart his foes was intensified by the fact that he had thought them cornered after the initial failure of impeachment in the House. "They are in a minority of their own party—and must stay there," he had told Lizzy Warriner in mid-December.[166]

Many observers regarded Fessenden's not-guilty vote as a betrayal of the Republican Party. One New York lawyer told him that he had always regarded the senator as "the great jurist and statesman of the party." However, he continued, a great leader "ought, when the crisis comes, to sacrifice himself to save his party rather than to sacrifice his party to save himself."[167] This was a misreading of Fessenden's action as he (Fessenden) saw it. The senator had always opposed impeachment because he feared it would divide the party, render it irresponsible in the eyes of the northern public, and thereby increase its vulnerability to a growing Democratic resurgence in the country. Impeachment, he had told his friend Freeman Morse in February, would "use us up, however it may result."[168] He had always resisted being told how to act as a politician. His pride, class, and self-image as an independent-minded U.S. senator prevented him from being dictated to by any individual or organization, but he had long regarded Republicanism as the nation's salvation. Fessenden was convinced that, if the president were convicted, the Republicans would lose the 1868 presidential election and that this result would be disastrous for the party and the country. "The old order of things will be restored," he predicted gloomily, "and ten more years will see us in the midst of another revolution."[169]

What is unclear is whether Fessenden was right to argue—as he did before, during, and after the trial—that opposing impeachment was the only way to save the party (and by extension the nation) from ruin. Judging by the results of the 1867 elections (and Republican losses in New Hampshire the following spring) *northerners* in general were growing impatient with the ruling party's preoccupation with Reconstruction and black rights. Wade, recently rejected by Ohioans, might have been a serious drag on the Republican ticket if he had secured the vice presidential nomination at Chicago (a not impossible scenario if impeachment had succeeded). Indeed, one correspondent from Philadelphia told Fessenden that he thought this development would cause the Republicans to lose several key states in the November election.[170] However, if saving the party had been his prime concern, the senator could have reasoned just as, if not more, convincingly that because a majority of *Republicans* wanted impeachment, a vote for acquittal would place intolerable strains on party unity and therefore threaten his co-partisans' ability to fight the upcoming election successfully. That he did not do so suggests that personality conflicts and

deep concerns for the future of American government and society were more significant factors in his decision to oppose conviction.

It is possible, of course, that the Radicals were right to suspect that their nemesis was motivated by his desire to cozy up to the administration in order to retain
friends like Morse in office. A Wade administration, short-lived though it would
have been, might well have moved against his allies. (Even though Fessenden was
the senior senator from Maine, the new Radical president would have had a powerful incentive to favor the disaffected Hamlin faction in state politics.) Johnson, on
the other hand, was so unpopular in the North by the spring of 1868 that Fessenden
was probably being honest when he informed his old law partner William Willis
that it would have been in his best interests politically to support impeachment and
that it had actually been hard to suppress his "strong impulses" to convict the willful
president.[171]

Did his action, a mixture of high principle and less elevated human imperfec-
tion, make a difference to Reconstruction? Many commentators believed that Fessenden played *the* critical role in the impeachment proceedings. "It might be almost
said," commented the *Boston Advertiser,* "that he held the issue of this great trial in
his hands, and took upon himself alone the responsibility of saying it should go no
further."[172] Rumors, however, abounded at the time that other, more cautious, Republicans were secretly ready to acquit if their votes were needed, so it is possible
that Johnson would have been saved even if some of the less prominent "recusants"
had not felt emboldened by Fessenden's conduct, as they surely did, to vote with the
majority. Yet by saving the president there is no doubt that Fessenden and the other
six centrists had delivered a major blow to the Radicals. Grant's nomination and
election were highly likely by this stage but, as Johnson's successor, Ben Wade would
have used his authority not only to promote inflationary policies but also to curb the
Rebel influence in the South and promote greater democratization of that troubled
region. This was why so many ex-Confederates were elated by Johnson's acquittal.
The day after the Senate vote on the eleventh article, a devastated Charles Sumner
received an anonymous letter from New Orleans. "Mr *Sumner,* and all the rest of the
Damned Yankee impeachers . . .," read the eloquent communication, "1,000 cheers
for our noble *Andy* Johnston [*sic*], who has beat you all at your own game, and three
small cheers for old Fowler, Henderson, Trumbull & co . . . Your yankee friends
down here will smell *hell* yet before the summer is out[.]"[173]

And so they would. Violence against southern black Unionists rose sharply during
the fiercely contested 1868 presidential election campaign. William Pitt Fessenden,

however, never regretted his decision to oppose the Radicals from the spring of 1867 onward. By his own lights he had acted the part of a patriotic American statesman throughout the postwar political crisis. He had, he believed, saved the republic from disaster by thwarting Andrew Johnson's dangerously lenient plan of Reconstruction, and then staved off an even greater menace to the country's welfare by trouncing the irresponsible Radicals at the moment of their expected triumph. These were impressive accomplishments for a prideful politician who had always regarded Reconstruction as a problem to be solved rather than an opportunity to be grasped. Even if they were not quite the product of high principle that Fessenden supposed them to be, they grew logically out of his consistent support for the Union cause, his determination to restore a healthy balance between the federal government and the states, and a profound desire for national unity and domestic peace that he shared with the majority of northerners. Only time would tell whether his achievements—as he saw them—would be recognized by his own party or whether his controversial vote in the impeachment trial would make him a political outcast in his own land.

Epilogue: 1868–1869

William Pitt Fessenden was seldom given to bouts of self-pity. Greatly discomfited by the debilitating bowel condition that would eventually kill him and by the intense criticism directed against him for his anti-impeachment vote, he retained his indomitable sense of purpose until the end of his life. Although some Republicans tried to expel him from the party, he resisted the urge to decamp and soon began to reassert his influence within the organization. He was still a force to be reckoned with just days before his death in the fall of 1869 and contemporaries, shocked by his sudden demise, rightly paid tribute to him as one of the most influential political figures of the Civil War generation.

At first it seemed that Fessenden might be overwhelmed by the ferocity of his opponents in May 1868. Even his political allies struggled to defend him. The editor of the *Portland Press*, normally one of the senator's strongest supporters, felt obliged to print a number of censorious articles to defend his own position before the court of local opinion. One described Fessenden's "whole mental constitution" as "conservative" and asked rhetorically if he had not sympathized with the reactionary wing of the Republican Party since the beginning of the Civil War. More convincingly, it disparaged Fessenden's claims that his stance had been determined solely by high principle. The anonymous writer noted the senator's patronage demands on the discredited president and concluded damningly that "His motives, like those of most of his compeers, are probably of average human purity, with a fair share of prejudice, personal dislike and interest present and prospective, while, like the rest of us he fancies that he is acting on the elevated plane of pure reason and in the atmosphere of judicial impartiality and disinterestedness."[1]

Stung by these attacks, Fessenden tried to fight back, pressing the editor to defend his course and insert more positive copy from Horace White's *Chicago Tribune*. It was an uphill struggle. A majority of Republicans had favored impeachment and concurred with Charles Sumner that Fessenden and his fellow "quibblers" had voted for acquittal on specious legal grounds and for their own base reasons.[2] Most of Fessenden's northern defenders were relatively conservative organs such as the *New*

York Times, the *Chicago Tribune*, and the *Springfield Republican*. Congratulatory letters tended to come from New England lawyers and bankers who lauded him for putting country above party.[3]

Fessenden was fortunate that wise heads in the Republican organization calculated that any attempt to expel the "recusants" would undermine party unity ahead of the presidential election. The Boston businessman John Murray Forbes bemoaned the failure to convict Johnson but thought it would be "sheer madness to add to this great disaster the risk of splitting up the Republican party, now the only bulwark of freedom. We owe it to the living and to the dead to keep together until we have absolutely secured the fruits of our dearly bought victories."[4] When the Republican national convention met at the Chicago Opera House shortly after the critical impeachment vote, hopes ran high that the seven senators would be dealt with, in the words of the *New-York Tribune*, as "deserters."[5] The fiery Radical general, John A. Logan, and Lincoln's old ally, Norman Judd, demanded their expulsion in speeches to the Illinois and southern delegations and a resolution calculated to achieve that end was drafted by the national council of the Union League. The expulsion efforts were thwarted, however, by non-Radicals like Carl Schurz and the final platform contained no explicit criticism of the anti-impeachers. Fessenden was still "sick at heart" over his friends' failure to laud his conduct but he was cheered by Grant's nomination and relieved that the convention had not caved into pressure from his enemies. "It now remains for us to decide whether we choose to stay in," he told Frank haughtily. "If the party desires to swap me off for Ben. Butler, I shall enter no protest. I owe the party nothing, and have no favours to ask."[6] Apparent confirmation that he had done the right thing came when a group of wealthy Boston businessmen and Brahmins, including Edward Atkinson, Francis Parkman, and Charles Francis Adams, Jr., thankful that the government had not been "Mexicanized" by impeachment or delivered into the hands of men committed to what they regarded as irresponsible economic policies, signaled strong support among New England's elite by announcing a public dinner in his honor.[7]

Given the severity of Republican attacks—one anonymous Down Easter denounced him as a *"villainous traitor"* and "Doubled-dyed Judas" and threatened to kill him when he returned home—Fessenden could have been forgiven for thinking about leaving the party.[8] He had not voted against impeachment to assist the political ambitions of Salmon Chase by breaking down the party of Lincoln, but, were the Democrats to nominate the chief justice for president, he knew he might be faced with a real dilemma. If his old ally received the nomination, he wrote on June 13, it would "be a great thing for the country whether he is elected or not, for it will be an abandonment of old democratic issues, and prove the dawn of a new era."[9]

Thoughts of jumping ship passed quickly. While Fessenden had always resisted party dictation, he had built his career on party loyalty. Grant's nomination confirmed that Radicals did not control party counsels and he was soon behaving like the leading Republican he had been for more than a decade. In late June he told his son William to secure the election of friendly delegates to Maine Republicans' state convention and subsequently ventured the unashamedly partisan hope that the Democrats' decision to nominate two conservative Unionists, Horatio Seymour and Francis Blair, Jr., would "save us."[10] It is true that in the Senate—where business went on until July—he exhibited further evidence of his independent streak, declining (out of continued concern for Republican control of the electoral college in the upcoming presidential election) to support the readmission of the reconstructed southern states as a matter of form and opposing, fruitlessly as he later admitted, more corrupting government subsidies for railroads.[11] He voted with the majority, however, to pass two more Reconstruction bills over Johnson's vetoes and was not the only Republican to oppose further increases in federal power.[12] Ten others, including Sumner, voted with him against a bill mandating an eight-hour day for federal employees. Fessenden, convinced that free labor meant the right to work hard, not to be cosseted by the government, dismissed this measure as "a humbug." All efforts to regulate work by legislation, he averred, tended "to bring all men to a level, a stupid man upon a level with a smart and capable one."[13] His outspoken backing, moreover, for a gradual return to specie payments by reducing the amount of greenbacks in circulation, by servicing the interest on the national debt in coin, and by using taxation to create the necessary financial surplus, was broadly in tune with the feeling of most eastern Republicans on the currency question.[14] By early July 1868 he felt confident enough to tell his friend James Pike, home from The Hague, that his position was improving. "I have never had any doubt that the storm would blow over and leave you unharmed," replied Pike. "Indeed I have sometimes held that your political position would be strengthened by your attitude on impeachment, and I am not by any means sure that this is not the true view of the case."[15]

Pitt Fessenden's readiness to campaign for the party in the state election was the clearest sign yet that he considered it in his best interests to remain a Republican. (Once the Democrats had rejected Chase for Seymour and Blair there was, in truth, nowhere else for him to go.) On the evening of August 31 he delivered one of the most impressive speeches of his career at a large Republican rally in Portland. It was his first major public appearance outside the Senate since the president's trial. In it he declared that he had always tried to do his duty as a Republican and a public man and that if he had ever differed from his co-partisans it would have to be ascribed to his "native obstinacy." He also poked fun at himself by claiming that he did not wish to speak ill of the Democrats because "recently they have spoken very respectfully of me." The comment elicited great mirth among the party faithful, who seemed willing to forgive him for his not-guilty verdict and eager to hear the city's most famous son resume combat with the old enemy.

Fessenden did not disappoint. Like all Republicans in 1868 he dwelt at length on the Democrats' opposition to the war—"quite as calamitous as if they had enlisted in the Confederate army"—and his own party's triumphs, including the abolition of slavery. He also reviewed his singular course on Reconstruction, observing that he had been less impatient, before and after passage of the Fourteenth Amendment, than many Radicals to readmit southern states to Congress. In the most memorable section of his address, the senator denounced pro-inflation Democrats such as George H. Pendleton of Ohio who held that the Union war debt should be paid off in greenbacks. The United States, he urged, had resources enough to service its debt in gold. This was, he insisted, "evidently the only way to act, to cultivate frugality, industry and the arts of peace, since national prosperity ever lies in the same path with national honesty." Republicans, he exhorted in a ringing appeal, "must repudiate the repudiators, whether in Massachusetts or Ohio, for they are unworthy [of] the confidence of an honest, God-fearing, intelligent people." After expressing faith in Grant and rehearsing the evils that would surely follow a Democratic victory (among them the repudiation of Union veterans' pensions), Fessenden took his bow amid cheers from the assembled throng.[16]

Having reasserted his influence at home during "the most active and exciting campaign that I have known," Fessenden looked anxiously for the result of the presidential election. The great problem, he told Freeman Morse, was the South. Republicans, he contended, could not count on the votes of the reconstructed southern states because, as he had maintained all along, they could not rely on "the aid of the negroes." "My opinion was," he wrote, "that once reorganized the wealth and intelligence of the States would rule them, and we had better let them stay out until after the election." If the three remaining unreconstructed states—Virginia, Texas, and Mississippi—voted in some form and if their votes proved the difference between Seymour and victory, there might be trouble. "I got my name of conservative by advising against the reconstruction acts," he added. Now the Radicals regretted "that, in this particular, they were not as conservative as I was."[17]

The 1868 election campaign was one of the most racist in American history. While the Democrats' vice presidential candidate Frank Blair, Jr., condemned Republicans for subjecting southern white women to the "unbridled lust" of freed black men, murderous violence against African American Unionists in the South intensified, especially in Georgia and Louisiana, where white terror made it difficult for them to vote at all.[18] Although anti-black violence would undermine all the Republican regimes fostered by congressional policy and end Reconstruction within a decade, it did not prevent Grant's election in November. Black and white Unionists played an important role in the general's success, delivering states like Tennessee, Alabama, and South Carolina into the Republican fold. But the fact that a majority of whites across the country actually voted for Seymour revealed that Fessenden's concerns about a Democratic revival had not been misplaced, even if he had shown few signs of understanding the plight of hard-pressed southern Republicans.[19] The senator welcomed the election result. "The nation is saved a terrible calamity," he rejoiced, "and we are afforded one more opportunity to secure what we fought for."[20]

There was no room for complacency. Even though Fessenden was confident in the president-elect's ability and patriotism, Grant did not have much of a political track record. The senator, moreover, had little idea whether his own power-base was still secure. On balance he was inclined to be optimistic. Grant, he reckoned, entertained kind feelings for him and, though supportive of impeachment, had countenanced against an internal witch-hunt after the trial. Besides, even his personal enemies were willing to admit that his vote had probably saved the party from electoral defeat. "Impeachment," he insisted, "was a great blunder . . . At the time I believed that my vote would destroy me politically. It looks now as if I should survive it."[21]

Fessenden traveled down to Washington via Boston at the beginning of December. James Grimes, mobile again after his stroke, accompanied him on the railroad journey and the Portlander was delighted to see his old friend looking so well. He found life at the capital largely to his satisfaction. Comfortably installed in his old boarding house, he told Lizzy that "My landlady is so tired of colored servants . . . that she prefers to do her own work, and thus far I perceive only improvement."[22] He was pleased too by the appearance of Senate affairs. Colleagues who had snubbed him after the trial seemed cordial enough once again. Predictably, however, Charles Sumner continued to annoy him. The Massachusetts senator attacked the recusants again in his eulogy to Thaddeus Stevens, who had died in the fall. "Sumner is a mean cowardly wretch," Fessenden growled privately. "Stevens time and again called him 'a d——d fool with considerable learning and no sense.'"[23]

Aware that he still had political ground to make up, the wounded senator was determined that the new administration should acknowledge his status by acceding to his patronage wishes. This desire assumed even greater urgency in mid-January 1869 when his ally Senator Lot Morrill was defeated for reelection by Hannibal Hamlin. Fearful of internecine warfare among Maine Republicans if his Augusta friends threw their weight against Hamlin and worried about the unpredictable political influence of Union veterans, Fessenden had opposed a countermovement to draft Governor Joshua Chamberlain. The problem was that even though Hamlin's allies reputedly viewed Fessenden's inaction as "highminded and honorable," this was no guarantee of future good behavior on the part of the ex-Democrat.[24] Fessenden suspected James Blaine of being intent on promotion and could not be sure that the ambitious congressman would not join forces with Hamlin or the popular Chamberlain to eject him from office.

He was lifted by several important developments in the early spring of 1869. First, he secured assurances of support from the Portland collector, Israel Washburn, Jr. (who had backed Hamlin against Morrill), and then saw his allies take control of the *Portland Press,* one of the most important Republican newspapers in southern Maine.[25] His next task was to persuade the Grant administration that it should not satisfy the Hamlinites' clamor for office at his expense. "I have insisted, and mean to claim," he told William pugnaciously, "that I am entitled to be heard, and I have now [*sic*] doubt the claim will be allowed. I don't know that there will be any war, but if there is to be I am quite ready to meet it."[26] Fessenden won the first major skirmish. His client Freeman Morse, American consul in London, was widely touted for dismissal. Tellingly, Blaine was among those Republicans who believed he could not be saved. Rightly seeing Morse's retention as a test of his strength, Fessenden used his influence with the new secretary of state, his friend Hamilton Fish, to secure Morse's job in the face of studied silence from the Maine delegation. He emerged from the bruising battle hurt by his colleagues' failure to render assistance but elated by his triumph. "I was much satisfied with the result," he told Morse, "not only for your sake, but because after certain people had been at great pains to inculcate the idea that my power was gone, they are rather chopfallen."[27]

Plagued by ill-health—he was now receiving painful injections for his bowel condition and adhering to a strict dietary regime—Fessenden managed to play an active role in Senate business during three brief consecutive sessions of Congress between December 1868 and April 1869. Although he remained a Republican, he shared his fellow centrists' lack of interest in further Reconstruction measures. He did indicate half-hearted support for the Fifteenth Amendment, which expressly prohibited states from disfranchising voters on the grounds of race or color.[28] Yet it was clear that he did not share his colleagues' belief that the amendment would make the South a Republican stronghold. Democratic Party election triumphs in Virginia and Tennessee subsequently confirmed his view that whites would continue to rule below the Mason-Dixon line and help to explain his lack of enthusiasm for more Reconstruction legislation. He revealed a discernibly conservative streak by supporting the restoration of the white-dominated militias in Virginia, Mississippi, and Texas, the last two of which were notoriously disordered states.[29]

Shortly after the close of the final session of the fortieth Congress, Fessenden received news of his father's death. Though he had always felt respect for the old Federalist, he was far from grief stricken. In fact the event led him to ponder his own mortality as much as it caused him to remember Samuel's long, eventful life. He would not be attending the funeral, he told Lizzy, for he was weak and busy with Senate affairs. "It will be my turn soon," he reflected, "and the idea is not so troublesome to me as it used to be." Yet, he added wistfully (thinking of his father's abolitionism), "I wish that my work had been as well performed as his."[30]

More eager than usual to return home to regain his health, Pitt Fessenden's placement on Sumner's Foreign Affairs Committee gave him little choice but to stay on for an executive session in April 1869. Discussion centered on a draft international treaty—negotiated by the U.S. minister in London, Reverdy Johnson, and the British foreign secretary, the Earl of Clarendon—intended to settle American claims arising out of Great Britain's actions during the Civil War. Fessenden had been as aggrieved as any northerner by Britain's failure to prevent the depredations of Confederate raiders like the *Alabama* and concurred with his fellow senators that the treaty fell short of what was required. Like his godfather Daniel Webster in the early 1840s, however, he had no yearning for another Anglo-American war. Thus, while he regarded the Johnson-Clarendon agreement as an inadequate settlement of U.S. claims, he did not endorse Zachariah Chandler's bellicose contention on April 19 that Britain should surrender Canada to pay for its wartime perfidy, nor was he entirely pleased with the aggressive tenor of Sumner's oration on the same subject three weeks later. Instead, in a letter to Secretary Fish, he counseled a strategy of patience grounded in the presumption, correct as it transpired, that it was in Britain's interests to express its regret ("something in the nature of a plaster for the sore") for its conduct during the Civil War.[31] Even though the Treaty of Washington, which settled the *Alabama* claims to the satisfaction of the American government, was not signed until after Fessenden's death, Fish later testified that the senator's influence had played a significant role in its inception.[32]

After the adjournment Fessenden sought refuge as usual in Portland. He was fit enough, however, to declare his intention to seek reelection and to begin making plans to secure that end. Ever the politician, he watched closely for any signs of opposition. In June he learned that one of his allies had been dismissed from a Treasury post. Immediately, he dispatched a letter to Washington requesting information and stating his concern "that some malign influence" might be at work.[33] He had little doubt that James Blaine was at the bottom of things. The congressman was, thought Fessenden, "a very artful and skilful manager, while I have no faculty that way." If Blaine designed to be a candidate, he would "prove himself false to his many professions of friendship for me, and of interest in my continued success."[34]

Anxious to shore up support in the Maine backcountry, Fessenden embarked on his last journey. On July 19 he left Portland for remote Aroostook County via the coastal town of Eastport.[35] It could not have been an easy trip for he was now in considerable discomfort because of his intestinal disorders. Among his stops was the village of Mattawaukeag, where he was met by his old sparring partner, Joseph Carr, who guided him around the district. Stoical as ever, the senator did not mention his maladies and appeared delighted by the tell-tale signs of economic improvement: well-tended farms, superior breeds of animals, and all manner of fruit trees and shrubs. Knowing his friend's love of horticulture, Carr promised to send him some cranberry and raspberry bushes. He then escorted him to Bangor from whence his illustrious guest departed for home.[36]

In the final days of August Fessenden continued to promote his reelection, writing about a patronage matter to Hamilton Fish and berating James Blaine for trying to stir up trouble between himself and ex-Senator Morrill.[37] On the evening of August 31, he retired to bed after a convivial game of whist with friends.[38] At midnight he cried out to William, who found him pacing the room in agony. Alarmed, his son promptly summoned a doctor who prescribed morphine to lessen the pain. The patient seemed to improve over the next few days but on September 2 he suffered a relapse. "You cannot imagine the sudden gloom & anxiety cast over our City by the illness of Mr Fessenden," reported one demoralized neighbor.[39] Despite the ministrations of three physicians, including a former surgeon-general of the army,

William Pitt Fessenden died at around 6:20 A.M. on Wednesday, September 8. The immediate cause of death was recorded as a ruptured lower intestine occasioned by longstanding irritation of the bowels.

Portlanders gathered three days later for the funeral at the First Parish (Unitarian) Church. Government offices were closed as a mark of respect and flags flew at half mast on city buildings and ships in the harbor. The Maine bar was well represented among the large crowd of mourners. So was the state's political elite, including Hannibal Hamlin, Lot Morrill, Israel Washburn, Governor Joshua Chamberlain, and John Lynch. Delegates were present from Bowdoin and Waterville colleges as well as the Ligonia Lodge of Odd Fellows of which Fessenden had long been a member. Dr. John Caruthers, a Congregational minister, preached the funeral sermon. He described the senator as "strong, steadfast, serenely conscious of right, and stern even to severity in the maintenance and avowal of well considered principles." No one, he added, "knew better the valuable right of self-control in popular discussion."[40]

The coffin was then taken from the church and a long procession escorted the body to the gravesite in Western Cemetery. Church bells tolled and minute-guns boomed as the mourners made their way slowly through the city streets. There were no further ceremonies and the senator was laid in earth to rest beside Ellen and his lost daughter Mary.

A Model Senator?

The eventful public career of William Pitt Fessenden commands attention because he secured and then exercised power at a crucial moment in U.S. history. Instrumental, like other leading Republicans, in confronting the slaveholding southerners whose reckless bid for independence nearly destroyed the American republic, he was equally responsible for helping the North defeat the Confederacy and subsequently for attempting to build a fairer and more stable Union. Although he was not an ideologue, he acted consistently on the basis of a composite ideology, the main elements of which he shared with other northerners: an enduring commitment to traditional republican values such as virtuous self-sacrifice in the public interest, a deep suspicion of unrestrained power, and a preference for balance in every walk of life; a strong belief that the North's meritocratic free-labor society was superior in every way to that of the slave South; and an obdurate determination not to let slaveholders destroy the Founding Fathers' precious experiment in nation-building.

While northerners' collective response to the Confederate attack on Fort Sumter demonstrated how deeply and widely these values were held, Fessenden's upbringing in a region heavily influenced by Congregationalism and Federalism made respect for ordered government central to his worldview. His ultimate readiness to go to war against the South had as much to do with his reverence for government and the law that underpinned it as it had with any romantic attachment to the imperfect antebellum Union.

Of course, Fessenden was not just driven by values, general or particular. He was ambitious for his own sake as well as that of his section and his country. Better placed than most of his contemporaries to find fortune and fame, he could not have gained high office without the sectional conflict any more than his fellow Whig-Republican, Abraham Lincoln, would have been able to secure the presidency had the political realignment of the 1850s not occurred. While they were both opportunists in their own not dissimilar ways, they were not unprincipled ones. Both men genuinely believed they were engaged in an urgent and principled struggle for control of the national government that they, their party, and their region had to win if the United States was to free itself from the pernicious domination of southern slave masters and their northern dependents. True, it was in their political interests to believe this. However, as Don Fehrenbacher and Ward McAfee have demonstrated, "the federal government had [by 1850] effectively become an agent of the slaveholding interest in addressing the South's concerns."[41] John Quincy Adams, for all his faults, was not mistaken in supposing that slavery's grip on the Constitution was growing stronger in the 1840s. Fessenden and Lincoln, therefore, had every reason to suppose that only a united and defiant North could disencumber the American republic from the clanking chains of proslavery Democratic rule.

The human cost of first promoting northern political unity at the expense of the inter-sectional second-party system and then defying the South on the battlefield was appalling. Primary responsibility for the carnage of 1861–65 lies with the proslavery secessionists who plotted to destroy the American republic and fired the first shot in anger, but there could have been no civil war without the "moderate" Republicans. A majority of northerners (as distinct from Republicans) were probably in favor of offering concessions to the South in early 1861.[42] Holding the balance of power within the Republican Party, centrists like Lincoln and Fessenden determined that war would come by opposing what they regarded as sell-out concessions over slavery that would demoralize the party of freedom and further corrupt the country.

Peaceable men radicalized by years of political warfare against proslavery advocates, they did not consciously set out to drench Columbia's woods and fields in blood. But death, disability, and destruction on a vast scale were as much the result of their decision to stand firm as was the saving of the Union and the emancipation of the slaves—the war's two great positive results that continue to fashion the dominant nationalist and civil rights-inflected scholarship on the American Civil War.

Would Fessenden have been willing to coerce the southern states back into the Union had he known that the ensuing conflict would take the lives of more than 620,000 Americans? We cannot know for sure but his willingness to fight another civil war in 1866 suggests that he believed that traitors must be confronted no matter what the cost. Unlike the melancholic Lincoln, who was visibly affected by the spiraling body count after Sumter, he was not unduly troubled by feelings of remorse, even after one of his own sons was killed and another was invalided by the war. When commentators compared him to Mount Katahdin, the highest peak in Maine, they had a point. Convinced, like a majority of New Englanders, that a Confederate triumph would dash his lofty, northern vision of American nationhood, he was as immovably committed to the Federal cause as the granite rocks of his home state.

William Pitt Fessenden was not quite the "noble statesman" mourned by his friend James Grimes upon his decease.[43] One of Charles Sumner's correspondents described him as "an incomplete man" because of his "inability to control a strong and violent temper."[44] There was some truth to this harsh judgment: "fervid elements" did, on occasions, "control his breast" as the sketch-writers Mansfield and Kelsey claimed in 1867.[45] Fessenden was a passionate, intelligent, and skilled politician who struggled to conceal his dislike of those he regarded as less able or less principled men than himself. Bourgeois in most respects, he was not temperamentally a moderate man. Like his father before him, but unlike the more forgiving Abraham Lincoln, he could not abide his political enemies, even those—*especially* those—in his own party. This fact alone throws his more positive achievements into greater relief. Fessenden did *try* to exercise self-restraint in the pursuit of northern victory. He did more than that. He tried hard and, as his wartime record as a bridge leader in the Senate shows, largely successfully. No historian attempting to explain how the North won the Civil War can do so thoroughly without comprehending the contribution of Congress and, specifically, the constructive brokerage role played by the brilliant chairman of the Finance Committee.

Fessenden's refusal to surrender the fruits of northern victory became clear in early 1866, when he broke with Andrew Johnson over Reconstruction and used his legislative skills to help craft and then pass the Fourteenth Amendment, a creative and enduring intra-party solution to the crisis occasioned by Johnson's leniency toward the vanquished South. His impressive *Report of the Joint Committee on Reconstruction* was a typically forthright demolition of the president's conduct as well as a lucid explication of Republican policy ahead of the crucial 1866 midterm elections that yielded damning public comment on the president's failure to secure northern war aims. Fessenden's preference at this juncture was to furnish government protection for southern Unionists and wait patiently for southern elites to demonstrate their willingness to accept northern terms and return as full members to the Union. He did so partly because he believed the nation would never be properly reunited if southern whites perceived congressional peace terms to be coerced. When Radical Republicans then moved to impose tougher measures on the South and his fellow centrists sought to make readmission automatic on ratification of the Fourteenth Amendment, he tried to hold the line during debates on the Military Reconstruction Bill in the spring of 1867. Though he failed to get his way, his efforts to thwart the Radicals' impeachment efforts (a product of mixed motives) culminated in success the following spring.

Racial and class prejudices constituted Fessenden's Achilles' heel during Reconstruction. He valued education highly—at least as highly as loyalty—and believed that most ex-slaves were unprepared to vote as independent citizens of the republic. Universal suffrage, he feared, would deliver the South into the hands of treason-tainted Democrats. He was not a racist demagogue who pandered to white voters' hostility toward blacks in order to gain votes. Nor did he believe, like the white supremacist authors of a pro-Johnson pamphlet in 1866, that it would take "centuries of instruction and experience" to elevate the Negro to the level of the Caucasian.[46] A tolerably compassionate man, he was fond of his black servant Moses, held that African Americans should be equal before the law, indicated support for black suffrage on an impartial basis, and evinced a commitment to black education by supporting the development of Storer College in the Unionist stronghold of West Virginia. But Fessenden was prone to casual racism in private and did not share the abolitionists' commitment to African Americans as a people. He knew he lacked the ability to empathize with the oppressed en masse and occasionally regretted it. He should, he told his father in late 1866, "think much better of myself if I had always been influenced and controlled by that love of my fellow men, and faithfulness to all my duties, which you have not only inculcated but practiced."[47] It was a revealing confession and one can only speculate at what might have been accomplished during Reconstruction had he felt impelled to act more positively upon this insight.

While the senator was wrong to underestimate African Americans' capacity for independent thought and action after emancipation, he was not alone in supposing that the effects of slavery on both races would linger long after passage of the Thirteenth Amendment. As the black abolitionist Frederick Douglass remarked in late 1862, "Slavery . . . has stamped its character too deeply and indelibly, to be blotted out in a day or a year or even a generation. The slave will yet remain in some sense a slave, long after the chains are taken from his limbs, and the master will retain much of the pride, the arrogance . . . and love of power, acquired by his former relation of master."[48] Fessenden's greatest mistake was his misplaced confidence that rational self-interest would, over time, induce the former slaveholders to come to terms with emancipation. In this respect both he and the former slaves were let down by his persistent faith in the South's "best men." His class bias was evident in his deeply felt statement that: "[I]t is very difficult for me to believe that respectable men, or men having the good of society among themselves at heart—and we must take it for granted that most of the men in power are so disposed—should not wish, if possible, to put an end to a state of society that renders their own lives and their own property . . . entirely unsafe."[49] As a humane and rational man of property, he could not imagine that the South's ruling class would stop at nothing to reassert its dominance over African Americans.

Perhaps one should not be too hasty to condemn the senator's actions in 1867 and 1868. Congressional Reconstruction was deeply flawed but the Fourteenth Amendment, in which he had a hand, proved to be one of the most formidable weapons of the modern civil rights movement precisely because it embedded the principle of equal rights under the law into the federal Constitution. The senator can even be credited with influencing the first stirrings of the movement. Storer College became one of the border South's most important black institutions of higher education, hosting the second conference of the Niagara Movement—forerunner to the National Association for the Advancement of Colored People—in 1906. Reconstruction *might* have taken a different course had he thrown his formidable political weight behind the Radicals, but it was bound to have limits because of the depth of American racism on both sides of the Mason-Dixon line, the virulence of southern opposition to Republican rule, northerners' yearning for peace after an exhausting conflict, and the fundamental similarities between northern and southern elites previously disguised by the political conflict over slavery. Fessenden himself had much in common with many of the southern leaders whom Andrew Johnson pardoned so hastily at the end of the war. It says a good deal about the emotional impact of the

North's collective sacrifice of 1861–65, the senator's determination to hold on to the reins of power once he had secured them, his desire for a durable peace, and his own racially inclusive vision of America's meritocratic future that he was unwilling to allow southern leaders back into Congress without new legal safeguards for the freedpeople. Had he been willing to sanction this in 1866, the rights revolution at the crux of Reconstruction might never have taken place at all.

Independent-minded though he was, Fessenden was a loyal Republican for the last decade and a half of his political career. The Republican Party, one veteran Yankee abolitionist mused, "has had the most difficult and responsible work that ever rested on any party in our country's history, and it has done it on the whole with unequalled ability and integrity. I never could see how anything but blood could was[h] out so much innocent blood as slavery had shed, but hoped it might be possible."[50] To be present at the creation of the Grand Old Party was to make history fast. Fessenden capitalized expertly on the realignment of the early 1850s and then, in conjunction with other northern free-soil leaders, used the new sectional organization to sweep proslavery Democrats from national power. When the ensuing bloodbath began in 1861, he devoted his efforts to finding the money required to defeat the Confederacy, a necessary precondition for the freeing of the slaves. He then strove to make and temper federal Reconstruction policy in order to maintain the Republican Party's grip on power and prevent a resurgence of Rebel Democracy that would have undone many of the North's hard-won gains. While the cost of these impressive achievements was undeniably high, it is likely a majority of twenty-first-century Americans would concur that the price in lives and treasure exacted by the Civil War was worth paying. If this is indeed the case they can be thankful that it was a previous generation of patriots like William Pitt Fessenden who chose to pay it.

Notes

WHF   William H. Fessenden
WPF   William Pitt Fessenden
WRHS   Western Reserve Historical Society

INTRODUCTION

1. Gienapp, *Origins of the Republican Party,* 71.

2. *New-York Daily Tribune,* March 7, 1854.

3. Gienapp, *Origins of the Republican Party,* 78.

4. *The Nation,* Sept. 16, 1869, 222.

5. Quoted in FF, *Life and Public Services of William Pitt Fessenden,* 2:349.

6. Bowers, *The Tragic Era,* 263. In his *History of the United States from the Compromise of 1850,* 5:592, 6:293, James Ford Rhodes described Fessenden as "the ablest debater in the Senate" and "a man in whom high legal learning, constructive ability and unselfish devotion to duty were combined to make a model senator."

7. McKitrick, *Andrew Johnson and Reconstruction,* 273.

8. Foner, *Free Soil, Free Labor, Free Men,* 205; Foner *Reconstruction: America's Unfinished Revolution,* 239; Benedict, *Compromise of Principle,* 28.

9. Bogue, *The Earnest Men,* 107–8.

10. Dennett, ed., *Lincoln and the Civil War in the Diaries and Letters of John Hay,* 202.

11. Cox, review of Jellison, *Fessenden of Maine,* in *Mississippi Valley Historical Review* 49 (1962): 528. Jellison's book provided two generations of scholars with a coherent life of Fessenden. However, it was written before Bogue, Benedict, and other accomplished exponents of the "cliometric" revolution located the senator more convincingly on the political continuum of the 1860s. The only other study of Fessenden's eventful career was the traditional life and letters account written by his third son at the beginning of the twentieth century. See note 5 above.

12. O'Brien, "Is Political Biography a Good Thing?" 60–66.

CHAPTER ONE

1. Smith and Hindus, "Premarital Pregnancy in America 1640–1971," 537–70.

2. DW to Samuel A. Bradley, Nov. 21, 1806, in Wiltse et al., eds., *Papers of Daniel Webster,* 1:85. According to the author of a sketch of Ruth's brother, Nathaniel, Webster was a frequent visitor to the Greens' farm during his time in Boscawen. "Memoir of Nathaniel Greene," 373. Webster left for Portsmouth to prepare for greatness in the late summer of 1807.

3. Grossberg, *Governing the Hearth,* 196–233.

4. Marini, "Religious Revolution in the District of Maine, 1780–1820," in Clark, Leamon, and Bowden, eds., *Maine in the Early Republic,* 118–45.

5. SF to MPF, July 8, 1809, FC.

6. SF to MPF, Dec. 7, 1811, FC.

7. SF, *An Oration Delivered Before the Federal Republicans of New Gloucester,* 7, 9, 12, 13. Dagon was a god of the Philistines demonized in the Old Testament.

8. Banner, *To the Hartford Convention*, 317–18.

9. Banks, *Maine Becomes a State*, 142–44.

10. SF to MPF, Sept. 29, 1810, FC.

11. SF to MPF, Dec. 7, 1811, FC.

12. Samuel and Deborah had a total of ten children together between 1815 and 1833. Fessenden, *Fessenden Family in America*, 2:511–55.

13. FF, unpublished ms. chapter for his biography of WPF, in Articles and Addresses (#16), FC; Theophilus P. Chandler to FF, Dec. 8, 1881, FC.

14. Chandler to FF, Dec. 8, 1881, FC.

15. FF, unpublished ms. chapter.

16. Ibid.

17. Hawthorne, "Nathaniel Hawthorne at Bowdoin," 246–79.

18. WPF to Deborah Fessenden, April 8, 1820, FC.

19. Thirty-three students graduated in the Bowdoin class of 1823. While most of them went on to forge professional careers, two became planters in the Southwest. *General Catalogue of Bowdoin College and the Medical School of Maine*, 53–54.

20. James Brooks, in *Memorial Addresses on the Life and Character of William Pitt Fessenden*, 70–71.

21. Gribbin, "Rollin's Histories and American Republicanism," 611–22.

22. WPF to SF, Dec. 18, 1820, FC; Bowdoin College, Executive Government Records, 1805–20, BC.

23. WPF to SF, Sept. 20, 1822, FC; Bowdoin College, Votes of the Executive Government, April 24, 1821–July 16, 1823, BC.

24. WPF to SF, Sept. [30?], 1822, FC.

25. Bowdoin College, Votes of the Executive Government, April 24, 1821–July 16, 1823, BC.

26. William Allen to Thomas A. Deblois, Aug. 22, 1823, FC.

27. WPF to SF, July 29, 1823, FC.

28. WPF to SF, Aug. 23, 1823, FC.

29. SF, Petition "To the President and Trustees of Bowdoin College," Sept. 2, 1823, Votes of the Governing Boards, BC.

30. Bowdoin College, Board of Trustees, Aug. 31, 1824, Votes of the Governing Boards, BC.

31. Allmendinger, *Paupers and Scholars*, 97–113; Novak, *The Rights of Youth*.

32. Hawthorne, "Nathaniel Hawthorne at Bowdoin," 260–61.

33. WPF, "Prospects of the South American States," Exhibition Parts, May 1823, Articles and Addresses (#5), FC.

34. WPF,GH   George Harrington
"Address before the Portland Benevolent Society . . . Oct. 1825," Articles and Addresses (#5), FC.

35. WPF, *Oration Delivered Before the Young Men of Portland*, 7, 12, 30.

36. King, "John Neal as a Benthamite," 47–65.

37. [Neal], "North American Politics," 355.

38. Characterized by technological innovation, rapid penetration of the market, and the growth of early corporations such as banks and railroads, this era has been dubbed variously by historians of the United States as "the transportation revolution," "the market revolution," and "the communications revolution." See Howe, *What Hath God Wrought*, 5–7, for a spirited advocacy of the latter.

39. The silhouette hangs on a wall in the Wadsworth-Longfellow House in Portland.

40. On the growth of Portland, see Butler, "Rising Like a Phoenix: Commerce in Southern Maine, 1775–1830," in Sprague, ed., *Agreeable Situations*, 15–35.

41. FF, unpublished ms. chapter.

42. Writing to his youngest son, Sam, in the 1850s, Fessenden urged upon him the importance of a thorough immersion in English history. It was, he said, "a part of our own history—lying at its foundation, and necessary to its illustration. I read a great deal of history, ancient and modern, when I was a boy, and it was well I did for my time has been otherwise occupied since I became a man." WPF to SFJr., Dec. 13, 1858, FC.

43. Justin S. Morrill, remarks in *Memorial Addresses on the Life and Character of William Pitt Fessenden*, 31. In the Senate obsequies held after Fessenden's death, Senator James W. Patterson of New Hampshire recalled tellingly that "[w]ith a fear bordering upon a morbid dread of pedantry, he [Fessenden] ordinarily concealed his literary attainments; but sometimes, in the seclusion of his chamber, he would rehearse a poem with such pathos and tender appreciation of its beauties as to surprise and entrance the privileged listener." Ibid., 40.

44. WPF to SF, Sept. 8, 1826, FC.

45. WPF to Sarah Fessenden, Oct. 28, 1826, FC.

46. On the use of "antislavery sectionalism" by New England Federalists and northern Jeffersonian Republicans in the early nineteenth century, see Mason, *Slavery and Politics in the Early American Republic*.

47. Thomas Fessenden to SF, Sept. 19, 1820, Samuel Fessenden Papers, MeHS.

48. After attending one of Garrison's radical lectures in Portland, Samuel Fessenden contributed $10 to sustain the printer's abolitionist newspaper *The Liberator* in November 1832 and helped to found the Maine Antislavery Society the following spring. William Lloyd Garrison to SF, Nov. 30, 1832, in Merrill et al., eds., *Letters of William Lloyd Garrison*, 1:192.

49. I am indebted to Marilyn (Green) Day, a direct descendant of Ruth Green, for this information in an e-mail communication of May 29, 2008.

50. WPF to SF, Oct. 30, 1827, FC.

51. Jellison, *Fessenden of Maine*, 5.

52. Ward, *Parental and Filial Obligation Illustrated and Enforced*, 10.

53. Neal had returned to the United States from London in 1827. King, "John Neal as a Benthamite," 55.

54. Joseph Carr to FF, Aug. 1883, FC.

55. Henry W. Longfellow to Zilpah Longfellow, Nov. 27, 1828, in Hilen, ed., *Letters of Henry Wadsworth Longfellow*, 1:282–83.

56. FF, *Life and Public Services of William Pitt Fessenden*: 1:6.

57. WPF, *Oration Delivered Before the Young Men of Portland*, 19–20.

58. WPF, "Address Delivered Sept. 2[,] 1828 Before the Athenaean Society of Bowdoin College at the Anniversary," Articles and Addresses (#8), FC.

59. *Portland Daily Evening Advertiser*, Aug. 22, 1831.

60. *Portland Daily Evening Advertiser*, Sept. 19, 1831.

61. WPF to Charles S. Daveis, Jan. 13, 1832, Charles Daveis Papers, MeHS.

62. Samuel E. Smith, Message to the Legislature, Journal of the Maine House of Representatives, 1832, Appendix, 1 (ms.).

63. For a broad assessment of the northeastern border dispute in 1831–32, see Jones, *To the Webster-Ashburton Treaty,* 15–19.

64. WPF to Daveis, Jan. 13, 1832, Daveis Papers, MeHS.

65. Moses Emery to John Holmes, Jan. 15, 1832, John Holmes Papers, MeHS.

66. *Portland Evening Advertiser,* Jan. 23, 1832.

67. *Portland Evening Advertiser,* March 16, 1832.

68. WPF to A. H. Everett, March 21, 1832, William Pitt Fessenden Papers, LC.

69. Josiah Pierce to George Pierce, Feb. 9, 1832, Pierce Family Papers, MeHS.

70. *Portland Evening Advertiser,* Feb. 28, 1832.

71. *Portland Evening Advertiser,* Feb. 18, 20, 1832.

72. *Portland Evening Advertiser,* Feb. 28, 1832.

73. WPF to Daveis, Jan. 13, 1832, Daveis Papers, MeHS.

74. *Portland Evening Advertiser,* March 9, 1832.

75. *Portland Evening Advertiser,* Feb. 24, 1832.

76. *Portland Evening Advertiser,* March 21, 1832.

77. Barry and Dominic, "Mr. Deering and His Mansion," 85–87; Fessenden, *Fessenden Family in America,* 2:513. In 1834 Pitt Fessenden and his new wife moved into a three-story brick house built for the new family by James Deering on his estate. *Portland Sunday Telegram,* April 12, 1903.

78. WPF, *Oration Delivered Before the Young Men of Portland,* 12–13.

79. John Holmes and Peleg Sprague had been elected as National Republicans in 1829 before the surge in Jacksonian turnout three years later.

80. *Portland Evening Advertiser,* Aug. 3, 1832.

81. *Portland Evening Advertiser,* Sept. 11, 1832.

82. WPF to Thomas Fessenden, Sept. 17, 1832, Ferdinand J. Dreer Autograph Collection, PaHS.

83. *Portland Evening Advertiser,* Oct. 29, 1832.

84. Remini, *Daniel Webster,* 369–87.

85. WPF, "Fourth of July," speech of July 4, [1833], Articles and Addresses (#12), FC.

86. Merrill, et al., eds., *Letters of William Lloyd Garrison,* 2:108.

87. Dow, *Reminiscences of Neal Dow,* 133.

88. Jellison, *Fessenden of Maine,* 22; Carr to FF, Aug. 1883, FC.

89. *Portland Daily Evening Advertiser,* Aug. 13, 1835.

90. *Portland Daily Evening Advertiser,* Aug. 17, 1835.

91. *Portland Daily Evening Advertiser,* Sept. 17, 1835.

92. Just over 1,300 blacks lived in Portland in 1840. Although adult males could vote, the population was poor and segregated. Murray, "Portland, Maine, and the Growth of Urban Responsibility," 361–67.

93. WPF to EMF, Aug. 9, 1836, FC.

94. The Whigs' poor showing relative to that of the National Republicans in 1832 reflected not only Maine Democrats' superior organization and popularity demonstrated in recent gubernatorial elections but also the boost that Van Buren's northern background gave him in New England. Holt, *Rise and Fall of the American Whig Party,* 45–47.

CHAPTER TWO

1. See, e.g., WPF to EMF, June 12, 1838 and [Jan. 1841], FC.

2. Howe, *What Hath God Wrought*.

3. Remini, *Daniel Webster,* 398–412.

4. Hiram Ketchum to WPF, March 22, 1837, William Pitt Fessenden Papers, WRHS.

5. WPF to EMF, June 6, 1837, FC.

6. WPF to EMF, June 18, 1837, FC.

7. WPF to William Willis, May 11, [1837], William Willis Papers, MeHS.

8. WPF to EMF, May 10, 1837, FC.

9. Ibid. Henry Clay was equally unimpressed with Webster's western tour. "Ambition has a powerful blinding effect," he wrote. "And I think Mr. Webster's case is a shocking proof of it." Remini, *Daniel Webster,* 469.

10. Ibid.

11. WPF to EMF, June 18, 1837, FC.

12. Ibid.

13. WPF to EMF, May 21, 1837, FC.

14. WPF to DW, Aug. 5, 1837, Webster Papers, reel 11.

15. Ketchum to WPF, Jan. 19, 1838, Fessenden Papers, WRHS.

16. WPF to DW, April 30, 1838, in Wiltse et al., eds., *Papers of Daniel Webster,* 4:290, 291. By "Locofocoism" Fessenden meant Jacksonian principles.

17. WPF to Josiah S. Little, May 31, 1839, FC.

18. *Portland Evening Advertiser,* Aug. 8, 1839.

19. *Portland Evening Advertiser,* Aug. 22, 1839. The *Advertiser* recorded that a committee to nominate candidates for office was appointed on Fessenden's motion. Tellingly, the Cumberland County Whigs nominated Clay only after declaring that Webster (who had now withdrawn from the race) had been their first choice. They were not the first New Englanders to declare for the Kentucky senator ahead of the 1840 presidential election. Their co-partisans in Rhode Island backed Clay as early as February 1838. Henry Clay to Joseph Childs in Hopkins et al., eds., *Papers of Henry Clay,* 9:143–44.

20. SF to WPF, July 7, 1839, FC.

21. *Portland Evening Advertiser,* Sept. 10, 1839.

22. Holt, *Rise and Fall of the American Whig Party,* 103.

23. Ketchum to WPF, Aug. 17, 1839, Misc. Mss. (WPF), NYHS.

24. WPF to Little, May 16, 1839, FC.

25. WPF to EMF, Jan. 1, 1840, FC; *Portland Evening Advertiser,* Jan. 2, 1840.

26. *Portland Evening Advertiser,* Jan. 15, 1840.

27. *Portland Evening Advertiser,* Feb. 8, 1840.

28. *Portland Evening Advertiser,* March 6, 1840.

29. *Portland Evening Advertiser,* March 6, 1840.

30. WPF to EMF, Feb. 15, 1840, FC.

31. WPF to EMF, March 7, 1840, FC.

32. SF to WPF, March 6, 1840, FC.

33. William C. Hammett to WPF, May 21, 1840, Fessenden Papers, WRHS.

34. Ketchum to WPF, March 7, [1840], Fessenden Papers, WRHS.

35. Freeman H. Morse to WPF, May 16, 1840, FC. As well as his Independence Day oration in Bath, Fessenden also spoke at Portland, New Gloucester, and Poland Corner in September. *Portland Evening Advertiser*, Sept. 5, 14, 1840. William Willis, Fessenden's law partner and fellow Whig, noted patronizingly that Morse was "a carver in wood & has no means of support but his daily labour, but is a man of talents & principle." Willis diary, Aug. 7, 1845, Portland Public Library.

36. *Portland Evening Advertiser*, July 10, 1840.

37. WPF, "Van Buren's Administration," speech of July 4, 1840, Addresses etc. (#10), FC.

38. *Portland Evening Advertiser*, July 10, 1840.

39. David Howler et al. to F. O. J. Smith, July 25, 1840, Francis O. J. Smith Papers, MeHS.

40. *Portland Evening Advertiser*, Sept. 15, 1840.

41. *Portland Evening Advertiser*, Oct. 10, 1840.

42. [Hallowell] *Advocate of Freedom*, Sept. 17, 1840.

43. Henry W. Longfellow to Stephen Longfellow, Sept. 18, 1840, in Hilen, ed., *Letters of Henry Wadsworth Longfellow*, 2:249.

44. WPF to Little, Jan. 24, 1841, FC.

45. John Hodgdon to Smith, Nov. 26, 1840, Samuel Holbrook to Smith, Dec. 11, 1840, Smith Papers, MeHS.

46. WPF to Little, Jan. 26, 1841, WPF to EMF, June 3, 1841, FC.

47. WPF to DW, Feb. 3, 1841, Webster Papers, reel 14. Nathaniel Greene [sic] was born in May 1797 and christened Peter. A journalist and scholar he edited Democratic newspapers in Concord and Boston before being appointed Boston postmaster in 1829. Dismissed from this position under Harrison, he was reappointed by President John Tyler and served again until 1849. He died in 1877. "Memoir of Nathaniel Greene," 373–78.

48. George Evans to WPF, Jan. 21, 1841, Fessenden Papers, WRHS.

49. Evans to WPF, March 19, [1841], Fessenden Papers, WRHS; WPF to EMF, June 3, 1841, FC. The successful applicant for U.S. surveyor at Portland, Bezaleel Cushman, was recommended by Samuel Fessenden. See SF and Samuel A. Bradbury to DW, Feb. 8, 1841, Applications for Appointments as Customs Service Officers, 1833–1910, Records of the U.S. Treasury, RG56, NA; WPF to EMF, June 3, 1841, FC.

50. Edward Kent to WPF, April 9, 1841, Fessenden Papers, WRHS.

51. WPF to Edward Stanly, July 20, 1844, Misc. Mss. (WPF), NYHS.

52. WPF to EMF, May 23, [1841], FC. This letter appears to be the only evidence that Fessenden met his mother after her surprise 1827 missive but there may have been other visits. Ruth's relationship with Moses Bailey, her second husband, had broken down. By this time she was living in Brookline, Massachusetts, with a customs house clerk. She died there in 1867, just a year before her old beau Samuel and less than two before Pitt. Marilyn (Green) Day to the author, May 29, 2008.

53. WPF to EMF, June 3, 1841, FC.

54. Balleisen, *Navigating Failure*, 103.

55. *CG*, 27 Cong., 1 sess., Appendix, 469–70.

56. Ibid., 470–71.

57. *CG*, 27 Cong., 1 sess., 350.

58. Adams diary, Aug. 11, 1841, in Adams, ed., *Memoirs of John Quincy Adams*, 10:529–30.

59. Henry W. Longfellow to Stephen Longfellow, Sept. 1, 1841, in Hilen, ed., *Letters of Henry Wadsworth Longfellow*, 2:325.

60. Adams diary, April 4, 1841, in Adams, ed., *Memoirs of John Quincy Adams*, 10:457.

61. WPF to SF, July 29, 1841, FC.

62. Ibid.

63. *CG*, 27 Cong., 1 sess., 303.

64. Peterson, *The Presidencies of William Henry Harrison & John Tyler*, 63–72.

65. WPF to EMF, Aug. 14, 1841, FC.

66. Remini, *Daniel Webster*, 531.

67. WPF to James Deering, Dec. 26, 1841, FC.

68. WPF to EMF, March 27, 1842, FC.

69. WPF to EMF, Aug. 14, Aug. 17, 1842, FC.

70. WPF to EMF, July 2, 1842, FC.

71. On Webster's secret efforts to promote a settlement of the Maine boundary question, see Crapol, *John Tyler*, 107–11.

72. Jones, *To the Webster-Ashburton Treaty*, 133. On the relative influence of Barings's interests and wider Anglo-American financial links on the Webster–Ashburton Treaty, see Sexton, *Debtor Diplomacy*, 31–38.

73. WPF to EMF, Aug. 23, 1842, FC.

74. WPF to EMF, Aug. 23, 1842, FC.

75. WPF to EMF, Feb. 4, 1843, FC.

76. *CG*, 27 Cong., 3 sess., 87–88, 99, 178–79.

77. Belohlavek, *Broken Glass*, 124.

78. Ibid., 146.

79. WPF to SF, Feb. 15, 1842, FC.

80. WPF to EMF, June 6, 1841, FC.

81. *CG*, 27 Cong., 1 sess., 63.

82. Adams diary, Jan. 24, 1842, in Adams, ed., *Memoirs of John Quincy Adams*, 11:70.

83. WPF to EMF, Jan. 26, 1842, FC.

84. WPF to EMF, Feb. 6, 1842, FC.

85. *CG*, 27 Cong., 2 sess., 214–15, 256.

86. [Hallowell] *Liberty Standard*, May 24, 1843.

87. Clifford voted against attempts to repeal the gag (House Rule 21) in each session of the Twenty-seventh Congress. With the exception of his vote on the Whig-engineered compromise in the special session, Fessenden supported repeal on each occasion. *CG*, 27 Cong., 1 sess., 27–28, 42, 56; 2 sess., 16–17; 3 sess., 32, 37–38, 39–40, 42. The abolitionists' charge that both men had spoken out on economic issues affecting the state rather than the immorality of slavery, however, was true. Clifford made a long speech against the idea of a protective tariff in July 1842, *CG*, 27 Cong., 2 sess., Appendix, 669–78. Fessenden did not speak on tariff issues but in the same month did vote to assist local commerce by increasing duties on firewood and timber for building wharves and to reduce the duties on

sugar. *CG,* 27 Cong., 2 sess., 758. His major speech in the Twenty-seventh Congress, of course, was on the Bankruptcy Bill.

88. WPF to Adams, June 2, 1843, Adams Papers, MassHS, reel 526; *Portland Daily Advertiser,* Aug. 4, 1843.

89. Adams to WPF, June 13, 1843, J. Q. Adams Letterbook (1839–1845), Adams Papers, MassHS, reel 154.

90. Adams diary, June 12, 1843, in Adams, ed., *Memoirs of John Quincy Adams,* 11:381.

91. *Portland Daily Advertiser,* Aug. 4, 1843.

92. *Portland Daily Advertiser,* Aug. 10, 1843. Walker's comments were first printed in a letter to the *Bangor Gazette* on August 3.

93. [Hallowell] *Liberty Standard,* Aug. 23, 1843.

94. WPF to Stanly, July 20, 1844, Misc. Mss. (WPF), NYHS.

95. Ibid.

96. WPF to ECW, Dec. 6, 1842, FC.

97. WPF to ECW, Jan. 21, 1843, FC.

98. WPF to SF, Feb. 15, 1842, FC.

99. WPF to EMF, May 21, 1842, FC.

100. Quoted in Remini, *Henry Clay,* 638n76.

101. See, e.g., *Portland Daily Advertiser,* July 17, 1844.

102. *Portland Daily Advertiser,* Aug. 9, 1844.

103. *Portland Daily Advertiser,* Aug. 13, 1844.

104. *Portland Daily Advertiser,* Aug. 27, Aug. 28, 1844.

105. *Portland Daily Advertiser,* Aug. 28, 1844.

106. *Portland Daily Advertiser,* Sept. 24, 1844.

107. Holt, *Rise and Fall of the American Whig Party,* 196–97.

108. Howe, *What Hath God Wrought,* 688.

109. WPF to Theophilus P. Chandler, Jan. 25, 1844, FC.

110. WPF to EMF, Jan. 23, 1842, FC

111. WPF to ECW, Aug. 8, 1847, FC.

112. For biographical details of Lizzy Warriner and her husband, see Fessenden, *Fessenden Family in America,* 2:561–62.

113. WPF to ECW, Dec. 6, 1842, FC.

114. WPF to ECW, Jan. 11, 1845, FC.

115. WPF to ECW, Aug. 31, 1845, FC.

116. WPF to ECW, Nov. 1, 1846, FC.

117. Murray, "Portland, Maine, and the Growth of Urban Responsibility for Human Welfare," 113.

118. Byrne, *Prophet of Prohibition,* 1–34.

119. WPF to EMF, Feb. 9, 1845, FC.

120. *Portland Daily Advertiser,* Oct. 10, 1845.

121. *Portland Daily Advertiser,* Oct. 1, 1845.

122. *Portland Daily Advertiser,* Oct. 9, 1845.

123. Neal Dow to WPF, July 21, 1846, Fessenden Papers, WRHS.

124. WPF to EMF, July 23, 1846, FC.

125. Jellison, *Fessenden of Maine*, 54.

126. Grant, *North Over South*, 1–18 and ff.

127. Ibid., 9.

128. *Portland Daily Advertiser*, Aug. 13, 1846.

129. *Portland Evening Advertiser*, Aug. 7, 1847.

130. *Portland Evening Advertiser*, Aug. 28, 1847.

131. Ketchum to WPF, May 1, 1848, Fessenden Papers, WRHS.

132. *Portland Daily Advertiser*, May 27, 1848.

133. Ketchum to WPF, May 30, 1848, Fessenden Papers, WRHS.

134. General Scott was a Virginian, a staunch American nationalist, and, like Taylor, another successful Whig general in the Mexican War. Though prone to political gaffes, he appealed to some northern Whig leaders because he was a non-slaveholding military hero.

135. WPF to EMF, June 3, 1848, FC.

136. WPF to EMF, June 5, 1848, FC.

137. WPF to EMF, June 7, 1848, FC.

138. CS to WPF, June 19, 1848, Charles Sumner Papers, reel 68.

139. WPF to William Fessenden, July 17, 1848, *The Collector* (Dec. 1908), Misc. Mss. Collection 422, MeHS.

140. *Portland Daily Advertiser*, Aug. 18, 1848.

141. WPF to Morse, Oct. 16, 1848, Freeman H. Morse Papers, WRHS.

142. See Holt, *Rise and Fall of the American Whig Party*, 368–81, for a detailed analysis of the 1848 election results.

143. WPF to ECW, Dec. 31, 1848, FC.

CHAPTER THREE

1. *Portland Daily Advertiser*, May 21, 1850.

2. Gienapp, *Origins of the Republican Party*; Holt, *Political Crisis of the 1850s* and *Rise and Fall of the American Whig Party*.

3. Gienapp, *Origins of the Republican Party*, 103–27.

4. WPF to EMF, Feb. 18, Feb. 25, 1849, FC.

5. WPF to EMF, Jan. 24, 1849, FC.

6. WPF to ECW, Feb. 18, 1849, FC.

7. WPF to William Fessenden, March 13, 1849, Etting Collection, PaHS; WPF to DW, May 27, 1849, in Wiltse et al., eds., *Papers of Daniel Webster*, 6:338–39; WPF to DW, Aug. 6, 1849, Daniel Webster Papers, reel 21; WPF to Franklin Pierce, July 21, 1849, William Pitt Fessenden Papers, LC.

8. WPF to ECW, Sept. 9, 1849, FC.

9. *Portland Daily Advertiser*, July 26, Sept. 10, 1849.

10. WPF to ECW, Jan. 13, 1850, FC.

11. *Portland Daily Advertiser*, Sept. 24, 1850.

12. William Willis to [Nehemiah?] Cleaveland, Feb. 12, 1855, FC.

13. U.S. Census, 1850: Portland, Maine, Ward 7, 265.

14. Holt, *Rise and Fall of the American Whig Party,* 371.

15. WPF to ECW, Sept. 9, 1849, FC.

16. Wescott, "History of Maine Politics 1840–1856," 123. Fessenden tried to secure an office for the talented Pike in the spring of 1849. See JSP to WPF, May 21, 1849, James S. Pike Papers, LC.

17. George A. Nourse to John Hubbard, May 19, 1850, John Hubbard Papers, BC. "Woolhead" was a racially charged reference to the curly hair of blacks used by conservative Maine Democrats to denigrate their antislavery opponents. The term "Wildcat" was used to denote disreputable, under-capitalized banks in antebellum America and presumably adopted by Wilmot Proviso Democrats to sap popular confidence in their intra-party foes.

18. WPF to ECW, March 10, 1850, FC.

19. WPF to HH, March 15, 1850, Hannibal Hamlin Papers, UMe.

20. *Portland Daily Advertiser,* July 2, 1850.

21. Orrin Blanchard to Charles P. Chandler, Aug. 12, 1850, Charles P. Chandler Papers, MeHS. Blanchard's claim that Pitt Fessenden approved the Free Soilers' shift to Hamlin sits uneasily with Neal Dow's subsequent claim that Fessenden and Henry Carter, editor of the *Portland Advertiser,* numbered among the very few local Whigs to be dissatisfied with Hamlin's election. See Neal Dow to Hamlin, Dec. 23, 1850, Hamlin Papers, UMe. There are three plausible explanations: (1) Blanchard exaggerated Fessenden's support in an effort to justify the Free Soilers' switch to Hamlin; (2) Fessenden subsequently concealed his aid for Hamlin from the majority of Portland Whigs in order negate any charges of treachery to the Whig Party; (3) Dow had not forgiven Fessenden for failing to back a strong prohibitory liquor law and therefore did not hesitate to blacken his fellow townsman's name before the powerful Hamlin. Given Fessenden's transparent determination to use realignment for his own purposes, a combination of explanations two and three would seem to be the most convincing. See also note 23 below, which bolsters the second of these explanations.

22. Blanchard to Chandler, Aug. 12, 1850, Chandler Papers, MeHS.

23. *Portland Daily Advertiser,* Aug. 2, 1850. To add to the intrigue, Fessenden's ally, Henry Carter, was a member of the resolutions committee that drew up the resolve condemning the Free Soilers.

24. *Portland Daily Advertiser,* Aug. 15, 1850.

25. *Portland Inquirer,* Aug. 22, 1850.

26. *Portland Daily Advertiser,* Sept. 5, Sept. 11, Sept. 14, 1850; *Portland Inquirer,* Sept. 5, 1850; Holt, *Rise and Fall of the American Whig Party,* 360. Fessenden carried Portland by 353 votes but lost heavily in outlying rural townships like Poland and Westbrook, where the Democrats were traditionally strong.

27. Israel Washburn, Jr. to Chandler, Sept. 20, 1850, Chandler Papers, MeHS.

28. *Portland Daily Advertiser,* Nov. 12, Nov. 19, 1850.

29. Fillmore had become president after Zachary Taylor's death in July 1850.

30. WPF quoted in Holt, *Rise and Fall of the American Whig Party,* 524.

31. Hiram Ketchum to WPF, Aug. 17, 1850, Misc. Mss. (WPF), NYHS.

32. WPF to EMF, Feb. 28, 1851, FC.

33. *Portland Daily Advertiser,* April 22, 1851.

34. Gienapp, *Origins of the Republican Party,* 47–48.

35. Anson Morrill to Hubbard, June 26, 1851, Hubbard Papers, BC.

36. Neal Dow, *Reminiscences of Neal Dow,* 444.

37. David Bronson to DW, Sept. 15, 1851, encl. in Bronson to Thomas A. Deblois, Sept. 15, 1851, FC; WPF to DW, Sept. 15, 1851, DW to WPF, Sept. 28, 1851, Webster Papers, reel 25. The appointment went to Massachusetts attorney, Benjamin R. Curtis, a prominent Whig, who was strongly favored by President Fillmore and well liked by Webster. See Charles W. Marsh to WPF, Sept. 25, 1851, FC. "The appointment made is an admirable one, and meets my entire approbation," Fessenden commented unconvincingly. WPF to Marsh, Sept. 28, 1851, FC. Webster claimed he had not received any papers recommending Fessenden and that Fillmore had already decided on Curtis before he spoke to him about the vacancy. This may have been true, but Maine Whigs' opposition to Webster's Compromise speech had done nothing to help his godson's ambitions. While expressing his continued "friendship & attachment" toward Fessenden, the secretary of state observed pointedly that "some of the good Whigs of Maine have no great loving kindness toward me." DW to WPF, Sept. 28, 1851, in Wiltse et al., eds., *Papers of Daniel Webster,* 7:275.

38. WPF to ECW, Nov. 10, 1851, FC.

39. Jellison, *Fessenden of Maine,* 49–50.

40. *Portland Daily Advertiser,* April 5, 1852.

41. WPF to ECW, May 9, 1852, FC.

42. Gienapp, *Origins of the Republican Party,* 48–49.

43. *Portland Daily Advertiser,* June 4, 1852.

44. WPF to EMF, June 14, 1852, FC.

45. *Portland Daily Advertiser,* July 2, 1852.

46. Holt, *Rise and Fall of the American Whig Party,* 716.

47. WPF to EMF, June 20, 1852, FC.

48. *Portland Daily Advertiser,* July 2, 1852.

49. *Portland Daily Advertiser,* Sept. 14, 1852.

50. WPF to ECW, Oct. 17, 1852, FC.

51. L. D. Campbell to Washburn, Nov. 4, 1852, Israel Washburn, Jr. Papers, LC.

52. WPF to HH, Nov. 17, 1852, Hamlin Papers.

53. *Portland Daily Advertiser,* Nov. 10, 1852.

54. WPF to ECW, Dec. 12, 1852, FC.

55. WPF to EMF, Jan. 29, 1853, FC.

56. Washburn to WPF, Feb. 12, 1853, William Pitt Fessenden Papers, WRHS.

57. WPF to ECW, Feb. 24, 1853, FC.

58. *Portland Daily Advertiser,* March 5, 1853.

59. Pierce to George F. Shepley, Sept. 15, 1853, Misc. Box Collection, MeHS.

60. Gienapp, *Origins of the Republican Party,* 51.

61. George Evans to WPF, Sept. 18, [1853], Fessenden Papers, WRHS.

62. WPF to ECW, Oct. 2, 1853, FC.

63. *Portland Inquirer* quoted in Wescott, "History of Maine Politics, 1840–1856," 198.

64. *Portland Inquirer,* Nov. 3, 1853.

65. William G. Crosby to WPF, Nov. 18, 1853, Fessenden Papers, WRHS.

66. Crosby to WPF, [1853?], Fessenden Papers, WRHS.

67. WPF quoted in Holt, *Rise and Fall of the American Whig Party,* 784.

68. WPF to HH, Dec. 27, 1853, Hamlin Papers, MeHS.

69. *Portland Inquirer,* Jan. 12, 1854.

70. *National Era,* Jan. 12, 1854.

71. Washburn to WPF, Feb. 11, 1854, FC; *Portland Inquirer,* Feb. 23, 1854.

72. *Portland Inquirer,* Feb. 16, 1854.

73. WPF to EMF, Feb. 23, 1854, FC.

74. WPF to EMF, Feb. 26, 1854, FC.

75. WPF to EMF, March 4, 1854, FC.

76. *CG,* 33 Cong., 1 sess., Appendix, 319–22.

77. *CG,* 33 Cong., 1 sess., Appendix, 322–23.

78. WPF to EMF, March 11, 1854, FC.

79. WPF to ECW, March 26, 1854, FC.

80. EMF to WPF, March 12, 1854, FC.

81. WPF to SF, March 6, 1854, FC.

82. Henry J. Raymond to WPF, June 14, 1854, FC.

83. WPF to Crosby, Feb. 11, 1854, Fessenden Papers, LC.

84. WPF to EMF, April 9, 1854, FC.

85. WPF to EMF, June 11, 1854, FC.

86. WPF to EMF, [June 1854?], FC.

87. WPF to EMF, July 19, 1854, FC.

88. Austin Willey to WPF, July 12, 1854, Fessenden Papers, WRHS.

89. WPF to JSP, Aug. 14, 1854, James S. Pike Papers, UMe.

90. Gienapp, "Nativism and the Creation of a Republican Majority in the North," 537.

91. WPF to ECW, May 8, 1847, FC; WPF to EMF, June 7, 1854, FC.

92. Wescott, "History of Maine Politics 1840–1856," 259–61.

93. *CG,* 33 Cong., 2 sess., Appendix, 219.

94. Edward Kent to WPF, May 21, 1855, Fessenden Papers, WRHS.

95. Kent to WPF, June 6, 1855, Fessenden Papers, WRHS.

96. WPF, "To the Whigs of Maine," [draft ms., 1855], Reports, Speeches, Opinions, etc. (#4), FC.

97. Wescott, "History of Maine Politics, 1840–1856," 279.

98. WPF, "The Slavery Speech: Damariscotta 1855," [draft ms.], Reports, Speeches, Opinions, etc. (#4), FC.

99. Gienapp, *Origins of the Republican Party,* 207.

100. Holt, *Rise and Fall of the American Whig Party,* 875.

101. WPF to ECW, Sept. 23, 1855, FC.

102. N. Abbot to HH, Nov. 2, 1855, Hamlin Papers, UMe.

103. WPF to FF, Dec. 20, 1855, FC.

104. WPF to EMF, Jan. 4, 1856, FC.

105. SPC to WPF, Dec. 13, 1855, FC.

106. WPF to EMF, Jan. 4, 1856, FC.

107. WPF to EMF, March 9, 1856, FC.

108. WPF to EMF, [June 1854?], FC.

109. WPF to EMF, June 24, 1854, FC.

110. CS to Julius Rockwell, Dec. 17, 1869, Charles Sumner Papers, reel 83; CS to WPF, Dec. 11, 1856, FC. Sumner's recollection postdated Fessenden's death.

111. Horace Greeley to JSP, Aug. 13, 1856, Pike Papers, UMe.

112. Jellison, *Fessenden of Maine,* 89–90; Nevins, *Hamilton Fish,* 59–60.

113. WPF to ECW, Feb. 10, 1856, FC.

114. WPF to WHF, Feb. 17, 1856, FC.

115. WPF to SFJr., May 4, 1856, FC.

116. WPF to WHF, June 16, 1856, FC.

117. James D. Fessenden to WPF, June 25, 1856, WPF to James D. Fessenden, June 25, 1856, J. D. Caton to WPF, July 20, July 21, July 24, 1856, E. S. Leland to WPF, July 26, 1856, Samuel Fessenden, Jr. Papers, MeHS; WPF to EMF, July 6, Aug. 1, 1856, FC; Nathaniel F. Deering to WPF, Oct. 20, 1856, Joseph A. Ware to WPF, Oct. 31, 1856, Misc. Mss. (WPF), NYHS.

118. WPF to ECW, June 15, 1856, FC.

119. WPF to EMF, July 6, 1856, FC.

120. Ibid.

121. WPF to William Willis, June 15, 1856, William Willis Papers, MeHS.

122. WPF to SFJr., June 15, 1856, FC.

123. WPF to EMF, July 10, 1856, FC.

124. *CG,* 34 Cong., 1 sess., 1722–23.

125. WPF to EMF, Aug. 3, [1856], FC.

126. WPF to John C. Frémont, Aug. 17, 1856, FC.

127. WPF to EMF, Aug. 6, 1856, FC.

128. George Morey to WPF, Aug. 21, Aug. 29, 1856, FC.

129. Hunt, *Hannibal Hamlin of Maine,* 88–98; Gienapp, *Origins of the Republican Party,* 390–92.

CHAPTER FOUR

1. *CG,* 34 Cong., 3 sess., 30–35.

2. WPF to CS, Dec. 18, 1856, Charles Sumner Papers, reel 15.

3. Ibid.

4. WPF to ECW, Dec. 14, 1860 [1856], William Pitt Fessenden Papers, LC.

5. SF to WPF, Jan. 16, 1857, FC.

6. WPF to FF, Jan. 4, 1857, FC.

7. SFJr. to WPF, Jan. 19, 1857, Samuel Fessenden, Jr. Papers, MeHS.

8. WPF to SFJr., Jan. 29, 1857, FC.

9. WPF to ECW, Jan. 27, [1857], FC.

10. *CG,* 34 Cong., 3 sess., 85–89.

11. Joseph A. Ware to WPF, March 12, 1857, Fessenden Papers, LC.

12. WPF to ECW, Feb. 8, [1857], EMF to WPF, [Feb.] 11, 1857, FC.

13. *Harper's Weekly,* March 28, 1857.

14. WPF to ECW, Feb. 23, [1857], WPF to ECW, March 1, 1857, FC.

15. Jellison, *Fessenden of Maine*, 102.

16. FF, *Life and Public Services of William Pitt Fessenden,* 1:88.

17. WPF to ECW, Aug. 9, 1857, FC.

18. Martha Fessenden to WPF, Aug. 15, 1857, FC.

19. Whalon, "Maine Republicans, 1854–1866," 41.

20. HH to Ellie Hamlin, Jan. 17, 1858, Hannibal Hamlin Papers, UMe.

21. WPF to WHF, Dec. 13, 1857, FC.

22. WPF to Hamilton Fish, Dec. 18, 1858, Hamilton Fish Papers, LC.

23. WPF to WHF, Jan. 16., 1858, FC.

24. WPF to SF, Feb. 6, 1858, FC.

25. *CG,* 35 Cong., 1 sess., 465.

26. *CG,* 35 Cong., 1 sess., 610, 614, 618.

27. William Willis to WPF, March 2, 1858, FC.

28. Edward Kent to WPF, March 9, 1858, Misc. Letters Collection 28, MeHS.

29. SPC to WPF, March 4, 1858, Gilder Lehrman Collection 2286, PML.

30. Fehrenbacher, *Prelude to Greatness,* 83, 93; Landis, "'A Champion Had Come'," 277–78; Burlingame, *Abraham Lincoln: A Life,* 1:464.

31. WPF to JSP, April 8, 1858, in Pike, *First Blows of the Civil War,* 411–12.

32. *CG,* 35 Cong., 1 sess., 1264–65.

33. WPF to ECW, April 11, 1858, FC.

34. WPF to Rufus Dwinel, April 25, 1858, FC.

35. Cole and McDonough, eds., *Witness to the Young Republic,* 327.

36. WPF to ECW, March 7, 1858 [?], FC.

37. WPF to ECW, June 26, 1859, FC.

38. WPF to ECW, Feb. 5, 1860, FC.

39. WPF to ECW, Dec. 29, 1860, FC. Fessenden had framed photographs of the Grimeses in his State Street bedroom. Salter, *Life and Times of James W. Grimes,* 240.

40. WPF to ECW, May 2, 1858, FC.

41. *CG,* 35 Cong., 1 sess., 1910, 2021–24.

42. *CG,* 35 Cong., 1 sess., 1964.

43. *CG,* 35 Cong., 1 sess., 1965.

44. Ibid.

45. WPF to FHM, June 22, 1858, Misc. American Autographs Collection, PML.

46. WPF to JSP, Aug. 24, 1858, James S. Pike Papers, UMe.

47. WPF to JSP, Sept. 26, 1858, Pike Papers, UMe.

48. WPF to ECW, Jan. 15, 1859, FC.

49. SF to WPF, Jan. 18, 1859, FC.

50. WPF to ECW, Jan. 28, 1859, FC.

51. WPF to SF, Jan. 30, 1859, FC.

52. Ibid.

53. *CG,* 35 Cong., 2 sess., 904.

54. *CG*, 35 Cong., 2 sess., 906.

55. *CG*, 35 Cong., 2 sess., 1121–22.

56. On May 27, 1858, Fessenden actually voted with southern senators to postpone a homestead bill—a clear case of his Whiggish principles winning out over his commitment to the free-soil ideology of the Republicans. Eastern Whigs had generally opposed the Jacksonian policy of selling off the national domain cheaply because they wanted to use federal land revenues to promote infrastructural development. *CG*, 35 Cong., 1 sess., 2426.

57. *CG*, 35 Cong., 2 sess., 742.

58. *CG*, 35 Cong., 2 sess., 627–8. Fessenden voted for a bill inviting private proposals to construct three lines to the Pacific on Jan. 27, 1859, *CG*, 35 Cong., 2 sess., 634. Largely because of sectional divisions, Congress failed to act decisively on construction of a transcontinental railroad until 1862.

59. *CG*, 35 Cong., 2 sess., 742.

60. WPF to JSP, May 1, 1859, Pike Papers, UMe.

61. WPF to JSP, April 17, 1859, Pike Papers, UMe.

62. Charles A. Dana to JSP, June 14, 1859, Pike Papers, UMe.

63. Dana to JSP, June 23, 1859, in Pike, *First Blows of the Civil War*, 441.

64. Solomon Foot to WPF, July 26, 1859, Misc. American Autographs Collection, PML.

65. WPF to JSP, July 23, 1859, Pike Papers, UMe.

66. Charles H. Upton to WPF, Sept. 24, 1859, Fessenden Papers, WRHS.

67. WPF to ECW, July 31, 1859, FC.

68. EMF to WPF, Feb. 28, 1854, FC.

69. Foot to WPF, July 26, 1859, Misc. American Autographs Collection, PML.

70. WPF to JSP, Sept. 4, 1859, Pike Papers, UMe.

71. On the connections between Helper's book, John Brown's raid, and the 1859 speakership contest, see Brown, *Southern Outcast*, 124–79.

72. WPF to WHF, Nov. 6, 1859, FC.

73. WPF to WHF, Dec. 9, 1859, FC.

74. *CG*, 36 Cong., 1 sess., 1100–1102. Predictably, Hyatt was unimpressed. In a letter to Abraham Lincoln he denounced "the sophistry and special pleading of Fessenden." Thaddeus Hyatt to AL, May 19, 1860, Abraham Lincoln Papers, LC.

75. *CG*, 36 Cong., 1 sess., 553.

76. *CG*, 36 Cong., 1 sess., 556.

77. *CG*, 36 Cong., 1 sess., 557–58. In June Fessenden did backtrack slightly on the issue of black citizenship. Responding to an Indiana Democrat's objection to the receipt of a petition from Connecticut blacks, he stated: "Suppose they are not citizens . . . I take it they are subjects; they live under the laws; they are persons; and I do not know that the right of petition is confined to citizens." *CG*, 36 Cong., 1 sess., 2908. The comment is probably best interpreted as an attempt by Fessenden to ensure receipt of the petition. Lawfully, of course, blacks were not considered U.S. citizens in the wake of the *Dred Scott* decision.

78. WPF to ECW, Jan. 29, 1860, FC.

79. WPF to SFJr., March 10, 1860, FC.

80. James G. Blaine to WPF, March 6, 1860, FC.

81. Fitz Henry Warren to JSP, Feb. 25, 1860, in Pike, *First Blows of the Civil War*, 496.

82. George F. Talbot to JSP, March 8, 1860, Pike Papers, UMe.

83. WPF to ECW, March 4, 1860, FC.

84. Rensellaer Cram to WPF, June 6, 1860, FC.

85. Blaine to WPF, May 16, 1860, FC.

86. Lot M. Morrill to WPF, May 17, [1860], Abraham Lincoln Collected Papers, WRHS.

87. WPF to ECW, May 20, 1860, FC.

88. *CG*, 36 Cong., 1 sess., 2319.

89. WPF to FHM, Aug. 15, 1860, Freeman H. Morse Papers, WRHS.

90. WPF to CS, Aug. 22, 1860, Charles Sumner Papers, reel 20.

91. JSP to WPF, Sept. 2, [1860], Pike Papers, LC.

92. WPF to JSP, Sept. 12, 1860, Pike Papers, UMe.

93. WPF to FF, Nov. 4, 1860, FC.

94. WPF to FHM, Nov. 18, 1860, Morse Papers, WRHS.

95. WPF to WHF, Dec. 2, 1860, FC.

96. SF to WPF, Dec. 11, 1860, in FF, "Account of General Samuel Fessenden and Family," FC.

97. WPF to Hamilton Fish, Dec. 15, 1860, Fish Papers, LC.

98. WPF to SF, Dec. 15, 1860, FC. Fessenden's son William reported that the reply had "made a new man" of Samuel. WHF to WPF, Dec. 23, 1860, FC.

99. WPF to FF, Dec. 17, 1860, FC.

100. WPF to WHF, Dec. 20, 1860, FC.

101. WPF to ECW, Dec. 22, 1860, FC. Fessenden was not the only Republican to muse privately that the country might be better off without the slave South. His fellow centrists Rutherford B. Hayes of Ohio and Justin S. Morrill of Vermont expressed similar views. Green, *Freedom, Union, and Power*, 64.

102. WPF to William Willis, Dec. 22, 1860, FC.

103. McClintock, *Lincoln and the Decision for War*, 121; *CG*, 36 Cong., 2 sess., 409.

104. WPF to ECW, Jan. 12, 1861, FC.

105. WPF to WHF, Jan. 14, 1861, FC.

106. Leonard Swett to AL, Jan. 5, 1861, Lincoln Papers, LC.

107. WPF to AL, Jan. 20, 1861, FC.

108. AL, memorandum, c. March 15, 1861, in Basler, ed., *Collected Works of Abraham Lincoln*, 4:284.

109. SF to WPF, March 11, 1861, FC; WPF to GH, April 3, 1861, Letters Received from the Congress, 1836–1910, Records of the United States Treasury, RG56, NA; WPF to ECW, April 14, 1861, FC; WPF to ECW, April 21, 1861, FC; C. W. Walton to HH, April 22, 1861, Hamlin Papers, UMe.

110. WPF to AL, March 26, 1861, FC.

111. *CG*, 36 Cong., 2 sess., 852.

112. WPF to SF, Feb. 16, 1860 [1861], FC.

113. *CG*, 36 Cong., 2 sess., 1405.

114. *CG*, 36 Cong., 2 sess., 1403.

115. *CG*, 36 Cong., 2 sess., 1401.

116. WPF to "My dear Sir," March 22, 1861, FC.

117. WPF to ECW, April 21, 1860, FC.

118. CS to WPF, April 16, 1861, in Palmer, ed., *Selected Letters of Charles Sumner*, 2:65.

119. WPF to ECW, April 21, 1861, FC.

120. WPF to ECW, [April 1861], FC.

CHAPTER FIVE

1. WPF to Simon Cameron, May 9, 1861, in U.S. War Department, *War of the Rebellion*, Series 3, 1:181–82.

2. WPF to ECW, May 26, 1861, FC.

3. Scott's "Anaconda Plan" was unpopular because it avoided a direct attack on the Confederacy but in many respects it served as the long-term blueprint for Union victory.

4. WPF to ECW, June 23, 1861, FC.

5. WPF to JSP, June 30, 1861, James S. Pike Papers, UMe.

6. WPF to ECW, July 7, 1861, FC.

7. Curry, *Blueprint for Modern America*, 149–50.

8. The two functions were not separated by the formation of a Senate Appropriations Committee until 1867.

9. WPF to JMF, June 22, 1861, FC.

10. WPF to JMF, July 19, 1861, FC.

11. WPF to JSP, Sept. 8, 1861, James S. Pike Papers, LC.

12. WPF to ECW, July 21, 1861, FC.

13. WPF to ECW, July 28, 1861, FC.

14. *CG*, 37 Cong., 1 sess., 265.

15. *CG*, 37 Cong., 1 sess., 259.

16. SF to WPF, July 27, 1861, FC.

17. *CG*, 37 Cong., 1 sess., 219; Siddali, *From Property to Person*, 92.

18. Jellison, *Fessenden of Maine*, 132.

19. *CG*, 37 Cong., 1 sess., 374, 453.

20. Flaherty, *Revenue Imperative*, 66.

21. *CG*, 37 Cong., 1 sess., 316.

22. *CG*, 37 Cong., 1 sess., 316–17.

23. *CG*, 37 Cong., 1 sess., 255. The bill was later amended in conference committee. In its final form the measure increased import duties, incorporated a direct tax, and imposed a 3 percent tax on incomes over $800. Curry, *Blueprint for Modern America*, 158; Richardson, *Greatest Nation of the Earth*, 115.

24. WPF to JWG, Sept. 26, 1861, FC.

25. JWG to WPF, Nov. 13, 1861, in Salter, *Life and Times of James W. Grimes*, 156–57.

26. Henry Martyn Smith to "My dear Bro. G.," [Oct. 1861?], Charles H. Ray Papers, HL.

27. WPF to JMF, Nov. 10, 1861, FC.

28. WPF to ECW, Dec. 1, 1861, FC.

29. WPF to FF, Dec. 6, 1861, FC.

30. WPF to SF, Dec. 12, 1861, FC.

31. *CG,* 37 Cong., 2 sess., 31.

32. *CG,* 37 Cong., 2 sess., 96.

33. Curry, *Blueprint for Modern America,* 158.

34. Flaherty, *Revenue Imperative,* 82.

35. Curry, *Blueprint for Modern America,* 189.

36. *CG,* 37 Cong., 2 sess., 764–65.

37. *CG,* 37 Cong., 2 sess., 800.

38. *CG,* 37 Cong., 2 sess., 804. The specie clause later passed the House although the majority of Republicans there voted against it. Fessenden was a member of the conference committee that oversaw final passage of the loan bill with the coin-interest clause intact. Curry, *Blueprint for Modern America,* 195–96.

39. *CG,* 37 Cong., 2 sess., 764.

40. WPF to his family, Jan. 14, 1862, in FF, *Life and Public Services of William Pitt Fessenden,* 1:259–60.

41. WPF to ECW, Jan. 19, 1862, FC. Lincoln counseled widely before appointing Stanton, for example, asking the Massachusetts Republican Henry L. Dawes whether he had turned up any incriminating evidence on the Ohio Democrat when investigating government contracts during the secession crisis. See Burlingame, *Abraham Lincoln: A Life,* 2:244.

42. WPF to SF, Jan. 20, 1862, FC.

43. *CG,* 37 Cong., 2 sess., 513.

44. *CG,* 37 Cong., 2 sess., 1472.

45. SF to WPF, May 9, 1862, FC.

46. WPF to SF, March 29, 1862, FC.

47. John A. Andrew to WPF, March 6, 1862, Civil War Collection, NYHS; WPF to SF, March 29, 1862, FC; *CG,* 37 Cong., 2 sess., 1526, 1815, 2618. Fessenden joked to his friend Freeman Morse that he relied on his vote to abolish slavery in Washington "to render my name immortal." WPF to FHM, April 23, 1862, Misc. American Autographs Collection, PML.

48. *CG,* 37 Cong., 2 sess., 1333, 1522, 1523.

49. For a discussion of voting patterns on the Militia Bill, see Bogue, *Earnest Men,* 160–67. On July 10 Fessenden voted against a Missouri War Democrat's motion to prevent the enlistment of slaves belonging to loyal masters. Five days later, he supported amendments to emancipate only Rebel-owned slaves who served in the U.S. armed forces and the immediate dependants of those liberated black soldiers. *CG,* 37 Cong., 2 sess., 3232, 3339, 3342, 3343.

50. *CG,* 37 Cong., 2 sess., 2724–25, 3099, 3232, 3233, 3339, 3342, 3343, 3351.

51. *CG,* 37 Cong., 2 sess., 993; Bogue, *Earnest Men,* 283.

52. *CG,* 37 Cong., 2 sess., 183.

53. *CG,* 37 Cong., 2 sess., 870.

54. *CG,* 37 Cong., 2 sess., 1011.

55. *CG,* 37 Cong., 2 sess., 1013–14.

56. WPF to ECW, June 1, 1862, FC. Other Republican centrists from New England, notably Charles Francis Adams, found Sumner's egoism and vanity equally irritating.

57. Legal action *in rem* is taken against property rather than persons.

58. WPF to ECW, Dec. 12, 1861, FC; Siddali, *From Property to Person,* 221. For a full discussion of the war power doctrine, see Carnahan, *Act of Justice.*

59. *CG*, 37 Cong., 2 sess., 1963.

60. *CG*, 37 Cong., 2 sess., 2202–3.

61. WPF to ECW, May 23, 1862, FC.

62. WPF to Hamilton Fish, July 15, 1862, Hamilton Fish Papers, LC.

63. *CG*, 37 Cong., 2 sess., 3376.

64. WPF to ECW, March 15, 1862, FC.

65. Bogue, *Earnest Men*, 81.

66. *CG*, 37 Cong., 2 sess., 2203.

67. *CG*, 36 Cong., 2 sess., 1951, 2634.

68. *CG*, 38 Cong., 1 sess., 652.

69. *CG*, 37 Cong., 2 sess., 2097. The possibility that Fessenden's sympathy for the Indians resulted as much from sectional hostility to the West as from humanitarian concern cannot be dismissed. He later defended General James Carleton, a onetime resident of Maine, for interning Navajo Indians at the Bosque Redondo in 1864, an infamous instance of abuse in the sorry history of white-Indian relations in the nineteenth century. *CG*, 40 Cong., 2 sess., 2016.

70. *CG*, 37 Cong., 2 sess., 2840. Fessenden's failure to speak out strongly against the Pacific Railroad Bill or to vote on final passage of the bill may have been induced partly by the persistent lobbying efforts of his colleague, James G. Blaine. The young Maine congressman boasted to Thomas Ewing, Sr., an investor in western railroads, that Fessenden was "rancorously hostile to the whole thing—d——d [*sic*] it soundly as a job—extravagant, inopportune and reckless . . . Had he taken this position in the Senate as Chmn of Finance he would have killed the bill. He was however kept quiet and quasi-acquiescent—if not openly consenting and approving. Herein I served you efficiently." Quoted in Green, *Freedom, Union, and Power*, 303.

71. Bogue, *Earnest Men*, 134.

72. JWG to WPF, July 3, 1864, William Pitt Fessenden Papers, WRHS.

73. For the most convincing effort to define "moderates" and "radicals" in the Civil War Senate, see Bogue, *Earnest Men*, 88–124.

74. Benedict, *Compromise of Principle*, 83.

75. WPF to ECW, April 25, 1862, FC.

76. *CG*, 37 Cong., 2 sess., 2421–22.

77. *CG*, 37 Cong., 2 sess., 2332.

78. Curry, *Blueprint for Modern America*, 172.

79. *CG*, 37 Cong., 2 sess., 2309–10, 2401–7, 2467.

80. *CG*, 37 Cong., 2 sess., 2467.

81. *CG*, 37 Cong., 2 sess., 2611. Amended subsequently in conference committee, the bill retained the income-tax provision. Curry, *Blueprint for Modern America*, 179, notes that it filled more than seventeen triple-column pages of fine print. Wartime income taxes proved relatively popular with voters because, as Fessenden had suggested in 1861, they attempted to spread the burden as widely as possible. However, appearances could be deceptive. Income taxes provided only a fraction of government revenue during the Civil War and ordinary consumers were hit hard by the sharp and, in revenue-raising terms, more significant rises in excise taxes. See Paludan, *"A People's Contest,"* 120–21.

82. WPF to FHM, April 23, 1862, Misc. American Autographs Collection, PML.

83. *CG,* 37 Cong., 2 sess., 3201. Five days later the *Chicago Tribune* greeted this forthright statement with the comment that when Fessenden moved, "it signifies that the whole glacier has started." Bogue, *Earnest Men,* 162.

84. WPF to JSP, Aug. 2, 1862, Pike Papers, UMe.

85. WPF to JWG, Sept. 25, 1862, FC.

86. Ibid.

87. Browning diary, Nov. 28, 1862, in Pease and Randall, eds., *Diary of Orville Hickman Browning,* 1:587.

88. WPF to JWG, Sept. 25, 1862, FC.

89. WPF to SPC, Oct. 23, 1862, Salmon P. Chase Papers, PaHS.

90. McPherson, *Battle Cry of Freedom,* 561–62.

91. WPF to JMF, Nov. 13, 1862, in Hughes, ed., *Letters and Recollections of John Murray Forbes,* 1:336–37.

92. JMF to WPF, Nov. 15, 1862, in ibid., 1:338. Radical congressman Thaddeus Stevens agreed on the need for cabinet changes. Seward was the prime candidate for dismissal, he thought. However, he feared it could not be done and did not share Forbes's view that Fessenden was the ideal replacement: "He has too much of the vile ingredient, called conservatism, which is worse than secession. He is not so great as at one time I hoped he would prove." Stevens to [Simon] Stevens, Nov. 17, 1862, in Palmer and Ochoa, eds., *Selected Papers of Thaddeus Stevens,* 1:328.

93. WPF to JMF, Nov. 13, 1862, in Hughes, ed., *Letters and Recollections of John Murray Forbes,* 1:337.

94. Joseph Medill quoted in Paludan, *Presidency of Abraham Lincoln,* 171.

95. Fessenden's narrative of the cabinet crisis is contained in Fessenden, *Life and Public Services of William Pitt Fessenden,* 1:233–50. The fullest modern accounts, all of which rely heavily on Fessenden's version of events, are Nevins, *War for the Union,* vol. 2, *War Becomes Revolution,* 350–65; Paludan, *Presidency of Abraham Lincoln,* 167–81; Donald, *Lincoln,* 398–406; Goodwin, *Team of Rivals,* 486–95; Burlingame, *Abraham Lincoln: A Life,* 448–59.

96. FF, *Life and Public Services of William Pitt Fessenden,* 1:234–36.

97. Ibid., 237.

98. Ibid.

99. Ibid., 241.

100. AL quoted in Goodwin, *Team of Rivals,* 491.

101. Nevins, *War for the Union,* 2:358.

102. Welles, *Diary of Gideon Welles,* 1:197; FF, *Life and Public Services of William Pitt Fessenden,* 1:245.

103. Ibid., 247.

104. Ibid., 247–48. Fessenden's tart recollection that "The President made several speeches in the course of the evening, and related several anecdotes, most of which I had heard before," spoke volumes about the difference between the two men. Ibid., 245.

105. Most scholarly assessments of the 1862 cabinet crisis, perhaps understandably, have focused on what it tells us about Lincoln. However, Allan Nevins observed many years ago that while "[t]he President was triumphant," the senators' motives were patriotic and their aims diverse and, up to a point, justified. Nevins, *War for the Union,* 2:364–65.

106. WPF to SF, Dec. 20, 1862, FC.

107. Curry, *Blueprint for Modern America*, 216, 228.

108. *Harper's Weekly*, Jan. 3, 1863.

109. Paludan, *Presidency of Abraham Lincoln*, 178–79; Donald, *Lincoln*, 405.

110. Curry, *Blueprint for Modern America*, 227.

111. *CG*, 37 Cong., 3 sess., 70.

112. *CG*, 37 Cong., 2 sess., 2016–17. On the development of what Williamjames Hull Hoffer terms "the second state" by Civil War-era and Gilded Age Republicans (a distinct phase of American state-building that he sees as characterized by sponsorship, supervisory and standardizing functions and one that spanned the antebellum republican and the regulatory Progressive states), see Hoffer, *To Enlarge the Machinery of Government*, vii–xiv and ff.

113. *CG*, 37 Cong., 3 sess., 931.

114. John Sherman to William T. Sherman, March 20, 1863, in Thorndike, ed., *Sherman Letters*, 194.

115. *CG*, 37 Cong., 3 sess., 897.

116. WPF to JSP, March 9, 1864, Pike Papers, LC.

117. WPF to JSP, April 5, 1863, Pike Papers, LC.

118. WHF to WPF, July 9, 1862, FC; A. S. Chadbourne to WPF, Feb. 2, 1863, William Pitt Fessenden Papers, Duke University.

119. *CG*, 37 Cong., 3 sess., 800, 1329. Fessenden also supported Sumner's amendment to limit the amount of bonds to be offered to loyal slave masters for the release of their slaves. *CG*, 37 Cong., 3 sess., 901.

120. Bogue, *Earnest Men*, 107–8. According to Bogue's scaling analysis only Sumner and Wilson of Massachusetts and Wade of Ohio compiled more radical voting records in the landmark third session of the Thirty-seventh Congress than Fessenden. This reflected the degree to which the latter was radicalized by the need for hard-war policies, not his conversion to neo-abolitionist Radicalism.

121. WPF to FHM, April 5, 1863, Freeman H. Morse Papers, WRHS.

122. WPF to JSP, April 5, 1863, Pike Papers, LC.

123. Fessenden's liking for Hooker, a consummate intriguer who, like McClellan, was a better organizer and administrator than battlefield commander, confirms his lack of military acumen. However, "Fighting Joe" was highly thought of by many Republican leaders, including Lincoln and Chase. Williams, *Lincoln and His Generals*, 175.

124. WPF to FF, May 31, 1863. For Warriner's obituary, see *Pittsfield Sun*, May 28, 1863.

125. John W. Forney to WPF, June 2, 1863, Misc. American Autographs Collection, PML.

126. Edwin M. Stanton to WPF, Aug. 3, 1863, Edwin M. Stanton Papers, LC, reel 14.

127. Gideon Welles to WPF, Aug. 29, 1863, William H. Seward Papers, LC, reel 79.

128. Whalen, "Maine Republicans, 1854–1866," 155.

129. Fred A. Pike to JSP, Oct. 11, 1863, Pike Papers, UMe.

130. WPF to ECW, Dec. 13, 1863, FC.

131. WPF to ECW, Jan. 23, 1864, FC.

132. WPF to ECW, Dec. 19, 1863, FC.

133. Flaherty, *Revenue Imperative*, 114.

134. *CG*, 38 Cong., 1 sess., 2513.

135. Richardson, *Greatest Nation of the Earth*, 251.

136. WPF to WHF, Jan. 24, 1862, FC.

137. Ibid.

138. *CG*, 38 Cong., 1 sess., 481.

139. WHF to WPF, Feb. 12, 1864, FC.

140. William Lloyd Garrison to Henry Wilson, Feb. 20, 1864, in Merrill, ed., *Letters of William Lloyd Garrison*, 5:191. Thomas Wentworth Higginson, a New England abolitionist who commanded eight hundred black troops in South Carolina, suppressed his ire but dispatched a strongly worded appeal to the senator. He had always heard of Fessenden, he wrote, "as a man of courage and justice" and urged the government not to "degrade itself" by betraying its "plain contract" with "these poor men." Higginson to WPF, Feb. 13, 1864, Misc. Mss. (Thomas Wentworth Higginson), NYHS.

141. WPF to WHF, March 2, 1864, FC.

142. *CG*, 38 Cong., 1 sess., 1183.

143. *CG*, 38 Cong., 1 sess., 481, 482, 870.

144. WHF to WPF, Feb. 12, 1864, FC.

145. *CG*, 38 Cong., 1 sess., 482.

146. *CG*, 38 Cong., 1 sess., 1811.

147. *CG*, 38 Cong., 1 sess., 1161, 1361, 1490. Less progressively, Fessenden voted for a conference committee report that limited the suffrage in Montana to whites and against Sumner's motion to enfranchise all Washington, DC taxpayers who could read and write. *CG*, 38 Cong., 1 sess., 2544.

148. Bogue, *Earnest Men*, 107–8, lists Fessenden at twentieth place in his moderate-radical scale during the first half of 1864.

149. *CG*, 38 Cong., 1 sess., 1182.

150. *CG*, 38 Cong., 1 sess., 3364.

151. *CG*, 38 Cong., 1 sess., 3368.

152. *CG*, 38 Cong., 1 sess., 370–71.

153. *CG*, 38 Cong., 1 sess., 1872–73.

154. *CG*, 38 Cong., 1 sess., 1894, 1896, 1897.

155. *CG*, 38 Cong., 1 sess., 654.

156. *CG*, 38 Cong., 1 sess., 652, 654.

157. *CG*, 38 Cong., 1 sess., 3076.

158. Ibid.

159. *CG*, 38 Cong., 1 sess., 2142.

160. *CG*, 38 Cong., 1 sess., 2207.

161. WPF to FF, March 23, 1864, FC. Frank Fessenden had been placed on Brigadier General William H. Emory's staff in Louisiana in early 1864. His father's first letter to him in his new post was a classic illustration of the senator's heavy reliance on close contacts and reciprocal obligations. After assuring Frank that he was "intimate" with Emory's brother-in-law, Fessenden added that the general also "has some reason to feel obliged to me, as I rendered some aid in restoring him to the Army. Genl. Franklin will be likely to treat you well as he knows Portland people so well. If you go to Mobile, and meet

Genl. Sherman there, get introduced to him. His brother John is my friend & associate in the Senate, as you know." WPF to FF, March 9, 1864, Misc. Mss. (WPF), NYHS. Emory's brother-in-law was the well-connected scientist Alexander Dallas Bache, a great-grandson of Benjamin Franklin.

162. Jellison, *Fessenden of Maine,* 178–79.

163. Simon Cameron to WPF, June 15, 1864, FC.

164. *CG,* 38 Cong., 1 sess., 3491.

165. Jellison, *Fessenden of Maine,* 175.

166. *CG,* 37 Cong., 2 sess., 767.

CHAPTER SIX

1. SPC diary, June 30, 1864, in Donald, ed., *Inside Lincoln's Cabinet,* 223.

2. Dennett, ed., *Lincoln and the Civil War in the Diaries and Letters of John Hay,* 202.

3. Welles diary, July 5, 1864, in Welles, *Diary of Gideon Welles,* 2:64–65.

4. AL, quoted in Burlingame, *Abraham Lincoln: A Life,* 2:625.

5. WPF to AL, July 1, 1864, FC.

6. WPF to ECW, July 3, 1864, FC. Francis Carpenter, a portrait painter in the White House in July 1864, recalled the same conversation in language that confirms the president's insistent tone while exaggerating his piety. "Fessenden," he remembered Lincoln saying, " *the* LORD *has not deserted me thus far, and He is not going to now,*—you must accept!" Carpenter, *The Inner Life of Abraham Lincoln,* 183.

7. WPF to ECW, July 3, 1864, FC.

8. SPC diary, July 1, 1864, in Donald, ed., *Inside Lincoln's Cabinet,* 227–28.

9. WPF to Edward Fox, July 3, 1864, FC.

10. Joseph A. Ware to WPF, July 5, 1864, Misc. Mss. (WPF), NYHS.

11. Carpenter, *Inner Life of Abraham Lincoln,* 183; George W. Davis to AL, July 2, 1864, FC.

12. Harris C. Fahnestock to HDC and Laura Cooke, July 4, 1864, Henry D. Cooke Papers, HL.

13. Edward Atkinson to unidentified correspondent, July 3, 1864, Edward Atkinson Papers, MassHS.

14. Francis P. Blair, Jr. to Montgomery Blair, July 9, 1864, Abraham Lincoln Papers, LC.

15. Fahnestock to JC, July 9, 1864, Jay Cooke Papers, PaHS.

16. WPF to ECW, July 9, 1864, FC.

17. Montgomery C. Meigs to Edwin M. Stanton, July 7, 1864, Letters Received from the War Department, 1832–1910, Records of the U.S. Treasury, RG56, NA.

18. WPF to ECW, July 17, 1864, FC.

19. George D. Lyman to AL, July 18, 1864, Lincoln Papers, LC; Fahnestock to JC, July 19, 1864, Jay Cooke Papers, PaHS.

20. Justin S. Morrill to WPF, July 17, 1864, Justin S. Morrill Papers, LC.

21. WPF, "To the People of the United States," Treasury Department circular, July 25, 1864, Misc. Mss. Collection, MeHS.

22. Fahnestock to JC, July 26, 1864, Jay Cooke Papers, PaHS.

23. Hooper to WPF, Aug. 3, 1864, Misc. American Autographs Collection, PML.

24. JC to SPC, Aug. 3, 1864, Jay Cooke Papers, PaHS.

25. JC to WPF, July 21, 1864, Misc. Mss. (WPF), NYHS.

26. Ibid.

27. Fahnestock to JC, Aug. 5, 1864, Jay Cooke Papers, PaHS.

28. WPF to GH, Aug. 12, 1864, George Harrington Papers, Bixby Collection, HL.

29. Berlin et al., *Freedom: A Documentary History of Emancipation 1861–1867,* ser. 1, vol. 3, 536–43.

30. The *Liberator,* Aug. 19, 1864.

31. *New-York Daily Tribune,* Aug. 8, 1864.

32. GH to John Eaton, Aug. 23, 1864, Letters Sent Relating to Restricted Commercial Intercourse, vol. 7, BE Series, 1861–1878, RG 56.

33. WPF to SF, Sept. 16, 1864, FC.

34. WPF to Stanton, Sept. 26, 1864, Letters Sent to Cabinet Officers, vol. 16, BC Series, 1861–66, RG 56; Lorenzo Thomas to E. D. Townsend, Jan. 1, 1865, Letters Received by the Division of Captured Property, Claims and Land, 1863–87, RG 56.

35. Josephine S. Griffing to AL, Sept. 24, 1864, Lincoln Papers, LC; Eaton to WPF, Nov. 14, 1864, Letters Received by the Division of Captured Property, Claims and Land, 1863–87, RG 56.

36. WPF to Zachariah Chandler, Jan. 30, 1865, Letters Sent Relating to Restricted Commercial Intercourse, vol. 8, BE Series, 1861–78, RG 56.

37. SPC diary, July 2, 1864, in Donald, *Inside Lincoln's Cabinet,* 229.

38. Welles diary, July 5, 1864, in Welles, *Diary of Gideon Welles,* 2:66.

39. Atkinson to AL, Sept. 3, 1864, Lincoln Papers, LC.

40. WPF to FHM, April 5, 1863, Freeman H. Morse Papers, WRHS.

41. Johnson, "Northern Profit and Profiteers," 101–2.

42. WPF to O. N. Cutler, Sept. 23, 1864, Letters Sent Relating to Restricted Commercial Intercourse, vol. 7, BE Series 1861–78, RG 56.

43. Stephen A. Hurlbut to AL, Sept. 26, 1864, Lincoln Papers, LC.

44. WPF, "Report of the Secretary of the Treasury," Dec. 6, 1864, *CG,* 38 Cong., 2 sess., Appendix, 30.

45. JWG to WPF, July 3, 1864, William Pitt Fessenden Papers, WRHS.

46. Johnson, "Northern Profit and Profiteers," 102–4. Johnson notes that while his deputies were up to their necks in cotton speculations, Fessenden "seems not to have been privy to most, if any, of the chicanery that went on." Ibid., 104.

47. WPF to EMS, Sept. 15, 1864, Letters Sent, Seventh Special Agency, RG56.

48. Burlingame, *Abraham Lincoln: A Life,* 2:764.

49. Welles diary, Jan. 3, 1865, in Welles, *Diary of Gideon Welles,* 2:220.

50. WPF to SPC, Aug. 4, 1864, Salmon P. Chase Papers, PaHS.

51. WPF to SPC, Sept. 6, 1864, Chase Papers, PaHS.

52. AL, "Memorandum," Aug. 23, 1864, Lincoln Papers, LC.

53. WPF to George F. Shepley, Aug. 22, 1864, George F. Shepley Papers, MeHS.

54. WPF to ECW, Aug. 27, 1864, FC.

55. WPF to ECW, Sept. 11, 1864, FC.

56. JC to SPC, Sept. 10, 1864, Jay Cooke Papers, PaHS.

57. SPC to JC, Sept. 8, 1864, Jay Cooke Papers, PaHS.

58. JC to SPC, Sept. 20, 1864, Jay Cooke Papers, PaHS.

59. HDC to JC, Oct. 15, 1864, Jay Cooke Papers, PaHS.

60. HDC to JC, Oct. 10, 1864, Jay Cooke Papers, PaHS.

61. HDC to JC, Oct. 19, 1864, Jay Cooke Papers, PaHS.

62. Oberholtzer, *Jay Cooke: Financier of the Civil War*, 1:435.

63. HDC to JC, Nov. 12, 1864, Jay Cooke Papers, PaHS.

64. HDC to JC, Nov. 14, 1864, Jay Cooke Papers, PaHS.

65. WPF, "Report," 24.

66. Ibid., 29, 30.

67. *New York Herald*, undated clipping, Dec. 1864, FC.

68. *Merchants' Magazine and Commercial Review*, Jan. 1865, 60.

69. Charles A. Dana to JSP, Dec. 12, 1864, James S. Pike Papers, UMe.

70. WPF to WHF, Dec. 15, 1864, FC.

71. Whalon, "Maine Republicans, 1854–1866," 179.

72. WPF to Israel Washburn, Jr., Nov. 18, 1865, Fessenden Papers, LC.

73. WPF to Judge——, Dec. 17, 1864, Fessenden Papers, LC.

74. William P. Frye to WPF, Jan. 7, 1865, FC.

75. HH to Ellie Hamlin, Jan. 8, 1865, Hannibal Hamlin Papers, UMe.

76. WPF to AL, Feb. 6, 1865, Lincoln Papers, LC.

77. WPF to JC, Jan. 28, 1865, Jay Cooke Papers, PaHS.

78. HDC to JC, Feb. 17, 1865, Jay Cooke Papers, PaHS.

79. Charles Francis Adams, Jr. to Charles Francis Adams, Jan. 30, 1865, in Ford, ed., *Cycle of Adams Letters*, 2:250; *Merchants' Magazine and Commercial Review*, Feb. 1865, 113.

80. Atkinson to [JMF?], Feb. 14, 1865, Atkinson Papers, MassHS; John Williams to Henry C. Carey, March 2, 1865, Henry C. Carey Papers, Edward Carey Gardiner Collection, PaHS. Williams edited the Philadelphia *Iron Age*.

81. Thomas W. Olcott to WPF, Feb. 15, 1865, FC.

82. *New-York Tribune*, March 4, 1865.

83. WPF to FHM, April 2, 1865, Morse Papers, WRHS.

84. Flaherty, *Revenue Imperative*, 140.

85. WPF to FHM, April 2, 1865, Morse Papers, WRHS.

86. WPF to HM, March 24, 1865, Hugh McCulloch Papers, LC.

87. WPF to GH, March 29, 1865, Harrington Papers, HL.

88. WPF to AL, Feb. 6, 1865, Lincoln Papers, LC.

89. WPF to HM, April 23, 1865, McCulloch Papers, LC.

90. WPF to HM, April 24, 1865, McCulloch Papers, LC.

91. WPF to Stanton, May 23, 1865, Edwin M. Stanton Papers, LC.

92. Joseph Medill to HM, June 16, 1865, McCulloch Papers, LC.

93. R. G. Greene to WPF, June 14, 1865, Fessenden Papers, WRHS.

94. Lot M. Morrill to WPF, July 19, [1865], FC.

95. WPF to FF, July 26, 1865, FC.

96. WPF to JWG, July 14, 1865, FC.

97. Supporters of *limited* suffrage favored imposing specific tests (e.g., Union military service, educational attainment, or property holding) on potential black voters. *Impartial* or *equal* suffrage required such tests to be imposed equally on whites and blacks, while *universal* suffrage involved the enfranchisement of most adult males regardless of color.

98. Henry Wilson to CS, Sept. 9, 1865, Charles Sumner Papers, reel 34.

99. James D. Fessenden to WPF, July 21, 1865, FC.

100. Fred A. Pike to his sister, Oct. 15, 1865, Pike Papers, UMe.

101. WPF to ECW, Dec. 3, 1865, FC.

102. CS to Francis Lieber, [Dec. 3, 1865], Sumner Papers, reel 64. At one point in the interview Johnson unwittingly (one assumes) used Sumner's hat as a spittoon.

103. WHF to WPF, Dec. 9, 1865, FC.

104. WPF to ECW, Dec. 10, 1865, FC.

105. *CG,* 39 Cong., 1 sess., 26.

106. *CG,* 39 Cong., 1 sess., 27.

107. HH to CS, Dec. 19, 1865, Sumner Papers, reel 34.

108. WPF to ECW, Dec. 24, 1865, FC.

109. WPF to ECW, Dec. 24, 1865, FC.

110. CS, remarks in *Memorial Addresses on the Life and Character of William Pitt Fessenden,* 13.

CHAPTER SEVEN

1. WPF to SF, Dec. 31, 1865, FC.

2. This tally of factional strength in the Joint Committee is based on the categories used in Benedict, *Compromise of Principle,* 348–53. Benedict lists Fessenden as a "conservative centrist" in the first session of the Thirty-ninth Congress. Allan Bogue's scaling analysis, however, lists the senator from Maine as the seventh most radical member of the upper chamber in the same session. Bogue, *Earnest Men,* 108. Fessenden's decision to break with John Sherman over the Civil Rights Bill certainly confirms his ability to think and act independently of the so-called moderates under the press of events.

3. Kendrick, *Journal of the Joint Committee,* 41.

4. Ibid., 50–51.

5. *Portland Daily Press,* Sept. 1, 1868.

6. Thaddeus Stevens quoted in Benedict, *Compromise of Principle,* 133; Kendrick, ed., *Journal of the Joint Committee,* 52.

7. *CG,* 39 Cong., 1 sess., 704.

8. *CG,* 40 Cong., 3 sess., 1032.

9. *CG,* 39 Cong., 1 sess., 704.

10. *CG,* 39 Cong., 1 sess., 708.

11. *CG,* 39 Cong., 1 sess., 365.

12. WPF to ECW, Jan. 28, 1866, FC. The phrase "bow drawn at a venture" was taken from 1 Kings 22:34. Doubtless remembered from his childhood recitations, Fessenden used it publicly on March 9, 1868. See *CG,* 40 Cong., 2 sess., 1752.

13. *CG,* 39 Cong., 1 sess., 367.

14. WPF to ECW, Jan. 28, Feb. 3, 1866, FC.

15. WPF to GH, Feb. 3, 1866, George Harrington Papers, Bixby Collection, HL; McKitrick, *Andrew Johnson and Reconstruction,* 282–83.

16. *CG,* 39 Cong., 1 sess., 673.

17. Ibid., 705, 708.

18. Kendrick, ed., *Journal of the Joint Committee,* 64–67.

19. WPF to ECW, Feb. 17, 1866, FC.

20. Andrew Johnson, speech of Feb. 22, 1866, in Bergeron, ed., *Papers of Andrew Johnson,* 10:149.

21. *CG,* 39 Cong., 1 sess., 984.

22. *CG,* 39 Cong., 1 sess., 986.

23. *CG,* 39 Cong., 1 sess., 988–91.

24. WPF to ECW, March 3, 1866, FC.

25. WPF to ECW, Feb. 25, 1866, FC.

26. *CG,* 39 Cong., 1 sess., 1147.

27. CS to the editors, *Boston Daily Advertiser,* March 15, 1866, Charles Sumner Papers, reel 80.

28. WPF to ECW, March 10, 1866, FC. Fessenden believed Sumner was motivated by "mortified vanity" induced by his failure to secure the post of chairman of the Joint Committee on Reconstruction. Ibid.

29. *CG,* 39 Cong., 1 sess., 1640, 1677. On the Stockton case, see Butler and Wolff, *United States Senate: Election, Expulsion and Censure Cases,* 127–29. Tellingly, though erroneously, the authors describe Fessenden as a Radical Republican.

30. WPF to WHF, March 31, 1866, FC. Fessenden's mood was darkened by the recent death of his friend, Senator Solomon Foot of Vermont. He was a pall-bearer at Foot's funeral and delivered a stirring eulogy in the Senate on April 12.

31. E. P. Walton to WPF, April 10, 1866, John Woodruff to WPF, May 7, 1866, William Pitt Fessenden Papers, WRHS.

32. Rufus P. Stebbins to CS, April 9, 1866, Sumner Papers, reel 36.

33. WPF to ECW, April 8, 1866, FC. Sumner married the Hoopers' daughter, Alice, in October 1866. The relationship was a notoriously unhappy one and the couple separated in September 1867.

34. Robert Dale Owen, "Political Results from the Varioloid," 664.

35. Ibid., 665–66. Jacob Howard of Michigan, a Radical, assumed leadership of the committee in Fessenden's absence.

36. Kendrick, ed., *Journal of the Joint Committee,* 101.

37. In committee Fessenden opposed disfranchising the former Confederates but, recognizing the need for party unity, voted to submit the amendment to Congress with the prohibition intact. Kendrick, ed., *Journal of the Joint Committee,* 105–6, 114; Benedict, *Compromise of Principle,* 185–86.

38. WPF to WHF, May 13, 1866, FC.

39. WPF to GH, May 12, 1866, Harrington Papers, HL.

40. WPF to ECW, June 2, 1866, FC.

41. WPF et al., *Report of the Joint Committee on Reconstruction, at the First Session Thirty-Ninth Congress,* viii, xi, xviii, xx.

42. Ibid., xiii, xvii.

43. *New-York Semi-Weekly Tribune,* June 12, 1866.

44. Thaddeus Stevens quoted in Foner, *Reconstruction: America's Unfinished Revolution,* 255.

45. The British consul reported that the fire left Portland's central business district "a region of desolation," destroying 1,700 houses and public buildings (the brick-built British consulate among them) worth between $10 and $15 million. Henry John Murray to the Earl of Clarendon, July 9, 1866, FO5/1076, National Archives, London.

46. WPF to WHF, July 11, 1866, FC; WPF to ECW, July 15, 1866, FC.

47. WPF to ECW, June 24, 1866, FC.

48. *CG,* 39 Cong., 1 sess., 3751–52.

49. *CG,* 39 Cong., 1 sess., 3842, 3992–93, 4219.

50. *CG,* 39 Cong., 1 sess., 3992–93. Fessenden did not add that Tennessee was also a distinctive case because it was Andrew Johnson's home state. Admitting its delegates to Congress was consistent with his own preference for maintaining relations with the president if possible.

51. *CG,* 39 Cong., 1 sess., 3433–34, 4221–22.

52. *CG,* 39 Cong., 1 sess., 3551.

53. *CG,* 39 Cong., 1 sess., 3763–64.

54. *CG,* 39 Cong., 1 sess., 3104–5.

55. Alexander Bullock et al. to WPF, July 31, 1866, FC. Fessenden declined the invitation, claiming that he was "[d]ebilitated by a long and most arduous session of Congress, and by repeated attacks of illness." WPF to Albert J. Wright, Aug. 8, 1866, FC.

56. WPF to HM, Sept. 7, 1866, Hugh McCulloch Papers, LC.

57. WPF to HM, Aug. 15, 1866, McCulloch Papers, LC. Like Doolittle, Edgar Cowan of Pennsylvania was a conservative Republican who sided with Johnson in the struggle over Reconstruction policy.

58. John Sherman to William T. Sherman, Oct. 26, 1866, in Thorndike, ed., *Sherman Letters,* 278.

59. *New-York Semi-Weekly Tribune,* Sept. 14, 1866.

60. WPF to HM, Sept. 11, 1866, McCulloch Papers, LC.

61. WPF to HM, Sept. 15, 1866, McCulloch Papers, LC.

62. WPF to FHM, Oct. 14, 1866, Freeman H. Morse Papers, WRHS.

63. Edwin D. Morgan to WPF, Oct. 16, 1866, FC.

64. WPF to Edwin M. Stanton, Oct. 20, 1866, Edwin M. Stanton Papers, LC.

65. WPF to HM, Nov. 3, 1866, McCulloch Papers, LC.

66. WPF to ECW, Dec. 1, Dec. 8, 1866, FC.

67. WPF to FHM, Nov. 21, 1866, Morse Papers, WRHS.

68. WPF to SF, Dec. 8, 1866, FC.

69. WPF to ECW, Dec. 8, 1866, FC.

70. L. P. Gudger to CS, Dec. 11, 1866, Sumner Papers, reel 37.

71. CS to Theodore Tilton, Dec. 23, 1866, Sumner Papers, reel 80.

72. WPF to SF, Jan. 19, 1867, FC.

73. WPF to Richard H. Dana, Feb. 9, 1867, Dana Family Papers, MassHS.

74. WPF to ECW, Dec. 8, 1866, FC.

75. *CG,* 39 Cong., 2 sess., 107, 109, 359, 360, 487. Fessenden's vote against James Dixon's literacy test amendment to the DC suffrage bill on December 13, 1866 represented an advance on the position he had

staked out in favor of equal suffrage the previous June. Possibly emboldened by the Republican victories in the 1866 midterm elections, he was clearly unwilling to allow his doubts about the freedmen's fitness for full citizenship to obstruct formulation of a viable Reconstruction policy with some form of black suffrage at its center. Fessenden's support for a popular referendum in Nebraska on Congress's black suffrage mandate (*CG*, 39 Cong., 2 sess., 486–87) highlighted his overwhelming preference for a consensual approach to Reconstruction that would render the government's rights revolution sustainable in all parts of the country.

76. *CG*, 39 Cong., 2 sess., 1905.

77. *CG*, 39 Cong., 2 sess., 385.

78. *CG*, 39 Cong., 2 sess., 469.

79. *CG*, 39 Cong., 2 sess., 550, 1966.

80. WPF to FF, Jan. 12, 1867, FC.

81. WPF to ECW, Jan. 19, 1867, FC.

82. WPF to ECW, Jan. 12, 1867, FC.

83. WPF to ECW, Feb. 2, 1867, FC.

84. *CG*, 39 Cong., 2 sess., 1007.

85. *CG*, 39 Cong., 2 sess., 1008.

86. *CG*, 39 Cong., 2 sess., 1053.

87. *CG*, 39 Cong., 2 sess., 1304.

88. *CG*, 39 Cong., 2 sess., 1303.

89. *CG*, 39 Cong., 2 sess., 1556.

90. Fessenden outlined this and the following reasons for his opposition to the caucus's decision in a subsequent public address. See WPF, "Notes for a Speech in the Grant-Seymour Campaign," in Manuscript Reports, Speeches, Opinions (#8), FC.

91. *New-York Semi-Weekly Tribune*, Feb. 19, 1867.

92. WPF to WHF, Feb. 17, 1867, FC.

93. Fessenden's conduct was revealed by Wade in debate on February 19. He did not deny the charge that he had gone to the House to defeat the bill. *CG*, 39 Cong., 2 sess., 1560.

94. *CG*, 39 Cong., 2 sess., 1556.

95. Ibid.

96. *CG*, 39 Cong., 2 sess., 1559.

97. Ibid.

98. WPF to ECW, Feb. 17, 1867. According to the *Brooklyn Daily Eagle*, Feb. 28, 1867, Fessenden actively campaigned for the post.

99. *CG*, 39 Cong., 2 sess., 1966, 1976.

100. *CG*, 40 Cong., 1 sess., 109.

101. *CG*, 40 Cong., 1 sess., 161.

102. *CG*, 40 Cong., 1 sess., 96.

103. *CG*, 40 Cong., 1 sess., 118. Although a majority of Senate Republicans opposed giving the provisional governments a decisive say in the Reconstruction process, they endorsed the principle that southerners should indicate their readiness to resume their erstwhile relations with the United States. The Supplementary Reconstruction Act of March 1867 required a majority of registered voters to vote in constitutional convention elections for those contests to be valid.

104. Maine philanthropist, John Storer, donated $10,000 toward this Free Will Baptist enterprise.

105. CS to Edward L. Pierce, March 11, 1867, Sumner Papers, reel 64.

106. WPF to ECW, April 21, 1867, FC.

107. WPF to JWG, May 2, 1867, FC.

108. *New-York Daily Tribune,* May 8, 1867.

109. WPF to Wendell Phillips, May 15, 1867, FC.

110. Kenneth Rayner to WPF, April 23, 1867, Misc. Mss. (Kenneth Rayner), NYHS.

111. WPF to Rayner, May 9, 1867, Misc. Mss. (Kenneth Rayner), NYHS. Fessenden made similar remarks in a letter to the Delaware senator, Thomas Bayard, written on the same day. Jellison, *Fessenden of Maine,* 218.

112. Richard Shannon, *Gladstone,* vol. 1, *1809–1865* (London: Hamish Hamilton, 1982), 468.

113. WPF to FHM, May 23, 1867, Morse Papers, WRHS.

114. WPF to JWG, June 18, 1867, FC.

115. WPF to Lot Morrill, June 21, 1867, Lot Morrill Papers, MeHS.

116. WPF to ECW, July 4, 1867, FC.

117. *CG,* 40 Cong., 1 sess., 498.

118. *CG,* 40 Cong., 1 sess., 492.

119. Jellison, *Fessenden of Maine,* 224.

120. Sumner effectively made this point earlier in the year. During debate on February 28 he announced rather wistfully that he coveted some of Fessenden's ability "in developing what I think the better cause. I wish that I could have in favor of what I think the true policy on this occasion the great powers that the Senator from Maine can so easily display. I know he can vindicate his side. I am only sorry that his side is not that which it seems to me at this moment the Senate ought to adopt. If we had his powerful support the Senate would not commit itself to a proposition which to my mind can have but disastrous influences." *CG,* 39 Cong., 2 sess., 1911.

121. Henry Wilson to CS, Sept. 9, 1865, Sumner Papers, reel 34.

122. WPF to William H. Seward, Aug. 9, 1867, Fessenden Papers, WRHS; WPF to FHM, Aug. 19, 1867, Morse Papers, WRHS.

123. WPF to HM, Sept. 2, 1867, McCulloch Papers, LC.

124. General William T. Sherman, unlike Fessenden a genuine conservative, suggested this strategy to the president in the fall of 1867. Johnson, he said, should "make overtures to such men as Fessenden, Trumbull, Sherman, Morgan, and Morton, who, though differing with him in abstract views of Constitutional Law and Practice, were not destructive." Sherman to John Sherman, [Oct. 1867?], in Thorndike, ed., *Sherman Letters,* 298.

125. WPF to FHM, Aug. 19, 1867, Morse Papers, WRHS.

126. WPF to HM, Sept. 2, 1867, McCulloch Papers, LC.

127. WPF to JWG, Sept. 20, 1867, FC.

128. Quoted in Trefousse, *Impeachment of a President,* 93.

129. WPF to JWG, Oct. 20, 1867, FC.

130. City of Portland Valuation Book, 1867, 97, Portland Public Library.

131. WPF, "Memorandum for my sons, appointed Executors of my last will and testament," Oct. 31, 1867, FC. While many important figures in history have ordered the destruction of their private papers,

it is tempting to interpret Fessenden's letter-burning instruction as proof of his desire to conceal a sexual relationship with Lizzy. However, it is possible to view it less conspiratorially as corroboration of his abiding love of order. Congressman John Lynch of Portland noted the connection between this trait and Fessenden's keen, logical mind. He recalled after Fessenden's death that the senator "had great order, not only in all business matters, but in his mental processes. Whether in his library at home, or in his committee-room or private apartments here [in Washington], this same order was observed. There were no piles of books and manuscripts, no confusion of papers, but all the surroundings were clear, clean, and orderly as the mind that presided over them. He kept himself unencumbered of all waste material, weeding out and rejecting everything superfluous, and retaining only the useful." *Memorial Addresses on the Life and Character of William Pitt Fessenden*, 60. At the very least, Fessenden's singling out of women's letters for destruction indicated his gendered belief that such "superfluous" private correspondence would not aid posterity in passing judgment on what was, for him, his all-important public career.

132. WPF to WHF, Nov. 23, 1867, FC.

133. Ibid.

134. Foner, *Reconstruction: America's Unfinished Revolution*, 335.

135. William Endicott, Jr. to CS, Feb., 29, 1868, Sumner Papers, reel 41.

136. WPF to SF, Dec. 7, 1867, FC.

137. William Alexander to CS, Jan. 6, 1868, Sumner Papers, reel 40.

138. WPF to ECW, Jan. 19, 1868, FC.

139. Benedict, *Impeachment and Trial of Andrew Johnson*, 102.

140. WPF to FHM, Feb. 22, 1868, Morse Papers, WRHS.

141. WPF to ECW, Feb. 22, 1868, FC.

142. Charles Dickens to W. H. Wills, Feb. 25, 1868, in House et al., eds., *Letters of Charles Dickens*, 12:59.

143. *New-York Semi-Weekly Tribune*, Feb. 28, 1868; *Portland Daily Press*, March 2, 1868.

144. WHF to WPF, March 3, 1868, FC.

145. WPF to SF, March 8, 1861, FC.

146. Benedict, *Impeachment and Trial of Andrew Johnson*, Chart 6, 127.

147. WPF to FF, March 29, 1868, FC.

148. WPF to ECW, March 31, 1868, FC.

149. WPF to ECW, April 12, 1868, FC.

150. Neal Dow to WPF, April 5, 1868, FC.

151. Dow to WPF, April 6, 1868, FC.

152. *New-York Semi-Weekly Tribune*, April 21, 1868.

153. Rufus Dwinel to WPF, April 26, 1868, FC.

154. CS to Francis Lieber, May 2, 1868, Sumner Papers, reel 81.

155. WPF to WHF, May 3, 1868, FC.

156. Edward L. Pierce to CS, May 7, 1868, Sumner Papers, reel 42.

157. JWG to Charles H. Ray, May 7, 1868, Charles H. Ray Papers, HL.

158. Trefousse, *Impeachment of a President*, 158–59.

159. Ibid., 168.

160. WPF, Opinion, in *CG*, 40 Cong., 2 sess., Impeachment Trial Supplement, 452, 457.

161. H. H. Jacobs to CS, May 13, 1868, Sumner Papers, reel 42.

162. Dwinel to WPF, May 13, 1868, FC.

163. WPF to WHF, May 13, 1868, FC.

164. *New-York Semi-Weekly Tribune,* May 19, 1868.

165. Ibid.

166. WPF to ECW, Dec. 15, 1867, FC.

167. Dexter A. Hawkins to WPF, May 14, 1868, FC.

168. WPF to Morse, Feb. 22, 1868, Fessenden Papers, WRHS.

169. Ibid.

170. M. W. Frazier to WPF, March 4, 1868, Heartman Collection, NYHS.

171. WPF to William Willis, May 16, 1868, FC.

172. *Boston Advertiser,* May 16, 1868, quoted in Benedict, *Compromise of Principle,* 310.

173. Anon. to CS, May 17, 1868, Sumner Papers, reel 42.

EPILOGUE

1. *Portland Daily Press,* June 5, 1868.

2. Sumner referred to the seven apostates as "quibblers" on several occasions after the trial. For example, he told Edward Atkinson on June 13 that their hands seemed to him to be "dripping with blood"— "Alas! for quibblers against justice—quibblers against humanity—quibblers against the Public Safety." Charles Sumner Papers, reel 82.

3. See, e.g., William Gray to WPF, May 16, 1868, Benjamin R. Curtis to WPF, May 18, 1868, FC.

4. JMF to WPF, May 23, 1868, in Hughes, ed., *Letters and Recollections of John Murray Forbes,* 164–65.

5. *New-York Semi-Weekly Tribune,* May, 19, 1868.

6. WPF to FF, May 23, 1868, FC.

7. Alexander H. Bullock et al. to WPF, June 2, 1868, FC.

8. "A Norridgewocker" to WPF, May 17, 1868, FC.

9. WPF to WHF, June 13, 1868, FC.

10. WPF to WHF, July 12, 1868, FC.

11. CG, 40 Cong., 2 sess., 3029, 3466 (admission of North Carolina, South Carolina, Louisiana, Georgia, and Alabama); 3677, 4437 (railroad subsidies). Fessenden confessed on January 25, 1869, that he realized opposition to federal subsidies for western railroads was "fruitless." CG, 40 Cong., 3 sess., 572.

12. CG, 40 Cong., 2 sess., 3363, 4236.

13. CG, 40 Cong., 2 sess., 3428–29. Fessenden also registered his opposition to what he saw as excessive use of federal power by opposing U.S. government assistance to education. CG, 40 Cong., 2 sess., 3508–9.

14. CG, 40 Cong., 2 sess., 3087, 3156–57, 3160.

15. JSP to WPF, July 5, 1868, Misc. Mss. (WPF), NYHS.

16. *Portland Daily Press,* Sept. 1, 1868.

17. WPF to FHM, Sept. 13, 1868, Freeman H. Morse Papers, WRHS.

18. Foner, *Reconstruction: America's Unfinished Revolution*, 340–43.

19. Ibid., 343.

20. WPF to GH, Nov. 7, 1868, George Harrington Papers, Bixby Collection, HL. For an account of the 1868 election, see Foner, *Reconstruction: America's Unfinished Revolution*, 338–45.

21. WPF to GH, Nov. 7, 1868, Harrington Papers, HL.

22. WPF to ECW, Dec. 6, 1868, FC.

23. WPF to William Willis, Dec. 18, 1868, FC.

24. Frederick Robie to WPF, Jan. 28, 1869, William Pitt Fessenden Papers, WRHS.

25. WPF to Israel Washburn, Jr., March 6, 1869, FC; Washburn to WPF, March 9, 1869, Fessenden Papers, WRHS; WPF to FF, March 18, 1869, FC; WHF to WPF, April 8, 1869, FC.

26. WPF to WHF, March 28, 1869, FC.

27. WPF to FHM, April 25, 1869, Morse Papers, WRHS.

28. *CG*, 40 Cong., 3 sess., 1032.

29. *CG*, 40 Cong., 3 sess., 80–81. Fessenden based his argument for restoration of the militias on the not unreasonable assumption that Congress was unwilling to increase the size of the army.

30. WPF to ECW, March 21, 1869, FC.

31. WPF to Hamilton Fish, May 23, 1869, Hamilton Fish Papers, LC.

32. FF to James D. Fessenden, Jan. 26, 1881, FC.

33. WPF to George S. Boutwell, June 29, 1869, Letters Received from the Congress 1836–1910, Records of the U.S. Treasury, RG56, NA.

34. WPF to FHM, July 5, 1869, Morse Papers, WRHS.

35. *Portland Daily Press*, July 20, 1869.

36. Joseph Carr to FF, Aug. 1883, FC.

37. WPF to Fish, Aug. 24, 1869, Fish Papers, LC; WPF to James G. Blaine, Aug. 26, 1869, FC.

38. The following account of Fessenden's last days is based on FF, *Life and Public Services of William Pitt Fessenden*, 2:330, and *Portland Daily Press*, Sept. 3, 4, 9, 1869.

39. A. L. Hobson to CS, Sept. 4, 1869, Sumner Papers, reel 48.

40. *Portland Daily Advertiser*, Sept. 11, 1869.

41. Fehrenbacher and McAfee, *The Slaveholding Republic*, xi.

42. McClintock, *Lincoln and the Decision for War*, 145.

43. JWG to Lyman Cook, Oct. 10, 1869, in Salter, ed., *Life and Times of James W. Grimes*, 378.

44. Maurice Wakeman to CS, Sept. 21, 1869, Sumner Papers, reel 48.

45. Mansfield and Kelsey, *Personal Sketches of the Members of the Fortieth Congress of the United States of America: Maine Delegation*.

46. National Union Executive Committee, *Negro Suffrage and Social Equality*, 6.

47. WPF to SF, Dec. 8, 1866, FC.

48. Frederick Douglass, speech of December 28, 1862, in Blassingame, ed., *Frederick Douglass Papers*, ser. 1, 3:545.

49. *CG*, 40 Cong., 3 sess., 81.

50. Austin Willey to WPF, May 4, [1869], Fessenden Papers, WRHS.

Bibliography

MANUSCRIPTS

Alexandria, VA

Charles Sumner Papers, Chadwyck-Healey, 1988

Ann Arbor, MI

Daniel Webster Papers, University Microfilms in collaboration with Dartmouth College Library, 1971

Bowdoin College, Brunswick, ME

Athenaean Society Records
Bowdoin College, Executive Government Records, 1805–20
Bowdoin College, Votes of the Executive Government, April 24, 1821–July 16, 1823
Bowdoin College, Votes of the Governing Boards
Fessenden Collection
John Hubbard Papers
William Willis Papers

Cambridge University Library, Cambridge, UK

Maine House of Representatives, Journals 1832, 1845, 1854 (microfilm)

Duke University, Durham, NC

William Pitt Fessenden Papers

Huntington Library, San Marino, CA

Hiram Barney Papers
Henry D. Cooke Papers
George Harrington Papers, Bixby Collection
Charles H. Ray Papers

Library of Congress, Washington, DC

Timothy Davis Papers
William Pitt Fessenden Papers
Hamilton Fish Papers
John W. Forney Papers
Abraham Lincoln Papers
Hugh McCulloch Papers
Justin S. Morrill Papers
William H. Seward Papers
James Shepherd Pike Papers
Edwin M. Stanton Papers
Lyman Trumbull Papers
Israel Washburn, Jr. Papers
Henry Wilson Papers

Maine Historical Society, Portland, ME

Shepard Cary Papers
Charles P. Chandler Papers
Nathan Clifford Papers
Charles S. Daveis Papers
Deering/Noyes Collection
Samuel Fessenden, Jr. Papers
John Holmes Papers
Lot Morrill Papers
George F. Shepley Papers
Daniel Walker Lord Papers
Miscellaneous Manuscripts Collection
John Mussey Papers
Pierce Family Papers
Portland Benevolent Society Records 1814–78
Francis O. J. Smith Papers
William Willis Papers

Massachusetts Historical Society, Boston

Adams Papers
Edward Atkinson Papers
Dana Family Papers
Norcross Collection

National Archives, London

Records of the British Consul at Portland, Maine, FO5

National Archives, Washington, DC

Records of the Civil War Special Agencies, Record Group 366
Records of the U.S. Senate, Record Group 46
Records of the U.S. Treasury, Record Group 56

New-York Historical Society, New York

Civil War Collection
Heartman Collection
Miscellaneous Manuscripts (William C. Bryant, Charles S. Daveis, William Pitt Fessenden, Thomas W. Higginson, Kenneth Rayner)

Pennsylvania Historical Society, Philadelphia

Salmon P. Chase Papers
Jay Cooke Papers
Ferdinand J. Dreer Autograph Collection
Etting Collection
Edward Carey Gardiner Collection
Simon Gratz Autograph Collection

Pierpont Morgan Library, New York

Gilder Lehrman Collection
Miscellaneous American Autographs

Portland Public Library, Portland, ME

Portland City Tax Books 1849–69
William Willis diary

University of Maine, Orono, ME

Samuel Fessenden Papers, Miscellaneous Collection
Hannibal Hamlin Papers
James Shepherd Pike Papers

Miscellaneous items

Western Reserve Historical Society, Cleveland, OH

William Pitt Fessenden Papers
Abraham Lincoln Collected Papers
Freeman H. Morse Papers

NEWSPAPERS AND PERIODICALS

[Brunswick, Augusta, Hallowell] *Advocate of Freedom*
Anglo-American Times
Brooklyn Daily Eagle
Congressional Globe
Harper's Weekly
The Liberator
[Hallowell] *Liberty Standard*
The Nation
National Era
Merchants' Magazine and Commercial Review
New York Times
New-York Tribune
Pittsfield Sun
Portland Advertiser
Portland Daily Press
Portland Inquirer

PUBLISHED PRIMARY SOURCES

Adams, Charles Francis, ed. *Memoirs of John Quincy Adams, Comprising Portions of His Diary from 1705 to 1848.* 12 vols. 1874–77. Repr. Freeport, NY: Books for Libraries Press, 1969.

Beale, Howard K., ed. *The Diary of Edward Bates 1859–1866.* Washington, DC: Government Printing Office, 1933.

Basler, Roy P. *The Collected Works of Abraham Lincoln.* 9 vols. New Brunswick, NJ: Rutgers University Press, 1953.

Beckett, S. B. *The Portland Reference Book and City Directory, for 1850–51.* Portland: Thurston, Tenley & Co., 1850.

Bergeron, Paul H., et al., eds. *The Papers of Andrew Johnson.* 16 vols. Knoxville: University of Tennessee Press, 1967–2000.

Berlin, Ira, et al. *Freedom: A Documentary History of Emancipation 1861–1867,* ser. 1, vol. 3, *The Wartime Genesis of Free Labor: The Lower South.* Cambridge: Cambridge University Press, 1990.

Blassingame, John W., ed., *The Frederick Douglass Papers,* ser. 1, *Speeches, Debates and Interviews,* vol. 3, *1855–63.* New Haven: Yale University Press, 1985.

Burlingame, Michael, ed. *An Oral History of Abraham Lincoln: John G. Nicolay's Interviews and Essays.* Carbondale and Edwardsville: Southern Illinois University Press, 1996.

———, ed. *With Lincoln in the White House: Letters, Memoranda, and Other Writings of John G. Nicolay 1860–1865.* Carbondale and Edwardsville: Southern Illinois University Press, 2000.

Carpenter, Francis B. *The Inner Life of Abraham Lincoln: Six Months in the White House.* Lincoln: University of Nebraska Press, 1995.

Chapman, George T. *Sketches of the Alumni of Dartmouth College from the First Graduation in 1771 to the Present Time, with a Brief History of the Institution.* Cambridge: Riverside Press, 1867.

Cole, Donald B., and John J. McDonough, eds. *Witness to the Young Republic: A Yankee's Journal, 1828–1870.* Hanover, NH: University Press of New England, 1989.

Dennett, Tyler, ed. *Lincoln and the Civil War in the Diaries and Letters of John Hay.* New York: Da Capo, 1988.

Donald, David, ed. *Inside Lincoln's Cabinet: The Civil War Diaries of Salmon P. Chase.* New York: Longmans, Green, 1954.

Dow, Neal. *The Reminiscences of Neal Dow: Recollections of Eighty Years.* Portland: The Evening Express Publishing Company, 1898.

Eaton, John. *Grant, Lincoln and the Freedmen: Reminiscences of the Civil War with Special Reference to the Work for the Contrabands and Freedmen of the Mississippi Valley.* New York: Longman, Green and Co., 1907.

Fessenden, Samuel. *An Oration, Delivered Before the Officers and Members of Cumberland, Oxford and Ancient Land-Mark Lodges, at New-Gloucester, June 25th, A.L. 5810, on the Festival of St. John the Baptist.* Portland: Arthur Shirley, 1810.

———. *An Oration Delivered Before the Federal Republicans of New Gloucester and the Adjacent Towns, July 4, A.D. 1811.* Portland: The Gazette Press, [1811].

Fessenden, Francis. *Life and Public Services of William Pitt Fessenden: United States Senator from Maine 1854–1864; Secretary of the Treasury 1864–1865; United States Senator from Maine 1865–1869.* 2 vols. Boston and New York: Houghton, Mifflin and Company, 1907.

Fessenden, William Pitt. *An Oration Delivered Before the Young Men of Portland, July 4, 1827.* Portland: James Adams, Jr., 1827.

Ford, Washington Chauncey, ed. *A Cycle of Adams Letters, 1861–1865.* 2 vols. Boston: Houghton Mifflin, 1920.

Hamlin, Charles Eugene. *The Life and Times of Hannibal Hamlin.* Cambridge: Riverside Press, 1899.

Hilen, Andrew, ed. *The Letters of Henry Wadsworth Longfellow*. 6 vols. Cambridge: Belknap Press of Harvard University Press, 1966–82.

Hopkins, James F., et al., eds. *The Papers of Henry Clay*. 10 vols. Lexington: University of Kentucky Press, 1959–1991.

House, Madeline, Graham Storey, and Kathleen Tillotson, eds. *The Letters of Charles Dickens*. 12 vols. Oxford: Clarendon Press, 1965–2002.

Hughes, Sarah Forbes, ed. *Letters and Recollections of John Murray Forbes*. 2 vols. Boston: Houghton, Mifflin and Co., 1899.

Kendrick, Benjamin B. *The Journal of the Joint Committee of Fifteen on Reconstruction, 39 Congress, 1865–1867*. New York: Columbia University Press, 1914.

McCulloch, Hugh. *Men and Measures of Half a Century: Sketches and Comments*. New York: Charles Scribner's Sons, 1889.

Mansfield, J. B., and D. M. Kelsey. *Personal Sketches of the Fortieth Congress of the United States of America: Maine Delegation*. Baltimore: The Authors, 1867.

"Memoir of Nathaniel Greene," *[New England] Historical and Genealogical Register* 32 (1878): 373–78.

Merrill, Walter, et al., eds. *The Letters of William Lloyd Garrison*. 6 vols. Cambridge: Belknap Press of Harvard University Press, 1971–81.

National Union Executive Committee. *Negro Suffrage and Social Equality*. [Washington, DC?]: n.p., [1866?].

[Neal, John]. "North American Politics." *Blackwood's Edinburgh Magazine* 18 (1825): 355–69.

Owen, Robert Dale. "Political Results from the Varioloid." *Atlantic Monthly* 35 (1875): 660–70.

Palmer, Beverly Wilson, ed. *The Selected Letters of Charles Sumner*. 2 vols. Boston: Northeastern University Press, 1990.

———, and Holly Byers Ochoa, eds. *The Selected Papers of Thaddeus Stevens*. 2 vols. Pittsburgh: University of Pittsburgh Press, 1997–98.

Pease, Theodore C., and James G. Randall, eds. *The Diary of Orville Hickman Browning*. 2 vols. Springfield: Trustees of the Illinois State Historical Library, 1925–33.

Pike, James S. *First Blows of the Civil War: The Ten Years of Preliminary Conflict in the United States from 1850 to 1860*. New York: The American News Company, [c. 1879].

Preble, George Henry. *William Pitt Fessenden: A Memoir, Prepared for the New England Historical and Genealogical Register for April 1871*. Boston: David Clapp and Son, 1871.

Salter, William. *The Life and Times of James W. Grimes, Governor of Iowa, 1854–1858; A Senator of the United States, 1859–1869*. New York: D. Appleton and Company, 1876.

Thorndike, Rachel Sherman, ed. *The Sherman Letters: Correspondence between General and Senator Sherman from 1837 to 1891*. New York: Charles Scribner's Sons, 1894.

U.S. Congress. *Report of the Joint Committee on Reconstruction, at the First Session Thirty-Ninth Congress*. 1866; Repr. Freeport, NY: Books for Libraries Press, 1971.

———. *Memorial Addresses on the Life and Character of William Pitt Fessenden, (A Senator from Maine,) Delivered in the Senate and House of Representatives, 41st Congress, 2d Session, December 14, 1869.* Washington, DC: Government Printing Office, 1870.

U.S. War Department. *The War of the Rebellion: A Compilation of the Official Records of the Union and Confederate Armies.* 128 vols. Washington, DC: Government Printing Office, 1880–1901.

Ward, Jonathan. *Parental and Filial Obligation Illustrated and Enforced. A Discourse delivered December 22, 1813 in Alna.* Augusta: Peter Eades, 1814.

Welles, Gideon. *Diary of Gideon Welles: Secretary of the Navy under Lincoln and Johnson.* 3 vols. Boston and New York: Houghton, Mifflin and Co., 1911.

Willey, Austin. *The History of the Antislavery Cause in State and Nation.* 1886. Repr. Miami: Mnemosyne Publishing Co., 1969.

Willis, William. *A History of the Law, the Courts, and the Lawyers of Maine, from its First Colonization to the Early Part of the Present Century.* Portland: Bailey & Noyes, 1863.

Wiltse, Charles M. et al., eds. *The Papers of Daniel Webster.* 14 vols. Hanover, NH: University Press of New England, 1974–89.

PUBLISHED SECONDARY SOURCES: BOOKS

Abbott, Richard H. *Cobbler in Congress: The Life of Henry Wilson, 1812–1875.* Lexington: University Press of Kentucky, 1972.

———. *The Republican Party and the South, 1855–1877: The First Southern Strategy.* Chapel Hill: University of North Carolina Press, 1986.

Ackerman, Bruce. *We The People 2: Transformations.* Cambridge: Belknap Press of Harvard University Press, 1998.

Allmendinger, David F., Jr. *Paupers and Scholars: The Transformation of Student Life in Nineteenth-Century New England.* New York: St. Martin's Press, 1975.

Altschuler, Glenn C., and Stuart M. Blumin. *Rude Republic: Americans and Their Politics in the Nineteenth Century.* Princeton: Princeton University Press, 2000.

Ashworth, John. *"Agrarians" & "Aristocrats": Party Political Ideology in the United States, 1837–1846.* London: Royal Historical Society, 1983.

———. *Slavery, Capitalism, and Politics in the American Republic,* vol. 1, *Commerce and Compromise, 1820–1850.* Cambridge: Cambridge University Press, 1995.

Balleisen, Edward J. *Navigating Failure: Bankruptcy and Commercial Society in Antebellum America.* Chapel Hill: University of North Carolina Press, 2001.

Banks, Ronald F. *Maine Becomes a State: The Movement to Separate Maine from Massachusetts, 1785–1820.* Middletown, CT: Wesleyan University Press, 1970.

Banner, James M., Jr. *To the Hartford Convention: The Federalists and the Origins of Party Politics in Massachusetts, 1789–1815.* New York: Alfred A. Knopf, 1970.

Bartlett, Irving H. *Daniel Webster.* New York: W. W. Norton, 1978.

Baxter, Maurice G. *One and Inseparable: Daniel Webster and the Union.* Cambridge: Harvard University Press, 1984.

Beckert, Sven. *The Monied Metropolis: New York City and the Consolidation of the American Bourgeoisie, 1850–1896.* Cambridge: Cambridge University Press, 2001.

Beale, Howard K. *The Critical Year: A Study of Andrew Johnson and Reconstruction.* 1930. Repr. New York: Frederick Ungar Publishing Company, 1958.

Belohlavek, John M. *Broken Glass: Caleb Cushing and the Shattering of the Union.* Kent, OH: Kent State University Press, 2005.

Belz, Herman. *Reconstructing the Union: Theory and Policy during the Civil War.* 1969. Repr. Westport, CT: Greenwood Press, 1976.

———. *A New Birth of Freedom: The Republican Party and Freedmen's Rights, 1861 to 1866.* Westport, CT: Greenwood Press, 1976.

Benedict, Michael Les. *The Impeachment and Trial of Andrew Johnson.* New York: W. W. Norton, 1973.

———. *A Compromise of Principle: Congressional Republicans and Reconstruction, 1863–1869.* New York: W. W. Norton, 1974.

Bensel, Richard Franklin. *Yankee Leviathan: The Origins of Central State Authority in America, 1859–1877.* Cambridge: Cambridge University Press, 1990.

Bloomfield, Maxwell. *American Lawyers in a Changing Society, 1776–1876.* Cambridge: Harvard University Press, 1976.

Blue, Frederick. J. *The Free Soilers: Third Party Politics 1848–54.* Urbana: University of Illinois Press, 1973.

———. *Salmon P. Chase: A Life in Politics.* Kent, OH: Kent State University Press, 1987.

Blumin, Stuart M. *The Emergence of the Middle Class: Social Experience in the American City, 1760–1900.* Cambridge: Cambridge University Press, 1989.

Bogue, Allan G. *The Earnest Men: Republicans of the Civil War Senate.* Ithaca: Cornell University Press, 1981.

———. *The Congressman's Civil War.* Cambridge: Cambridge University Press, 1989.

Bond, James E. *No Easy Walk to Freedom: Reconstruction and the Ratification of the Fourteenth Amendment.* Westport, CT: Praeger, 1997.

Borritt, Gabor, ed. *Why the Civil War Came.* New York: Oxford University Press, 1996.

Bowers, Claude G. *The Tragic Era: The Revolution After Lincoln.* New York: Houghton, Mifflin Company, 1929.

Brewer, Holly. *By Birth or Consent: Children, Law, and the Anglo-American Revolution in Authority.* Chapel Hill: University of North Carolina Press, 2005.

Brock, W. R. *An American Crisis: Congress and Reconstruction, 1865–1867.* New York: St. Martin's Press, 1963.

————. *Parties and Political Conscience: American Dilemmas 1840–1850.* Millwood: KTO Press, 1979.

Brown, David. *Southern Outcast: Hinton Rowan Helper and The Impending Crisis of the South.* Baton Rouge: Louisiana State University Press, 2006.

Brown, Thomas, ed. *Reconstructions: New Perspectives on the Postbellum United States.* New York: Oxford University Press, 2006.

Burlingame, Michael. *Abraham Lincoln: A Life.* 2 vols. Baltimore: Johns Hopkins University Press, 2008.

Butler, Anne M., and Wendy Wolff. *United States Senate: Election, Expulsion, and Censure Cases 1793–1990.* Washington, DC: Government Printing Office, 1995.

Byrne, Frank L. *Prophet of Prohibition: Neal Dow and His Crusade.* Madison: State Historical Society of Wisconsin, 1961.

Carnahan, Burrus M. *Act of Justice: Lincoln's Emancipation Proclamation and the Law of War.* Lexington: University of Kentucky Press, 2007.

Carwardine, Richard J. *Evangelicals and Politics in Antebellum America.* New Haven: Yale University Press, 1993.

————. *Lincoln.* Harlow, UK: Pearson Education, 2003.

Clark, Charles E., James S. Leamon, and Karen Bowden, eds. *Maine in the Early Republic: From Revolution to Statehood.* Hanover, NH: University Press of New England, 1988.

Coffin, Charles Carleton. *The History of Boscawen and Webster. From 1733 to 1878.* Concord, NH: The Republican Press Association, 1878.

Congressional Quarterly's Guide to U.S. Elections. 2nd ed. Washington, DC: Congressional Quarterly Inc., 1985.

Cooper, William J., Michael F. Holt, and John McCardell, eds. *A Master's Due: Essays in Honor of David Herbert Donald.* Baton Rouge: Louisiana State University Press, 1985.

Cox, LaWanda. *Lincoln and Black Freedom: A Study in Presidential Leadership.* Columbia: University of South Carolina Press, 1981.

Crapol, Edward. *John Tyler: The Accidental President.* Chapel Hill. University of North Carolina Press, 2006.

Curry, Leonard P. *Blueprint for Modern America: Non-Military Legislation of the First Civil War Congress.* Nashville: Vanderbilt University Press, 1968.

Donald, David. *Charles Sumner and the Coming of the Civil War.* New York: Alfred A. Knopf, 1960.

————. *The Politics of Reconstruction 1863–1867.* Baton Rouge. Louisiana State University Press, 1965.

————. *Charles Sumner and the Rights of Man.* New York: Alfred A. Knopf, 1970.

————. *Lincoln.* 1995. London: Pimlico, 1996.

Dunning, William A. *Reconstruction: Political and Economic 1865–1877.* New York: Harper and Bros, 1907.

Durden, Robert Franklin. *James Shepherd Pike: Republicanism and the American Negro, 1850–1882*. Durham: Duke University Press, 1957.

Engerman, Stanley, and Robert E. Gallman, eds. *The Cambridge Economic History of the United States,* vol. 2, *The Long Nineteenth Century.* Cambridge: Cambridge University Press, 2000.

Epps, Garrett. *Democracy Reborn: The Fourteenth Amendment and the Fight for Equal Rights in Post-Civil War America.* New York: Henry Holt, 2006.

Faust, Drew Gilpin. *This Republic of Suffering: Death and the American Civil War.* New York: Alfred A. Knopf, 2008.

Fehrenbacher, Don E. *Prelude to Greatness: Lincoln in the 1850s.* Stanford: Stanford University Press, 1962.

———, and Ward M. McAfee. *The Slaveholding Republic: An Account of the United States Government's Relations to Slavery.* New York: Oxford University Press, 2001.

Fessenden, Edwin Allan. *The Fessenden Family in America.* 2 vols. [Vestal, NY?]: n.p., 1971.

Flaherty, Jayne. *The Revenue Imperative: The Union's Financial Policies during the American Civil War.* London: Pickering & Chatto, 2009.

Foner, Eric. *Free Soil, Free Labor, Free Men: The Ideology of the Republican Party.* New York: Oxford University Press, 1970.

———. *Reconstruction: America's Unfinished Revolution 1863–1877.* New York: Harper and Row, 1988.

Fredrickson, George M. *The Inner Civil War: Northern Intellectuals and the Crisis of the Union.* New York: Harper Torchbook, 1968.

Freehling, William W. *The Road to Disunion: Secessionists Triumphant 1854–1861.* New York: Oxford University Press, 2007.

Gara, Larry. *The Presidency of Franklin Pierce.* Lawrence: University of Kansas Press, 1991.

General Catalogue of Bowdoin College and the Medical School of Maine: A Biographical Record of Alumni and Officers, 1794–1950. Portland: Anthoenson Press, 1950.

Gerteis, Louis S. *From Contraband to Freedmen: Federal Policy Toward Southern Blacks 1861–1865.* Westport, CT: Greenwood Press, 1973.

Gienapp, William E. *The Origins of the Republican Party 1852–1856.* New York: Oxford University Press, 1987.

Gillette, William. *The Right to Vote: Politics and the Passage of the Fifteenth Amendment.* Baltimore: Johns Hopkins University Press, 1965.

Goodwin, Doris Kearns. *Team of Rivals: The Political Genius of Abraham Lincoln.* New York: Simon and Schuster, 2005.

Grant, Susan-Mary. *North Over South: Northern Nationalism and American Identity in the Antebellum Era.* Lawrence: University of Kansas Press, 2000.

Green, Michael S. *Freedom, Union, and Power: Lincoln and His Party during the Civil War.* New York: Fordham University Press, 2004.

Greven, Philip. *The Protestant Temperament: Patterns of Child-Rearing, Religious Experience, and the Self in Early America*. New York: Random House, 1978.

Grossberg, Michael. *Governing the Hearth: Law and the Family in Nineteenth-Century America*. Chapel Hill: University of North Carolina Press, 1985.

Guelzo, Allen C. *Abraham Lincoln: Redeemer President*. Grand Rapids: William B. Eerdmans, 1999.

Harris, William C. *With Charity for All: Lincoln and the Restoration of the Union*. Lexington: University of Kentucky Press, 1997.

Hess, Earl J. *Liberty, Virtue, and Progress: Northerners and Their War for the Union*. 2nd ed. New York: Fordham University Press, 1997.

Hoffer, Williamjames Hull. *To Enlarge the Machinery of Government: Congressional Debates and the Growth of the American State, 1858–1891*. Baltimore: Johns Hopkins University Press, 2007.

Holt, Michael F. *The Political Crisis of the 1850s*. New York: John Wiley, 1978.

———. *The Rise and Fall of the American Whig Party: Jacksonian Politics and the Onset of the Civil War*. New York: Oxford University Press, 1999.

Holzer, Harold. *Lincoln President-Elect: Abraham Lincoln and the Great Secession Winter 1860–1861*. New York: Simon and Schuster, 2008.

Howe, Daniel Walker. *The Political Culture of the American Whigs*. Chicago: University of Chicago Press, 1979.

———. *What Hath God Wrought: The Transformation of America, 1815–1848*. New York: Oxford University Press, 2007.

Hunt, H. Draper. *Hannibal Hamlin of Maine: Lincoln's First Vice-President*. Syracuse: Syracuse University Press, 1969.

Hyman, Harold M., and William M. Wiecek. *Equal Justice Under Law: Constitutional Development 1835–1875*. New York: Harper and Row, 1982.

Iseley, Jeter A. *Horace Greeley and the Republican Party 1853–1861*. Princeton: Princeton University Press, 1947.

Jellison, Charles A. *Fessenden of Maine: Civil War Senator*. Syracuse: Syracuse University Press, 1962.

Johannsen, Robert W. *Stephen A. Douglas*. New York: Oxford University Press, 1973.

Jones, Howard. *To the Webster-Ashburton Treaty: A Study in Anglo-American Relations, 1783–1843*. Chapel Hill: University of North Carolina Press, 1977.

Keller, Morton. *Affairs of State: Public Life in Late Nineteenth Century America*. Cambridge: Belknap Press of Harvard University Press, 1977.

Koistinen, Paul A. C. *Beating Plowshares into Swords: The Political Economy of American Warfare, 1606–1865*. Lawrence: University of Kansas Press, 1996.

Krug, Mark M. *Lyman Trumbull: Conservative Radical*. New York: A. S. Barnes and Company, 1965.

Kutler, Stanley I. *Judicial Power and Reconstruction Politics.* Chicago: University of Chicago Press, 1968.

Larson, Henrietta M. *Jay Cooke: Private Banker.* Cambridge: Harvard University Press, 1936.

McClintock, Russell. *Lincoln and the Decision for War: The Northern Response to Secession.* Chapel Hill: University of North Carolina Press, 2008.

McCormick, Richard P. *The Second American Party System: Party Formation in the Jacksonian Era.* Chapel Hill: University of North Carolina Press, 1966.

McKitrick, Eric L. *Andrew Johnson and Reconstruction.* Chicago: University of Chicago Press, 1960.

McPherson, James M. *The Struggle for Equality: Abolitionists and the Negro in the Civil War and Reconstruction.* Princeton: Princeton University Press, 1964.

———. *Battle Cry of Freedom: The Civil War Era.* New York: Oxford University Press, 1988.

———. *Tried By War: Abraham Lincoln as Commander in Chief.* New York: Penguin Press, 2008.

———. and William J. Cooper, Jr., eds. *Writing the Civil War: The Quest to Understand.* Columbia: University of South Carolina Press, 1998.

Mason, Matthew. *Slavery and Politics in the Early American Republic.* Chapel Hill: University of North Carolina Press, 2006.

Mitchell, Wesley Clair. *A History of the Greenbacks with Special Reference to the Economic Consequences of Their Issue: 1862–65.* Chicago: Chicago University Press, 1903.

Morrison, Michael A. *Slavery and the American West: The Eclipse of Manifest Destiny and the Coming of the Civil War.* Chapel Hill: University of North Carolina Press, 1997.

Myers, John L. *Senator Henry Wilson and the Civil War.* Lanham, MD: University Press of America, 2008.

Nagel, Paul C. *John Quincy Adams: A Public Life, a Private Life.* Cambridge: Harvard University Press, 1997.

Neely, Mark E., Jr. *The Boundaries of American Political Culture in the Civil War Era.* Chapel Hill: University of North Carolina Press, 2005.

Nelson, William E. *The Fourteenth Amendment: From Political Principle to Judicial Doctrine.* Cambridge: Harvard University Press, 1988.

Nevins, Allan. *Hamilton Fish.* New York: Dodd, Mead and Company, 1936.

———. *The War for the Union,* vol. 2, *War Becomes Revolution.* New York: Charles Scribner's Sons, 1960.

Niven, John. *Salmon P. Chase: A Biography.* New York: Oxford University Press, 1995.

Novak, Steven J. *The Rights of Youth: American Colleges and Student Revolt, 1798–1815.* Cambridge: Harvard University Press, 1977.

Oberholtzer, Ellis Paxson. *Jay Cooke: Financier of the Civil War.* 2 vols. Philadelphia: George W. Jacobs & Co., 1907.

———. *A History of the United States Since the Civil War.* 5 vols. New York: Macmillan, 1917–37.

Paludan, Phillip Shaw. *A Covenant with Death: The Constitution, Law, and Equality in the Civil War Era.* Urbana, Chicago, and London: University of Illinois Press, 1975.

———. *"A People's Contest": The Union and Civil War 1861–1865.* New York: Harper and Row, 1988.

———. *The Presidency of Abraham Lincoln.* Lawrence: University Press of Kansas, 1994.

Perman, Michael. *Reunion Without Compromise: The South and Reconstruction, 1865–1868.* Cambridge: Cambridge University Press, 1973.

Peterson, Norma Lois. *The Presidencies of William Henry Harrison & John Tyler.* Lawrence: University Press of Kansas, 1989.

Potter, David M. *Lincoln and His Party in the Secession Crisis.* New Haven: Yale University Press, 1942.

Rayback, Robert J. *Millard Fillmore: Biography of a President.* East Aurora, NY: Henry Stewart, 1972.

Remini, Robert V. *Henry Clay: Statesman for the Union.* New York: W. W. Norton, 1991.

———. *Daniel Webster: The Man and His Time.* New York: W. W. Norton, 1997.

Rhodes, James Ford. *History of the United States from the Compromise of 1850.* 7 vols. New York: Macmillan, 1893–1906.

Richards, Leonard L. *The Slave Power: The Free North and Southern Domination 1780–1860.* Baton Rouge: Louisiana State University Press, 2000.

Richardson, Heather Cox. *The Greatest Nation of the Earth: Republican Economic Policies During the Civil War.* Cambridge: Harvard University Press, 1997.

———. *The Death of Reconstruction: Race, Labor, and Politics in the Post-Civil War North, 1865–1901.* Cambridge: Harvard University Press, 2001.

Riddleberger, Patrick W. *1866: The Critical Year Revisited.* Carbondale: Southern Illinois University Press, 1979.

Rotundo, E. Anthony. *American Manhood: Transformations in Masculinity from the Revolution to the Modern Era.* New York: Basic Books, 1993.

Sellers, Charles. *The Market Revolution: Jacksonian America, 1815–1846.* New York: Oxford University Press, 1991.

Sexton, Jay. *Debtor Diplomacy: Finance and American Foreign Relations in the Civil War Era 1837–1873.* Oxford: Clarendon Press, 2005.

Shannon, Richard. *Gladstone*, vol. 1, *1809–1865.* London: Hamish Hamilton, 1982.

Sharkey, Robert P. *Money, Class and Party: An Economic Study of Civil War and Reconstruction.* 1959. Repr. Baltimore: Johns Hopkins University Press, 1967.

Siddali, Silvana R. *From Property to Person: Slavery and the Confiscation Acts, 1861–1862.* Baton Rouge: Louisiana State University Press, 2005.

Silbey, Joel. *Storm Over Texas: The Annexation Controversy and the Road to Civil War.* New York: Oxford University Press, 2005.

Simpson, Brooks D. *The Reconstruction Presidents*. Lawrence: University of Kansas Press, 1998.

Smith, Adam I. P. *No Party Now: Politics in the Civil War North*. New York: Oxford University Press, 2006.

Sprague, Laura Fecych, ed. *Agreeable Situations: Society, Commerce, and Art in Southern Maine, 1780–1830*. Kennebunk, ME: The Brick Store Museum; Boston: Distributed by New England Universities Press, 1987.

Stampp, Kenneth M. *And the War Came: The North and the Secession Crisis 1860–1861*. Baton Rouge: Louisiana State University Press, 1950.

Temin, Peter, ed. *Engines of Enterprise: An Economic History of New England*. Cambridge: Harvard University Press, 2000.

Thomas, Benjamin P., and Harold M. Hyman. *Stanton: The Life and Times of Lincoln's Secretary of War*. New York: Alfred A. Knopf, 1962.

Trefousse, Hans L. *Benjamin Franklin Wade: Radical Republican from Ohio*. New York: Twayne, 1963.

———. *The Radical Republicans: Lincoln's Vanguard for Racial Justice*. New York: Alfred A. Knopf, 1969.

———. *Impeachment of a President: Andrew Johnson, the Blacks, and Reconstruction*. Knoxville: University of Tennessee Press, 1975.

Unger, Irwin. *The Greenback Era: A Social and Political History of American Finance 1865–1879*. Princeton: Princeton University Press, 1964.

Vorenberg, Michael. *Final Freedom: The Civil War, the Abolition of Slavery, and the Thirteenth Amendment*. Cambridge: Cambridge University Press, 2001.

Wang, Xi. *The Trial of Democracy: Black Suffrage and Northern Republicans, 1860–1910*. Athens: University of Georgia Press, 1997.

Williams, T. Harry. *Lincoln and His Generals*. New York: Alfred A. Knopf, 1952.

PUBLISHED SECONDARY SOURCES: ARTICLES

Adams, John W., and Alice Bee Kasakoff. "Wealth and Migration in Massachusetts and Maine: 1771–1798." *Journal of Economic History* 45 (1985): 363–68.

Altschuler, Glenn C., and Stuart M. Blumin. "Limits of Engagement in Antebellum America: A New Look at the Golden Age of Participatory Democracy." *Journal of American History* 84 (1997): 855–85.

Barry, William David, and Randolph Dominic. "Mr. Deering and His Mansion." *Down East* 28 (1982): 85–87.

Benedict, Michael Les. "Constitutional History and Constitutional Theory: Reflections on Ackerman, Reconstruction, and the Transformation of the American Constitution." *Yale Law Review* 108 (1999): 2011–38.

Feller, Dan. "Politics and Society: Toward a Jacksonian Synthesis." *Journal of the Early Republic* 10 (1990): 135–61.

Formisano, Ronald P. "The New Political History and the Election of 1840." *Journal of Interdisciplinary History* 23 (1993): 661–82.

———. "The 'Party Period' Revisited." *Journal of American History* 86 (1999): 93–120.

Gerteis, Louis S., "Salmon P. Chase, Radicalism, and the Politics of Emancipation, 1861–1864." *Journal of American History* 60 (1973): 42–62.

Gienapp, William E. "Nativism and the Creation of a Republican Majority in the North." *Journal of American History* 72 (1985): 529–59.

———. "The Myth of Class in Jacksonian America." *Journal of Policy History* 6 (1994): 232–59.

Gribbin, William. "Rollin's Histories and American Republicanism." *William and Mary Quarterly* 29 (1972): 611–22.

Hawthorne, Manning. "Nathaniel Hawthorne at Bowdoin." *New England Quarterly* 13 (1940): 246–79.

Johnson, Ludwell H. "Contraband Trade during the Last Year of the Civil War." *Mississippi Valley Historical Review* 49 (1963): 635–52.

———. "Northern Profit and Profiteers: The Cotton Rings of 1864–1865." *Civil War History* 12 (1966): 101–15.

Johnson, Reinhard O. "The Liberty Party in Maine, 1840–1848: The Politics of Antislavery Reform." *Maine Historical Society Quarterly* 19 (1980): 135–76.

Kaczorowski, Robert J. "To Begin the Nation Anew: Congress, Citizenship, and Civil Rights after the Civil War." *American Historical Review* 92 (1987): 45–68.

King, Peter J. "John Neal as a Benthamite," *New England Quarterly* 39 (1966): 47–65.

Landis, Michael Todd. "'A Champion Had Come': William Pitt Fessenden and the Republican Party." *American Nineteenth Century History* 9 (2008): 269–85.

O'Brien, Patrick. "Is Political Biography a Good Thing?" *Contemporary British History* 10 (1996): 60–66.

O'Connor, Thomas. "Lincoln and the Cotton Trade." *Civil War History* 7 (1961): 20–35.

Ratcliffe, Donald J. "Antimasonry and Partisanship in Greater New England, 1826–1836." *Journal of the Early Republic* 15 (1995): 199–239.

Roske, Ralph J. "The Seven Martyrs?" *American Historical Review* 64 (1959): 323–30.

Ross, Stephen Joseph. "Freed Soil, Freed Labor, Freed Men: John Eaton and the Davis Bend Experiment." *Journal of Southern History,* 44 (1978): 213–32.

Schriver, Edward O. "Antislavery: The Free Soil and Free Democratic Parties in Maine, 1848–1855." *New England Quarterly* 42 (1969): 82–94.

Smith, Daniel Scott, and Michael S. Hindus. "Premarital Pregnancy in America 1640–1971: An Overview and Interpretation." *Journal of Interdisciplinary History* 5 (1975): 537–70.

Whitmore, Allan R. "'A Guard of Faithful Sentinels': The Know-Nothing Appeal in Maine, 1854–1855." *Maine Historical Society Quarterly* 20 (1981): 151–97.

THESES

Murray, Constance Carolyn. "Portland, Maine, and the Growth of Urban Responsibility for Human Welfare, 1830–1860." Boston University, PhD thesis, 1960.

Wescott, Richard. "'A History of Maine Politics 1840–1856: The Formation of the Republican Party." University of Maine, PhD thesis, 1966.

Whalon, Michael Winters. "Maine Republicans, 1854–1866: A Study in Growth and Political Power." University of Nebraska, PhD thesis, 1968.

Index